ET   3 3 6 19

DRUG USE
EPIDEMIOLOGICAL
AND SOCIOLOGICAL
APPROACHES

THE SERIES IN GENERAL PSYCHIATRY

Daniel X. Freedman · Consulting Editor

FISHER AND FREEDMAN · *Opiate Addiction: Origins and Treatment*

JOSEPHSON AND CARROLL · *Drug Use: Epidemiological and Sociological Approaches*

DRUG USE

EPIDEMIOLOGICAL
AND SOCIOLOGICAL
APPROACHES

EDITED BY **ERIC JOSEPHSON**

COLUMBIA UNIVERSITY SCHOOL OF PUBLIC HEALTH

AND **ELEANOR E. CARROLL**

CENTER FOR STUDIES OF NARCOTIC AND DRUG ABUSE
NATIONAL INSTITUTE OF MENTAL HEALTH

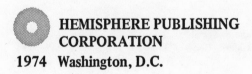

HEMISPHERE PUBLISHING
CORPORATION
1974   Washington, D.C.

A HALSTED PRESS BOOK

JOHN WILEY & SONS
New York   London   Sydney   Toronto

033619

Copyright © 1974 by Hemisphere Publishing Corporation. All rights reserved. No part of this book may be reproduced in any form, by photostat, microform, retrieval system, or any other means, without the prior written permission of the publisher.

Hemisphere Publishing Corporation
1025 Vermont Ave., N.W., Washington, D.C. 20005

Distributed solely by Halsted Press, a Division of John Wiley & Sons, Inc., New York.

Library of Congress Cataloging in Publication Data

Main entry under title:

Drug use: epidemiological and sociological approaches.

    (The Series in general psychiatry)
    "Papers prepared for an international conference . . . held in San Juan, Puerto Rico, February 12-14, 1973, under the auspices of the Columbia University School of Public Health and the University of Puerto Rico School of Public Health."
    Includes bibliographies.
    1. Drug abuse—Congresses. 2. Drug abuse—Social aspects—Congresses. 3. Drug abuse—Treatment—Congresses. 4. Drug and youth—Congresses.
I. Josephson, Eric, ed. II. Columbia University. School of Public Health and Administrative Medicine. III. Puerto Rico. University. School of Public Health. [DNLM: 1. Drug abuse—Congresses. 2. Drug abuse—Occurrence—Congresses. 3. Drug addiction—Congresses. 4. Drug addiction—Occurrence—Congresses. WM270 D7951 1973]
HV5800.D782   362.2'93   74-19056
ISBN 0-470-45082-7

Printed in the United States of America

CONTENTS

033619

v

   REPORTING SYSTEM OF DRUG DEATHS, *Dan J. Lettieri*
   and Michael S. Backenheimer **159**

   Introduction **159**
   Objectives and Aims **160**
   Sources and Availability of Data **160**
   The Current Model **162**
   Preliminary Issues and Definitions in a
       Model System **165**
   Directions for the Future **173**
   References **173**

Part III. YOUTH AND DRUGS

10 TRENDS IN ADOLESCENT MARIJUANA USE,
    Eric Josephson **177**

    The Problem **177**
    Conceptual and Methodological Issues **179**
    General Trends in Marijuana Use **183**
    Adolescent Marijuana Use, 1971-73 **189**
    Interpretation **201**
    References **203**

11 INTERPERSONAL INFLUENCES ON ADOLESCENT ILLEGAL
    DRUG USE, *Denise Kandel* **207**

    Method **212**
    Findings **216**
    Discussion and Conclusion **235**
    References **238**

12 PATTERNS OF COLLEGE STUDENT DRUG USE AND
    LIFESTYLES, *W. Eugene Groves* **241**

    Survey Methodology **242**
    Prevalence and Incidence Findings **249**
    Drug Use in Different Schools **255**
    Usage Associations among Different
        Drugs **258**
    Explaining Drug Use **266**
    Student Lifestyles **268**
    Lifestyles and Drug Use **271**
    Discussion **272**
    References **274**

PREFACE

This book presents papers prepared for an international conference on the epidemiology of drug use held in San Juan, Puerto Rico, February 12-14, 1973, under the auspices of the Columbia University School of Public Health and the University of Puerto Rico School of Public Health.* More than sixty researchers from thirteen states of the United States, the District of Columbia, Puerto Rico, Canada, and the United Kingdom participated.

What prompted the conference was the need for critical assessment in a field of research beset by serious conceptual and methodological problems. Defining the various terms of drug behavior heads any such list of problems. How to measure drug use at any moment in time or over periods of time comes next. Who is doing what with which drugs—heroin, marijuana, hallucinogenic drugs, stimulants, and psychotherapeutic drugs in particular? What do we currently know and need to learn about individual and group trends in their use and about the factors related to those trends? Then there is the question of how treatment programs, such as methadone maintenance, should be evaluated. These are among the issues to which the San Juan meeting was addressed. In the variety of drugs considered and in its concern with ways of studying drug behavior, this conference was the first of its kind ever held in North America. The ultimate aim was to produce state-of-the-art reports on the epidemiology of drug use in the early 1970s as well as directions for future research.

*The conference and publication of this volume were supported by grant number 1 R13 DA00526 from the Center for Studies of Narcotic and Drug Abuse, National Institute of Mental Health (now the National Institute of Drug Abuse) to the Columbia University School of Public Health.

Several recent developments make this an appropriate time for just such an assessment. One is the worldwide phenomenon of youthful experimentation with a variety of mood-changing substances and the widespread concern such behavior has aroused. Second is the increasing use of large-scale population surveys as a means of finding out about drug use—especially but not only among youth. Not the least of the methodological problems at issue here is that these surveys vary widely in their definition and measurement of drug use; they also often deal with illicit behavior. Nevertheless, and whatever their limitations, it is only in the last half-dozen years that such surveys have made it possible for us to begin to map basic social patterns and trends in drug use. Still another development is the rapid growth of treatment systems for drug users, particularly users of heroin; these programs provide an unprecedented opportunity for researchers to learn about the dynamics of drug use—at least in treated populations—and to wrestle with the thorny task of evaluating attempts to control such behavior.

This book presents a considerable amount of original data based on recent social surveys and on the study of drug users receiving treatment. It is addressed to persons interested in deviant behavior in general and drug use in particular, those engaged in epidemiological and social science research on drug behavior, those involved in providing various forms of treatment to drugs users, and those responsible for developing social policy regarding drug use and its control. Part I deals with conceptual issues in the study of drug use. Part II focuses on heroin use, including the British drug scene, the recent heroin "epidemic" in the United States, the "careers" of heroin users, and the evaluation of heroin treatment. Part III deals with drug behavior and its correlates among youth of high school and college age in the United States. Part IV consists of overviews of hallucinogenic and stimulant drug use in the United States. The book ends with an overview of psychotherapeutic drug use in the United States.

A planning group for the San Juan Conference consisted of Eleanor E. Carroll, Center for Studies of Narcotic and Drug Abuse, National Institute of Mental Health; Mitchell B. Balter, Psychopharmacology Research Branch, National Institute of Mental Health; Ira H. Cisin, Social Research Group, George Washington University; Jack Elinson, Anne Zanes, and Eric Josephson (who served as conference chairman), all of the Columbia University School of Public Health.

It remains for me to acknowledge with thanks the contributions a number of people made to the meeting. Special appreciation is expressed to Ms. Zanes for her dedication in handling preconference arrangements. Grateful acknowledgments are also due Dr. José Nine Curt, dean of the University of Puerto Rico School of Public Health, and his assistant, Ms. Martha Burns, for their hospitality and their generous help with arrangements for the meeting. Some of Dr. Nine's challenging remarks appear in the introduction to this book. Finally, acknowledgments are due the discusssants and other participants. Unfortunately, limitations of space have made it impossible to include their statements, which in many cases were stimulating and provocative. However, we hope that the dialogues which took place during the San Juan conference as well as the work presented here will be reflected in future advances in epidemiological research on drug use.

Eric Josephson

INTRODUCTION*

Eric Josephson

THE DRUG "PROBLEM"

"Perhaps the greatest feature which distinguishes man from the other animals," Sir William Osler once said, is his "desire to take medicine." Another distinguishing characteristic of man is his tendency to worry about drug taking. What some people do with drugs and medicines is the subject of this book. But precisely because drug taking and its study are so heavily influenced by social responses to drugs, the nature of those responses—often disapproving and punitive, even hysterical—requires some consideration at the outset.

In many parts of the world the use of drugs has recently come to be regarded as a major social problem, if such a problem is determined by the great attention given it by the mass media; a high level of public concern, if not alarm; and the considerable number of governmental commissions of inquiry, conferences, and books devoted to it. What makes it a problem? History teaches us that the current drug scare is by no means the first and, given man's pharmacological inventiveness as well as his curiosity about mood-changing substances, probably will not be the last. History also suggests that in many countries there has long been a tendency to attribute demoniacal powers to drugs (Blum & associates, 1969, Ch. 14); thus the age-old image of the "dope fiend." However, none of this explains just why there is so much concern today.

*I wish to acknowledge with thanks the helpful criticism of Jack Elinson regarding this introduction and also Ch. 10.

Many factors contribute to that concern, which is very much a study in its own right (Goode, 1972; Young, 1971; Zinberg & Robertson, 1972). Only a few of those factors, however, are singled out here. Presumably, increasing numbers of people are doing things with drugs that they should not be doing; this is the conventional and prevailing view. But which people and what drugs?

Without question, a major factor in the current scare is the entry of middle-class youth into the drug scene on a large scale. This is unprecedented. In recent years advantaged youth, in particular, have led the way in experimenting with a variety of drugs, notably marijuana, amphetamines, and LSD (Josephson, Groves, McGlothlin, Ellinwood, this volume). Part of adult concern about such behavior has to do with the real or imagined health hazards associated with the use of these drugs and with the belief, so far unsubstantiated, that the use of certain drugs, such as marijuana, inexorably leads to the use of others, such as heroin (Goode, 1972). Much concern is based on the assumption that unconventional drug use by middle-class youth threatens self-control and the work ethic and therefore the very moral fabric of society. This assumption has been reinforced by the "countercultural" advocates of mood-changing drug use as a symbol of protest against or even a way of changing an alienating society. It is worth noting that unconventional drug use by less advantaged youth, while by no means approved, is perceived in a different light by those with influence; that is, as more of a threat to the civil than to the moral order.

This perception reveals a second major factor in the current drug scare: the public's identification of unconventional drug use with disadvantaged minority groups. This has been a recurrent feature of drug panics, especially but not only in the United States, where the century-old crusade against drugs has focused successively on the opium dens of Chinese immigrants; the use of cocaine by blacks in the South (although whites were apparently just as likely to be sharing the experience); and, more recently, the use of heroin by blacks, Puerto Ricans, and Chicanos in urban ghettos (*Drug Use in America: Problem in perspective*, 1973, p. 17; Musto, 1973, p. 245). The movement to prohibit consumption of alcoholic beverages in the United States was also motivated in part by nativistic resentment against "un-Americans," i.e., immigrants from Europe, Catholics, and big-city dwellers in general (Gusfield, 1963).

To be sure, the forms and patterns of drug use among the disadvantaged in any society often differ from what prevails among the advantaged. Thus, heroin use in the United States today *is* concentrated among blacks, Puerto Ricans, and Chicanos. However, although there is evidence of variation among as well as between them in their taste for heroin (Lukoff, this volume), the tendency to stereotype and scapegoat certain minority groups as users and proselytizers of unconventional drug use remains a feature of the current drug scare. To illustrate, in Britain during the 1960s, West Indian immigrants were blamed by some for the increasing use of heroin in that country, although they were no more likely to be using it than were native-born white people (Hawks, this volume).

Another factor in the current drug scare in the United States as well as in other countries is the public's association of heroin use with criminal behavior. Indeed, it can be argued with some justification that this more than anything else is responsible for the panic. The salience of drug-related crime is indicated by the results of a national public-opinion survey conducted in the United States in 1971. Presented with a list of things that had "gone wrong" in the country, 47% of the respondents mentioned drug use, a higher figure than recorded for any other problem on the list, including the war then raging in Vietnam, which was mentioned by 40%. In presenting these findings, the investigators who had collected them noted that a

> new spectre [was] haunting the American scene, the taking of drugs. Its position at the top of the list indicates an almost obsessive concern with its effect on American life. It overshadows nearly everything else, and probably includes two distinct sources of anxiety: crime by addicts, and the willingness of young people to turn on [*The Roper Report*, July 1971].

Public concern about youth and drugs has already been noted. As for crime, data available from several countries indicate that although many drug users do indeed commit crimes to pay for the drugs they want, their delinquent careers often begin before—not after—they begin to use the drugs (Goode, 1972; Hawks, Lukoff, this volume). Moreover, the amount of drug-related crime in general and violent crime in particular may be considerably smaller than the public believes (*Drug Use in America: Problem in perspective*, 1973; Singer, 1971).

There is, however, another way of looking at the issue of drug-related crime. As long as such crime was perceived as contained within disadvantaged communities (it is still concentrated in them), there was relatively little general, although much localized, concern about the problem. But with the spread of drug-related crime into middle-class communities, thereby "democratizing" the risks of being victimized, concern mounted rapidly on the part of an influential public.

Class interests have therefore played a major part in the current drug scare; they have also helped to determine society's response. This may be illustrated by the recent trend in a number of countries toward reduced penalties for the possession of marijuana: middle-class parents do not want their children convicted of felonies.

Still another factor in the drug panic is the belief that modern societies are becoming "overmedicated." Here the idea is that as a result of advertising and promotion by pharmaceutical manufacturers and excessive prescribing by physicians, increasing numbers of people are being given mood-changing substances they do not need, especially tranquilizers and antidepressants, to cope with "everyday" problems of life and thereby escape those problems (Lennard, Epstein, Bernstein, & Ransam, 1971). The implication is that this is bad. No doubt there are cases of overmedication; but data recently collected in the United States indicate that most physicians and most patients are cautious rather than reckless in their prescription and use of mood-changing drugs (Mellinger et al., this volume). Another charge is that the overmedication of adults encourages young people to use drugs in unconventional and dangerous ways. Again, however, the evidence available indicates that young people are far more heavily influenced in their drug taking by the behavior of their peers than by what their parents and elders do with drugs (Kandel, this volume).

While by no means exhausting the many factors contributing to the contemporary drug scare, the four considered so far—drug use among middle-class youth; heroin use, in particular, among disadvantaged minorities; the issue of drug-related crime; and the notion of an overmedicated society—appear high on any list. This book addresses itself to each of these four areas of concern. Before proceeding further, however, it is appropriate to take a more general look at drug use, its classification, and the response to it.

What is meant by the term "drug"? To pharmacologists, one authority has written,

> any substance that by its chemical nature alters structure or function in the living organism is a drug. . . . Pharmacological effects are exerted by foods, vitamins, hormones, microbial metabolites, plants, snake venoms, stings, products of decay, air pollutants, pesticides, minerals, synthetic chemicals, virtually all foreign materials (very few are completely inert), and many materials normally in the body [Modell, 1967, p. 345].

To this list may be added water.

Pharmacologists not only define, they also classify drugs. Thus, they distinguish between substances that actually change people's psychological states or are perceived as doing so, the so-called "psychotropic" drugs, and those without this effect. Since mood-changing drugs have different effects, further classification is needed. Among the major pharmacological types are sedatives, such as alcohol and barbiturates; stimulants, such as caffeine, nicotine, cocaine, and amphetamines; tranquilizers; antidepressants; narcotics, such as heroin, morphine, codeine, and demerol; and hallucinogens, such as marijuana and LSD.

What makes any one of these drugs harmful is not inherent in its chemistry but rather in the context in which it is used. This simple but fundamental truth about drug taking has yet to penetrate public opinion, let alone the laws regarding drugs. For most people the term "drug" is associated with substances about which they are concerned, such as heroin or marijuana, and to a lesser degree with the antidepressants and tranquilizers physicians prescribe; alcohol and tobacco, probably the most widely used of all drugs, are not popularly regarded as such and therefore are less likely to arouse public concern.

As for the law, it is often quite arbitrary in its classification of drugs. Thus, until 1973 British law set the same penalties for the possession of marijuana as for the possession of heroin. In the United States seven states classify marijuana as a narcotic and one classifies it as a depressant or stimulant. A current New York State law classifies cocaine, which is a stimulant, as a narcotic. Defending the law, a special narcotics prosecutor recently said:

> The classification of drugs in the Penal Law does not serve a medical or pharmacological function: it establishes degrees of criminality and punishment. The legislature can define "narcotic drugs" to include *whatever drugs it wishes* as long as the substances classified as narcotics are clearly enumerated so that the public knows exactly which drugs are prohibited [*The New York Times*, Nov. 15, 1973, italics added].

Equal if not greater ambiguity marks both public discourse and presumably scientific discussions of the ways in which people use drugs or are used by them. This is illustrated by the tendency to equate drug "abuse" with any use of drugs; but it is also illustrated by confusion regarding the meaning of "addiction." To most people, an "addict" is someone who becomes a "slave" to some habit; i.e., the habit has him in its power. Though the term is perhaps most commonly used with reference to mood-changing substances, it can also be applied to a number of other things to which people can and do become habituated, such as work or watching television. Thus, Laurie (1971, p. 12) includes trousers in a list of drugs to illustrate

> the similarity between drug-oriented behavior and other relationships that we consider perfectly normal. We depend quite intensely on this substance, both mentally and physically, its withdrawal causes discomfort, mental distress, and is a well-known weapon in brain-washing.

Expert opinion so far has not been particularly successful in clarifying such terms (Balter, Smart, this volume). Thus in dealing with addiction, pharmacologists distinguish between psychological and physical "dependence" on drugs. This has led to endless difficulties. One of them has to do with drawing the boundaries between the two sets of dependencies. Another difficulty is caused by the fact that the use of some drugs may lead to one dependency and not the other, whereas the use of other drugs may lead to both physical and psychological dependence. Opiate drugs such as heroin, as well as alcohol, it is generally agreed, have the potential for leading to both physical and psychological dependence. But how then explain those persons who use heroin "only" on weekends or those who stop using it altogether? And how explain the fact that most people who consume alcoholic beverages do not become "addicted" to the drug? With some justification, it has been proposed that such terms as "abuse" and "addiction" be abandoned, at least in talking about drugs.

Still further ambiguity lies in the distinction often made between medical and nonmedical drug use. The implication is that the former is good because it is legitimized by physicians, the latter (which by definition includes self-medication or the use of over-the-counter drugs) bad because it is not. But even if fears regarding an overmedicated society are exaggerated, the potential for harm is as great in medically approved as in nonmedical drug taking.

Another and perhaps more fruitful way of approaching the problem of drug classification is to distinguish between socially acceptable substances and unacceptable drugs. Acceptable drugs generally include substances prescribed by the medical profession (or by medicine men), but they also include other drugs, the production and use of which are sanctioned by custom and law; they may not always be good for one's health, but they are substances most people regard as beneficial, feel "comfortable" with, or believe they can control. Unacceptable drugs, which are not necessarily bad for one's health, are those about which many people feel concerned or whose use they believe cannot be controlled; they are likely to be the proscribed drugs.

What makes one drug socially acceptable and another unacceptable has less to do with their pharmacological properties or with the risks to health which their use poses than with the threat to the moral order they symbolize and with the legitimacy of investment in their production and distribution. To be sure, drug tastes change: what was prohibited in the past may in time become acceptable. Many countries have reacted strenuously, even violently, to the introduction of new drugs or to new patterns of drug use. This is illustrated by past attempts to ban such drugs as coffee, tobacco, and alcoholic beverages and to punish their users, until tastes changed and/or economic interest (meaning investment in the cultivation, production, and marketing of the drugs) prevailed over moral and health considerations.

Does this mean that once introduced, every drug ultimately wins public acceptance? Opinion differs here, but history suggests that this need not necessarily be the case. Thus, the nonmedical use of opium (an ancient drug) was probably much more widespread in the past than at present, particularly in the Middle East and in Asia; but in no country on earth today is such use sanctioned either by custom or law. On the other hand, marijuana has undoubtedly become acceptable to increasing numbers of young people in North America and Western Europe; but it is by no means certain that it will in due course become an approved drug.

As for the health hazards presented by the use of acceptable and unacceptable drugs, in the United States several hundred thousand persons die prematurely every year from diseases associated with smoking cigarettes or drinking alcoholic beverages. However, in 1971 the citizens of the United States spent more than $30 billion on liquor and tobacco (an amount equal to half the gross national product of all of Africa) and hundreds of thousands of Americans are employed in the production and distribution of these drugs. Moreover, despite warnings from health authorities, per capita consumption of cigarettes in the United States has again begun to rise (most notably among youth), and in the past 20 years per capita consumption of distilled spirits has nearly doubled. But as noted, tobacco and alcohol are not generally regarded as drugs, although they have probably done more damage to health than all other drugs put together. In contrast, only a handful of people die from heroin "overdoses" (as ill defined as addiction itself; Lettieri & Backenheimer, this volume) and probably none from using marijuana. If the production and distribution of heroin for nonmedical use are also highly profitable, that is due almost entirely to its prohibited status.

Conventional views of the drug problem have therefore been subjected to a number of criticisms. One is that they focus attention on the "wrong" drugs; i.e., use of these substances may be morally reprehensible, but they are less harmful than other drugs protected by custom or law. If health were the primary consideration, this criticism could be leveled at the present volume, since it gives relatively little attention to alcohol and to tobacco; but then, as noted, health hazards are not the only factors underlying public concern about drugs.

Another criticism of the conventional wisdom is that it exaggerates the dimensions of drug use today in comparison with the past. Thus, very possibly there were more nonmedical opiate users in Western Europe and North America during the 19th century (when patent medicines containing a heady mixture of opium and alcohol were readily available) than at present; but apart from a few celebrated figures like Thomas de Quincey, most "addicts" of a century ago were not usually recognized as such and therefore rarely stigmatized or punished (Musto, 1973). Still another criticism is that overzealous bureaucrats have acquired a vested interest in the drug problem, much as a succession of politicians and bureaucrats in capitalist countries have exploited the "Red menace" ever since 1917.

In short, it is argued that the public has overreacted to drug use, that its concern is misplaced, and that there are far more serious problems worthy of its attention, such as poverty, malnutrition, population growth, environmental pollution, political corruption, and war. This may very well be true; but then it is not always experts who decide just what constitutes a social problem.

Our perceptions of the drug problem and our classifications of drugs and drug taking represent just some of the ways in which society responds to the use of mood-changing substances. What we do or try to do about drug use also needs to be classified, as several commentators have suggested (Joyce, 1973; Zacune & Hensman, 1971).

One response to drug taking is to do little or nothing about it. The rationale for this is provided by the libertarian philosophy of John Stuart Mill, who argued that adult misbehavior should not be interfered with or punished as long as it causes no harm to others. Since it has never been easy to draw the line between what is harmful to oneself and what is harmful to others and since in any case most forms of drug use are either considered reprehensible or profitable or both, this approach has rarely been tried in practice. Nevertheless, it is illustrated somewhat imperfectly by the tolerance shown most users of opiate patent medicines in Western Europe and North America during the 19th century, by the general acceptance of aspirin use and coffee drinking in many countries, and by the current effort of some to "decriminalize" the possession of marijuana for personal use.

A second and more common response is to profit from drug making and drug selling by licensing and taxing these activities. This is standard policy regarding tobacco and alcoholic beverages in many countries and a major source of revenue for them; it has also been proposed as a way of dealing with marijuana use today. Not the least of the consequences is the establishment of quality controls over the drugs produced and sold. The cigarettes smoked and the alcohol drunk today have approximately the same effects on their users—and are equally dangerous; but neither statement can be made about the marijuana or heroin available in most countries.

A third response to the taking of drugs is to curtail their supply. This takes several forms. One is to reduce production, as a number of governments have attempted to do in the case of amphetamines. Another is to ban the drug—or try—as the United States tried to prohibit the consumption of alcoholic beverages between 1918 and 1933 and as it is now trying to enforce the prohibition against marijuana and heroin. The recent, abortive United States effort to subsidize Turkish farmers to refrain from growing opium also belongs in this category.

A fourth response to drug use is to punish the seller and/or the users of drugs by stigmatizing them, imprisoning them, even executing them. In trying to enforce drug prohibitions and deal with offenders, some governments have made heavy demands on their police forces (in the United States half a million are arrested annually for drug-possession offenses). As for more violent reactions, a 17th century Sultan of Constantinople decreed the death penalty for smoking tobacco, although to no avail in discouraging its use (Brecher, 1972, p. 212); and similar punishment has been recommended for heroin traffickers today. Recently it has been suggested that the United States cut off aid to Turkey or even declare war to punish that country for resuming the cultivation of opium (much of which is intended for legitimate medical use in the form of morphine).

A fifth response is to call drug users "sick" and treat them. The fact that no form or pattern of drug use is a disease in any clinical sense of the term, although it may result from pathology or lead to it, makes little difference as far as this perception is concerned. Thus in the United States in 1973 approximately 160,000 persons were receiving various forms of medical and pseudomedical treatment for drug "abuse," including individual and group therapy as well as the substitution of one drug (methadone) for another (heroin). Among many other solutions which have either been attempted or proposed are permitting physicians to prescribe narcotics to their patients (as the United States did until passage of the Harrison Narcotics Act in 1914 and as the British did on a very small scale with heroin until 1968) and developing a vaccine that will immunize people against the effects of heroin for years if not a lifetime.

These responses are neither mutually exclusive nor exhaustive of the many things, some of them bizarre, that people have done or are doing about drug taking. To illustrate, some countries have increased taxes on alcoholic beverages to reduce their consumption. Another approach is represented by the proposal to quarantine narcotics users and force them to "accept" treatment. Not included in these approaches are efforts to discourage the use of drugs by educating people about their real or alleged dangers. Nor do these categories include efforts to punish those who interfere with drug taking, a prime case being the 19th-century British war against China to protect Britain's lucrative opium trade there.

The relative effectiveness of these responses to drug use cannot easily be determined since they are intended to achieve different objectives, and no society has experimented with a variety of policies regarding some particular form of drug use. To do nothing about drug use may have some appeal in principle, but is unthinkable in practice regarding the use of disapproved drugs; something will be done, however ineffective or counterproductive. Increasing the price of drugs such as tobacco and alcoholic beverages through taxation has apparently failed to reduce their consumption in any significant way; one reason is that no government has dared to tax them at a prohibitive level. Reducing the availability of a drug will of course lower its consumption; but there may be unanticipated consequences. Thus the United States experiment with alcohol prohibition may have reduced the death rate from cirhossis of the liver, but it also helped create a highly organized criminal underworld. To take another example, a recent outbreak of methedrine ("speed") injecting among young people in Britain was checked when manufacturers were persuaded to withdraw the drug from distribution to pharmacists; one consequence was the shifting by those who had used methedrine to other drugs, such as marijuana and LSD (de Alarcon, 1972). The punitive approach, the oldest of all "solutions," has been notoriously unsuccessful in deterring people from using drugs; thus, marijuana has become increasingly popular among young people despite thousands of arrests in many countries. As for the effectiveness of various treatment programs for drug "abusers," opinion differs here; but it is probably safe to say that few programs launched so far have been able to achieve their intended objectives, the chief one being to make people drug free. One of the few countries on earth that claims to have eliminated its major drug problem—the use of opium—is the People's Republic of China; but reliable information as to how much of its reported success is due to unique methods of social control, to the self-exile of drug users, or to more violent means of dealing with them has yet to be shared with other countries.

STUDYING DRUG USE

Whatever the social policies regarding drug use, they are not likely to be particularly effective without reliable information about what people are doing with drugs as well as about the effectiveness of programs intended to control such behavior. Still another response to drug use, therefore, is to study it, which some cynics regard as the equivalent of doing nothing at all. That study has followed various paths, one (psychopharmacology) having to do with the effects of drugs, another with law and public policy. Still another area of study, the subject of this book, has to do with social patterns and trends in drug use. Presumably, increasing numbers of people, particularly youth, are using disapproved drugs or approved drugs in unacceptable ways; this, as noted earlier, has aroused public opinion. What factors have contributed to this phenomenon?

It would be a gross understatement to suggest that there are any easy answers to such a question. For one thing, we are dealing with different kinds of drug use by different kinds of people—e.g., heroin "addiction" among the disadvantaged in the United States and experimentation with LSD by middle-class youth. To be sure, both are mood-changing drugs; but that is perhaps all that they, let alone their users, have in common. Another difficulty is presented by the lack of information about people who use drugs in unacceptable ways; much simply remains unknown. However, none of this has inhibited a large number of commentators and researchers from trying to "explain" drug use.

One approach to the problem has been to relate increased drug use to other major social and cultural trends, real or alleged. Thus it has been attributed to increased affluence and leisure; hedonism; the breakdown of community and of traditional ethical values; the declining influence of family, church, and school, and alienation—to name just a few. The difficulty here lies first in defining and measuring such broad social trends and second, in demonstrating that they have in fact contributed to increased drug use. At best this approach, which has considerable public support, is speculative.

Another approach has focused on population trends which are presumably associated with increasing drug use. To illustrate, in the United States during the 1960s, as a result of the postwar baby boom, there was an unprecedented increase of nearly 14 million in the size of the population aged 14 to 24 years to a total of over 40 million by the end of the decade. One feature of this youthful population explosion has been a great increase in the numbers attending colleges and universities (from under 3 million in 1950 to nearly 9 million in 1971) and the postponement of their entry into the labor force. The rise of large, age-segregated university communities has presumably provided fertile ground for the growth of a youth culture with its own values, unlike if not opposed to those of older people. One expression of such communities allegedly has been an increased willingness to experiment with drugs. There is much that is plausible, if simplistic, about this approach: if there were not so many young people spending an ever larger portion of their lives in institutions of higher learning, there would of course be fewer student drug users.

Still another population trend associated with increased drug use, at least in the United States, is the growing concentration of black people and other minority groups in big cities. To illustrate, the black population in these cities doubled between 1950 and 1970 (rising from 6.6 million to 13.1 million), while the white population of these cities increased less than 5% during this period. One feature of this population shift has been an extremely high unemployment rate among youth: in 1971 nearly 4 out of 10 nonwhite youths 16–19 years in urban low-income areas were out of work. It is in just such communities that heroin use is concentrated.

Although changes in cultural values and such trends as the growth of student and of ghetto populations provide a background for approaching contemporary drug problems, those trends cannot determine just what predisposes some people to use drugs in unacceptable ways and others to refrain from doing so. In many countries millions of people now spend an increasing part of their young adulthood in colleges and universities, but not all by any means engage in disapproved forms of drug use. In the United States black people and other minority groups are increasingly concentrated in urban ghettos, but all of them do not become "addicted" to heroin.

Similar considerations apply to the use of other drugs. To illustrate, in most modern societies drugs such as tobacco and alcoholic beverages are readily available to all above a certain age who wish to use them. Yet nowhere do all persons old or affluent enough to consume these drugs actually do so. Thus in the United States more than half of all adults do not smoke cigarettes, nearly one-third do not drink alcohol, perhaps 1 in 10 has ever "tried" marijuana, and fewer still have ever used heroin. Moreover, as noted earlier, there are fairly sharp class and ethnic differences in the particular forms as well as in the rates of drug use. Finally, there is the question as to trends in drug use. Some drugs have become increasingly popular, others, such as glue sniffing, have apparently declined in popularity regardless of their availability.

The question that presents itself then is to try to determine not only collective trends or fads in drug use but individual predispositions to use drugs in unacceptable ways. The challenge as well as the difficulties presented here are encompassed in a summary statement regarding the "causes" of nonmedical drug use, which appeared in the final report of the Canadian Commission of Inquiry into the nonmedical use of drugs:

> There are factors in the personality or psychological make-up of the prospective user, in his close personal relations and environment in the family, school, and the peer group, in social and economic conditions, and in the general attitude of the society towards drug use, as reflected by advertising, the media and the practice of the adult population, which predispose and encourage the individual to engage in

non-medical drug use [*Final report of the Commission of Inquiry into the non-medical use of drugs,* 1973, p. 35].

In considering these four sets of predisposing factors, we will have an opportunity briefly to review the contributions the social sciences have made to our understanding of drug use.

With regard to the first set of factors mentioned by the Canadian Commission, "the personality or psychological state of the prospective user," research has so far been unable to identify any single, let alone any combination of, personality characteristics that predispose some people to use drugs in unacceptable ways. If there is a "drug-prone" personality, it has yet to be discovered. Perhaps the main reason for this is the lack of reliable psychological data about individuals *before* they initiate drug use; most of the data available pertain to them *after* they have started to use drugs and therefore cannot shed light on predisposing factors. However, psychologists have contributed much to our knowledge of habitual drug use as learned or conditioned behavior and to what we know about the effects of drugs on people who use them (Chein, 1969; Wikler, 1973). So too, our understanding that individual as well as group "settings" or contexts in which drugs are taken may have as much to do with their effects as their pharmacological properties is a major contribution of psychology to the field of drug research. But none of this indicates just what predisposes some people to use drugs.

As for the second set of factors noted by the Canadian Commission, "close personal relations and [the] environment [of] family, school, and . . . peer group," the assumption here is that they all somehow predispose to drug use. We have already noted that what parents do with drugs has relatively little influence on adolescent drug taking; far more influential is the behavior of peers, most of whom are encountered in school (Kandel, this volume). What one's friends do with drugs is therefore a powerful predictor of one's own drug use; but again, this finding does not necessarily identify predisposing factors. Do friends choose drugs or do drugs choose friends? This question remains unanswered.

Regarding "social and economic conditions" that predispose toward unconventional drug use, the third set of factors listed by the Canadian Commission, some sociologists have claimed that this, like other forms of deviant behavior, is determined by the "opportunity structure." Put otherwise, the argument is that those deprived of the opportunity to get ahead in society—the poor—are more likely than the advantaged to engage in such escapist or "retreatist" behavior (Cloward & Ohlin, 1960).[1] Thus, as noted,

[1] A variation on this theme is the argument, heard particularly in the United States, that the ruling class covertly tolerates and even profits from heroin trafficking and now promotes the substitution of methadone for heroin to "pacify" and thereby control the disadvantaged. But if the ruling class were so clever, why did it not continue the legal dispensing of heroin after 1914, thereby making it unnecessary for users to commit crimes in order to obtain their drugs, and why the harsh penalties for those in possession of as well as trafficking in heroin? (For a statement on this issue, see *HEALTH/PAC Bulletin,* June 1970).

heroin use in the United States is concentrated in disadvantaged communities. Even in those communities, however, most residents refrain from heroin use; and those who do become involved are not necessarily at the bottom of the social ladder (Lukoff, this volume). But even if certain forms of drug use could be explained by disadvantage, this explanation would of course contribute little or nothing to our understanding of drug use among the advantaged.

No more than personality characteristics does one's position in the class structure alone predict who will and who will not engage in unconventional forms of drug use. A more promising approach, applied so far most notably in the study of deviant drinking behavior, seeks to integrate just such sociological and psychological perspectives (Jessor, Graves, Hanson, & Jessor, 1968).

As for the Canadian Commission's statement regarding "general attitudes towards drug use," the basic assumption here is that the mass media have helped shape a culture distinguished by pain avoidance and hedonism. To be sure, drugs of various kinds are advertised in the mass media (as well as in medical journals), and it would be absurd to claim that such promotion is entirely without effect; drug advertisers certainly do not think so. Certain popular arts also "promote" drug experiences, and millions of young people have been exposed to them. Attributing drug use to the media, however, seems no more justifiable than placing major blame on them for violence. As noted earlier, the evidence available suggests that despite advertising, most people are careful in their use of drugs, just as most television viewers are ordinarily nonviolent. Nor is there evidence that all persons exposed to drug-oriented popular arts are "turned on" by them.

Attempts to interpret unconventional drug use in terms of some one set of predisposing factors—personality characteristics, primary group influences, the social structure, or general attitudes regarding drugs—have so far been unsuccessful. To suggest, as does the Canadian Commission, that *all* these factors contribute to drug use only compounds the difficulties, since no one has been able to determine just what the relative influence of each may be. A major problem here has to do with defining and measuring any one of these sets of factors, let alone "interrelating" them. Another difficulty, noted earlier, is that we are dealing with a variety of drugs used in different ways with different effects.

Still another approach, reflected in the work of an influential group of sociologists, focuses not on the factors that predispose to drug use but rather on the social response to drug taking itself; some of the dimensions of that response have been reviewed earlier. According to this view, very much simplified here, unconventional drug users, like other nonconformists, are *made* into deviants by the stigmatization, punishment, or treatment imposed on them (Duster, 1970; Young, 1971). In directing our attention to the often irrational nature of the social response to drug taking as well as in its descriptions of the consequences of that response for drug users, this group of sociologists has made an important contribution to our understanding of the drug problem. It is to them that we are particularly indebted for descriptions of drug subcultures and the ways in which they introduce people to drugs or help them to survive in a hostile environment (Goode, 1970; Johnson, 1973; Young, 1971).

A strong case can be made for the argument that it is not what some people do with drugs but how others react to them that constitutes *the* drug problem. But even if this were the case, it would contribute little to our understanding of just what predisposes some people to use drugs.

That understanding has come hard since, as noted earlier, we are dealing with various forms of drug taking and no theory offered so far has been able to satisfactorily account for them. The main reason for this state of affairs is the lack of reliable, valid information about different rates of drug use as well as about the factors related to them.

The exploration of such phenomena is a task for epidemiology, a research discipline which studies the distributions and determinants of health-related problems—its aim being not just to describe but to alleviate or help prevent those problems. Historically, epidemiology emerged as part of the effort to combat the infectious diseases. However, with their decline as threats to health in developed countries, epidemiological research in these countries has in recent years focused on a number of behavioral problems that affect individual and community health, such as accidents, mental disorders, smoking, eating, drinking, and other forms of drug use. This enterprise has engaged researchers from many disciplines—public health, medicine, psychiatry, psychology, sociology, and anthropology—and to it they bring a variety of intellectual as well as methodological orientations.

Epidemiological research on behavioral problems also reflects a tendency to apply the disease label and extend the medical response to more and more forms of deviant behavior, such as drug use. The ideological implications of such "moral entrepreneurship" need to be considered here (Freidson, 1972, Ch. 10). At first glance, it may seem more humanitarian to call some form of deviant behavior a medical rather than a criminal or moral problem. But this may be more apparent than real. The underlying assumption is that if one is sick or diseased, he is not responsible for his condition and will not be punished. However, the history of disease and of medicine shows that few if any major health problems have been divorced from moral considerations, whether the problem is madness, tuberculosis, or venereal disease. Moral considerations have been used to justify authoritarian public health control measures in the eradication of disease, measures that may conflict with notions of individual freedom. The proposal to quarantine "addicts" is in this tradition. As Room (1973) notes in a discussion of the epidemiological approach to drug use, "Ideologically (although not always practically), the eradication of disease is a moral imperative; calling something a disease is not only labelling it undersirable and abnormal, but also issuing a call for action against it." And yet, as noted earlier, in the clinical sense there is no form of drug use which is a disease, although diseases may result from or lead to particular kinds of drug use.

Similar considerations apply to the contagion model which is suggested by the name of the game—epidemiology—and it is hardly surprising that one may read in both the popular and scientific literature about "epidemics" of heroin "addiction," marijuana use, and the like, some of them involving only a few dozen cases, others involving thousands. Nor is it surprising that the contagion model has been applied in the study of drug use since many forms of drug taking (including smoking and drinking) do spread by a process of social contact, with friends or peers, rather than germs being the "agents." Indeed, some of the most imaginative research in the epidemiology of drug use, particularly as regards heroin, has adopted a model of contagion in tracing the social networks or "chains" in which the drug is introduced by one person to another (de Alarcon, 1969; Hughes, Barker, Crawford, & Jaffe, 1972; Hughes & Crawford, 1972). Like sociometric studies of friendship groupings, the contagion model describes the processes by which drug use spreads. However, no more than other theories can it determine why some people are more susceptible than others.

If the contagion model helps one understand how drug use spreads, it is also instructive regarding the stabilization or decline of drug taking. The history of infectious diseases offers several notable instances of "spontaneous" or "natural" remission or flattening out, often independently of and prior to public health or medical intervention; scarlet fever provides one example of this phenomenon (Dubos, 1959, Ch. 6). Other diseases, such as smallpox, have declined only after public health control measures were undertaken.

Data on trends in drug use are somewhat scarce. However, there is some evidence that marijuana use in the United States has begun to stabilize, possibly because the potential market for the drug is reaching the saturation point but certainly not because of the prohibition against it (Josephson, this volume). Another example of possible stabilization is provided by the reported decline of heroin use among United States veterans of the Vietnam war after they returned home (Robins, 1973b). This has been attributed in part to the breakup by demobilization of the chains or social networks that had facilitated the spread of heroin use among soldiers in Vietnam; another interpretation is that the drug was more readily available in Southeast Asia than in the United States. Whether such chains can be broken in civilian populations and with the same consequences remains to be determined.

Precisely because of the ideological as well as the policy implications of the disease model for studying and dealing with drug use, not all those engaged in epidemiological research on drug taking are prepared to accept this approach to the problem. Whether there can be "value-free" research on drug use, considering the high level of public concern and the determination, however misguided, to do something about it, is an issue that merits far more discussion than it has received. Similar questions, of course, can be raised about research on any other social problem.

Quite apart from such ideological questions, major conceptual and methodological issues confront the epidemiology of drug use. Conceptually, the chief problem has to do with the definition of terms regarding use itself. We have already noted the confusion among specialists as well as the public regarding terms such as "addiction" and "abuse." A major obstacle to progress in the epidemiology of drug use is the failure of researchers to agree on the meanings of the terms they employ. Both the United States National Commission on Marihuana and Drug Abuse and the Canadian Commission on the Non-Medical Use of Drugs have drawn attention to this confusion; both have also proposed ways of overcoming it (*Drug use in America: Problem in perspective*, 1973, pp. 93-98, 121-140; *Final report of the Commission of Inquiry into the non-medical use of drugs*, 1973, Appendix C).

In principle, data are required on the extent and level or intensity of drug use in any given population. Extent of use refers to the numbers or proportions who are using some particular drug at any one moment in time (what epidemiologists call "prevalence") or who begin to use it during some period of time (what epidemiologists call "incidence"). This may be illustrated by the statistics available in many countries on per capita consumption of alcoholic beverages or tobacco.

Level of use refers to the frequency with which individuals in any given population have "ever" used or are currently using a particular drug. Here numerous difficulties present themselves. To call drug users those who have "ever" tried a drug means including some who have done so only once as well as others who may have stopped. Current use is therefore preferable, if agreement can be reached on what is "current." Another difficulty has to do with differences among drugs in the way their use is distributed. This may be illustrated in several ways. For example, substantial proportions of those who consume tobacco or alcoholic beverages do so "regularly," i.e., on a daily basis. On the other hand, among those who use marijuana, relatively few do so regularly; for most it is an occasional or irregular experience. To take another example, monthly use of marijuana cannot be equated with monthly use of LSD.

Various typologies of drug use have been proposed. The National Commission on Marihuana and Drug Abuse differentiates between experimental use, social or recreational use, circumstantial or situational drug use, intensified use, and compulsive use. The Canadian Commission of Inquiry distinguishes between experimental, occasional, and regular drug use. Although these typologies appear to represent an improvement over earlier classifications, the practical problem for researchers has been to achieve agreement on the definition of such categories and to apply them to a variety of drugs. Failure to reach any such agreement regarding either the time periods being covered or the categories of use levels has made it difficult if not impossible to obtain comparable findings (Elinson, Haberman, Hervey, & Allyn, 1974).

The conceptual issues discussed so far pertain to levels of drug use at some particular moment or period of time. Still another problem is presented by the fact that many people change their levels and patterns of drug use over time—some of them initiating use, some increasing their consumption, others decreasing or stopping use, and still others switching from one drug to another or using a combination of drugs. As the Canadian Commission of Inquiry notes, "The examination of this social process or 'career' of drug use can be viewed as the study of how an individual changes his position in the per capita consumption distribution over time (which is a within-subject analysis over time, as opposed to a between-subject analysis at a given point in time) [*Final report of the Commission of Inquiry into the non-medical use of drugs,* 1973, p. 673]." Studies of the "natural history" of drug careers have so far been attempted most notably with reference to heroin users (Winick, this volume) and the techniques for undertaking such studies differ from what is involved in determining consumption levels.

Regarding the measurement of drug use, several issues present themselves. Perhaps the main issue is that many—not all—of the drugs about which we are concerned can only be obtained illicitly. The production and consumption data available for legally manufactured substances such as tobacco, alcoholic beverages, prescription drugs, and over-the-counter drugs are missing, of course, for heroin, marijuana, or LSD; guesses about the amount of trafficking in illicit drugs, some of them quite ingenious, are no more than that—guesses. Rates of arrest for possession of illicit drugs or the numbers receiving treatment of various sorts, though significant indicators of the social response to drug taking, are unreliable as measures of consumption rates or of trends in use. To be sure, several countries have attempted to "register" narcotics users; but with the possible exception of the United Kingdom (Hawks, this volume), most such registers tend to understate the actual numbers involved. However, drug registers and the recent rapid expansion of treatment facilities with their large "captive" populations of drug users provide unusual opportunities for research on drug careers as well as for the evaluation of treatment programs (Lukoff, this volume).

Lacking the kinds of data available for legally manufactured drugs, epidemiological research on levels of illicit drug use has relied to a considerable extent on population surveys in which respondents are asked about their past or present use of drugs. Until fairly recently, most of these surveys have been conducted with selected populations, particularly secondary school and college students, in which levels of drug use are presumably high. Relatively few surveys of general populations have been undertaken so far; one reason for this is that they are unlikely to uncover many cases of uncommonly used drugs, e.g., cocaine or heroin.

These surveys vary widely in quality; but all present questions about the reliability, validity, and generalizability of their findings regarding illicit drug use. Surveys of deviant behavior are by no means new, but they all face the risk of encountering underreporting or overreporting of the behavior being studied. Thus the question as to the validity or truthfulness of what people report about illicit drug use has yet to be studied systematically. Such techniques as examining the contents of medicine cabinets to check on the reported use of psychotherapeutic and over-the-counter drugs are of no help here. Indeed, with the possible exception of matching urinalyses with self-reports of heroin use, there are as yet no practicable ways of validating survey data on illicit drug use. As for the generalizability of such data, this is a function of the population being studied; the many surveys of selected populations which have been conducted do not provide a reliable base for drawing inferences about general levels of drug use or trends in consumption.

Another problem with much of the epidemiological research on drug use undertaken so far is that it has relied on cross-sectional studies, that is, surveys conducted with particular populations at one moment in time. These studies are informative regarding the extent and levels of drug use as well as the correlates of such behavior; if repeated, they can also provide data on trends in drug consumption. This method is unsuitable, however, for getting at the processes of individual change in drug use. To achieve this objective—i.e., to better understand the interplay of social and personal factors that predispose some people to use drugs in unacceptable ways and to understand more fully the careers of drug users—the appropriate method is longitudinal research, prospective as well as retrospective. The difficulties of conducting longitudinal research on drug use are formidable, not least because of the time required, and relatively few studies of this kind have been undertaken so far (O'Donnell, 1973; Robins, 1973a).

One of the greatest difficulties that epidemiological research on drug use faces is that the drug scene is always subject to change over time and in place—and sometimes very rapid change. In several countries it is believed that the heroin "epidemics" which began during the 1960s have peaked and that "the" problem of today is multidrug use. Whether this is indeed true and, if so, what may explain such cycles remain to be determined. The monitoring of trends in drug use is a primary task for epidemiological research. Also needed is comparative study of drug use and the response to it in countries with different traditions and patterns of drug taking; but relatively few such cross-cultural studies have been undertaken so far.

These are only some of the conceptual and methodological issues that present themselves in the epidemiology of drug use. They as well as others are discussed more fully in the following chapters.

Epidemiology is an applied discipline, its ultimate purpose being to help communities deal with their health problems. The question as to how epidemiological research on drug use can be utilized and the role to be played in this process by social scientists themselves was put directly by Dr. José Nine Curt, dean of the University of Puerto Rico School of Public Health, in his welcoming address to the San Juan conference which led to this book. In the course of his remarks, Dr. Nine said:

> Some of my best friends are behavioral scientists. Many of them are loaded with statistics. They attend meeting after meeting, present paper after paper, figure out correlation after correlation, and trend after trend. But those of us who are engaged in the training of health workers and in the delivery of health services read about trends and correlations and must nevertheless cope with an incoherent, illogical and ineffective drug policy. . . .

> Instead of being applied, drug research seems to have become an end in itself. Let me ask: Have you learned from each other's experiences? Have your own projects been well-evaluated? Or is your success in obtaining grants determined by who has the more novel or esoteric idea? We need not deprecate creativity; but I believe that we must evaluate the utility of the research we do; otherwise, we isolate ourselves and become irrelevant.

> More specifically, we all know that it is much easier to deal with the addict than to prevent drug abuse. . . . However, the preventive techniques of the past are no longer effective; we must think in terms not only of the proximal etiological factors related to drug abuse but also of the distal factors. How much more could have been accomplished in the past if our orientation had been truly preventive? For many years we have been taking boys out of the poverty of rural farms in Puerto Rico or out of the urban slums and sending them to Fort Jackson and then on to Vietnam. Along the way they learned about guns, mines and sophisticated radio equipment; but why didn't they learn about the dangers of heroin?

> I have been and am a strong supporter of the integration of the behavioral sciences in the delivery and evaluation of health care. To be sure, not all health workers want to be "integrated." Nor do all behavioral scientists want to be integrated with health workers, even though the former have often been among the integrators. However, public health is a relatively young profession and behavioral scientists are newcomers to public health. Although we know how to administer vaccinations, we know little about dealing with such problems as drug abuse. What we want is to bring the drug abuser into the community. To do so, we need the help of behavioral scientists—as integrators.

> Epidemiology itself provides a key to integration. Just as cancer has forced us to engage all the biomedical disciplines in an integrated attack on the disease, so too social problems such as drug abuse require a similar integration and attack. However, we not only need more white-coated professionals; we also need "barefoot" epidemiologists. And I cannot emphasize enough the importance of including behavioral scientists in this endeavor. To them I say—you cannot permit yourselves complacently to think that the application of your findings is someone else's problem; it is yours as well as ours. . . . There are those of us who are committed to improving the health of our people. Let us all reassess and renew that commitment.

Whether epidemiologists and social scientists can meet Dr. Nine's challenge remains to be seen. Even if they can, there is the question as to how many social "casualties" any society is prepared to tolerate and what, if any, alternatives it can provide them. Meanwhile, the present volume is intended as a contribution to that effort.

REFERENCES

Blum, R. H., & Associates. *Society and drugs.* San Francisco: Jossey-Bass, 1969.

Brecher, E. M., & the Editors of Consumer Reports. *Licit and illicit drugs.* Mount Vernon, N.Y.: Consumers Union, 1972.

Chein, I. Psychological functions of drug use. In H. Steinberg (Ed.), *Scientific basis of drug dependence.* London: Churchill, 1969.

Cloward, R., & Ohlin, L. E. *Delinquency and opportunity.* Glencoe, Ill.: Free Press, 1960.

de Alarcon, R. The The spread of heroin abuse in a community. *Bulletin on Narcotics,* 1969, 21(3), 17–22.

de Alarcon, R. An epidemiological evaluation of a public health measure aimed at reducing the availability of methylamphetamine. *Psychological Medicine,* 1972, 2(3), 293–300.

Drug use in America: Problem in perspective. Second Report of the National Commission on Marihuana and Drug Abuse. Washington, D.C.: U.S. Government Printing Office, Mar. 1973.

Dubos, R. *Mirage of health.* New York: Anchor Books, 1959. ·

Duster, T. *The legislation of morality: Law, drugs, and moral judgment.* New York: Free Press, 1970.

Elinson, J., Haberman, P. W., Hervey, L., & Allyn, A. L. Operational definition of terms in drug-use research. Report prepared for the Special Action Office for Drug Abuse Prevention. Division of Sociomedical Sciences, School of Public Health, Columbia University, May 1974.

Final report of the Commission of Inquiry into the non-medical use of drugs. Ottawa: Information Canada, 1973.

Freidson, E. *Profession of medicine.* New York: Dodd, Mead, 1972.

Goode, E. *The marijuana smokers.* New York: Basic Books, 1970.

Goode, E. *Drugs in American society.* New York: Knopf, 1972.

Gusfield, J. R. *Symbolic crusade: Status politics and the American temperance movement.* Urbana, Ill.: University of Illinois Press, 1963.

HEALTH/PAC Bulletin. June 1970.

Hughes, P. H., Barker, N. W., Crawford, G. A., & Jaffe, J. H. The natural history of a heroin epidemic. *American Journal of Public Health,* 1972, 62(7), 995–1001.

Hughes, P. H., & Crawford, G. A. A contagious disease model for researching and intervening in heroin epidemics. *Archives of General Psychiatry,* 1972, 27(2), 149–155.

Jessor, R., Graves, T. D., Hanson, R. C., & Jessor, S. L. *Society, personality and deviant behavior.* New York: Holt, Rinehart & Winston, 1968.

Johnson, B. D. *Marihuana users and drug subcultures.* New York: Wiley, 1973.

Joyce, C. R. B. Some possible reactions to drug abuse. *Proceedings of the Anglo-American conference on drug abuse.* London: The Royal Society of Medicine, 1973.

Laurie, P. *Drugs: Medical, psychological and social facts.* (2nd ed.) Harmondsworth: Penguin Books, 1971.

Lennard, H. L., Epstein, L. J., Bernstein, A., & Ransom, D. E. *Mystification and drug misuse.* San Francisco: Jossey-Bass, 1971.

Modell, W. Mass drug catastrophes and the roles of science and technology. *Science,* April 21, 1967, 156, 346–351.

Musto, D. F. *The American disease: Origins of narcotic control.* New Haven: Yale University Press, 1973.

The New York Times. Nov. 15, 1973.

O'Donnell, J. A. The methodology of retrospective studies. *The epidemiology of drug dependence.* Copenhagen: Regional Office for Europe, World Health Organization, 1973.

Robins, L. N. The methodology of prospective studies of drug abuse. *The epidemiology of drug dependence.* Copenhagen: Regional Office for Europe, World Health Organization, 1973. (a)

Robins, L. N. *A follow-up of Vietnam drug users.* Special Action Office for Drug Abuse Prevention. Washington, D.C.: U.S. Government Printing Office, 1973. (b)

Room, R. The epidemic model and its assumptions. *The Drinking and Drug Practices Surveyor,* Aug. 1973, 8, 16–21.

The Roper Report. July 1971, **1.**

Singer, M. The vitality of mythical numbers. *The Public Interest,* Spring 1971, **23,** 3–9.

Wikler, A. Dynamics of drug dependence: Implications of a conditioning theory for research and treatment. S. Fisher & A. M. Freedman (Eds.), *Opiate addiction: Origins and treatment.* Washington, D.C.: V. H. Winston & Sons, 1973.

Young, J. *The drugtakers: The social meaning of drug use.* London: Paladin, 1971.

Zacune, J., & Hensman, C. *Drugs, alcohol and tobacco in Great Britain.* London: Heinemann Medical Books, 1971.

Zinberg, N. E., & Robertson, J. A. *Drugs and the public.* New York: Simon & Schuster, 1972.

PART I
CONCEPTUAL ISSUES

1
DRUG ABUSE: A CONCEPTUAL ANALYSIS AND OVERVIEW OF THE CURRENT SITUATION*

Mitchell B. Balter
Psychopharmacology Research Branch
National Institute of Mental Health

ANALYSIS OF THE CURRENT SITUATION

In the midst of the current social crisis over drug abuse it is helpful to distinguish two sets of separate but related problems:

- The widespread and increasing misuse of drugs and the attendant human casualties, social costs, and social liabilities.
- Society's reaction, in most instances overreaction, to the actual and threatened consequences of widespread illicit drug use—especially among the young.

Part of society's overreaction to the problem can be attributed to a common tendency toward all-or-none thinking, which does not recognize any refined or subtle distinctions between the concept of illicit use and the realities of hard-core abuse. The net result is a lumping together in the public mind of all kinds of illicit drug behavior, which extends from minor technical transgressions to dependency and serious involvement. In this type of thinking, the danger is equivalent to the number of people who have used drugs illicitly; thus, by definition, there exists an overwhelming and threatening problem.

There also has been a general failure to recognize the extent to which unexamined attitudes, values, and opinions are imbedded in the issue; and there has been a tendency to react on the basis of a priori feelings and assumptions rather than careful analysis of the facts. This is equally true of the young proponents of drug use and the older members of society who strongly oppose it.

*This chapter is extracted from "Character and Extent of Psychotherapeutic Drug Usage in the United States", *Proceedings of the Vth World Congress of Psychiatry, Mexico, 1971.* Amsterdam: Exerpta Medica Foundation, 1973.

Current reaction frequently borders on hysteria, which seriously impedes the kind of constructive thought and action that is required to mount a significant attack on the core problem of casualties, costs, and consequences of drug abuse to which this chapter is mainly addressed.

At the risk of oversimplification, positions currently being taken in the United States can be characterized in ideological terms as "hawk," "moderate," and "dove."[1] The distribution is neither uniform nor bell-shaped. There are many indications that the majority, primarily older persons and those with adolescent children at risk, are hawkishly disposed. A significant vocal minority, mainly recruited from the young, white, middle class, can be classified as doves; and a much smaller heterogeneous group of persons who hold moderate attitudes and opinions can be found in various age and social-class strata. Unfortunately, moderate, informed voices are seldom heard above the general din. Many hawks have mixed feelings because they do not want to see their children arrested or exposed in a fashion that will threaten future careers.

In this highly charged atmosphere of contrary attitude and opinion, rational public discourse is rare. It is difficult—and without special effort on the part of opinion leaders it will continue to be difficult—to entertain novel solutions and to develop, implement, or gain acceptance for realistic programs of remedial action contrary to invested prejudices. Except in the case of heroin addiction, the distribution of opinion and intensity of concern over illicit drug usage bears little relationship to the facts about the overall occurrence of adverse consequences. Compared with such problems as alcoholism, mental illness, automobile injuries, and fatalities, the problem of drug abuse is relatively small. Response to the problem probably should be titrated to the need rather than the outcry. With the present high public concern and stiff competition for public monies, one should be wary of inflated and unrefined estimates of the magnitude of the problem—estimates that could be self-serving.

Overreaction to the threatened consequences of illicit drug use among the children of the middle class has, in many instances, led to public policies and actions that were hastily drawn, ill considered, and destined for failure. The strong pressure of public opinion has led many to grasp at the most readily available solutions and to err in the direction of overcontrol through externally imposed sanctions on behavior, which to date have had little or no effect.

Reaction to the economic and social costs of heroin addiction in the ghetto has been more considered, but evidence of overreaction to the specter of the violent addict can be seen in the somewhat premature willingness of professionals and public officials to accept methadone maintenance as an

---

[1] To my knowledge Dr. Gerald Klerman, Professor of Psychiatry, Harvard University, was the first person to apply these popular terms to drug abuse.

established treatment and the pell mell rush to get thousands of addicts on the drug without due consideration of the possible long-term consequences.

Not only may hasty and ill-considered policies be ineffective, but they may generate qualitatively different types of casualties and adverse consequences of a medical, social, and legal nature. Some of these consequences are loss of respect for the law, extensive arrest records among the young for only technical or minor violations, and accidental deaths and levels of dependence hitherto unknown as a function of leaks in widely dispersed and often poorly conceived methadone maintenance programs.

Lack of agreement on a definition of drug abuse within and outside government makes it difficult to develop coherent and comprehensive plans for a national program of prevention, treatment, and rehabilitation. When drug abuse is variously defined as a legal, moral, medical, or social problem, programmatic goals and actions frequently conflict with one another. The legal definition equates drug abuse with the mere act of using a proscribed drug or using a drug under proscribed conditions. The moral definition is similar, but greater emphasis is placed on the motivation or purpose for which the drug is used. The medical model opposes unsupervised usage but emphasizes the physical and mental consequences for the user, and the social definition stresses social responsibility and adverse effects on others. It probably would be most practical to seek agreement on a set of goals emphasizing the consequences to be avoided and the conditions of use likely to give rise to those consequences.

Another common failure worth mentioning is the failure to realize that illicit drug use is both a symptom and a cause. It is not an isolated or unitary phenomenon but a powerful social-cultural indicator that reflects the quality and character of life in the United States. A proper understanding of who uses what drugs for what purposes can provide insights into American character structure and reveal much about current social dynamics. Heroin addiction, for example, can be viewed as a response to frustration by those who have been denied access to the mainstream of American life. Use of marijuana and LSD by middle-class youth can be viewed as an attempt to avoid or overcome the dreariness and dissatisfactions of conventional middle-class life which they can neither fully accept nor completely reject.

Ready attribution of the drug-abuse problem to gross phenomena such as the Vietnam war, extensive use of drugs by middle-class parents, TV advertising, or to poverty as such is a convenient form of scapegoating that does not go to the heart of the matter or, even if true, get to a level of causation that is applicable to the individual drug abuser. Realistic programs for prevention, treatment, and rehabilitation cannot be built on negative abstractions, unexamined and undocumented premises, or vague postulates about distal social forces.

Basic value conflicts certainly are involved in the problem of drug abuse among middle-class youth, but these conflicts are more of the type that pits the traditional virtues of safety, deliberateness, and moderation against a position that sees virtue in risk and immediate spontaneous experience.

SOME BASIC ASSUMPTIONS

Drug use inside and outside the medical system differs in several important respects, but there are also many similarities among the various types of drug use. These similarities can be cast in the form of a set of assumptions or hypotheses, which could be of great theoretical and practical importance in the area of drug abuse.

Coping

The use of psychoactive drugs can be seen as but one alternative among many for coping with the subjective needs, desires, and problems of life. If so, the critical questions are: Why this alternative as opposed to some other? Why this alternative to the exclusion of all others? and What factors increase or decrease the likelihood that the individual will resort to drugs?

Choice

Most drug use can be viewed as a matter of choice, whether inside or outside the medical system, for seldom is the person so ill or in such distress that there is no other recourse. This implies that there are wide individual differences in personal criteria of illness and tolerance for discomfort. Decisions to visit the physician or seek drugs directly need not be rational or deliberate, but the action suggests that at some level a choice among available alternatives has been made.

Interaction of Drugs and Needs

Individuals take drugs that fit their needs or that are deemed desirable by their important reference group. In the physician's office, the patient is prescribed a drug that fits his complaints; if he does not like it he rejects it and gets another. On the street, he searches about and finds a drug or class of drugs that fits his needs, or he takes the drugs that produce effects valued by his reference group.

This approach is generally in keeping with what we know about the heroin, psychedelic, and alcohol subcultures, although the fit is far from perfect. It argues for an approach to the problem which emphasizes a thorough understanding of both the drugs and the subcultures.

Benefit-Risk Ratio

There is a benefit-risk ratio associated with use of all drugs whether inside or outside the medical system, and illicit drug users are making choices similar to those made inside the medical system but with much less precision and with much less reliable knowledge at their disposal. Immediate threats of psychosis did not stop LSD users, but inconclusive evidence about possible chromosome damage did.

Cost-Benefit Ratio

There is also a cost-benefit ratio associated with all drug use in terms of personal and social consequences. The cost-benefit question applies to the use of drugs versus other coping mechanisms, the use of one drug versus another, the use of drugs in an otherwise hopeless situation, and so on. The heroin user may find immediate relief in the drug, but its use will obviously have some bad personal and social consequences. The key question to be asked is what other personal and social alternatives are readily available to him.

Compensatory Behavior

Finally, the model anticipates the occurrence of compensatory behavior and assumes that if an individual—for personal, social, economic, or cultural reasons—does not appear in the medical system, he may appear in some other system where he gets the drugs that meet his needs. If, however, he has alternative coping mechanisms or other social pathways readily available, he may find it unnecessary or undesirable to use drugs. It is significant that young black, Puerto Rican, and Mexican males, who are underrepresented in visits to physicians, are overrepresented in the population of heroin addicts.

SCOPE AND SPECTRUM OF DRUGS OF ABUSE

The spectrum of drugs and other substances with psychoactive properties and potential for abuse is wide and will no doubt continue to grow, partly as a function of our conventional drug development system and partly as a function of the increasing knowledge, sophistication, and mobility of illicit drug users. Many drugs currently unavailable on the street, THC for example, are likely to appear there at some future date as are mixtures and combinations not yet discovered by the drug cognoscenti. The list of "culpable" drugs is long and could reasonably include the following: caffeine, alcohol, minor tranquilizers, barbiturates, nonbarbiturate hypnotics, stimulants, opiates and derivatives, cocaine, psychedelics, marijuana-hashish-THC, and inhalants. Other such drugs are many over-the-counter (OTC) preparations containing scopolamine, atropine, or other belladonna alkaloids, as well as many natural products such as morning glory seeds, wood rose, and so on. Methadone is culpable, as are OTC nasal sprays containing epinephrine and some bronchial dilators containing ephedrine. The list is practically endless. Attempts to closely control all these substances would be cumbersome and make serious inroads into the freedom of the majority of Americans who use drugs in a responsible manner.

It is also difficult to anticipate which drugs will be judged attractive and become popular on the street. A case in point is LSD. Prior to 1958, who would have guessed that a drug with its frightening hallucinogenic properties would dance out of the laboratory and be so enthusiastically embraced by the educated middle class? Our record of hindsight is second to none: the next wave of abuse is usually upon us by the time we can classify a new dangerous drug or control the supply.

Given the almost endless variety of substances that can be abused and the millions of people disposed to try them, it seems unreasonable to assume that in the long run the problem can be solved by further imposition of external controls or the elimination of all drugs of abuse. The main hope would seem to lie in the direction of increased knowledge and appropriate internal sanctions coupled with a nonpunitive environment that would encourage those with drug problems to step forward freely for treatment and/or support.

Ultimately, as with alcohol and other freely available drugs, the best we can hope for is responsible and moderate behavior toward drugs on the part of most people in the society.

WHAT DRUGS CAN DO

When discussing abuse, it is common practice to refer to dangerous drugs rather than dangerous people and to thus assume that the fault lies solely with the drug. An examination of this complex issue may help clarify matters.

Myths

Part of the basic attraction of any drug, including heroin, is the set of myths and claims that surround it. These become part of the rationale for using the drug and also serve as a set of guidelines for the effects to be sought and valued. In the case of marijuana, LSD, and other psychedelic drugs, the myths and claims have taken on the character of a "party line" and are thus difficult to dispel. Grand claims for marijuana have diminished as the drug has become more widely used but persist for LSD and other hallucinogenic agents because of their impressive potency. The marked alterations of consciousness produced by LSD can be influenced by prior expectations and lend themselves to various interpretations by the user, a situation that tends to promote belief in the original contentions. The user finds it hard to believe that a drug with such powerful acute subjective effects cannot in some way produce significant and lasting changes in personality or outlook. He may then take the drug repeatedly in search of those changes and become increasingly confused, to the point of losing touch with reality. Therein lies one of the great dangers associated with hallucinogenic drugs, in the interaction between myths or expectations and the clinical effects of the drugs—factors that tend to reinforce one another in circular fashion.

To the extent that myths are part of the inherent dangers associated with drugs, they should be addressed directly through research and systematic accumulation of data on drug careers of heavy or involved users. Data on the validity of current contentions about drugs may not be the whole answer, but it is difficult to proceed rationally without having such information readily at hand. To obtain information of this type in any reasonable period of time, it is necessary to have a free climate for research and investigation. Drugs of interest must be freely available to legitimate researchers, who must be in a position to pursue their topic of choice in acceptable scientific fashion. In many instances state laws and regulations prevent such research, as does a federal posture of fear and distrust. The argument need not be restricted to the topic of investigating drug myths; it is generally applicable to the whole field of research and treatment in the area of drug abuse.

More Basic Questions About Drugs

When discussing or classifying drugs of abuse, it is helpful to recall that their effects are dose related and dependent on the manner in which they are taken. Certain consequences follow from particular dosage regimens, routes of administration, and patterns of use and not from others. These principles hold even for heroin, although the safety range is much smaller than for many other drugs. Acute administration of a drug at high dosage may be harmful, chronic administration at low dosage may not. Chronic intermittent use may be innocuous, chronic regular use extremely dangerous. The consequences of oral administration may be mild, the consequences of injection disastrous.

The effects of long-term chronic administration of illicit drugs such as marijuana and LSD in man are essentially unknown and probably will have to be established by statistical association, as was done with cigarette smoking. The long-term effects of high- and low-dosage methadone in man are also unknown—which should give some pause to treatment programs proposing indefinite maintenance as a therapeutic goal.

The major point to be made, one that is often lost sight of in current styles of all-or-none thinking about drug abuse, is that in general drugs are as dangerous as the conditions and circumstances under which they are being taken. Although one can produce paranoid psychoses in most people in a fairly short period of time by administering successively larger doses of amphetamine at a rapid rate, very few people have ever taken the drug in this manner of their own accord. In most instances, danger can be translated into mode of drug administration and pattern of acquisition and use.

It is often assumed that drug abuse can be defined by the simple expedient of combining formal concepts of drug classification with the notion of unsupervised use—a proposition that does not stand up under close scrutiny.

Once we formally recognize the existence of various patterns of illicit drug use and a hierachy of consequences, some more serious than others, it becomes possible to deal with the problem in a more realistic manner through a series of graded actions and alternatives. We might want to provide young people who are using drugs occasionally with information on the quality and character of available street drugs to protect them from harm. We might provide prophylactic information to the young street addict—whom we cannot yet reach for treatment—that will enable him to avoid serious infection or death from an overdose.

From a medical-sociological point of view, the critical distinctions between use and abuse come down to the following questions: In what manner is the drug being used, in what situations, for what purposes, and with what consequences?

A working definition of drug abuse that might help organize thinking and action in the areas of prevention, treatment, and rehabilitation would be the following:

Use of a drug or other substance with central nervous system activity in excessive amounts, or in a fashion, whether on one occasion or repeatedly, so as to produce:

1. Significant physical or psychological dependency.
2. Serious mental or personality disturbances, psychoses, or serious and/or prolonged states of disorientation.
3. Serious impairment of personal and/or social functioning, including significant toxicity of behavior, e.g., impulsivity, poor judgment, and psycho-motor instability.
4. Death or behavior endangering the life of oneself or others.
5. Serious interference with growth of personality and/or social development, particularly among younger persons.
6. Physical damage or debility—physiological, biochemical, genetic, neuro-logical, etc.

This definition emphasizes the more immediate consequences of drug taking per se rather than the highly probable secondary social consequences such as arrest, incarceration, or crimes committed in the interest of obtaining needed drugs. While important, these secondary consequences are mainly a function of society's legal stance with respect to drugs and its reaction to drug abusers rather than being intrinsic consequences of drug ingestion.

The virtue of the position is that it is realistic and permits specific actions to be directed toward specific consequences for specific purposes. It does not equate moderate or occasional use of a drug in the service of pleasure, comfort, or efficiency with serious involvement with drugs. In the past we have too easily assumed that if a drug is not administered or ordered by a physician, or taken under his supervision, or is not one that is in his official repertoire, the action should immediately be condemned and labeled abuse. The issues are obviously more complex than that, and the traditional position simply will not bear up as long as alcohol continues to be freely available and freely abused by a significant number of Americans. It may not be possible to eliminate serious abuse of drugs, but it may be possible to reduce the problem to tolerable limits and minimize many adverse consequences that are currently associated with it.

MATRIX OF DANGER

Arriving at decisions about what constitutes a dangerous drug of abuse and then ranking or classifying drugs accordingly is the most natural point to begin deliberations about action. To avoid confusion, the discussion should be addressed to the intrinsic characteristics of the drug and its effects under various circumstances of use rather than indirect consequences which are derivatives of current laws, regulations, norms, or social practices.

The following dimensions of analysis constitute what might be termed a "matrix of danger" for drugs of abuse:[2]

1. Attractiveness of the drug—the extent to which most people find the immediate effects of the drug intrinsically pleasing.

2. Mode of administration—associated dangers.

3. Ease with which tolerance to the drug develops, if at all.

4. Ease with which significant physical or psychological dependency can be established, if at all.

5. Intensity of physical or psychological dependency.

6. Death liability—likelihood or danger of death from overdose, high dosage, or excessive use.

7. Behavioral toxicity—adverse behavioral consequences of excessive use.

8. Side effects and/or serious adverse effects on the organism associated with long-term or excessive use.

9. Character and severity of withdrawal syndrome, if any.

A brief discriptive analysis of some key drugs of abuse in terms of this matrix of danger will help place the drugs in appropriate perspective for later discussions and deliberations.

Heroin

Attractiveness: Very pleasing effect for most people.

Mode of administration: Some snorting, but primarily by injection.

Tolerance: Develops rapidly and easily, initiated by repeated administration of small dosages, increases directly with dosage, requires increase in dosage to obtain same psychological effects.

Occurrence of dependence: Physical dependence develops early and increases indefinitely with dosage.

Intensity of dependence: Severe physical and psychological dependence can be established.

[2] This approach is meant to be illustrative rather than exhaustive.

Death liability: Death from overdose is easily accomplished.

Behavioral toxicity: Mild, primarily associated with acute intoxication.

Side effects/adverse effects: constipation, loss of appetite, and reduced libido.

Withdrawal syndrome: Symptoms appear within few hours of last dosage; many symptoms including vomiting, diarrhea, aches and pains, tremors, and sweating. Abrupt withdrawal not usually life threatening, however.

Barbiturates

Attractiveness: Moderate.

Mode of administration: Oral or injection, but mainly oral.

Tolerance: Develops fairly rapidly with low doses, but there is a limit to which the person can become tolerant.

Occurrence of dependence: Physical and psychological dependence develop, but establishment of physical dependence usually requires repeated ingestion of doses well above therapeutic dose levels.

Intensity of dependence: Can reach very severe levels.

Death liability: Very high, death rather easily accomplished, particularly in combination with alcohol.

Behavioral toxicity: Severe and persistent if person has exceeded his level of tolerance: ataxia, motor incoordination, confusion, accident proneness, instability, and assaultiveness.

Side effects/adverse effects: Mental disturbances, coma, respiratory failure, shock after long-term chronic administration on high dosages.

Withdrawal: Occurs 24–48 hours after last dosage and reaches peak in 2–3 days. Symptoms severe and often life threatening: grand mal seizures, depression of respiratory functions, delirium tremens, major psychotic episodes, etc.

Amphetamines

Attractiveness: High.

Mode of administration: Oral or by injection; oral administration much more frequent and effects by this route much less severe.

Tolerance: Develops slowly but persists even at high dosage levels; tolerance to euphoric effects occurs much more rapidly than to negative effects of irritability, nervousness, and insomnia.

Occurrence of dependence: Psychological dependence, but no physical dependence despite tolerance.

Intensity of dependence: Severe, almost compulsive psychic dependence can occur.

Death liability: Death from high dosages can occur via convulsions or coma; cerebral hemorrhages with very large acute dosages, but the event is rare.

Behavioral toxicity: Pronounced at high dosages and includes impulsivity, accident proneness, assaultiveness and antisocial behavior, and erratic actions.

Side effects/adverse effects: Bizarre mental effects such as delusions, hallucinations, and toxic psychoses of a paranoid type. Much more likely to occur after intravenous administration.

Withdrawal: No characteristic withdrawal syndrome as such, but symptoms of depression and gross fatigue are common when drug is suddenly stopped after chronic use at high dosages.

Marijuana

Attractiveness: Moderate.

Mode of administration: Primarily smoked, but sometimes put in food.

Tolerance: Very little if any when smoked, but may be more pronounced for new liquid form of THC.

Dependence: No physical dependency and only mild to moderate psychological dependency.

Death liability: Death by overdose or from excessive use not known to occur.

Behavioral toxicity: Some motor incoordination and ataxia associated with acute intoxication; some possible slowing of reactions after long-term frequent use.

Side effects/adverse effects: Amotivational syndrome and indolence in some heavy users and rare panic or paranoid states in naive users.

Withdrawal: No known symptoms or sequelae when drug is stopped.

LSD

Attractiveness: Low to moderate.

Mode of administration: Oral or injection but oral much more typical.

Tolerance: Very rapid to single high dose, but also disappears rapidly.

Occurrence of dependence: No physical dependency, some psychological dependency.

Intensity of dependence: Psychological dependency mild, with ready willingness to substitute other drugs.

Death liability: Deaths from overdose are unknown.

Behavioral toxicity: Acute state is dangerous because of sensory distortion, but chronic behavioral effects, if any, tend to be mild.

Side effects/adverse effects: Panic states, psychoses—temporary and more permanent, and other mental disturbances can be precipitated by the drug. Frightening flashbacks are also fairly common; death or other dangers can ensue from hallucinatory or delusional states precipitated by acute administration of the drug.

Withdrawal: Does not occur; however, the occurrence of some increased sensitivity to succeeding dosages is suspected.

Cocaine

Attractiveness: Very high.

Mode of administration: Sniffed, injected intravenously, or swallowed. However, injection is prime route.

Tolerance: No tolerance develops, and drug is so rapidly destroyed in organism that large quantities can be taken in 24-hour period by repeated administration of small dosages at short intervals.

Occurrence of dependence: No physical dependence, but frequent psychological dependence.

Intensity of dependence: Profound and dangerous psychological dependence can and does occur.

Death liability: Deaths from convulsions and respiratory failure occur; the drug can be quite toxic in very high dosages, but lethal dose in man is unknown.

Behavioral toxicity: Pronounced and dangerous in character; includes such things as violence, overestimation of capabilities, extreme impulsivity, etc.

Side effects/adverse effects: Usually severe in the inveterate user. Paranoid delusions and auditory, visual, and tactile hallucinations are common; user's life becomes disorganized. Nausea, sleeplessness, tremors, and digestive disorders are also common among heavy users.

Withdrawal: No characteristic abstinence syndrome has been observed, but depression may occur and delusions may persist for some time after withdrawal.

HOW PEOPLE ARE USING DRUGS

Ultimately the basic issues in drug abuse come down to questions about what people are doing and are likely to do with respect to drugs and what the consequences of their behavior might be. The drug-abuse scene has been changing rapidly during the past few years. Yesterday's information and perceptions of the situation can go out of date quickly.

Since patterns of use are so important in evaluating risk and these can change rapidly over time, we must monitor the situation carefully through repeated cross-sectional studies and repeated longitudinal studies in users and in the general population. When the activity is both disreputable and clandestine (e.g., heroin addiction), such studies obviously are difficult to carry out. This problem, however, is partially offset by the fact that in the long run overt manifestations and consequences of heroin addiction are difficult to hide: chronic and heavy users tend to surface somewhere in the health care or correctional systems.

Knowledge about typical drug careers is critically important because this gives us a basis for planning treatment and rehabilitation programs and extrapolating risks. For example, although incidence of marijuana use among college students has increased sharply during the past few years, a significant proportion of users continue to try the drug a few times and then quit. On the other hand, it is now also apparent that a significant proportion of the users have continued to use the drug on a once-or-twice-a-week basis over a fairly long period of time.

The major advantage of population data is that risk can be placed in the larger perspective of use. It is on the occurrence of casualties that we must base our decisions about the use of particular drugs and the actions taken with respect to them. The critical question is, What level of casualties are we willing to accept?

SCHEMA FOR EVALUATING DRUG PROBLEMS

What constitutes a dangerous drug and what we mean by abuse potential are complex questions that have important ramifications for policy, treatment, and prevention. By examining these questions carefully and teasing apart the issues we can move toward a framework which will help us evaluate drug problems and develop some policy decisions.

From one point of view, almost all drugs are dangerous if taken in sufficient dosage for a sufficient length of time. However, not all drugs have abuse potential. Most so-called drugs of abuse are drawn from among those with psychoactive properties—drugs that have significant effects on mental processes, mood, and behavior—but not all drugs with psychoactive properties have significant or equal abuse potential. Chlorpromazine, for example, has powerful psychological effects, but has little or no abuse potential in the popular sense of the term.

The term "abuse potential" currently refers to one or more of the following: (a) the intrinsic attractiveness of a drug, (b) the number of people who are using a drug illicitly, (c) the number of people who are seriously abusing a drug, (d) the capacity of the drug to produce physical or psychological dependence—sometimes referred to as addiction or dependence liability, and (e) the capacity of the drug to produce other adverse consequences. Drug abuse as a problem area, unfortunately, is fraught with this kind of confusion about meanings and concepts.

What is needed at present is a refined set of concepts which will help us reach decisions about necessary and proposed actions. Let us begin with the idea of a probability statement about the likelihood of a drug user becoming physically or psychologically dependent on the drug or suffering rather severe adverse consequences from its use. For any drug, this probability could be expressed as a simple risk ratio (number of users who are dependent or suffering adverse consequences/total number of users). In these terms heroin would be rated as a high-risk drug, LSD would be rated as a moderate risk, and marijuana would be a drug of low risk. Whatever the term employed, the important issue is that we recognize a distinction between the *possible* occurrence of dependence and/or adverse consequences among a particular population of users and the *probable* occurrence. The probable occurrence can be either estimated or determined empirically.

This type of analysis would argue that, other things being equal, prevention and treatment efforts should be directed first toward users of high-risk drugs. However, rate of occurrence of dependency and/or adverse consequences in a drug-using population is by itself an insufficient criterion for making final decisions about action and the allocation of resources because it ignores the issues of overall prevalence and the relative or absolute severity of adverse consequences.

In addition to risk ratio, the following factors should definitely be considered in arriving at decisions about action and in planning and allocating resources for prevention, treatment, and rehabilitation:

1. The severity of the consequences, both personal and social, associated with the illicit use of a particular drug or class of drugs.

2. The absolute size of the core problem (the total number of people dependent on the drug or suffering adverse consequences from its use).

3. The number of people using the drug illicitly.

4. The number of people in the nonusing population who, within a certain time span, are likely to try the drug and in turn suffer adverse consequences from its use.

Adverse consequences certainly should include social costs and liabilities, as follows: (*a*) those directly attributable to drug effects and/or membership in a drug culture and (*b*) those associated with problems and difficulties of acquiring the drugs of choice.

Value judgments could and should enter the deliberations leading to the choice of actions, but these judgments should be made explicit. One way that this can be accomplished is by assigning a set of subjective weights to various kinds of adverse consequences. We may decide that casualties are less tolerable in young people than in older persons or that harm visited on innocent persons is less acceptable than harm visited on the drug abuser, and so on. Once established, these factors can be used to form a decision matrix in which the problems associated with various drugs can be evaluated and compared and from which reasonable actions or alternatives can be deduced. One of the strengths of this approach is that it permits one to set objective priorities on various goals and actions. A drug that was widely used and had a moderate risk ratio but was low rated on severity of adverse consequences would get a fairly low priority and might be ignored, whereas a drug that was much less widely used but had a high risk ratio and severe adverse consequences might get a high priority and demand immediate action.

Application of these concepts should clarify some of the problems of drug abuse and objectify our thinking about specific aims and goals.

FUNCTIONS THAT DRUGS SERVE[3]

Although it is possible and useful for some purposes to characterize the main motivational thrust that underlies the use of many illicit drugs, from a

---

[3] This section draws heavily on the work of Isidor Chein (1969). I have retained portions of the original but have modified and supplemented the material in important respects.

clinical point of view it is more important to recognize that drugs serve a variety of functions for different individuals and these functions often shift at different points in a drug career. The phases in a typical drug abuse career might be characterized as initiation, maintenance, escalation, and dependence or heavy involvement (inability or unwillingness to stop dangerous or excessive use). The concept of stages is introduced to underline the point that drug abuse is not a monolithic behavior, and there are various points along the way where different types of intervention may be indicated. The situation will be somewhat different for certain individuals and certain drugs; but the general approach should have heuristic value for planning prevention, treatment, and rehabilitation programs.

Four major classes of functions with general applicability to illicit drug usage are the following:

Functions Associated with Direct Pharmacologic Properties of Drugs

The person uses drugs specifically to produce positive feelings, to relieve anxiety, to become disinhibited, to relieve depression, to avoid emotional pain, etc.—in a therapeutic or pseudotherapeutic fashion. This usually follows previous exposure to the drug but may be present at the outset, if the person is aware of claims for the drug or its general indications. This function is probably important in the early phases of heroin addiction and, the demands of dependency notwithstanding, remains so as time goes on. Whatever reasons are given for starting a drug—and curiousity is the one most commonly reported for almost all drugs—a significant number of persons continue on with the drug or become heavily involved with it because it fulfills an immediate psychological need. For many young male heroin addicts, the drug is a form of self-treatment that enables them to protect their masculinity; to avoid the passive-dependency of the sick role; and, at the same time, maintain a positive public image or facade of "hip" bravado. The implications for treatment and medical care are obvious, but it is also obvious that in this group of young males we should anticipate resistance to medically oriented treatment offerings—an expectation that is already being borne out in the mushrooming methadone-maintenance programs. Similar problems of resistance to conventional therapy can be expected with heavily involved LSD users and young people who are mainlining amphetamines.

Licensing or Masking Functions

Some persons use drugs and their well-known effects as an occasion and semi-acceptable rationalization (enabling mechanism) for openly acting out in ways that would otherwise be unacceptable to the person or society. Homosexuality, violence, crime, sexual excesses, pathological dependency, and autistic flights of fantasy come readily to mind. For other persons, drugs may mask underlying fears or inadequacies, prevent impulses from surfacing, or permit the person to avoid unpleasant responsibilities or situations. The particular drug or class of drugs is important, but mainly in the sense that it must have some general properties or secondary effects that fit the intent of the user or could be reasonably associated with the observed behavior.

Many people feel that heroin addiction and its associated lifestyle fulfill the masking-blocking function quite well; many addicts enter the heroin culture or stay in it for these or similar reasons. Drugs like marijuana and alcohol, which disinhibit, could readily serve a licensing function.

Instrumental Functions

For many people there is secondary gain associated with taking drugs illicitly in situations where the pharmacological effects of the drug are relatively less important or even irrelevant.

The use of the drug may simply be the means whereby the person obtains and maintains companionship or achieves intimacy, or he may achieve status or identity by becoming a drug aficionado. He may like the excitement of obtaining the drug in a clandestine manner, or he may like the ritual or ceremonial aspects of taking drugs in group fashion. He may get heavily involved with the drugs because of secondary reinforcements within the group process without having great subjective needs for drugs or without enjoying them greatly; or in some situations personal desires and interpersonal rewards may interact.

The secondary gain seems to be an important factor in marijuana use among college students and other young people and a potent force among repeated users of LSD who are often found in small close-knit groups with a cultish orientation.

Secondary gain or instrumental aspects of drug behavior appear to be less important for heroin addiction, which, as time goes on, tends to be a more solitary pastime and to breed mistrust among fellow addicts. Social reinforcement may play a role at the outset and may have relevance for recruitment into addiction, but its influence probably drops out rather quickly as the drug habit becomes more firmly established.

Meaning and Values with Which
Drug Taking Is Invested

To a large extent these functions have to do with a priori expectations about the effects of drugs and secondary interpretations of their use. Some of the more common and important symbolic functions that can be identified on the current scene are the following.

Hostility-expressing functions. For society at large, use of drugs like marijuana, LSD, and heroin is not only illegal but is a disreputable act. As a consequence, for some, use of these drugs is a way of expressing hostility or defiance toward the society, parents, and others with a vested interest in respectability. As Chein has eloquently pointed out, delinquency is characterized by a versatility of acts, and which one is fastened upon may simply be an accident of opportunity. In this context drugs may be viewed as one way of misbehaving among many.

It is probably safe to assume that this hostility-expressing function is common and is a theme that runs through all illicit drug use, but it is particularly applicable to those who use drugs repeatedly in rather open fashion.

Consciousness-expanding functions. There are many young people today who feel there is truth in drugs that cannot be obtained any other way and if you haven't tried them you can't really know. The experiences in turn are valued as real insights that are far superior to any obtained through more rational processes or conventional channels. Claims are also made that drugs provide a quick and ready form of social deconditioning.

The principle of mind expansion and creative freedom through drugs can be viewed as a radical extension of the middle-class intellectual preoccupation with broadening one's experience in the interests of growth and development. Most early recruits to LSD were well-established intellectuals and creative people who saw in it a pathway to superior knowledge and a higher level of functioning. LSD is not popular in the practical environment of the ghetto or among heroin addicts who do not value the introspective experiences it produces.

Status-conferring functions.[4]   In the youth culture, use of drugs is highly valued in certain important reference groups. Use of drugs and achievement of certain effects is often the important goal, and special status can be attained by using a variety of drugs and ingesting high dosages of drugs for which special claims can be made. As the use of drugs has become more widespread among young people, drug taking—especially the use of marijuana—has become more akin to a puberty rite than an act of daring. Among the very young, at high school and junior high school level, use of marijuana is probably still a daring thing to do. The status-conferring function is still an important factor among blacks, Puerto Rican, Mexican, and Indian males who often try heroin for this reason and then get quickly caught up in the trap of addiction.

Use of drugs in the service of higher principles.   Some people still claim to be using drugs because the act serves the interest of a higher principle such as "People ought to have a right to do with their bodies as they see fit." Others equate the use of drugs, marijuana in particular, with civil disobedience aimed at a reactionary and unjust society and see opposition to its use as a form of hypocrisy on the part of those who are generally lacking in wisdom. The importance of these issues of principle has also diminished as use of marijuana has become more popular and commonplace: there is more frank admission that marijuana is being tried or used merely for excitement and pleasurable

[4] Although status-conferring functions were touched on in the section on instrumental behavior, they merit a separate discussion because of their general importance on the contemporary scene.

social purposes or to avoid being regarded as unsophisticated. The whole issue has become more low key, and much less profound or symbolic significance is attached to the use of the drug than was true but a few years ago. It might be wise for government and society to adopt a similar attitude and position.

General Characterizations

With due caution, we can also characterize the use of certain illicit drugs or classes of drugs in general motivational terms that summarize the major intentions of the users. This approach is of value when we are searching for themes around which to organize our thinking about certain drugs or usage patterns and when we attempt to deal with the drug-abuse problem in terms of the typical user.

Despite the many profound theories advanced to explain marijuana use, statistically speaking, the key words for marijuana are curiosity, kicks, and social rewards. Repeated use of LSD and the other potent hallucinogens probably is best understood as a striving toward goals of revelation, conversion, and personal transformation. In heroin addiction, aside from the demands of the dependency-withdrawal cycle, the central element is probably the search for total emotional relief or true analgesia.

SOME GENERAL CONSIDERATIONS

Stereotyping Users

The youth culture in general has tended to reject the truly invested drug "heads" and "freaks" and in a sense has already identified the core problem for the rest of us. To group the moderate or occasional users together with the heavily invested users in the planning and implementation of prevention, treatment, and rehabilitation programs for "soft" drug abusers is to confuse matters badly. Such generalizations probably will impede efforts to reach the heavily involved abusers by generally consolidating opposition among the young. We will probably need the cooperation of young people at the grass roots level if casefinding and intervention efforts are to be successful.

There is an analogue to this problem in and around the heroin culture of the inner city where, despite claims to the contrary, most youthful triers of drugs like marijuana, amphetamines, barbiturates, and wine do not go on to heroin. We may want to try an experimental accommodation with deviance in the interests of establishing a "buddy system" or some other peer mechanism that could save some or many from the ravages of heroin addiction. Who but his peers is really in contact with the potential young addict at the critical juncture?

Drug Progression

Among college students, evidence suggests that about 25% of marijuana users have used LSD and that most of them have used marijuana prior to their use of LSD. Reversing the question, we find that 90% of LSD users have used marijuana, most, but not all, before LSD. A similar situation exists in the heroin cultures of the inner cities with respect to marijuana and other drugs, but there is also surprising evidence that as many as 33% of heroin addicts may go directly to heroin. These findings suggest a two-pronged attack, one designed to minimize entry into drug use and another directed toward the more imminent problem of progressive involvement with drugs.

Special Treatment Problems

Dependent or heavily invested multiple-drug abusers probably will be a difficult treatment and rehabilitation problem because they are difficult to manage and often violate the criteria for admission and retention in current treatment/rehabilitation programs. The issue is raised to point up the difficulties encountered in establishing uniform standards for treatment and rehabilitation programs and to underscore the fact that there are many aspects of treatment and rehabilitation about which we know very little. We can therefore expect that a significant portion of treatment and rehabilitation activity will of necessity be innovative.

A Caveat

Some of the more realistic and promising approaches to the problem of drug abuse may run contrary to established moral and legal positions. These conflicts must somehow be resolved if we are to proceed toward the high-priority common goal of minimizing the casualties, costs, and liabilities of serious abuse.

It becomes increasingly apparent that drug misbehavior that stems from deep-seated value conflicts, personal pathology, or pathological social conditions simply does not yield readily to exhortation or punitive action.

GENERAL REFERENCES

Blum, R. H., & associates. *Students and drugs.* San Francisco: Jossey-Bass, 1970.

Chein, I. Psychological functions of drug use. In H. Steinberg (Ed.), *Scientific basis of drug dependence.* London: Churchill, 1969.

Eddy, N. B., Halbach, H., Isbell, H., & Seevers, M. H. Drug dependence: Its significance and characteristics. *Bulletin of World Health Organization,* 1965, *32,* 721–733.

Goodman, L. S., & Gilman, A. *The pharmacological basis of therapeutics.* New York: Macmillan, 1960.

Nurco, D., Balter, M. B., et al. Maryland drug abuse study. State of Maryland, 1969.

2

ADDICTION, DEPENDENCY, ABUSE, OR USE: WHICH ARE WE STUDYING WITH EPIDEMIOLOGY?

Reginald G. Smart
Addiction Research Foundation
Toronto, Canada

The epidemiology of drug abuse has never rested on a solid conceptual framework. Epidemiology began as the science of epidemics, originally investigating the source, spread, and control of communicable diseases (Rogers, 1965). Such investigations remain an important aspect of epidemiology in many parts of the world, but in North America more attention is given to epidemiological studies of noncommunicable diseases. A further development is the application of epidemiological methods to behavior pathologies such as mental illness, drug abuse, and drug use in which physical illness is a minor element. Broadly speaking, epidemiology is "the study of all factors (and their interdependence) that affect the occurrence and course of health and disease in a population [Rogers, 1965]." It is this broader definition into which current studies of drug use fit since they rarely bear directly on disease or pathology. Most such studies are concerned with counting the numbers of users of various drugs and less often with the broader aspects of factors that affect their occurrence. Questions about the general purposes of epidemiology are rarely considered. A prime purpose with regard to drug use is to achieve sufficient understanding to prevent harmful drug use, however that comes to be defined. One of the purposes here is to discuss the concept of prevention, what is to be prevented, and how we might go about it.

The various uses of epidemiology have been outlined by several writers but in most detail by Morris (1964). The uses of epidemiology, according to Morris, are to accomplish the following:

1. Study the history of the health of populations and of the rise and fall of diseases and changes in their character.

2. Diagnose the health of the community and the condition of the people.
3. Study the working of health services with a view to their improvement.
4. Estimate from the group experience the individual risks and chances, on average, of disease, accident, and defect.
5. Complete the clinical picture of chronic disease and describe its natural history.
6. Identify syndromes by describing the distribution, association, and dissociation of clinical phenomena in the population.
7. Search for causes of health and disease and, by means of these, search for the methods of definition.

Probably the last is of greatest interest to those concerned with drug-abuse epidemiology. Drug abuse, in general, is seen as an undesirable state that ought to be modified. All could agree on that, even without a definition of abuse. A major problem given insufficient attention is that the various methods of conceptualizing drug "abuse" or drug problems have little clarity. It is worth examining some concepts to determine how epidemiologists can contribute to the development of usable definitions. Among the most undesirable aspects of drug problems would be addiction, habituation, or dependency, together with a few less well known aspects called drug "abuse", nonmedical use, or misuse of drugs. Unhealthy drug use is usually meant by these terms; they describe the "disease" referred to by Morris. Healthy drug use is seen as the lack of addiction, dependency, or abuse.

It cannot be emphasized too strongly that we ought to know what we are studying to have any reasonable chance of success in prevention. One purpose of this study is to discuss the meanings of the concepts—addiction, habituation, dependence, drug abuse, and nonmedical use of drugs. This report indicates the manner in which the concepts are used, whether there is agreement on their conceptualization, and what problems exist in their interpretation. In addiction, this study shows how the concepts actually are used in epidemiological research on drugs. A final purpose is to argue for a retreat from all such terms and for the need to study drug *use* and its consequences. Only when drug use is understood will it be possible to modify drug "abuse," however that comes to be defined. It probably will be necessary to decrease drug use in order to decrease heavy, excessive use or abuse.

CONCEPTS EMPLOYED IN THE STUDY
OF DRUG-RELATED PROBLEMS

Conceptual clarity has never been prominent in the field of alcohol and drug research. Terms such as addiction, dependency, habituation, drug abuse, drug misuse, and the like are used—sometimes differently, sometimes interchangeably. Few of them, with the possible exception of "addiction," have any clear referent to observable events. Several terms have come and gone as there appear to be fashions and fads in the use of such terms. For example, drug "addiction" was defined by the World Health Organization (WHO) in 1950 (WHO, 1950). A definition of "habituation" was added in 1957 (WHO, 1957). Both were apparently replaced in 1964 (WHO, 1964) by the term "drug dependence." Now it seems that all will be swept away by the new term "drug abuse." This term seems to be more and more popular, but is an additional step away from clarity. Miscellaneous terms such as "drug misuse" and "nonmedical use of drugs" are also new and somewhat popular. Thorough analyses of the empirical and lexical consequences of all these definitions have not been made. Christie and Bruun (1969), however, have made an analysis of the term "dependency" as stated by the WHO. They recommend that "fat words" such as "drug dependence" be exterminated but argue that "a more precise and clear terminology would only seemingly complicate communication." They also state, however, that "it would force experts to talk so specifically about substances, as well as dangers, that experts from other fields and nonexperts from all fields would be provided with opportunities for evaluation of the experts' evaluations." Another consideration is that improved clarity would also allow experts in the drug field to be sure that they understand each other. It is not certain that experts have a high degree of mutual understanding now. Naturally, improved clarity also would make empirical referents for concepts more readily available. Such referents are particularly required in epidemiology, where a vast number of meanings and definitions can be employed either explicitly or implicitly. We need as much certainty as possible that we are all using terms such as "addiction" and "abuse" in the same way.

Addiction

Definitions of "addiction" are more numerous and controversial than might be expected. The related term "addict" is often used to apply to anyone who is being treated at a clinic for drug problems or perhaps as "synonymous with almost any unapproved use of drugs." It is often believed (e.g., Glasscote, Sussex, Jaffe, Ball, & Brill, 1972) that "it can apply only to those drugs that create physical dependence." The National Clearinghouse for Drug Abuse Information equates addiction with physical dependence on a drug. This is probably the older and more acceptable pharmacological definition of addiction. Many definitions, however, have not made physical dependence a requirement. For example, *Webster's New International Dictionary* (3rd ed.) defines addiction as "the compulsive uncontrolled use of habit forming drugs" and the addict as "one who habitually uses and has an uncontrollable craving for an addictive drug." Presumably an addictive drug is only one that can generate uncontrollable craving and not one that regularly or always leads to physical dependence or withdrawal symptoms.

The definition preferred by Maurer and Vogel (1962) also does not require physical dependence:

Drug addiction may be defined as a state in which a person has lost the power of self-control with reference to a drug and abuses the drug to such an extent that the person or society is harmed . . . . . In addition one or more of the following related but distinct phenomena are always present:

(a) Tolerance,
(b) Physical dependence with resulting abstinence illness when the drug is withheld,
(c) Habituation or emotional dependence.

The "sine qua non" of addiction is not seen to be dependence but loss of self-control over use, as well as drug use to the extent of harmful consequences for the user or society. "Harm" in this context is left open to interpretation. Physical dependence may be involved, but is not a necessary symptom; tolerance and habituation are made to count equally with physical dependence. A similar definition to that of Maurer and Vogels has been suggested by Chapman (1962): "drug addiction is the repetitive and compulsive use of some natural or synthetic substance to the detriment of self or society."

Definitions suggested by Lindesmith (1947) require physical dependence, but also some craving or psychological recognition of the connection between use and the disappearance of withdrawal symptoms. Lindesmith states:

Addiction occurs only when opiates are used to alleviate withdrawal distress, after this distress has been properly understood or interpreted, that is to say, after it has been represented to the individual in terms of linguistic symbols and cultural habits which have grown up around the opiate habit. If the individual fails to conceive of his distress as withdrawal distress brought about by the absence of opiates he cannot become addicted . . . all of the evidence supports this conclusion.

This definition seems to rule out the possibility of "real" addiction in nonhuman animals, infants born to heroin addicts, some types of medical "addiction," etc. Indeed, all organisms without the use of symbols could become addicted in Lindesmith's sense.

A somewhat different approach is taken under the Narcotic Rehabilitation Act of 1966 (quoted in Rappolt, 1972): an addict is "any individual who habitually uses any narcotic drug so as to endanger the public morals, health, safety or welfare, or who is so far addicted to the use of such narcotic drugs as to have lost the power of şelf-control with reference to addiction." In these terms, an addict could be any frequent user who creates a moral, health, or safety problem, or he may be only a user with no control over his use. The necessity for physical dependence or withdrawal symptoms is not there. This is not the place to debate the issue of whether anyone ever "has control" over his behavior or whether all behavior is determined. Statements about self-control over addiction, however, are too vague to have much practical use.

Probably the best known and most often quoted definition of addiction is the one proposed by the World Health Organization in 1950 and 1957. It was devised by the Expert Committee on Addiction-Producing Drugs in 1957 to be a definition of drugs applicable to those coming under international control. The 1957 definition stated:

> Drug addiction is a state of periodic or chronic intoxication produced by the repeated consumption of a drug (natural or synthetic). Its characteristics include: (i) an overpowering desire or need (compulsion) to continue taking the drug and to obtain it by any means; (ii) a tendency to increase the dose; (iii) a psychic (psychological) and generally a physical dependence on the effects of the drug; and (iv) detrimental effect on the individual and on society.

This definition does not describe pharmacological addiction. Physical dependence is not a requirement for addiction, only a possibility. The essential elements are overpowering desire, tendency to increase the dose, and detrimental effects on society and the individual. Clear specification of statements such as "overpowering" desire and "tendency" to increase the dose have not been made; it is doubtful whether they could easily be specified. "Detrimental effects" is such a value-laden concept that agreement on the nature of these effects will be often impossible. In addition, it has been admitted that "psychic dependence" is difficult to determine. As late as the 16th WHO report of the Expert Committee on Drug Dependence (WHO, 1969) it was stated that "evidence concerning the presence and degree of psychic dependence is drawn mainly from case histories, subjective statements and general observation." Experimental studies of this phenomenon's existing without physical dependence are rare. On the other hand, methods for the study of physical dependence and withdrawal symptoms have been developed in a variety of species (WHO, 1969). Of all the elements in the 1952 WHO definition of addiction, only tolerance and physical dependence—a nonessential element—have been carefully studied. The tolerance aspect is apparently not essential since only a "tendency" is required; it is uncertain how much tolerance development is necessary to have a tendency to increase the dose.

One of the aims of the WHO definition of addiction was to clarify and standardize usage. It has almost certainly not done so, although it is probably more often used than other definitions in general discussions of drug issues. Unfortunately, it is not a definiiton that can easily be used in epidemiological or treatment studies. Defining observable behaviours related to the major elements has apparently been too difficult to make it of practical utility. It is also clear that the WHO definition departs significantly from those of Lindesmith, Maurer and Vogel, and Chapman, to name only a few. One of the most commonly used definitions of addiction is that it applies to persons seeking treatment at centers for the treatment of opiate problems. This is rarely made explicit, but frequently such places apply only the physical-dependency criterion to begin treating patients.

Habituation

In 1957 a WHO committee suggested a definition of habituation (WHO, 1957). The term "habituation" was to be separate from "addiction" and probably meant to indicate a problem of lesser magnitude for the individual. Presumably it was not to replace or overlap with the concept of addiction, but to be supplementary to it. Drug habituation was defined as a state of periodic or chronic intoxication produced by the repeated consumption of a drug (natural or synthetic). Its characteristics include the following:

1. An overpowering desire or need (compulsion) to continue taking the drug and to obtain it by any means;
2. A tendency to increase the dose;
3. Some degree of psychic dependence on the effect of the drug, but absence of physical dependence and hence of any abstinence syndrome;
4. Detrimental effects, if any, primarily on the individual.

The main elements are repeated consumption and an overpowering desire to consume; but psychic dependence is relatively weak, and detrimental effects may be nonexistent (i.e., "if any"). Habituation differs from addiction in that addiction requires psychic dependence, tendency to increase the dose, and *some* detrimental effects on the individual or society. Habituation, then, is nearly identical to addiction except for the certainty of psychic dependence and of detrimental effects. Examination of habituation will also show that it is not very different from the "habit" described by psychologists of the 1940s and 1950s, e.g., Hull (1952). Habituation, in fact, would seem to refer only to a rather strong habit in Hull's sense, e.g. the law of Habit Formation: "If reinforcements follow each other at evenly distributed intervals, everything else constant, the resulting habit will increase in strength or a positive growth function of the number of trials according to the equation [Hull, 1952]." All that is added is the "overpowering desire" and "tendency" to increase the dose. It is not surprising, therefore, that the term "habituation" as proposed by WHO has been rarely used or quoted in discussions of drug problems.

Christie and Bruun (1969) have also pointed out the impossibility of really differentiating between addiction and habituation. Using Haakansson's work they "spell out the basic ambiguities in this attempt to discriminate between addiction and habituation." In fact, they see six relevant dimensions: desire, physical dependence, psychic dependence, tendency to increase the dose, detriment to society, and detriment to the individual. These can be dichotomized as overpowering desire versus no overpowering desire; psychic dependence strong versus weak; detrimental to the individual and not detrimental to the individual. Christie and Bruun (1969) took the various dichotomized dimensions and arrived at a table with 64 cells. One of these cells represents addiction in the WHO sense; and habituation falls into 47, 48, 63, and 64 according to a strict definition, but also 45, 46, 61, and 62 if a less strict one is employed. Almost none of the possible cells is covered by the WHO definitions of addiction and habituation. However, none of the other definitions proposed for addiction would fill many of them either; and few have attempted to define habituation differently from WHO. An important question, naturally, is, What about all the other cells—are there no drug problems or conditions that fit them? Obviously, the one cell involving none of the six variables is "no problem": this could be cell 64—no physical dependence, no detriment to individual or society, no overpowering desire, and psychic dependence weak, depending on whether "weak psychic dependence" alone is sufficient to cause concern.

Drug Dependence

Officials of WHO realized that the "difficulties in terminology become increasingly apparent with the continuous appearance of new agents with various and perhaps unique pharmacological profiles and with changing patterns of drugs already well known [Eddy, Halbach, Isbell, & Seevers, 1965]." Accordingly in 1964 a new attempt was made at a definition—"drug dependence." This definition was meant to replace the two earlier terms and to "cover all kinds of drug abuse." The main component in common is taken to be "dependence," whether psychic or phsyical or both. In general, "drug dependence" is defined as "a state of psychic or physical dependence or both, on a drug, arising in a person following administration of that drug on a periodic or continuous basis." The real characteristics of the dependence, however, "vary with the agent involved"; e.g., dependence of the morphine type, barbiturate type, LSD type, and khat type are all described.

The WHO definition is frequently used and quoted; it is almost a standard appendage to any discussion of drug problems. Exactly what is covered by the definition? At least two vastly different phenomena are brought under one phrase, "drug dependence." These are psychic and physical-dependence states. The latter is a well-studied and easily recognized phenomenon for those drugs where it occurs. "Psychic" dependence is "a feeling of satisfaction and a psychic drive that require periodic or continuous administration of the drug to produce pleasure or avoid discomfort." It seems that dependence occurs when people take drugs and derive satisfaction from them and then use them again sometimes to get that same satisfaction. This could presumably occur with the infrequent smoking of marijuana. Under the same category of "drug dependence" is brought pharmacological addiction, e.g., continuous use of narcotic drugs to stave off withdrawal symptoms. Such vastly different social, psychological, and drug-use problems are squeezed under the same rubric that confusion is almost certain. The only type of drug use that is nondependent would be that in which the user derived no satisfaction from continuing to use that drug. This is an extremely wide net. It should also be considered that basically the same six features used in the earlier WHO definitions of addiction and habituation are used without greater specificity in general terms; i.e., they are independent of a particular drug.

Several types of dependency—e.g., morphine type and barbiturate-alcohol type—are essentially pharmacological addiction in the old sense. Several

033619

others—e.g., drug dependence of the cannabis type, khat type, and LSD type—are similar to the old "drug habituation." What is really being said is that addiction and habituation are part of the same phenomenon— dependency. As Christie and Bruun note, if one wants to know more about dependence one has to look at the features of the drug itself and its effects. What then is the purpose of bringing such a diversity of events under the same phrase?

Drug Abuse

The term "drug abuse" is currently in vogue, at least in North America. Many works concerning drug abuse are being published currently but it is surprising how many of these contain no definition of drug abuse (e.g.,Arndt & Blockstein, 1970; Cole & Wittenborn, 1969; Dawtry, 1970). One of the most commonly used booklets for drug education in schools is entitled *Drug Abuse: Escape to Nowhere: A Guide for Educators* (1968). This booklet, however, contains no reference to drug abuse, although the WHO definitions of addiction, habituation, and dependence are described. The impression can sometimes be gained that drug abuse is meant to refer to anything bad that happens concerning the use of drugs. It may be that "drug abuse" is an all-inclusive term to cover addiction, dependency, and habituation; but this is not made clear in publications reviewed so far.

Several writers have attempted explications of drug abuse and sometimes with rather unusual results. For example, Glasscote, et al. (1972) define addiction and dependence and then add:

> Another term is "drug abuse"—it is the least specific of the common terms and for that reason perhaps the most useful and often the most accurate. Its applicability ranges all the way from a single experimental use of marijuana to "addiction" to heroin.

Further definition than this is not given, but a chapter follows on theories of the causation of drug abuse. However, this chapter seems to describe only causation of illicit *use.* It is most unusual to find that the less specific a definition the more useful and accurate it is.

Other writers also appear to equate drug abuse with mere use. The term "drug abuse" was defined for the President's Advisory Commission on Narcotic and Drug Abuse (Rappolt, 1972) as when an individual uses drugs under the following circumstances:

> (a) in amounts sufficient to create a hazard to his own health or to the safety of the community, or
> (b) when he obtains drugs through illicit channels, or
> (c) when he takes drugs on his own initiative rather than on the basis of professional advice.

Drug abuse then includes all illicit use, however frequent or harmful. It also includes all use of alcohol, tobacco, aspirins, etc. unless under "professional advice." This is so clearly ridiculous it hardly requires comment.

One may feel that the definition of drug abuse presented by the President's Advisory Commission is an unusually poor one. The WHO definition (1969), however, is nearly identical. That is, "persistent or sporadic excessive drug use inconsistent with or unrelated to acceptable medical practice." Certainly, drinking alcoholic beverages and smoking cigarettes are unrelated to and perhaps even "inconsistent" with acceptable medical practice. When it is realized that a "drug" (WHO, 1969) is *any substance that when taken into the living organism may modify one or more of its functions* [italics supplied]," the possibilities for drug abuse are limitless. It must not be intended that so wide a definition is created, but perhaps it is.

Sometimes drug abuse is made to refer to use other than for medical reasons, but often other criteria are added as well. The Le Dain Commission (1970) equates drug abuse with use outside acceptable medical practice. Similarly, Phillipson (1970) asserts that drug abuse entails "consumption of a drug apart from medical need or in unnecessary quantities." Drug abuse requires acquisition from illegal sources or "unjustified prescribing" by medical practitioners. Surprisingly, Cohen (1969) supplies a definition of drug abuse that is quite similar to the older definitions of addiction. His definition is that "drug abuse is the persistent and usually excessive self-administration of any drug which has resulted in psychological or physical dependence or which deviates from approved social patterns of the culture." It would be fair to say then that there is no generally agreed upon definition of "drug abuse." Some appear excessively wide and some very narrow, but few agree.

Summary and Conclusions on Definitions of Terms

The preceding discussion of definitions nearly defies summary. In general, a number of caveats are probably in order first. At the outset it should be agreed that not all possible definitions of addiction, dependency, and abuse have been outlined or discussed. A comprehensive review of every such definition would be an enormous task, and this is not attempted here. An effort was made to examine the most commonly used definitions, especially those of the World Health Organization and other official bodies. In addition, definitions employed in some recent books have been included. The ones selected would appear to be representative of those used in the field. It is also the case that not all terms indicating drug use "pathology" have been discussed, e.g., drug misuse and drug problems; but these terms appear to be less frequently used than are addiction, habituation, dependency, and abuse. It might also be argued that we understand ourselves much more adequately than indicated here. Perhaps definitions are tacitly held and consensus about them exists outside the concepts reviewed here. However, this is most unlikely.

In summary, there is no real agreement about concepts such as addiction and abuse. Agreements on habituation and dependency are better perhaps because these concepts have been so rarely used and only WHO has taken much interest in their nature. Addiction, for instance, sometimes involves physical dependence and sometimes not, sometimes requires craving and sometimes not. The same can be said for tolerance and the need to increase the dose. "Drug dependence" and "habituation" involve vague concepts such as overpowering desire, psychic dependence, and detriment to the individual and society. Similar difficulties with the concept of "drug abuse" have occurred. Many researchers use the concept with no definition, and those who use it achieve no consensus. Many times "drug abuse" is meant to apply to any sort of illicit drug use. However, it may also be applied to any drug use outside of acceptable medical practice, including, apparently, all forms of smoking and drinking, plus all aspects of addiction, habituation, and dependence.

The words "addiction," "dependence," and "abuse" are what Christie and Bruun (1969) referred to as "fat words." They cover too much and attempt to bring under single rubrics types of drug use that are extremely disparate. Christie and Bruun have also suggested that there are good reasons for the continuing vagueness and confusion. For example, lack of clarity helps to maintain, among competing parties in a dispute, the idea that one side has won. It is important for future research, law, health administration, and public education, however, that we begin to use the same terms in the same ways. Would this require some overall agreement on what terms to use in what way? Should WHO again set out definitions to be used in all cases? Such an approach probably would encourage use of the old terms in some new, clearly defined, ways; much recommends this approach.

Other approaches could also be taken. One of these would be to suspend the use of all terms such as addiction, habituation, dependence, and abuse until sufficient research has been done to give all of the conceptual elements empirical meaning. For example, exactly what is the meaning of overpowering desire, psychic dependence, and tendency to increase the dose?

Another approach might be to consider drug use, and not drug addiction, drug dependence, or drug abuse. This approach would, I believe, have much to recommend it. Among the most important considerations would be that drug use and problems arising from drug use are probably related; therefore, to reduce "problems," it probably will be necessary to reduce per capita drug use of a general sort. In all definitions of addiction, "dependence" and "abuse" proposed the one common element is drug use. One has to consume or take drugs to be eligible for any consideration as an addict, drug-dependent person, or drug abuser. We ought to know far more about drug use and how it relates to specific problems of use.

THE NEED TO EMPHASIZE
THE STUDY OF DRUG USE

Drug use, not "abuse," should be studied because prevention is the most important "use" of epidemiology. It is not one of the "uses" listed by Morris

(1964), although he does see it as a subset of the last "use," i.e., studies of causes. One should expect, however, that the "use" of epidemiology would be, finally, the prevention of drug problems (however we define them). In fact, most epidemiological studies of drug use involve merely descriptions of the nature and frequency of use. The great majority of studies of high school and college populations are descriptions of the frequency of drug use. Some of these involve an examination of those demographic characteristics associated with drug use (see Berg, 1970; and Mercer & Smart, 1972, for reviews). The majority of studies, however, make no attempt to get at psychological variables or even a broad range of social variables. Where many variables are studied, multivariate or regression analyses are not often performed. In short, few epidemiological studies are designed to illuminate the causes of drug use or even the necessary or sufficient conditions for use. It is of interest to know which social and demographic variables are associated with use, e.g., age, sex, and grade average; but these are indicators, not causative factors. It is also true that preventive efforts related to drug use are rarely based upon epidemiological work. Existing preventive efforts are based on educational programs, e.g., courses run through school systems or alternative programs such as involvement in nonusing group activities (Ungerleider, 1969). Normally, these programs make no use of epidemiologic findings; they are typically applied to the whole population and not merely those at high risk. Rarely do they take account of what indicators are known to be important. One reason is that so little epidemiological work is seen to be relevant to the prevention of drug use or drug problems. It could also be argued that much epidemiological work, while primarily studying drug use, has not studied drug problems at the same time.

Often it appears that any drug use is taken to be problem use. Investigators then feel no need to specify what level of use is associated with the occurrence of various problems. This approach is rather different from that taken with alcohol. The concept of social drinking is well recognized to be a normal, nonharmful level of consumption. We may argue as to what the nonharmful level is, but the idea that not all alcohol use is problem generating is well accepted. With regard to heroin, speed, cocaine, and other illegal drugs—even marijuana in some quarters—no level of use is conceived without likely harmful consequences. I want to point out that I am not arguing for more recreational or social use of these drugs. We do not know, however, how frequent the use of these drugs must be to result in particular problems, e.g., school dropouts, bad trips, personality changes, treatment for drug problems, and withdrawal symptoms.

A program to study how drug-use frequency (and quantity) relates to "problems" has been underway for some time in the alcohol-research area. Research has begun with nonalcoholic drugs but is at a much less well developed stage. It is worthwhile to look at the approaches in these two areas and to see what they contribute to epidemiology in general and to a preventitive approach based on epidemiology.

CONSUMPTION LEVELS AND DRINKING
PROBLEMS: IMPLICATIONS FOR PREVENTION

It can be argued that the final outcome of epidemiological work on drugs should be social policy, particularly concerning prevention. This outcome probably has been realized to a great extent for research on alcohol use and alcoholism. A variety of epidemiologic researches have sought to establish rates of use of alcohol and how they relate to problem alcohol use. There are at least two approaches to the provision of social policy concerning alcohol control and sale. One of these is the "distribution of consumption" model, based primarily on studies of consumption in large populations. The other is the "sociocultural" model, based more on studies of drinking in smaller social and ethnic minorities with especially high or low rates of alcohol problems. It is impossible here to summarize all relevant evidence on these approaches; this report, however, will (a) indicate their general outline, (b) show how the study of consumption levels in epidemiology relates to principles of prevention, and (c) show how epidemiology can contribute to social policy concerning prevention.

The distribution-of-consumption model was first suggested by Ledermann (1956), but many aspects were not pursued by him because of his untimely death. Most work on this model has been done by DeLint and Schmidt at the Addiction Research Foundation in Toronto. At the time of their first paper (DeLint & Schmidt, 1968), Ontario required that all alcohol beverages be purchased using sales slips containing the purchaser's name and address. This made it possible to determine how many purchases of alcoholic beverages were being made by given individuals. Purchase forms were collected for some 63,009 transactions made in representative areas of Ontario during 1962 and 1964. Analysis of the forms indicated that those who buy more usually consume more (since purchasers of large numbers of bottles typically made many separate purchases). The frequency of purchases in Ontario describes a logarithmic normal curve according to Ledermann's model. This is a curve in which there are many infrequent purchasers, a somewhat smaller number of more frequent purchasers, and even fewer very frequent purchasers. The curve is a smooth one with no large discontinuities. It is also unimodal. This research indicates that there is no clear difference in consumption between social drinkers, heavy drinkers, and alcoholics. All categories gradually shade into one another and cannot be clearly distinguished. This finding, however, is contradictory to a commonly held clinical viewpoint that alcohol consumption should be bimodal; i.e., alcoholics or problem drinkers should stand out from normal drinkers in their extent of consumption.

A variety of studies have shown that the log normal fit holds for alcohol consumption in several countries. Ledermann's early work showed that the fit was good for Finland and selected populations of American drivers and French hospital patients. Later surveys using interviewing techniques have established that the log normal distribution describes alcohol consumption in Finland at several points in time (Ekholm, 1972).

DeLint and Schmidt (1968) have also studied the levels of consumption associated with different aspects of problem drinking. For example, the average per diem consumption for most (84%) Canadian drinkers is 5 cl. per day or less of absolute alcohol, 5-10 cl. for 10% of drinkers. Fewer than 3% drink 15 cl. per day or more. However, 15 cl. is the average amount consumed by alcoholics seen at clinics (DeLint, 1968). Amounts in excess of 10 cl. per day taken regularly are associated with marked increases in the risk of liver cirrhosis. The use of liver cirrhosis as an alcohol-problem indicator rests both on the known effect of alcohol on the liver and on the high rates of liver disease found among alcoholics. These arguments have been made even stronger by data showing a significant correlation between liver-cirrhosis mortality and per capita consumption in several countries (DeLint & Schmidt, 1971). These data show spatial and time series correlations for a variety of periods in Australia, Belgium, Canada, Finland, France, Holland, Sweden, and the United States. In summary, the distribution approach suggests that (a) the distribution of alcohol consumption is similar in character from place to place, (b) alcohol consumption relates to liver cirrhosis, and (c) it may be necessary to reduce per capita consumption to reduce alcohol-related problems.

This research is of interest in the light of the earlier developed sociocultural theory of alcoholism. This approach attempted to explain the differences between alcoholism rates of ethnic minorities and national groups with reference to different norms about drinking. For example, drinking was believed to be a problem among Irish-Americans because cultural norms allowed "institutionalized intoxication." On the other hand, norms among Jewish drinkers emphasize careful use and the avoidance of intoxication. The contrasting rates of alcoholism among Irish-American and Jewish Americans are well known and presumably related to these norms. Analyses of this sort have led to a sociocultural hypothesis; e.g.,

> in any group or society in which drinking customs, values and sanctions ... are well established, known to and agreed upon by all, consistent with the rest of the culture and are characterized by prescriptions for moderate drinking and proscriptions against excessive drinking, the rate of alcoholism will be low [Blacker, 1966].

This model suggests that social and cultural factors are most important and that a set of proscriptive and prescriptive norms allowing controlled, integrated drinking should be established. Essentially, this approach has ignored research on the distribution model, and its proponents have tended to assume that the total volume of drinking or per capita consumption does not matter in preventing alcohol problems. Whitehead (1972) has shown that these two positions are not as far apart as has seemed since they emphasize different aspects of alcohol problems—drunkenness in the sociocultural approach and liver cirrhosis in the distribution approach. Unfortunately, most approaches taken on the sociocultural model (e.g., improving the acceptability of bars and taverns as social centers and fostering wine drinking with meals) would increase overall per capita consumption.

Opportunities to test the implications of either model experimentally have been rare. Governments usually do not change laws on alcohol consumption with any particular preventive model in view. It is recognized that prohibition did result in remarkable reductions in liver-cirrhosis death rates in the United States (DeLint & Schmidt, 1971). More recently, an interesting social experiment occurred in Finland (Makela, 1972) with regard to alcohol policy. According to some sociocultural theories, one might expect that less drunkenness would result from creating a shift to low alcohol beverages, e.g., beer and wine. It has been suggested that if the use of such beverages were promoted, moderate drinking habits, e.g., drinking with meals, would be generated. On the suppositions of the distribution model, however, unless per capita alcohol consumption (from all sources) decreased, there would not be fewer problems from alcohol.

In Finland in 1969 laws were changed to allow the sale of beer in retail liquor stores rather than in state-operated outlets (Makela, 1972). Retail liquor stores were also established in rural areas at the same time. The aims were to make low alcohol beverages more readily available through sources such as grocery stores and hopefully to moderate drinking practices. Surveys done in 1969 and 1971 showed a 48% increase in consumption. Beer accounted for much of the increase but the consumption of liquor occurred at the same rate as earlier. The distribution of consumption described a log normal function both before and after the change (Ekholm, 1972) but with a shift toward much higher per capita consumption. The numbers of drinkers reaching consumption levels involving health hazards also rose. It appears that the liberalization merely encouraged people to add a new drinking habit to those already held, without getting them to relinquish any of the older ones. Thus, changing drinking habits by encouraging new ones may be more difficult than formerly imagined. It also suggests that volume of consumption and per capita use must be reduced or held constant before sociocultural or normative changes will reduce the hazards of consumption. There is also a suggestion that psychoactive drugs made newly available will not replace those already in use unless some special concern for this problem is taken.

There are substantial problems in using the distribution data for alcohol to affect prevention through alcohol policy. One research problem is that no situation has yet been found where per capita consumption is falling so that the effect on the distribution and rate of hazardous drinking can be studied. Consumption seems to be going up everywhere. More generally, to try to reduce or maintain present per capita consumption appears to be against all contemporary ideologies about alcohol control. Most such ideologies in western countries seem to demand more availability of alcohol: decreasing age limits, increasing numbers and types outlets, and allowing more advertising and promotion. If epidemiological research is to have a real effect on social policy and personal behavior, many people must be involved in preventive public health. There should be involvement of large sections of the drinking population if there is to be a great effect on per capita consumption. With regard to policy changes, Whitehead (1972) has suggested that experiments be made with increasing the cost of alcohol, increasing legal purchase ages, elimination of beverage advertising, and decreasing bottle sizes. Many of these suggestions are at least worth a trial.

CONSUMPTION LEVELS AND DRUG USE: IMPLICATIONS FOR PREVENTION

As outlined in the previous section, the study of the epidemiology of alcohol use has generated major preventive and social policy implications. Work along these same lines has been initiated for drugs other than alcohol. The success of the distribution model for alcohol has created a need to determine whether the same or different relationships might hold for all psychoactive and hallucinogenic drugs. Fortunately, the major implications of the distribution model may not be so difficult to accept for "drugs" as for alcohol. This investigator has argued elsewhere (Smart, 1972) that most legal and social policy related to drug control assumes that drug use and not mere "abuse" or heavy or "addictive" use is to be controlled. Control measures, however, are not explicitly based on arguments from epidemiological theory but more on the supposition that all drug use is "abuse." Nevertheless, dissenting views (e.g., Le Dain, 1972) maintain that increasing the frequency of drug use would not necessarily increase the number of users who are harmed.

Research on the relationship between the distribution of drug use and drug problems is much less developed than for alcohol. There are several reasons for this paucity. One is the vague nature of the problem [set] believed to be associated with nonalcoholic drugs. As discussed previously, the concepts addiction, habituation, dependence, and abuse have no agreed-upon meaning. Individual definitions usually do not include enough sufficiently clear statements to be useful in epidemiological research; terms such as "psychic dependence" or "overpowering desire" are rarely useful. Unlike the field of alcohol studies, clear indicators of pathological consumption have been difficult to determine and have not been related to drug use. Perhaps the exception would be withdrawal symptoms and increased tolerance in the case of narcotics and some other drugs; but these symptoms are of little use in the study of hallucinogenic drugs such as MDA and LSD. There is no one symptom of excessive drug use such as liver cirrhosis, which is a useful indicator of problem alcohol use. An additional problem is, of course, the wide range of drugs that can be used. Drug use among adolescents typically involves multidrug use so that the volume of use of any particular drug may be too small to create any special organic effect. Multidrug use, of course, also makes it difficult to associate any consequence with the use of a single type of drug. Insufficient attention has been given so far as to how drug problems can be identified in epidemiological work and how their occurrence is associated with the frequency of drug use. Even with narcotics it is impossible to say how many doses must be taken before the risk of withdrawal symptoms increases substantially. The same problem occurs with tolerance: How much heroin must be taken or how often before tolerance is developed? With regard to multidrug use, the most likely indicants of problems are social and psychological and may involve the following: bad trips, dropping out from school or other social and familial institutions, personality changes, long-term psychotic reactions, suicide, spontaneous recurrences, or treatment for a variety of drug-related problems. Not all observers would classify all these as problem indicators rather than a sign of health, but there is sufficient agreement on most. Nevertheless, the risks of encountering any such problems cannot be specifically related to consumption levels in the same way as can liver cirrhosis.

Some research relevant to the distribution hypothesis or model has been done for nonalcoholic drugs. Smart, Whitehead, and Laforest (1971) collected data on drug-use frequency for five samples of high school students. These samples involved students in Toronto (in 1968 and 1970), in Niagara Counties (in 1970), Montreal (in 1969), and Halifax (in 1969). A variety of sampling methods were employed, but all studies used adequately chosen samples; the total number of students involved was 27,022. A drug-use score was computed for each student indicating the number and frequency of drug use. The drugs used were alcohol, tobacco, glue, marijuana, LSD, other hallucinogens, opiates, tranquilizers, stimulants, and barbiturates—10 drugs in all. All five studies inquired about the use of all 10 drugs and, depending on the frequency of use, drug scores could vary from 1.5 to 75.0. In all five studies the distributions were smooth and unimodal, and they roughly approximated a log normal distribution. Even in Toronto, where per capita drug use increased substantially between 1968 and 1970, the basic character of the distribution remained the same. Similar distributions were found (Smart & Whitehead, 1972a) for drugs when considered separately, i.e., in three studies in Canada. The distributions of the frequency of the use of marijuana, LSD, speed, solvents, stimulants, tranquilizers, and barbiturates among high school students were continuous and approximately log normal (with a few exceptions). For high school students, both multidrug use and use of individual drugs are similarly distributed—even though some of the drugs are legal and some illegal, and they have a wide variety of effects. It would be best, of course, to have comparable data for many other groups in North America and for groups in other countries as for alcohol distributions. An unpublished study by Smart and Whitehead (1972b) has shown that there is some generality to these findings. They found that data from a group of British university students also described continuous roughly log normal distributions. Data for a large sample of Canadian adults did not fit the log normal expectancy well (statistically speaking) but the distribution of scores was continuous, unimodal and somewhat similar to the expectancy.

Work on this aspect of epidemiology is shifting from a concern with the character of the consumption distribution to studies of how "problems" relate to per capita consumption. A survey of drug use among high school students in Toronto (in 1970) involved some 15 districts. Each district was a unit comprising a high school and the several feeder schools associated with it. It was found that the 15 districts varied enormously in rates of drug use: some were low in all types of use, some high, and some varied with the type of drug. The average "drug use score" was examined for each district. These scores involved the frequency of use of alcohol, tobacco, glue, marijuana, LSD, other hallucinogens, opiates, tranquilizers, stimulants, and barbiturates. Each user's score could vary from 1.5 to 75.0 for the 10 drugs. The average score and the proportion of students receiving scores of 30 or more were computed for each district. The mean scores, however, were computed with the 30 or more scores removed so there was no forced correlation between the two. The score of 30 or more was selected somewhat arbitrarily, but also because this score seemed to be the minimal held by persons seeking treatment for drug problems. A Spearman rank correlation between the two was .75 ($p < .001$), indicating that within a given population where average drug consumption is high, heavy use is also high, even when heavy users have been excluded. Essentially, this sort of analysis has been made for alcohol consumption and liver cirrhosis. The data for the latter comparison, however, are far more extensive in that they cover a variety of years and are cross-national in scope.

These data are germane to problems of drug-use control through reducing availability, increasing penalties, and providing alternatives to drug use. Data produced by Whitehead and Aharan (1972), however, are relevant to educational and attitude-change problems. They have studied attitudes toward the desirability of intoxication with drugs other than alcohol and have found scores to be log normally distributed and positively correlated with drug-use frequency. This finding suggests that efforts to reduce favorable attitudes to intoxication may be accompanied by a reduction in drug use. It also suggests that efforts will fail unless they are directed at changing attitudes of the total population rather than just those of heavy users.

Efforts also are being made to determine the drug-use scores usually achieved by persons in treatment for drug problems. A study of the Toronto high school population in 1972 asked students whether they had been treated for any drug-related problem. Relative risks of being in treatment have been estimated, and it appears that relative risk increases greatly at scores of about 26 to 30, or when four or five drugs have been used at least seven times in a 6-month period. Although this work is not completely developed, it indicates the way in which drug use can be studied in relation to specific drug problems. The number of such "problems" studied so far is very small; it would be useful to be able to plot such problems as personality change and school and social dropout according to drug consumption. It may be that the problems of drug "abuse" (or problem) prevention are similar to those for alcoholism prevention. Of course, much more work on all relevant aspects is needed. Data available to date for drug use do suggest the following:

1. Drug use and heavy use are correlated; where one is high, so is the other.

2. Drug-use consumption is unimodal and often log normally distributed.

3. It may be necessary to reduce per capita consumption of drugs by the population at large to reduce the numbers of heavy users.

4. A series of experiments in reducing various types of drug use by reducing availability would allow a more convincing test of some of these propositions. This might involve reducing advertising of drugs, removing drugs from the prescription rota, and other such measures.

SUMMARY AND CONCLUSIONS

It has been argued that a major aim of epidemiology is the creation of principles of prevention. These principles should be sufficiently well described to be of use in social-policy decisions. Few studies of the epidemiology of drug use, however, are designed to provide information about preventive approaches. Part of the difficulty is that there are too few clear definitions of what is to be prevented. Ultimately we probably wish to prevent drug problems or harmful drug use. Traditionally, drug problems have been seen as addiction, habituation, dependency, and drug abuse. Unfortunately, an examination of how these terms are frequently used shows (a) little agreement among various definitions of the same word and (b) a lack of clarity and empirical referents in many of the terms used. Words such as addiction, dependency, and abuse, therefore, are unlikely to be of much use in discovering principles of prevention. What unites all these "disease" or pathological states is drug use.

Studies along these lines have progressed most quickly with alcohol consumption, although work on drug use is also progressing. The net result of all this work is to suggest the following:

1. Drug and alcohol problems are most common where per capita consumption is highest.

2. To reduce problems it may be necessary to get many people, not just

addicts or "abusers," to use fewer drugs. This process may take several generations to achieve and depend on social-policy approaches as yet untried.

3. Social experiments should be conducted as an attempt to reduce drug use and determine whether drug problems also would be reduced.

REFERENCES

Arndt, J. R., & Blockstein, W. L. *Problems in drug abuse.* Madison: University of Wisconsin, 1970.

Berg, D. The non-medical use of dangerous drugs in the United States: A comprehensive view. *International Journal of the Addictions,* 1970, 5, 777–834.

Blacker, E. Socio-cultural factors in alcoholism. *International Psychiatry Clinics,* 1966, 3, 51–80.

Chapman, K. W. The General Problem. In W. C. Bier (Ed.), *Problems in addiction, alcoholism, and narcotics.* New York: Fordham University Press, 1962.

Christie, N., & Bruun, K. Alcohol problems: The conceptual framework. *Proceedings of the 28th International Congress on Alcohol and Alcoholism,* Vol. 2. Rutgers: Hillhouse Press, 1969.

Cohen, S. *The drug dilemma.* New York: McGraw-Hill, 1969.

Cole, J. O., & Wittenborn, J. R., *Drug abuse.* Springfield, Ill.: Charles C Thomas, 1969.

Dawtry, F. *Social problems of drug abuse.* London: Butterworths, 1970.

DeLint, J. Alcohol use in Canadian society. *Addictions,* 1968, 14–28.

DeLint, J., & Schmidt, W. The distribution of alcohol consumption in Ontario. *Quarterly Journal of Studies on Alcohol,* 1968, 29, 968–973.

DeLint, J., & Schmidt, W. Consumption averages and alcoholism prevalence: A brief review of epidemiological investigations. *British Journal of Addiction,* 1971, 66, 97–107.

Eddy, N. B., Halbach, H., Isbell, H., & Seevers, M. H. Drug dependence: Its significance and characteristics. *Bulletin of the World Health Organization,* 1965, 32, 721–733.

Drug abuse: Escape to nowhere: A guide for educators. Philadelphia: Smith, Kline, & French. 1968.

Ekholm, A. The Lognormal distribution of blood alcohol concentrations in drivers. *Quarterly Journal of Studies of Alcohol,* 1972, 33, 508–512.

Glasscote, R. M., Sussex, J. N., Jaffe, J. H., Ball, J., & Brill, L. *Treatment of drug abuse: Programs, problems, prospects.* Washington, D.C.: Joint Information Service of the American Psychiatric Association and the National Association for Mental Health, 1972.

Hull, C. L. *A behaviour system.* New Haven: Yale University Press, 1952.

LeDain, G. *Interim report of the Commission of Inquiry into the non-medical use of drugs.* Ottawa: Information Canada, 1970.

LeDain, G. *Cannabis. A report of the Commission of Inquiry into the non-medical use of drugs.* Ottawa: Information Canada, 1972.

Ledermann, S. *Alcool, alcoolisme, alcoolisation.* Donnees Scientifiques de Caractere Physiologiques, Economique et Social (Institut National d'Etudes Demographiques, Travaux et Documents, Cahier (No. 29). Paris: Presses Universitaires de France, 1956.

Lindesmith, A. *Opiate addiction.* Evanston: Principia Press, 1947.

Makela, K. Consumption level and cultural drinking patterns as determinants of alcohol problems. *Proceedings of the 30th International Congress on Alcoholism and Drug Dependence.* Amsterdam, 1972.

Maurer, D. W., & Vogel, V. H. *Narcotics and narcotic addiction*, Springfield, Ill.: Charles C Thomas, 1962.

Mercer, W., & Smart, R. G. *The epidemiology of psychoactive and hallucinogenic drug use.* Vol. 1 (in Press). *Recent advances in drug abuse research.* New York: Wiley, 1972.

Morris, J. N. *Uses of epidemiology.* Edinburgh: Livingstone, 1964.

Phillipson, P. V. *Modern trends in drug dependence and alcoholism.* London: Butterworths, 1970.

Rappolt, R. T. In J. M. Singh, L. H. Multer, & H. Lal (Eds.), *Drug addiction, clinical and socio-legal aspects,* Vol. 2. Mt. Kisco: Futura Publishing Co., 1972.

Rogers, F. B. (Ed.) *Studies in epidemiology.* New York: Putnam, 1965.

Smart, R. G. *The ethics and efficacy of the prevention of drug dependence.* WHO Conference on Epidemiology of Drug Use, London, 1972.

Smart, R. G., & Whitehead, P. C. The consumption patterns of illicit drugs and their implications for prevention of abuse. *U.N. Bulletin on Narcotics,* 1972, 24, 39–47. (a)

Smart, R. G., & Whitehead, P. C. The prevention of drug abuse by lowering per capita consumption distributions of consumption from Canadian adults and British university students. Unpublished manuscript. Toronto: Addiction Research Foundation, 1972. (b)

Smart, R. G., Whitehead, P., & Laforest, L. The prevention of drug abuse by young people: An argument based on the distribution of drug use. *U.N. Bulletin on Narcotics,* 1971, 23, 11–15.

Ungerleider, J. T. Information about project dare. Los Angeles: Drug Abuse Research and Education Foundation, 1969.

Whitehead, P. *The prevention of alcoholism: An analysis of two approaches.* London: Addiction Research Foundation, 1972.

Whitehead, P. C., & Aharan, C. H. Drug using behaviours and attitudes: Their distributions and implications. London: Addiction Research Foundation, 1972.

World Health Organization, Expert Committee on Mental Health. *Drugs liable to produce addiction: Report on the 2nd session of the WHO Expert Committee, 1950* (WHO Technical Report Series, 21), Geneva, 1950.

World Health Organization, Expert Committee on Mental Health. *Addiction-producing Drugs: 7th report of the WHO Expert Committee, 1957* (WHO Technical Report Series, 116), Geneva, 1957.

World Health Organization, Expert Committee on Mental Health. *Addiction-producing drugs: 13th report of the WHO Expert Committee, 1964,* (WHO Technical Report Series, 273), Geneva, 1964.

World Health Organization, Expert Committee on Drug Dependence, *16th report* (WHO Technical Report Series, 407), Geneva, 1969.

PART II
HEROIN

3

THE EPIDEMIOLOGY
OF NARCOTIC ADDICTION
IN THE UNITED KINGDOM

David Hawks
Addiction Research Unit
Institute of Psychiatry
University of London

The use of the term "epidemiology" in discussions of drug dependence is not uniform. Some argue that the lack of a physical agent of contamination precludes the use of this term and its methodology in the study of drug dependence. Dissenters from this classical view of epidemiology argue, however, that the transmission of drug dependence, involving as it does the transaction of a physical agent and often implicating known associates (de Alarcon, 1969; de Alarcon & Rathod, 1968), so closely approximates the epidemic model as to suggest that epidemiological methods are likely to illuminate the progression and causation of drug dependence.

HISTORY OF NOTIFICATION

The discernment of the epidemiology of drug dependence, defined as "the study of the distribution and determination of disease frequency" (MacMahon & Pugh, 1970), requires agreement as to the characteristics of those cases to be regarded as dependent. Although it is convenient to confine the present discussion to cases of narcotic addiction, it must be admitted that the machinery of notification (i.e., reporting) in the United Kingdom has never been such that the addicts notified represented the total.

Prior to the enactment of the Dangerous Drugs (Notification of Addicts) Regulations in February 1968, Home Office statistics were compiled on the basis of a routine examination of pharmacists' records. Before these regulations were introduced, doctors were not required to notify addicts, either therapeutic or nontherapeutic, and those who submitted reports presumably did so for a variety of reasons. The annual statistics published before 1968 showed only those addicts known to have taken drugs repeatedly during the previous year. The statistics excluded those who were not known to be *currently* taking drugs, e.g., those addicts in prison or abroad, and more important, those who obtained their drugs entirely from illicit sources.

Despite the nonstatutory nature of reporting and its consequent incompleteness, the drug scene in the United Kingdom, prior to 1967 at least, was probably so cohesive that few people using narcotics on a regular basis were unknown to the authorities. Prior to 1968 when notification legally required a doctor's assessment, the Home Office employed a variety of sources of varying credibility in compiling evidence of a person's dependence. It employed a tiered system of recording, only part of which reflected medical opinion.

COMPLETENESS OF NOTIFICATION

Two studies (de Alarcon & Rathod, 1968; Kosviner, Mitcheson, Myers, Ogborne, Stimson, Zacune, & Edwards, 1968) conducted prior to the implementation of the regulations for notification suggested that this system of recording was starting to seriously underrepresent the true nature of the problem. It was probably true that the number of new persons becoming dependent from 1966–67 was such that the accuracy of the existing, rather informal, recording system broke down. The extent to which it underrepresented the true situation is reflected in the sizable increase in the number of notifications that resulted as soon as the new regulations were introduced. Kosviner et al. (1968) found that of the 37 who were eventually identified as using heroin in the particular town investigated by them, six were unknown to official sources. De Alarcon and Rathod (1968), using a variety of screening techniques, found a total of 50 using heroin, of whom only eight were known.

While the present system of notification is statutory, there remains some evidence of its incompleteness. The Chief Medical Office of the Department of Health and Social Security (hereafter referred to as DHSS, 1971) has acknowledged that

> ... on some occasions in 1970 heroin coming forward for treatment and being immediately transferred to methadone were wrongly notified as being addicts to methadone so that in 1970 the number of valid first notifications for addiction to heroin should have been somewhat higher and the corresponding figure for methadone should have been lower [p. 131].

In addition, while the provisions for statutory notification cover dependence on methadone, there has been some doubt as to whether patients addicted to methadone have invariably been notified, particularly by general practitioners.

Quite aside from the administrative confusion regarding the grounds on which patients should be notified, patients may have been using narcotics on a regular basis for some time before first attending clinics. Blumberg, Cohen, Dronfield, Mordecai, Roberts, and Hawks (1973) found that of patients newly notified in the 12 months November 1970 to November 1971, the median interval of narcotic use was 3 years. The median duration of regular narcotic use (defined as at least daily for 7 days) was 2 years. For 37% of the sample, regular use had been continuous over this period. Bransby, Curley, and Kotulansha (1973) found that of patients notified for the first time between March 1970 and December 1971, one-half claimed to have started using heroin, methadone, or cocaine 2 years before attending the hospital, while 13% claimed to have used these drugs 5 or more years previously. Although use may not have been continuous, most addicts had been getting drugs for daily use from an illegal source for at least 6 months before coming to the hospital for the first time. The number known to be using narcotics on a regular basis, as derived from the treatment records of the drug treatment centers, is likely to be a considerable underestimate of the true situation. That patients may be some time approaching clinics is confirmed by the evidence (Blumberg et al, 1973) that approximately 50% of the narcotic-using associates of those newly notified are not under treatment.

It may be true, of course, that at some stage those not currently known come to the notice of official agencies; what one witnesses, therefore, may be a delayed notification rather than a permanently submerged segment of the total narcotic-using population.

SOURCES OF INFORMATION

Official

At present there are in the United Kingdom three primary sources of information[1] regarding the characteristics of narcotic addicts. The first of these is statutory, the details of which are set down in the Dangerous Drugs (Notification of Addicts) Regulations, 1968. These particulars, notified to the Chief Medical Officer of the Home Office, comprise the one obligatory source and provide the basis for all official declarations. In addition, and on a voluntary basis, consultants notifying addicts are requested by the Department of Health and Social Security to complete a more extensive questionnaire, which includes additional details. This questionnaire and the modified form completed at regular intervals on all people still under care provide the basis of a central data bank, access to which was to be available to all bona fide research workers (Bransby, 1971b). Recently, questions regarding the confidentiality of this information and access to it have emerged. The present situation is that hospital questionnaire data are not made available to anyone without the consent of the psychiatrist in charge.

[1] Questionnaires may be obtained from David Hawks, Addiction Research Unit, Institute of Psychiatry, University of London, 101 Denmark Hill, London, SE5 8AF.

While it was intended that the initial questionnaire be completed as people were first notified, the number notified in the first few months of the clinics' operation was such that the majority of the initial questionnaires were completed retrospectively using available case notes. The discernment of the status of patients on notification was therefore dependent on the adequacy of these case notes. Of a total of 2,580 notified by hospitals during the period covered by the study (February 1968–February 1970), forms were completed on 2,187 (84%). While the incompleteness of the case notes may, in some instances, have resulted in an understatement of the findings, Bransby (1971b) has observed that the completeness of recording allowed a confident interpretation of the findings at least in broad terms, even though addicts themselves were the source of the particulars. Followup questionnaires were to have been completed on people still under treatment. This intention has since been abandoned.

In addition to these two returns, the one statutory and the other voluntary, the clinics are required at 2-month intervals to check their current caseload against previous returns and notify any changes.

In context, these sources allow the publication (for internal purposes only) of the number of inpatient admissions during the month, the number of inpatients at the end of the month, the number of new outpatients during the month, the number of outpatients at the end of the month, and the number of outpatient attendances during the month. This information is published for the London area separately, other areas, and all England (excluding Wales). In addition, clinics notify the quantities of heroin and methadone prescribed to outpatients, from which average quantities can be caluclated for each of the clinics.

Unofficial

In addition to official sources of information, a number of research investigations provide data relevant to a discussion of the epidemiology of narcotic dependence. Some of these relate to patients under treatment with particular clinics (Bewley, James, & Mahon, 1972; Boyd, Layland, & Crichmay, 1971; Chapple & Gray, 1968; Chapple, Somekh, & Taylor, 1972a, 1972b; Gardner & Connell, 1971; Hicks, 1969; Mahon, 1971), while others have involved representative samples of all those under treatment. Some investigators have studied all those newly notified during a specified period (Blumberg et al. 1973; Stimson & Ogborne, 1970a, 1970b). These studies are of particular relevance, since they provide information which is independent of and in some cases inaccessible to the clinics.

Stimson and Ogborne (1970a, 1970b) found, for example, that of those patients receiving prescriptions for heroin, 84% were also using drugs obtained from illicit sources in the month before interview. Twenty-four percent claimed to have no friends who were not using drugs of some sort, and 37% were engaged in illegal activities independent of their use of illicit drugs. The expectation that addicts, if given a regular prescription for heroin, would lead "stable" lives was only borne out for a minority.

Blumberg et al. (1973) showed that newly notified addicts had been using narcotics on a regular basis for some time before first approaching clinics and that approximately half of their narcotic-using associates were not under treatment. They also found that 89% had used powdered heroin ("Chinese" heroin) prior to their notification and that 83% had injected barbiturates.

DEVELOPMENT OF NARCOTIC DEPENDENCE

The gross features of the development of heroin dependence in the United Kingdom are generally known; they are documented in a number of sources (Bewley, 1966; Hawks, 1971; Spear, 1969). Before 1950 the number known to be abusing narcotics was relatively static, varying between 400 and 600. Those involved tended to be middle-aged, more often than not female, and disproportionately drawn from the medical and paramedical professions. In most cases addiction had a therapeutic origin, and the drugs involved were usually morphine and pethidine. Almost coincidental with the publication of the First Report of the Interdepartmental Committee on Drug Addiction (Brain Committee, 1961) there originated a series of changes that have continued in the same direction until very recently, when they have shown some slight divergence.

There appeared both an increase in the number of people known to be dependent on narcotics and an increasing tendency for their addiction to be nontherapeutic in its origin. Those persons concerned also tended to be younger and predominately male. There was evidence that the drug preferred was heroin rather than morphine and indications that other drugs were being increasingly abused. Whereas the misuse of illicitly obtained drugs was originally confined to London, the problem also spread to other parts of the country. (See Tables 1-5).

Following the enactment in early 1968 of the regulations affecting the treatment and notification of addicts, there was a considerable and entirely predictable increase in the number of persons known to be dependent on narcotics. The increase was predictable since the previous system of recording was in no way obligatory. The number of addicts first notified as dependent on heroin in 1968 was 1,306, whereas the number first known to the Home Office as dependent in 1967 was 745. The vast majority of those notified in the first few months of the clinics' operation were using heroin, and a substantial proportion of them were subsequently prescribed heroin by the treatment centers. While more than 500 licences to prescribe heroin and cocaine were issued, 71% of those notified as addicted to heroin in 1968 were listed with clinics in the Greater London area. The number of new notifications, while it did not again approximate the influx of the first few months of the clinics' operation, did not abate until February 1970 and is

TABLE 1

Characteristics of Known Narcotic Addicts in the United Kingdom, 1962–71: Number of Addicts, Type of Drug Taken, Origin, and First Notifications

Characteristic	1962	1963	1964	1965	1966	1967	1968	1969 Year total	1969 As at Dec. 31, 1969[a]	1970 Year total	1970 As at Dec. 31, 1970[a]	1971 Year total	1971 As at Dec. 31, 1971[a]
Number taking specified drug:[b]													
Heroin	175	237	342	521	899	1,299	2,240	1,417	499	914	437	959	385
Methadone	54	55	61	72	156	243	486	1,687	1,011	1,820	992	1,927	1,160
Cocaine	112	171	211	311	443	462	564	311	81	198	57	178	58
Morphine	157	172	162	160	178	158	198	345	111	346	105	346	103
Pethidine	112	107	128	102	131	112	120	128	83	122	80	135	73
Number of specified origin:													
Therapeutic	312	355	368	344	351	313	306	289	247	295	231	265	218
Nontherapeutic	212	270	372	580	982	1,385	2,420	2,553	1,196	2,321	1,177	2,457	1,313
Unknown	8	10	13	3	16	31	56	59	23	45	22	47	24
Number of valid first notifications for heroin addiction	72	90	162	259	522	745	1,306	652	–	353	–	535	–
Total number known addicts	532	635	753	927	1,349	1,729	2,782	2,881	1,466	2,661	1,430	2,769	1,555

[a]Statistical data from 1969 are presented differently from those of preceding years. Previously these data had been based on the total number of addicts coming to the notice of the Home Office during the course of the year. New recording procedures have made it possible to give details of those addicts known to have been receiving supplies of drugs at the end of the year as well as the total number of cases during the year.

[b]These figures refer to drugs used alone or in combination with other drugs. Thus an addict using both heroin and cocaine was included under both drugs; all but a handful of the cocaine addicts shown were also using heroin.

TABLE 2

Characteristics of Known Narcotic Addicts in the United Kingdom, 1962-71: Age, Sex, and Professional Class

Characteristic	1962	1963	1964	1965	1966	1967	1968	1969 Year total	1969 As at Dec. 31, 1969[a]	1970 Year total	1970 As at Dec. 31, 1970[a]	1971 Year total	1971 As at Dec. 31, 1971[a]
Age													
Under 20 years:													
Total number of addicts	3	17	40	145	329	395	764	637	224	405	142	338	118
Number taking heroin[b]	3	17	40	134	317	381	709	598	221	365	136	304	111
20-34 years:													
Total number of addicts	132	184	257	347	558	906	1,530	1,789	897	1,813	959	2,010	1,123
Number taking heroin[b]	126	162	219	319	479	827	1,390	1,709	872	1,705	921	1,912	1,088
35 years and over:													
Total number of addicts	381	426	449	425	448	421	406	415	320	411	307	382	291
Number taking heroin[b]	46	58	83	68	103	90	98	147	109	145	108	141	108
Age unknown:													
Total number of addicts	16	8	7	10	14	7	82	40	25	32	22	39	23
Number taking heroin[b]	–	–	–	–	–	1	43	26	13	18	10	19	9
Sex													
Number of male addicts	262	339	409	558	886	1,262	2,161	2,295	1,067	2,071	1,053	2,134	1,135
Number of female addicts	270	296	344	369	463	467	621	586	399	590	377	635	420
Professional classes (medical or allied)													
Total number	57	56	58	45	54	56	43	43	26	38	26	44	22

Note.– Derived from Drugs Branch, Home Office, London.
[a]New recording procedures have made it possible to give details of those addicts known to have been receiving drugs at the end of the year as well as the total number of cases during the year.
[b]From 1969 this figure is for addicts to heroin and/or methadone. A deliberate policy was adopted by hospital clinics in the treatment of heroin addiction by weaning patients from heroin on to methadone; thus, methadone has supplanted heroin as the drug most commonly used by addicts.

TABLE 3

Characteristics of Known Narcotic Addicts in the United Kingdom, 1968-70:
Place of Birth, by Sex

Place of birth	Percentage of drug addicts, by sex		
	Male (N = 1,786)	Female (N = 401)	Both sexes (N = 2,187)
England	82.1	81.5	82.1
Wales	0.9	0.5	0.8
Scotland	3.5	5.7	3.9
Northern Ireland	1.7	0.8	1.5
Eire	4.4	1.5	3.8
Other European	1.3	3.7	1.8
United States	1.8	2.2	1.9
Canada	1.9	1.5	1.8
West Indies	0.3	0.3	0.3
Africa	0.3	0.8	0.4
India and Pakistan	0.4	–	0.3
Other Asian	0.3	–	0.3
Elsewhere	0.6	1.2	0.7
Unknown	0.5	0.3	0.4

Note.—Based on hospital notification, Apr. 1, 1968, to Feb. 28, 1970. Source: Bransby, E. R. Note for discussion. *Department of Health and Social Security Study of Drug Dependent Patients* [CCDD/(71)3], 1971.

currently of the order of 50 per month. Most recently, the number has risen slightly. Whereas in 1970 there were only 353 valid first notifications of addiction to heroin (compared with 652 in 1969), in 1971 the number rose to 535. By 1970 methadone was frequently the drug of primary dependence, probably reflecting the policy of the clinics to increasingly substitute methadone for heroin and the consequent scarcity of heroin on the illicit market.

The vast majority of addicts are polymorphous drug users and the prescribing of other drugs is less stringently controlled than is prescribing of heroin and cocaine. Therefore, changes in the supply of these drugs have had consequences for the use of others. The injection of methylamphetamine assumed brief, though devastating vogue, until a voluntary restriction on its prescription resulted in its at least temporary demise (de Alarcon, 1972). The use of barbiturates, particularly their intravenous injection, continues to be a cause for concern.

Over time, the number prescribed heroin alone by the clinics has decreased, and the number prescribed methadone alone has increased. While general practitioners retain the right to prescribe methadone, in fact few availed themselves of this dubious privilege; the principal source of both drugs is the drug treatment centers.

Both the total quantity and average amount of heroin prescribed per patient have fallen. This decrease may reflect better opportunities for assessment now available to the clinics. In addition, the administrative practice of publishing for internal circulation the total and average amounts prescribed by each center might be expected to have leveled out the initially discrepant practices of the clinics. The decrease in heroin prescription, however, may have deleterious consequences.

The decrease in the total amount of heroin prescribed was initially compensated for by an increase in the total amount of methadone prescribed, though individual addicts may not have been compensated in this way. Over time, however, both have leveled out.

At present, approximately one-third of patients attending clinics for the first time and seeing a doctor receive no prescription for opiates, at least initially (Blumberg et al., 1973); of those who receive a prescription, only 16% receive heroin. The amounts presently prescribed to new patients are such that the system can no longer be justifiably regarded as a maintenance system, but rather must be described as an abstinence-oriented system.

TABLE 4

Characteristics of Known Narcotic Addicts in England and Wales, 1968–70: Education, Work Status, and Social Class of Father, by Sex and Place of Birth

Characteristic	Percent male		Percent female	
	Born in England	Born outside England	Born in England	Born outside England
Education and work:				
Still attending full-time education	1.5[a]		>1[a]	
Terminated education under age 16	71	54	62	47
Continued education to 18 years or over	6	12	6	13
Working full or part-time[b]	40[a]		28[a]	
Social-class rating of father's usual occupation:				
I	5	6	12	2
II	14	21	19	43
III (nonmanual)	12	9	12	14
III (manual)	41	37	39	29
IV	23	21	14	7
V	5	6	4	5

Note.—Based on hospital notification, Apr. 1, 1968, to Feb. 28, 1970. This table relates only to those patients where a *positive statement* was made. Source: Bransby, E. R. Note for discussion. *Department of Health and Social Security Study of Drug Dependent Patients* [CCDD/(71)3], 1971.

[a]This figure includes all birthplaces.

[b]The majority were in fact working full-time.

TABLE 5

Characteristics of Known Narcotic Addicts in England and Wales, 1968–70:
Marital Status, Special Schooling, Attendance at Child Guidance Clinic, and
Criminal Offenses, by Place of Birth and Sex

Characteristic	Place of birth (percentage) (N = 2,187)			
	England	Wales, Scotland, N. Ireland, and Eire	United States and Canada	All other places[a]
Marital status				
Male:				
Never married	83	83	47	
Married	12	9	33	
Separated or divorced	5	8	13	
Widowed	0	0	7	
Female:				
Never married	66			65
Married	20			22
Separated or divorced	14			11
Widowed	0			2
Special schooling, child guidance clinic, and criminal offences				
Special schooling:				
Male	1	3	–	–
Female	2	–	–	–
Child guidance clinic:				
Male	5	4	2	5
Female	6	–	–	2
On probation currently:				
Male	28	22	12	13
Female	24	–	–	15
Guilty of offence in juvenile court:				
Male	45	41	24	29
Female	25	–	–	22
Guilty of an offence involving drugs:				
Male	42	50	57	40
Female	35	–	–	36

Note.—Based on hospital notification, Apr. 1, 1968, to Feb. 28, 1970. Source: Bransby, E. R. Note for discussion. *Department of Health and Social Security Study of Drug Dependent Patients* [CCDD/(71)3], 1971.

[a]For females, "all other places" refers to all places of birth other than England.

CHARACTERISTICS OF NARCOTIC ADDICTS

Research to date has largely been descriptive; even so, it suggests that the development of narcotic addiction in the United Kingdom has been different from that in the United States. Whereas within the last 20 years at least, narcotic addiction in the United States has appeared to be closely associated with poverty and minority-group status, neither has been a particular feature of addiction in the United Kingdom.

Socioeconomic Status

While the socioeconomic status of addicts as ascertained by reference to their fathers' occupation provides only an uncertain index of their current socioeconomic status, studies done in the United Kingdom consistently show that the socioeconomic background of addicts does not diverge significantly from the general population norm. In some studies (e.g., Kosviner et al., 1968) it even appeared to be skewed toward the higher socioeconomic classes; this finding, however, may have been a peculiarity of the particular town investigated. More representative studies (Bransby, 1971a, 1973; Stimson & Ogborne, 1970a) suggest that material disadvantage has not been a feature of the background of narcotic addicts. Underachievement on the part of the incipient addict, however, appears to be a characteristic. A number of studies allude to the fact that addicts frequently leave school at younger ages or else withdraw from further training, or if employed work in less skilled capacities than their fathers (the latter is perhaps hardly surprising, given the age differential).

Furthermore, in a comparatively benevolent welfare society where treatment is provided under a National Health Service, addiction does not lead inevitably to the abject poverty observed in some other settings. There is some suggestion (Connell, 1965a, 1965b), however, that amphetamine users tend more often to derive from working-class backgrounds where poverty is a more common experience.

Ethnicity

Ethnicity does not appear to be a significant correlate of narcotic dependence in the United Kingdom. Most studies of known narcotic addicts show that the vast majority are born in the United Kingdom (Bransby, 1971a, 1973). Although the majority of registered addicts attend treatment centers in London, fewer of them were born in London, suggesting that the concentration of both licit and illicit sources of narcotic drugs in London results in their migration from other areas.

The majority of studies makes no distinction between place of birth and ethnicity. To be born in the United Kingdom provides only an unreliable indication of racial background. In the one study to make the differentiation (Bewley et al., 1972), 92% of 491 addicts treated at three London centers had either British, Irish, or Scottish nationality, while 75% were born in the United Kingdom or Eire. Ninety-seven percent were white. Bewley et al. make the observation that the characteristics of these patients appear to be typical of those of the addict population of London as a whole.

It has been suggested that one group played a significant role in the development of narcotic addiction in the United Kingdom. This group was the Canadians who emigrated to England between 1959 and 1969 under the privileged status accorded British subjects from Commonwealth countries. While at one time (1962) a considerable number of Canadians were receiving treatment in the United Kingdom, usually from a limited number of general practitioners, there is no evidence that they were instrumental in creating the epidemic observed in 1967-68 (Spear & Glatt, 1971). On the contrary, they appear to have been a relatively self-contained group, known to one another, but largely atypical of the average British-born addict, having both a much longer history of addiction and imprisonment and usually in receipt of much larger prescriptions of narcotics. A study done in 1969 (Zacune, 1971) indicated that of the 91 Canadian addicts known to have emigrated to Britain, 50% had either returned to Canada or been deported, while those who remained continued to be different from the average British addict; the Canadians who stayed in Britain were more often employed and less involved in the drug scene than the British addict.

Contrary to what might have been supposed, West Indians and Indians do not appear to have contributed significantly to the development of narcotic dependence in the United Kingdom. Although official data are unavailable, the number of West Indians represented in the total addict population is not disproportionate, and Indians and Pakistanis are noticeably underrepresented. This may reflect a variety of influences including the selective factors affecting immigration, the increased or alternatively decreased scrutiny of such populations by the police, and the successful integration of these ethnic groups into British society.

Criminality

The association of narcotic dependence with criminality is a more complex matter. It was a basic tenet of the British approach that addicts, if given a regular legal prescription, would have no need or incentive to engage in illegal activities. Nor was it supposed, except insofar as their use of drugs was an illegal activity, that addicts would have predominately criminal backgrounds. For addicts, even those under treatment, to have no need to engage in illegal activities assumes, of course, that such activities were not part of their lifestyle before they became addicted and that they receive sufficient amounts of the drug of their choice to have no need to supplement it from illicit sources. In actuality, neither assumption has proved to be well founded. A significant proportion (about 50%) of notified addicts have criminal records that predate their drug use and do not involve the use of drugs. A significant proportion (about 50%) continue to engage in illegal pursuits of a type not closely related to their drug dependence, though they are at the time in receipt of a prescription (Bewley et al., 1972; Bransby, 1971b). It can be argued that no activity engaged in by an addict is irrelevant to his addiction; these offenses, however, are not classified as drug offenses.

Although the amount of narcotics said to be needed by addicts on first attendance did not decrease over the 12 months of the intake period, the amounts prescribed decreased (Blumberg et al., 1973). In addition, one-third of those newly notified were prescribed no opiates initially. Given that the amount said to be needed and the amounts said to be used in fact both exceeded the amounts prescribed, it is obvious that the balance must be made up from illicit sources. Even in the benevolent context described by Stimson and Ogborne (1970a) where all the patients questioned were receiving heroin prescriptions, 84% were also using drugs obtained illicitly in the month prior to interview.

It must be concluded, therefore, that the somewhat naive assumption that British addicts would not have any need to engage in illegal activities has not provided an insurance against the probability of their engaging in criminal activities. What does appear to be true, at least until recently, is that the supply of illicit heroin has not been as organized as it is in the United States. Most of the heroin available on the black market before 1968 derived from the overgenerous prescribing of a few doctors (DHSS, 1965). Following the implementation of the new regulations, the chief sources of supply were probably the treatment centers themselves, whose lack of experience and means of assessment undoubtedly contributed to surplus prescribing. More recently the clinics' policy of substituting methadone for heroin and prescribing both in diminishing quantities has meant that very little English heroin at least has found its way to the black market. (The black-market price of English heroin has increased significantly.) On the other hand, contaminated (Chinese) heroin has become a more prevalent commodity on the black market, indicating that the market has become more organized and that initially legal sources are no longer the principal sources of supply.

Causation

A review of the British literature shows it to be curiously deficient in its analysis of causation. Such a deficiency, in part, reflects the relative infancy of such research in the United Kingdom; nevertheless, it is a manifestation of the failure to test explicitly causal hypotheses with the implications for employing comparison groups which this inevitably involves. There has been no lack of etiological hunches: it has been variously suggested that narcotic addiction reflects a preexisting delinquent lifestyle, a neurotic predisposition, and a disillusionment with the opportunities offered. Dependence on narcotics has been consistently shown to be associated with leaving school at an early age, truancy, initial occupational instability, and precocious use of legal drugs.

Drug dependence undoubtedly is facilitated by living in particular areas and being involved in a friendship network that includes drug users. The addict population also appears to be characterized by a high incidence of familial separation and disturbance.

It is highly unlikely that any one or several of these correlates will provide an adequate explanation of the development of narcotic dependence. Research must assume an order of complexity and subtlety that to date it has lacked. An understanding of demographic characteristics is essential for preemptive legislative action; but, at present, research concerning the relation of such characteristics to drug dependence frequently lacks normative data or comparison groups.

Progression beyond the present demographic level of research will also require that sufficient numbers be included in the sample to allow their subdivision into a number of preconceived categories. The relationship between these categories can then be investigated, employing methods of multifactoral analysis. The subdivision of samples on socioeconomic grounds can be expected to permit a closer study of those more subtle psychological factors that supposedly account for the many exceptions observed when only gross social and economic variables are examined.

Course

The description of prognosis is hampered in the United Kingdom by the recency of the problem and the lack of studies that have followed narcotic addicts over considerable periods of time. Those studies in existence, usually involving patients treated by a particular clinic or clinics (Bewley & Ben-Arie, 1968; Chapple et al., 1972a, 1972b; Mahon, 1971) over different lengths of followup, indicate that approximately 40% of those at one time under treatment are known still to be taking opiates while 15% have died. Approximately 20% appear to be drug free at follow-up, the remainder being of indeterminate status (some of whom are in institutions of one kind or another).

The only study to attempt personal followup of patients purportedly off narcotics is that reported by Chapple et al. (1972a). Of the 108 followed up over 5 years, 17 were found on personal interview and clinical assessment to be off opiates; and for a further eight it was possible to establish that they had adopted a new lifestyle inconsistent with the continued illicit use of opiates.

A retrospective study (Hawks, D. V., & Smith, L. Unpublished manuscript, Addiction Research Unit, 1972) pursued narcotic addicts known to the Home Office in 1965 (therefore predating compulsory notification); official sources were employed in the followup. This study revealed that 14% were known to have died and 37% were know to be still dependent on narcotics. The exact status of the remainder was indeterminate: they were not known to be dead or under treatment with the drug-dependence centers.

The system of prescribing by clinics has not prevented comparatively high mortality and recurrent hospitalization for drug-related reasons. Bewley, Ben-Arie, and James (1968) suggested that the mortality of United Kingdom addicts was twice that among New York addicts, a difference that partly may reflect the different conventions of reporting death in the two countries and the relative strengths and dosages of heroin injected.

Most observers agree that whereas the narcotics problem in the United Kingdom may have been contained in the sense that the number of new notifications no longer approximates the epidemic proportions characteristic of 1967 and 1968, few addicts are *known* to have been abstinent from drugs for a prolonged period of time. A considerable number are known to be no longer in touch with treatment centers. Although a percentage of these are probably drug free, a significant proportion are undoubtedly still using narcotics obtained from illicit sources.

The present system of monitoring is deficient in that it does not provide for the routine followup of addicts no longer in touch with the treatment centers. There are a number of research investigations underway that provide for the personal followup of those no longer under treatment, but their results are not yet available. Preliminary indications are that approximately one-third of those notified are not known to be under treatment 10 months later.

VALIDITY

Aside from those general considerations affecting validity already discussed, the representativeness of the addict samples studied, the existence of an uncharted periphery of narcotic use, and the incompleteness of the case notes or notifications employed in a number of studies, there are a number of problematic issues peculiar to the study of narcotic addicts. In the absence of biochemical tests allowing the assessment of the exact quantity and quality of drugs ingested, the determination of such information must necessarily rely on verbal report. Even if such tests were available, their use would be limited to the immediate past and would indicate nothing about the addict's previous drug use. The fact that the nontherapeutic use of drugs is an illegal activity except when the drug is supplied by one of the drug treatment centers increases the unreliability of self-report in any context where it is felt by the addict that the information supplied might affect his ability to get more drugs. The effect of drugs themselves on the accuracy of self-report is itself largely unknown.

Despite these qualifications, most information as to the personal and social history of drug addicts has been based entirely on the addict's self-report. Criminal, medical, and employment histories may be checked, but the reliability and validity of the more personal and probably more pertinent aspects of an individual's history are largely untested. The historical nature of many of the events inquired about adds further to their inaccessibility. No one questions the importance of social factors in the initiation and maintenance of drug dependence, but we are at present comparatively inept at assessing such factors in those settings presented by the addict.

Much of the research on which this account of the epidemiology of narcotic dependence is based has its origins in the clinical centers treating addicts. While it is possible to check some features of the addict's account, other aspects are both inaccessible to testing and more likely to be affected by the ambivalent doctor/patient relationship characteristic of these settings. Other investigations have had the advantage of being independent of the treatment process and thus perhaps party to information that would not have been volunteered to the clinics treating patients. On the other hand, such investigators have lacked the clinics' ability to insure the patient's cooperation with the investigation. What is lacking in the United Kingdom is any prospective study of "at risk" groups where the development of narcotic dependence is observed without the double disadvantage of a retrospective orientation and identification with "treatment."

ORGANIZATION OF RESEARCH

The way in which research is organized in the United Kingdom inevitably bears on the adequacy of the description of narcotic addiction. The drug scene in the United Kingdom is, by comparison with the United States, a fairly cohesive one; in like manner, research in the United Kingdom is organized on a much more coordinated basis than is probably true in the United States. One reason for the difference, of course, may be the different size of the problem in the two countries.

Following the recommendations of the Second Brain Committee Report, the Medical Research Council established in 1969 three working parties concerned with the biochemistry/pharmacology, treatment, and epidemiology of drug dependence. After taking a census of research that was underway to determine the gaps in existing knowledge, each party published its recommendations. A single Working Group on Drug Dependence, including representatives from the Medical Research Council, Social Science Research Council, Home Office, and the Department of Health and Social Security, was then charged with the responsibility of enacting these recommendations. The working party on epidemiology recommended that the following five aspects of the problem needed more detailed study:

1. Prevalence of drug taking—including casual and "soft" drug use in defined geographical areas and involving certain groups in different areas.

2. Dissemination of drugs—how and where drugs became available in the community.

3. Natural history of drug taking—the process of initiation of drug use, its continuance, and its treatment. These wide-ranging studies should employ appropriate control groups as necessary.

4. Central collection of data and monitoring of trends—using data from the Home Office, the Department of Health and Social Security, the Scottish Home and Health Department, and the National Health Service Pricing Bureau.

5. Refinement of methodology—refining techniques in field surveys and establishing the reliability and validity of such instruments.

The Home Office for some time has maintained a directory of research in drug dependence, the details of which are furnished by the research workers themselves. In addition, the Medical Research Council has published a list of projects supported by them. In 1971 the Home Office listed 109 projects, including work on biochemistry, pharmacology, assay techniques, genetics, pathology, animal studies, treatment studies, sociopsychological studies, and research with delinquents. Such research was carried out in 49 centers under the aegis of hospitals, universities, and research institutes. In addition to supporting research at the Addiction Research Unit, the Medical Research Council supports a Drug Dependence Research Team at Graylingwell Hospital. The Department of Health and Social Security, in addition to providing partial support for the Addiction Research Unit, supports a unit at the Maudsley Hospital (Clinical Research and Drug Dependence Treatment Unit). The Scottish Home and Health Department supports a unit at the University of Strathclyde (Drug Dependence Research Project).

The Working Group on Drug Dependence has representation from all major grant-giving agencies in this field and thus has the facility for insuring the financial support of research. The Medical Research Council took the rather unusual step of declaring research in this field to be a priority area, and the Social Science Research Council has a small working party specifically concerned with the encouragement of social science research in the field of drug dependence.

A rather unusual and certainly atypical situation exists in the United Kingdom in that more than enough money is available for research and at least some degree of coordination is exercised over the development of research. Total centralization, however, has not occurred. In addition to the government-supported research mentioned previously, a large number of projects are pursued by university departments, whose initiation and direction has a much more individual origin.

Another characteristic of the research organization in the United Kingdom is that, in theory at least, research likely will affect policy. Not only are results disseminated through the professional journals, but the Department of Health and Social Security, by virtue of commissioning at least some of the studies, has direct access to the results. The department holds regular meetings with psychiatrists in charge of drug centers and includes on the agenda the discussion of research findings relevant to the management of drug dependence. The Advisory Council on the Misuses of Drugs reviews research carried out in this area. Thus, in the United Kingdom, favorable circumstances exist for the support of research and its translation into policy.

REFERENCES

de Alarcon, R. The spread of heroin abuse in a community. *Bulletin on Narcotics,* 1969, 21, 17-22.

de Alarcon, R. An epidemiological evaluation of a public health measure aimed at reducing the availability of methylamphetamine. *Psychological Medicine,* 1972, 2, 293-300.

de Alarcon, R., & Rathod, M. H. Prevention and early detection of heroin abuse. *British Medical Journal,* 1968, 2, 549-553.

Bewley, T. H. Recent changes in the pattern of drug abuse in the United Kingdom. *Bulletin on Narcotics,* 1966, 28, 1-9.

Bewley, T. H., & Ben-Arie, O. A study of 100 consecutive in-patients, *British Medical Journal,* 1968, 1, 727-730.

Bewley, T. H., Ben-Arie, O., & James, I. P. Morbidity and mortality from heroin dependence. I. Survey of heroin addicts known to the Home Office. *British Medical Journal,* 1968, 1, 725-726.

Bewley, T. H., James, I. P., & Mahon, T. Evaluation of the effectiveness of prescribing clinics for narcotic addicts in the United Kingdom (1968-70). In C. T. D. Zarajonetis (Ed.), *Drug abuse: Proceedings of the international conference.* Philadelphia: Lea & Febiger, 1972.

Blumberg, H. H., Cohen, D. S., Dronfield, B. E., Mordecai, E. A., Roberts, J. C., & Hawks, D. V. British opiate users: I. People approaching London treatment centers. *International Journal of the Addictions,* 1973, in press.

Boyd, P., Layland, W. R., & Crichmay, T. R. Treatment and followup of adolescents addicted to heroin. *British Medical Journal,* 1971, 2, 604-605.

Brain Committee: The report of the interdepartmental committee on drug addiction. London: HMSO, 1961.

Bransby, E. R. A study of patients notified by hospitals as addicted to drugs: First report. *Health Trends,* 1971, 3, 75-78. (a)

Bransby, E. R. Note for discussion. *Department of Health and Social Security study of drug dependent patients.* CCDD/(71)3. 1971. (b)

Bransby, E. R., Curley, G. O., & Kotulansha, M. T. A study of patients notified by hospitals as addicted to drugs: Second report. *Health Trends,* 1973, 5, 17-20.

Chapple, P. A. L., & Gray, G. One year's work at a center for treatment of addicted patients. *Lancet,* 1968, 1, 908-911.

Chapple, P. A. L., Somekh, D. F., & Taylor, M. E. A five year followup of 108 cases of opiate addiction: general findings and a suggested method of staging. *British Journal of Addiction,* 1972, 67, 33-38. (a)

Chapple, P. A. L., Somekh, D. E., & Taylor, M. E. Followup of cases of opiate addiction from the time of notification to the Home Office. *British Medical Journal,* 1972, 2, 680-683. (b)

Connell, P. H. Adolescent drug taking. *Proceedings of the Royal Society of Medicine,* 1965, 58, 409-412. (a)

Connell, P. H. The assessment and treatment of adolescent drug takers with special reference to the amphetamines. *Proceedings, Leeds symposium on behavioural disorders, March, 1965.* London: May & Baker, 1965. (b)

Department of Health & Social Security. *Second report of the Interdepartmental Committee on Drug Addiction.* London: H.M.S.O., 1965.

Department of Health & Social Security. *On the state of the public health.* London: H.M.S.O., 1971.

Gardner, R., & Connell, P. H. Opiate users attending a special drug dependence clinic 1968-1969. *Bulletin on Narcotics,* 1971, 23(4), 9-15.

Hawks, D. V. The dimensions of drug dependence in the United Kingdom. *International Journal of Addiction,* 1971, 6, 135-160.

Hicks, R. C. The management of heroin addiction at a general hospital drug addiction treatment center. *British Journal of Addiction,* 1969, 64, 235-243.

Kosviner, A., Mitcheson, M., Myers, K., Ogborne, A., Stimson, G. V., Zacune, J., & Edwards, G. Heroin use in a provincial town. *Lancet,* 1968, 1, 1189-1192.

MacMahon, B., & Pugh, T. *Epidemiology: Principles and methods.* Boston: Little, Brown, 1970.

Mahon, T. A. An exploratory study of hospitalized narcotic addicts in Great Britain. *Acta Psychiatrica Scandinavica,* Suppl. 227, 1971.

Morris, T. N. *Uses of epidemiology.* Edinburgh: Livingstone, 1957.

Spear, H. B. The growth of heroin addiction in the United Kingdom. *British Journal of Addiction,* 1969, 64, 245-255.

Spear, H. B., & Glatt, M. M. The influence of Canadian addicts on heroin addiction in the United Kingdom. *British Journal of Addiction,* 1971, 66, 141-149.

Stimson, G. V., & Ogborne, A. C. Survey of addicts prescribed heroin at London clinics. *Lancet,* 1970, 1, 1163-1166. (a)

Stimson, G. V., & Ogborne, A. C. A survey of a representative sample of addicts prescribed heroin at London clinics. *Bulletin on Narcotics,* 1970, 22, 13-22. (b)

Zacune, J. A comparison of Canadian narcotic addicts in Great Britain and Canada. *Bulletin on Narcotics,* 1971, 23, 41-49.

4

SOME EPIDEMIOLOGICAL CONSIDERATIONS OF ONSET OF OPIATE USE IN THE UNITED STATES[1]

Carl D. Chambers
Department of Epidemiology
University of Miami School of Medicine
and
Resource Planning Corporation
Washington, Miami, New York

THE PROBLEM

Epidemiologists working within the field of drug abuse have been seeking to assess the significance of three hypotheses suggested by clinical researchers:

- The age at which persons begin to use opiates (age of onset) has decreased in recent years. Persons who use opiates have done so increasingly at younger ages.
- The onset of opiate use is influenced by such cultural factors as stylistic peer group behavioral patterns and availability of specific drugs. Because of these cultural changes certain years can be characterized as eruption years because of the increased incidence of onset.
- The elapsed time between the onset of opiate use and the seeking of formal treatment for addiction to the opiates has been reduced significantly. Persons addicted to the opiates seek treatment much earlier than in the past.

[1] This study would not have been possible without the cooperation and support of the following agencies: Special Action Office for Drug Abuse Prevention; National Institute of Mental Health (NIMH); California Human Relations Agency; Georgia Department of Public Health; New York State Narcotic Addiction Control Commission; West Philadelphia Community Mental Health Consortium; University of Chicago, Illinois Drug Abuse Program; University of Miami, Dade County Drug Program; University of Missouri, St. Louis State Hospital Drug Program; and Texas Christian University, Institute of Behavioral Research. Interpretations or viewpoints stated in this document do not necessarily represent positions or policies of any of these cooperating and supporting agencies.

This report is an analysis of data compiled to address these three hypotheses.

SCOPE AND METHOD OF STUDY

In this assessment of onset of opiate use in the United States we were guided by the following principles: (a) to secure contemporary onset data from known "hard data" files throughout the United States and (b) to present detailed data in compiled aggregate form so as to permit other epidemiologists immediate access to the data for supplemental interpretation and discussion.

For ease of description, the following assumptions were made:

1. Only treatment files where "addiction" is a criterion for inclusion were solicited.

2. Any person seeking treatment for opiate use was considered to be addicted. While the investigator is completely aware of the inaccuracy of this assumption, there is no valid means of identifying and separating users, abusers, and addicts in most treatment programs.

3. Files from different geographic areas or states were searched. Any person reported in one of the files was considered to be unique for the time period studied and not to be in any of the other seven.

In accordance with the hypotheses, the study was designed to address four specific issues:

1. What had been the pattern of age at onset during the 1960s?
2. What sex differences, if any, could be identified?
3. What race/ethnicity differences, if any, could be identified?
4. What had been the pattern of elapsed time between onset of use and entering treatment?

STUDY POPULATION

Eight data files were searched:

1. A New York State Narcotic Addiction Control Commission file, which includes addicts from the civil commitment program; volunteers on the Beth Israel Methadone program; and volunteers from 12 community-based programs, e.g., Daytop, Odessey House, etc. The file contained admissions for 1965-71.

2. A California file that includes addicts from the state civil commitment program. The file contained admissions for 1966-70.

3. The NIMH Clinical Research Center file, which includes the addicts who had been sent to Lexington under the National Addict Rehabilitation Act federal civil commitment program. The file contained admissions for 1967-71, representing persons from throughout the United States.

4. An Illinois file that includes volunteers for the multimodality, state treatment program. The file contained admissions for 1968-71.

5. A Georgia file that includes volunteers for the multimodality, state-coordinated, community-based treatment programs. The file contained admissions for 1971-72.

6. A Philadelphia file that includes volunteers for the largest community-based methadone maintenance program in the city. The file contained admissions for 1968-71.

7. A St. Louis file that includes volunteers for a State Hospital-based methadone maintenance program. The file contained admissions for 1967-70.

8. A Miami file that includes volunteers for county, community-based methadone maintenance and detoxification programs. The file contained admissions for 1969-72.

These combined admissions include persons seeking treatment in all the major modalities and include all major civil commitment programs as well as some of the largest voluntary community-based programs.

The investigator is painfully aware of the methodological problems inherent in "mixing" data from these diverse files and in assuming the validity of the data obtained from each. The very fact that they *do* represent admissions in all the major modalities and from programs operating within various legal entities makes them noncomparable at one level. Nonetheless, the need to include as much "nationwide" data in this most preliminary analysis was deemed more important than attempting to fully resolve the comparability issue. Hypotheses generated from this "global" approach and future analyses around them must, of course, be framed within more precise cohorts. With regard to validity, few programs attempt an independent verification of self-reported data collected during the intake or admissions process. Future investigators must somehow address this issue beyond the recognition level now employed.

Each agency was asked to submit six sets of data for *each client* in its files:

1. Age at onset of opiate use
2. Year of onset of opiate use
3. Age at current treatment admission
4. Year of current treatment admission
5. Sex of client
6. Race/ethnicity of client

The agencies were permitted to submit these data in the most convenient form for that agency. Data were submitted on printouts, cards, and computer tape. All data were converted and a master file constructed at the University of Miami Division of Addiction Sciences. The master file includes data for 69,887 opiate abusers. These 69,887 persons are distributed as indicated in Table 1.

TABLE 1

Distribution of the Study Population

File	Males	Females	Total
New York	38,996	9,787	48,783
California	8,023	1,106	9,129
Kentucky	3,965	1,042	5,007
Illinois	3,082	826	3,908
Georgia	832	292	1,124
Philadelphia	622	166	788
St. Louis	559	106	665
Miami	371	112	483
Total	56,450	13,437	69,887

RESULTS

Age at Onset

In the study population of 69,887 addicts, age-at-onset distributions were recorded (Table 2).[2] Among these 69,887 addicts, 1.7% were using opiates before age 12, 22.3% were using opiates before age 16; 45.9% were using

[2] These grouped distributions were dictated by the way in which California ($N = 9,129$) groups onset data at the time the data are collected.

TABLE 2

Number and Percent Distribution of
Addicts by Age at Onset

Age at onset,[a] in years	Number	Percent
11 or less	1,192	1.7
12-13	3,583	5.1
14-15	10,798	15.5
16	8,221	11.8
17	8,229	11.8
18	7,553	10.8
19-20	10,668	15.3
21-24	10,661	15.2
25-29	4,852	6.9
30 or more	4,130	5.9
Total	69,887	100.0

[a] Based on groupings found in the California data.

opiates before age 18; 72.0% were using opiates before age 21; and all but 5.9% were opiate users before age 30.

Sex Differences in the Age at Onset

In the total study population of 69,887 addicts, 56,450 (80.8%) were males and 13,437 (19.2%) were females. Distributions by sex are shown in Table 3. Although these data would suggest that a minor sex difference does exist in the onset of opiate use, with males beginning to use opiates slightly earlier than females, these differences are not statistically significant. Neither the sex composition of the study population nor the slightly earlier onset pattern for males was unexpected. Both patterns are reflected in the literature. (See Ball & Chambers, 1970, for a variety of references showing these two patterns have been about the same at least since 1965.)

Race/Ethnicity Differences in the Age of Onset

In the total study population of 69,887 addicts, race/ethnicity was distributed as follows:

Race/ethnicity	Number	Percent
Black	30,537	43.7
White	24,538	35.1
Spanish-speaking	13,618	19.5
Other	1,194	1.7
Total	69,887	100.0

In this study population 22.3% began using opiates prior to age 16, 45.9% began prior to age 18 and fully 87.2% began opiate use prior to age 25. Some minor race/ethnicity differences were noted in the distribution of ages at onset (Tables 4–7).[3] Tables 6 and 7 exclude the onset data for California addicts to expand the age-at-onset presentation.

Year of Onset

To determine if any "eruption" years had occurred, the data were grouped to determine what year the onset of opiate use had occurred. Distributions derived from this grouping are shown in Tables 8 and 9.

Grouping of these data according to year of onset produced the following findings:

• Among these 69,887 addicts, significantly greater proportions of both black and Spanish-speaking addicts began their opiate use prior to 1960. Almost one-third of the black and Spanish-speaking addicts began using

[3]In collapsing the age categories to assess onset *prior* to age 18, statistical significance of differences was noted. However, these differences may be artifacts due to the size of the cells.

TABLE 3

Percent Distribution of Addicts by Age at Onset and Sex

Age at onset, in years	Males ($N = 56,450$)	Females ($N = 13,437$)	Total ($N = 69,887$)
11 or less	1.9	1.2	1.7
12–13	5.1	5.0	5.1
14–15	15.6	14.9	15.4
16	12.1	10.6	11.8
17	12.0	10.8	11.8
18	11.0	10.3	10.8
19–20	15.4	14.8	15.4
21–24	14.7	17.5	15.2
25–29	6.5	8.2	6.9
30 or more	5.7	6.7	5.9
Total	100.0	100.0	100.0

opiates prior to 1960 as compared with some one-fifth of the white addicts.

- Among these 69,887 addicts, males more frequently began opiate use prior to 1960. Twenty-nine percent of all males but only 21% of all females began use prior to 1960.
- The low values for onset during the 1970s are probably due, in part, to agencies not having up-to-the-minute reporting systems and, in part, to fewer years at risk.
- It would appear that the years 1965–69 were "eruption" years for the onset of opiate use in the United States (Table 10). For these 69,887 opiate addicts, the pattern was one of gradual increase, the eruption, a leveling off, and the *possibility* of a gradual decrease. This pattern would appear to be the same for both sexes and all three of the race/ethnicity cohorts.

Age at Time of Current Admission for Treatment

As part of the attempt at determining if addicts are seeking treatment earlier in their addiction careers, distributions by sex and race/ethnicity were compiled for the ages at which the current treatment was begun (Tables 11 and 12).

Grouping these data according to the beginning of treatment produced the following findings:

- In this study population of 69,887 addicts, over one-fourth were under age 21 when they began treatment and more than one-half were under age 25.

TABLE 4
Number and Percent Distribution of Addicts by Age at Onset and Race/Ethnicity

Age at onset, in years	Black		White		Spanish-speaking		Other		Total	
	Number	Percent	Number	Percent	Number	Percent	Number	Percent	Number	Percent
11 or less	474	1.5	344	1.4	344	2.5	30	2.5	1,192	1.7
12–13	1,246	4.1	1,509	6.2	735	5.4	93	7.8	3,583	5.1
14–15	4,165	13.6	4,278	17.4	2,188	16.1	167	14.0	10,798	15.5
16	3,410	11.2	3,139	12.8	1,552	11.4	120	10.1	8,221	11.8
17	3,522	11.5	3,069	12.5	1,515	11.1	123	10.3	8,229	11.8
Total, under 18	—	41.9	—	50.3	—	46.5	—	44.7	—	45.9
18	3,191	10.5	2,894	11.8	1,357	10.0	111	9.3	7,553	10.8
19–20	4,693	15.4	3,843	15.7	1,981	14.5	151	12.6	10,668	15.3
21–24	5,185	17.0	3,163	12.9	2,163	15.9	150	12.6	10,661	15.2
25–29	2,715	8.9	1,036	4.2	1,018	7.5	83	6.9	4,852	6.9
30 or more	1,936	6.3	1,263	5.1	765	5.6	166	13.9	4,130	5.9
Total	30,537	100.0	24,538	100.0	13,618	100.0	1,194	100.0	69,887	100.0

TABLE 5

Percent of Opiate Users Under Age 21, by Race/Ethnicity

Race/ethnicity	Opiate use under age 16	Opiate use under age 18	Opiate use under age 21
White	24.9	50.3	77.7
Spanish-speaking	24.0	46.5	71.0
Black	19.2	41.9	67.7

- Female addicts appear to seek treatment earlier than male addicts.
- White addicts appear to seek treatment earlier than black addicts.
- Black addicts appear to seek treatment earlier than Spanish-speaking addicts.

Elapsed Time Between Onset and Treatment

The data support the hypothesis that opiate addicts are seeking treatment earlier in their addiction careers. Two separate analyses were performed.

In the first analysis, the years since onset were determined for all addicts seeking treatment in given years (Table 13). Prior to 1965, when the data suggest an onset "eruption" was beginning, only 12.1% of the addicts who sought treatment had been using opiates 3 years or less. Among those seeking treatment at the onset of the "eruption" (1966), 25.9% had been using opiates 3 years or less. The seeking of treatment continued to increase during the peak years of the "eruption":

- 1967–31.3% of the 5,895 addicts seeking treatment had been using opiates 3 years or less.
- 1968–36.8% of the 8,186 addicts seeking treatment had been using opiates 3 years or less.
- 1969–38.6% of the 12,865 addicts seeking treatment had been using opiates 3 years or less.

In 1970, when the data suggest that the rate of increase in the incidence of new cases might be decreasing, the pattern of seeking treatment early in one's addiction career appears to have remained constant. For example, of 19,059 addicts who sought treatment during 1970, 39.5% had been using opiates 3 years or less.

In the second analysis of the elapsed time between onset and seeking treatment, the year in which treatment was sought was determined for all addicts who began using opiates in a given year (Table 14). The second analysis also revealed a pattern of the increasing search for early treatment. For example, of the 4,726 addicts who began using opiates during 1965, less than 10% appear to have sought treatment during the first and second year of

TABLE 6

Percent Distribution of Addicts by Age at Onset of Opiate Use and
Sex for 60,758 Addicts

Age at onset, in years	Males (N = 47,595)	Females (N = 13,163)	Total (N = 60,758)
10 or less	1.5	0.9	1.4
11	0.7	0.5	0.6
12	1.8	1.7	1.7
13	3.9	4.0	3.9
14	6.8	6.4	6.7
Total, under 15	14.7	13.5	14.3
15	10.4	9.2	10.2
16	12.9	10.8	12.5
17	12.4	10.7	12.1
18	10.7	9.8	10.6
19	7.9	8.3	7.9
Total, 15-19	54.3	48.8	53.3
20	6.4	6.6	6.4
21	4.9	5.4	5.1
22	3.5	4.2	3.7
23	2.9	3.7	3.0
24	2.2	3.1	2.4
Total, 20-24	19.9	23.0	20.6
25	1.9	2.3	2.0
26	1.4	1.9	1.5
27	1.1	1.7	1.2
28	0.9	1.3	1.0
29	0.7	0.9	0.7
Total, 25-29	6.0	8.1	6.4
30 or more	5.1	6.6	5.4
Total	100.0	100.0	100.0

Note.—California addicts (N = 9,129) were excluded. California groups onset ages *prior to* processing the data file, thus preventing retrieval of the actual age of California addicts reported in the section.

Table 7

Number and Percent Distribution of Addicts by Age at Onset of Opiate Use and Race/Ethnicity for 60,758 Addicts

Age at onset, in years	White		Black		Spanish-speaking		Other		Total	
	Number	Percent	Number	Percent	Number	Percent	Number	Percent	Number	Percent
10 or less	208	1.0	344	1.2	242	2.3	19	1.7	813	1.4
11	136	.7	130	.4	102	1.0	11	1.0	379	0.6
12	426	2.1	350	1.2	227	2.1	35	3.2	1,038	1.7
13	1,022	5.1	874	3.0	457	4.3	57	5.2	2,410	3.9
14	1,601	8.0	1,603	5.5	798	7.5	78	7.1	4,080	6.7
15	2,440	12.1	2,514	8.7	1,136	10.7	87	7.9	6,177	10.2
Total, under 16	–	29.0	–	20.0	–	27.9	–	26.1	–	24.5
16	2,841	14.1	3,343	11.7	1,295	12.1	112	10.2	7,591	12.5
17	2,614	13.0	3,431	11.9	1,188	11.1	112	10.2	7,345	12.1
18	2,282	11.4	3,025	10.6	988	9.3	103	9.3	6,398	10.6
Total, 16-18	–	38.5	–	34.2	–	32.5	–	29.7	–	35.2
19	1,610	8.0	2,375	8.2	745	7.0	79	7.2	4,809	7.9
20	1,213	6.0	2,004	6.9	623	5.8	55	5.0	3,895	6.4
21	895	4.5	1,576	5.3	535	5.0	47	4.3	3,053	5.1
Total, 19-21	–	18.5	–	20.4	–	17.8	–	16.5	–	19.4
22	558	2.8	1,253	4.3	408	3.8	35	3.2	2,254	3.7
23	410	2.0	1,049	3.6	330	3.1	29	2.6	1,818	3.0
24	302	1.5	895	3.1	261	2.5	16	1.4	1,474	2.4
25	234	1.2	719	2.5	233	2.2	18	1.6	1,204	2.0
Total, 22-25	–	7.5	–	13.5	–	11.6	–	8.8	–	11.1
26	172	.9	571	2.0	163	1.5	12	1.1	918	1.5
27	120	.6	477	1.6	141	1.3	18	1.6	756	1.2
28	99	.5	376	1.3	131	1.2	8	0.7	614	1.0
29	74	.4	279	1.0	96	0.9	13	1.2	462	0.7
Total, 26-29	–	2.4	–	5.9	–	4.9	–	4.6	–	4.4
30 or more	822	4.1	1,725	6.0	565	5.3	158	14.3	3,270	5.4
Total	20,079	100.0	28,913	100.0	10,664	100.0	1,102	100.0	60,758	100.0

Note.—California addicts (*N* = 9,129) were excluded from this table. California groups onset ages *prior to* processing the data file, preventing the retrieval of the actual age of California addicts reported in this section.

TABLE 8

Percent Distribution of Addicts by Year at Onset of Opiate Use and Sex

Year at onset, in years	Males (N = 56,450)	Females (N = 13,437)	Total (N = 69,887)
Pre-1960	28.8	21.2	27.4
1960	3.6	2.7	3.4
1961	4.0	2.8	3.7
1962	4.4	3.2	4.1
1963	5.2	4.4	5.1
1964	6.1	5.5	6.0
1965	7.9	7.6	7.9
1966	9.9	10.4	10.0
1967	11.0	13.1	11.4
1968	9.9	13.7	10.7
1969	6.2	10.1	7.0
1970	2.4	4.3	2.7
1971	0.6	1.0	0.6
Total	100.0	100.0	100.0

use. This compares with 32.9% of the 7,099 addicts who began using opiates in 1967. If the pattern continues, one might expect that as many as 40% or 50% of newly initiated addicts will seek treatment during their first year of addiction and as many as 95% will probably seek treatment during the first 2 years of their addiction. *At least among addicts who seek treatment, this treatment is being sought earlier in their addiction careers.* One seems forced to conclude that if treatment services are provided, the addict will seek them out permitting an early intervention attempt.

Corroborative Data

The primary focus of this study was to compile data that would produce descriptions of trends in the epidemiology of onset. The design also included having a comparative study population of only those addicts seeking treatment at the present time. Such a comparison group *should* reflect all the patterns identified as having occurred during the 1960s. Texas Christian University (TCU) and NIMH provided data for 1,026 admissions that occurred during March 1972. The major findings were verified in this comparative group.

- *Males begin using opiates slightly earlier than females.*
- *Females seek treatment for their drug use earlier than males.* The differences are even more pronounced in the TCU study group than in the larger study population: 33.3% of all the females were under age 21 when admitted for treatment as compared with 18.4% of all males.

TABLE 9

Number and Percent Distribution of Addicts by Year at Onset of Opiate Use and Race/Ethnicity

Year at onset	White		Black		Spanish-speaking		Other		Total	
	Number	Percent	Number	Percent	Number	Percent	Number	Percent	Number	Percent
Pre-1960	5,166	21.0	9,372	30.7	4,153	30.5	426	35.7	19,117	27.4
1960	892	3.6	856	2.8	610	4.5	38	3.2	2,396	3.4
1961	1,010	4.1	895	2.9	656	4.8	36	3.0	2,597	3.7
1962	1,192	4.9	939	3.1	695	5.1	41	3.4	2,867	4.1
1963	1,501	6.1	1,197	3.9	815	6.0	50	4.2	3,563	5.1
1964	1,740	7.1	1,538	5.0	902	6.6	37	3.1	4,217	6.0
1965	2,339	9.5	2,012	6.6	1,067	7.8	90	7.6	5,508	7.9
1966	2,716	11.1	2,853	9.3	1,316	9.7	105	8.8	6,990	10.0
1967	3,020	12.3	3,535	11.6	1,311	9.6	145	12.1	8,011	11.4
1968	2,596	10.6	3,591	11.8	1,122	8.2	121	10.1	7,430	10.7
1969	1,609	6.6	2,464	8.1	688	5.1	75	6.3	4,836	7.0
1970	589	2.4	1,034	3.4	253	1.9	23	1.9	1,899	2.7
1971	162	0.7	246	0.8	30	0.2	7	0.6	445	0.6
1972	6	0.0	5	0.0	–	0.0	–	0.0	11	0.0
Total	24,538	100.0	30,537	100.0	13,618	100.0	1,194	100.0	69,887	100.0

TABLE 10

Number and Percent Distribution of
Addicts by Year of Onset, 1960-69

Year of onset	Number	Percent
1960	2,396	4.9
1961	2,597	5.4
1962	2,867	5.9
1963	3,563	7.4
1964	4,217	8.7
1965	5,508	11.4
1966	6,990	14.4
1967	8,011	16.5
1968	7,430	15.4
1969	4,836	10.0
Total	48,415	100.0

- *White addicts are more likely to be recent initiates to opiate use than either black or Spanish-speaking addicts.* For example, 77.3% of the white addicts entering treatment began using opiates during 1965 or later. This compares with 69.5% of the black and 47.0% of the Spanish-speaking addicts.
- *The "eruption" years for opiate onset were 1966-69; the rate of increase appears to be decreasing.* In the TCU study group, 48.0% began using opiates during these 4 years.
- *Addicts are seeking treatment early in their careers.* In the TCU study group, 43.0% had been using opiates 3 years or less; and 29.5% had been using 2 years or less.

SUMMARY AND CONCLUSIONS

This study has attempted to provide national data pertaining to the onset of opiate abuse which will benefit both behavioral scientists and social policy-makers. The more salient of these findings are as follows.

In this study population of 69,887 addicts, 22.3% had begun to use opiates before age 16, 45.9% before age 18, and 72.0% before age 21. Males began using opiates earlier than females, and white and Spanish-speaking addicts began use earlier than black addicts.

Sixty-nine percent of all addicts began using opiates during the 1960s. It would appear that the major "eruptions" of opiate use occurred during the period 1965-69, and these eruptions began to subside after that time. This eruption period was noted among all race/ethnic and sex cohorts. *To what extent the epidemic has abated is still to be determined.*

TABLE 11
Percent Distribution of Addicts by Age at Treatment and Sex

Age at treatment, in years	Males (N = 56,450)		Females (N = 13,437)		Total (N = 69,887)	
	Percent	Total (%)	Percent	Total (%)	Percent	Total (%)
15	.8		2.2		1.1	
16	1.6		2.6		1.8	
17	3.5	25.4	4.6	30.1	3.7	26.4
18	5.3		6.1		5.5	
19	6.8		7.3		6.9	
20	7.4		7.3		7.4	
21	7.5		7.5		7.5	
22	7.2		7.4		7.2	
23	7.0	32.6	6.0	31.2	6.8	32.2
24	5.8		5.7		5.7	
25	5.1		4.6		5.0	
26	4.4		4.0		4.3	
27	3.9		3.7		3.8	
28	3.4	17.6	3.4	16.4	3.4	17.3
29	3.1		2.7		3.0	
30	2.8		2.6		2.8	
31	2.5		2.1		2.4	
32	2.2		2.2		2.2	
33	2.0	10.4	1.8	9.9	2.0	10.3
34	1.9		1.9		1.9	
35	1.8		1.9		1.8	
36	1.7		1.6		1.7	
37	1.6		1.4		1.6	
38	1.4	7.2	1.3	6.7	1.4	7.1
39	1.4		1.3		1.3	
40	1.1		1.1		1.1	
41	1.0		1.0		1.0	
42	.8		.8		.8	
43	.7	3.7	.7	3.3	.7	3.6
44	.6		.4		.6	
45	.6		.4		.5	
46	.4		.3		.4	
47	.3		.2		.3	
48	.3	1.3	.2	.9	.3	1.3
49	.3		.2		.3	
50 or more	1.8		1.5		1.8	
Total		100.0		100.0		100.0

Table 12
Number and Percent Distribution of Addicts by Age at Treatment and Race/Ethnicity

Age at treatment, in years	White		Black		Spanish-speaking		Other		Total	
	Number	Percent	Number	Percent	Number	Percent	Number	Percent	Number	Percent
15	316		259		122		48		745	
16	410		577		216		37		1,240	
17	879		1,215		436		45		2,575	
18	1,407	29.8	1,717	25.2	652	22.7	66	28.3	3,842	26.4
19	1,993		1,984		793		67		4,837	
20	2,298		1,936		867		75		5,176	
21	2,361		1,921		928		78		5,288	
22	2,222		1,881		926		57		5,086	
23	2,009	39.5	1,775	27.3	936	32.1	63	25.0	4,783	32.3
24	1,697		1,446		836		57		4,036	
25	1,396		1,308		739		43		3,486	
26	1,071		1,158		727		47		3,003	
27	916		1,086		637		49		2,688	
28	784	16.3	1,026	16.6	551	20.6	24	16.3	2,385	17.3
29	659		933		455		42		2,089	
30	573		878		442		33		1,926	
31	470		799		378		25		1,672	
32	440		734		352		18		1,544	
33	346		671		341		18		1,376	
34	296		656		316		22		1,290	
35	264		687		294		21		1,266	
36	232		668		257		18		1,175	
37	177		658		221		13		1,069	
38	162		585		211		17		975	
39	156		583		177		14		930	
40	113	14.4	500	30.9	141	24.6	13	30.4	767	24.0
41	105		473		124		10		712	
42	90		387		104		5		586	
43	78		336		82		8		504	
44	55		279		61		7		402	
45	52		246		53		7		358	
46	35		200		44		2		281	
47	35		146		23		3		207	
48	27		139		20		4		190	
49	25		124		18		5		172	
50 or more	389		566		138		133		1,226	
Total	24,538	100.0	30,537	100.0	13,618	100.0	1,194	100.0	69,887	100.0

TABLE 13

Percent of Addicts Who Sought Treatment, Showing Elapsed Time Between Onset and Treatment, by Year of Admission

Years since opiate onset	Year of admission									
	Pre-1965 (N = 41)	1965 (N = 101)	1966 (N = 1,694)	1967 (N = 5,895)	1968 (N = 8,186)	1969 (N = 12,865)	1970 (N = 19,059)	1971 (N = 21,586)	1972 (N = 465)	Total (N = 69,887)
1	2.4	2.0	13.0	14.8	17.0	15.0	12.7	7.5	23.0	12.2
2	7.3	2.0	7.4	8.6	11.1	13.3	13.9	10.9	23.7	12.0
3	2.4	5.9	5.5	7.9	8.7	10.3	12.9	13.2	19.1	11.4
4	7.3	6.9	6.4	6.8	6.7	8.3	10.3	11.7	12.7	9.6
5	7.3	4.0	6.4	6.4	6.4	6.7	7.9	10.0	5.8	8.0
6	2.4	3.0	5.7	5.5	4.9	5.4	5.6	7.3	2.8	6.0
7	2.4	7.9	5.6	6.0	4.4	4.2	4.5	5.3	2.4	4.8
8	4.9	6.9	5.4	4.9	4.9	3.6	4.0	4.5	0.6	4.3
9	2.4	3.0	3.7	4.3	4.1	3.1	2.8	3.1	0.9	3.2
10 or more	61.2	58.4	40.9	34.8	31.8	30.1	25.4	26.5	9.0	28.5

TABLE 14

Percent of Addicts Who Sought Treatment, Showing Elapsed Time Between
Onset and Treatment, by Year of Onset

Addict sought treatment at least by the	Year of onset				
	1965 (N = 4,726)	1966 (N = 6,130)	1967 (N = 7,099)	1968 (N = 6,728)	1969 (N = 4,359)
1st year of use	0.1	0.1	12.7	21.7	44.2
2nd year of use	6.6	11.5	20.2	34.9	53.8
3rd year of use	11.5	18.8	31.2	42.5	2.0
4th year of use	19.5	28.8	35.6	0.9	
5th year of use	28.7	35.2	0.4		
6th year of use	33.4	0.2			
7th year of use	0.2				

It was apparent that addicts have begun seeking treatment early in their addiction careers. In 1970, for example, 19,059 addicts sought treatment with the eight agencies cooperating in this study. A total of 12.7% had been using opiates only 1 year; 26.6%, 2 years or less; and 39.5%, 3 years or less. One is forced to acknowledge the necessity for providing meaningful treatments for these novice addicts before they become "hard core." There is evidence that more than 40% of the addicts will seek treatment during the first year of their addiction.

While one must be understandably concerned about the continued early onset of opiate use, one must also be encouraged by the leveling off and possible subsiding of the eruption period noted during 1965-69 and by the early seeking of treatment by those initiated during the eruption period. We *must* continue to provide meaningful services during this initial intervention opportunity. Only through relevant services will we be able to terminate these early addiction careers. If the number of new cases entering the addiction pool has become stabilized or is decreasing and these new cases enter the treatment system early, major reductions in the addiction pool can be accomplished by increasing the effectiveness of treatment techniques and modalities.

There are a number of questions this research has left unanswered and research goals which must still be pursued. These include the following:

What specific relationships exist between age at onset and seeking treatment? For example, do those with an early onset seek treatment earlier in their addiction careers?

What treatment variables are most relevant to the person seeking treatment early in his career versus late in his career? For example, what is the novice addict looking for in treatment? What would bring those *not* seeking treatment into programs?

If persons start using opiates early and seek treatment early, what should that treatment be? For example, must we learn to habilitate rather than rehabilitate?

What geographic variations exist, if any, in all of these patterns?

Onset patterns must be monitored continually to see if addiction is on a decline, as these data indicate. Indeed, there is a definite need for a standardized annual epidemiological census of onset factors. The need for a national data system is obvious.

We must also learn to monitor the onset patterns for debilitating drugs other than the opiates. While addiction to opiates could be decreasing, casualties could be increasing in the other patterns. Indeed, there is some evidence of a polydrug pattern where some opiate use occurs on a fairly regular basis but never to the point of a dysfunctional addiction.

What has happened to the addicts who began using drugs during the 1950s? This current study did not identify many of these addicts who were in treatment or seeking treatment.

One would hope the resources can be made available to pursue these goals.

REFERENCE

Ball, J. D., & Chambers, C. D. *The epidemiology of opiate addiction in the United States.* Springfield, Ill.: Charles C Thomas, 1970.

5
IS THE ONSET OF NARCOTIC ADDICTION AMONG TREATED PATIENTS IN THE UNITED STATES REALLY DECLINING?

Alex Richman
Mount Sinai School of Medicine
City University of New York
and
Beth Israel Medical Center

The onset of opiate use in the United States was recently described by Chambers[1] as "... subsiding ... stabilized ... or decreasing ...." Since Chambers presented detailed data, supplemental interpretation of the source of these conclusions was possible. Epidemiologic review of the source data not only questions the conclusion that the incidence of addiction has been decreasing, but supports the converse—the number seems to be increasing.

BACKGROUND

The data represent 69,887 admissions to facilities, reporting from eight geographic areas. Admissions are included from national, state, and municipal treatment programs, including methadone maintenance and other modalities; and they represent both voluntary and commitment programs. About 70% of the patients were from New York State and 13% from California. Nearly 60% were admitted in 1970 and 1971.

YEAR OF ONSET

Chambers grouped the data by year of onset of opiate use in order to determine if any "eruption" years had occurred. Table 1 shows this grouping by number of addicts.

[1] Chambers, C. D. Some epidemiological considerations of onset of opiate use in the United States. This volume.

TABLE 1

Number of Addicts by
Year of Onset

Year of onset	Number
1960	2,396
1961	2,597
1962	2,867
1963	3,563
1964	4,217
1965	5,508
1966	6,990
1967	8,011
1968	7,430
1969	4,836
Total	48,415

Source. –Chambers, this volume, Table 10.

Chambers concluded:

The years 1965-69 were "eruption" years for the onset of opiate use in the United States. . . . Of the . . . opiate addicts with an onset during the 1960's. The pattern was one of gradual increase, the eruption, and the *possibility* of a gradual decrease. This pattern would appear to be the same for both sexes and all three of the race/ethnicity cohorts.

TABLE 2

Number and Percent of Addicts Admitted for Treatment by Year
Admitted and Number of Years Since Onset

Year admitted	Number admitted	Percentage of admissions entering treatment within:	
		1 year of onset	3 years of onset
1966	1,694	13.0	25.9[a]
1967	5,895	14.8	31.3
1968	8,186	17.0	36.8
1969	12,865	15.0	38.6
1970	19,059	12.7	39.5
1971	21,586	7.5	31.6

Source. –Chambers, this volume, Table 13.
[a]Corrected from 22.4% in Chambers text.

IS INCIDENCE DECLINING?

Data shown in Table 2 are taken from Chambers' Table 13, data he presented to support the hypothesis that opiate addicts are seeking treatment earlier in their addiction careers.

Chambers states that "the data suggest that the rate of increase in the incidence of new cases might be decreasing".

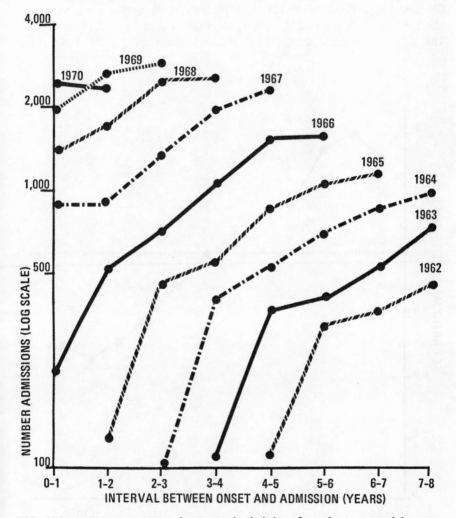

FIG. 1. Interval between year of onset and admission, for cohorts grouped by year of onset.

There are two possible sources for the claim that the number of cases with onset in recent years is decreasing. First, the largest number of onsets were reported during 1967, and successively fewer admissions reported onset during the following 2 years, 1968 and 1969 (Table 1).

Second, the percentage of admissions with onset less than 1 year before admission successively decreased from 17.0% in 1968 to 7.5% in 1971. From 1968-71, as treatment was apparently becoming more available, the percentage of cases with recent onset progressively reduced (Table 2).

Both observations can be explained in a different way. Table 13 in Chambers' report was converted from percentages to absolute numbers and number of addicts grouped by year of *onset* rather than by year of admission. The group with onset during 1967 includes admissions during 1967 with

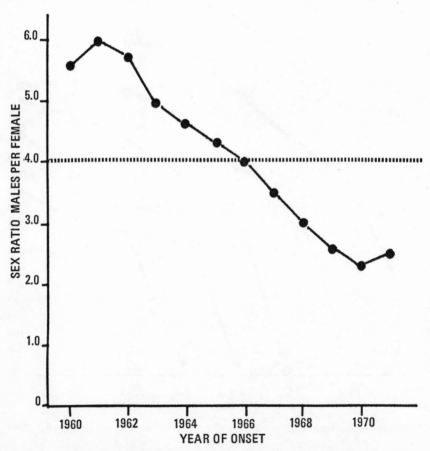

FIG. 2. Sex ratio: Males per female, by year of onset, 1960–71.

0-1-year interval since onset, admissions during 1968 with 1-2-year interval since onset, admissions during 1969 with 2-3-year interval since onset, etc. When graphed by year of onset, we see a progressive increase in the number of addicts admitted in successive intervals following onset (derived from Chambers' Table 13): The cohort with onset during 1967 had 872 admitted within 0-1 years of onset; 908 admitted within 1-2 years of onset; 1,325 admitted within 2-3 years of onset; 1,963 admitted within 3-4 years of onset; 2,159 admitted within 4-5 years of onset (Figure 1).

Secondly, it is evident that the decrease in the number from 8,011 with onset in 1967 to 7,430 with onset in 1968 to 4,836 with onset in 1969 shown in Table 1 is due to having truncated reporting; that onset during 1967 was reported by those admitted in 1967-71; onset during 1968 and 1969 was reported by admissions during a smaller number of years. It is obvious from Figure 1 that the onset has progressively increased from 1962 up to 1969; that the number of patients admitted with 0-3 years of onset was higher for the cohort with onset in 1969 than for the cohort with onset in 1968, and that the 1968 onset cohort was higher than the 1967 onset cohort.

POSSIBLE EXPLANATION FOR APPARENT DECREASE AMONG 1971 ADMISSIONS OF PERSONS WITH RECENT ONSET

Admissions in 1971 were less likely to be admitted within 2 years of onset than were admissions during 1970. Among the 21,586 admissions during 1971, 18.4% were admitted within 2 years of onset compared with 26.6% of the 19,059 admitted during 1970 (see Chambers' Table 13). To what extent does this represent, not a decrease in cases of recent onset, but the admission policies of the expanded number of methadone maintenance programs in recent years, which require a prior history of 2 years of opiate use before admission?

OTHER STRIKING FINDINGS

There has been a consistent decrease in the sex ratio of addicts with onset between 1961 and 1970. The ratio of males to females progressively decreased from 6.0:1.0 among those with onset during 1961 to 2.3:1.0 among those with onset during 1970 (Figure 2) (Derived from Chambers' Table 8). This large-scale progressive change is striking and requires further study.

CONCLUSION AND SUMMARY

Secondary epidemiologic analysis of Chambers' source data does not support the conclusion that the number of new cases in the addiction pool has stabilized or is decreasing. The data do not support the conclusion that there were more cases with onset during 1967 than in 1968 or 1969. The converse is true, that the number of new cases has increased each year up to 1969.

A decrease in the proportion of recent admissions with onset less than 2 years before admission is likely related to the admission policies of methadone maintenance treatment programs.

A long-term progressive increase in the percentage of women among cohorts with onset between 1961 and 1970 is of major interest and requires further epidemiologic analysis.

6
EPIDEMIOLOGY OF HEROIN ADDICTION IN THE 1970s: NEW OPPORTUNITIES AND RESPONSIBILITIES[1]

Patrick H. Hughes
University of Chicago Department of Psychiatry
and
Gail A Crawford[2]
Illinois Drug Abuse Programs

Prior to the 1970s epidemiological studies of heroin addiction were largely descriptive and theoretical. The rapid expansion of community-based treatment services during recent years, however, has permitted epidemiology to enter the stage of experimental and applied research. Experimental research is the systematic testing of intervention programs aimed at reducing the incidence and prevalence of heroin addiction in defined communities or populations. Applied research is the use of epidemiological knowledge and techniques to assist program planners in developing more effective public health approaches to prevention and control of heroin addiction.

Due to the paucity of literature on this substantive area, we will describe our own experience during the past several years in developing an epidemiological research and planning unit for the Illinois Drug Abuse Program, the largest treatment system for heroin addicts in the Midwest. The multidisciplinary team includes investigators with backgrounds in public health psychiatry, clinical and social psychology, sociology, and anthropology. By reviewing achievements and problems, we may be of assistance to other epidemiological researchers who enter this challenging area.

[1] These projects were supported by National Institute of Mental Health Grants MH 18248 and MH 16409 and by the Illinois Drug Abuse Program.
[2] Dr. Patrick H. Hughes is currently a Drug Abuse Council Fellow and Director, Drug Abuse Epidemiology Unit, Department of Psychiatry, University of Chicago. Dr. Gail A. Crawford is a Research Sociologist with the Department of Psychiatry, University of Chicago, and the Illinois Drug Abuse Program.

EPIDEMIOLOGICAL INTERVENTION EXPERIMENTS
IN ADDICTION CONTROL

Our primary mission was to explore ways in which community treatment programs might organize their therapeutic activities around the goal of reducing the incidence and prevalence of heroin addiction in defined communities or populations. This broad and complex mission carried us into many areas of epidemiological inquiry and required the use of a variety of epidemiological methods and techniques. The series of studies to be reviewed does not represent a comprehensive description of the epidemiology of heroin addiction, for our research has only touched on such important areas as primary etiology and the natural history of heroin outbreaks.

Other studies (MacMahon & Pugh, 1970; Morris, 1957; World Health Organization, in press) discuss the full range of activities that might be included in a truly comprehensive description of the epidemiology of heroin addiction. In addition, a number of excellent studies relate specifically to incidence and prevalence of heroin addiction (Ball, Englander, & Chambers, 1970; Dai, 1937; Kavaler, Denson, & Krug, 1968; Kobrin & Finestone, 1965; Sheppard, Smith, & Gay, 1972; Terry & Pellens, 1928), to subcultural dynamics (Finestone, 1957; Preble & Casey, 1969; Sutter, 1966), to natural history (Ball, 1970; Robins & Murphy, 1967; Vaillant, 1966; Winick, 1964), to narcotic addict death rates (Cherubin, McCusker, Baden, Kavaler, & Amsel, 1972; Sapira, Ball, & Penn, 1970), and to etiology (Ball, Chambers, & Ball, 1970; Chein, Gerard, Lee, & Rosenfeld, 1964; Feldman, 1968).

Developing an Epidemiological Field Team

In our early search for operational field research and intervention frameworks, we reviewed recent progress in the field of public health psychiatry. We were unable, however, to find appropriate mental health program models or field concepts for reducing the incidence and prevalence of emotional disorder in defined communities. The history of contagious disease control, on the other hand, provided us with a rich source of public health approaches to disease control. In our review of various strategies used to control communicable diseases, i.e., disorders spread by interpersonal contact, we noted that epidemiological field teams play a key role in the identification of new outbreaks and the involvement of contagious and chronic cases in treatment.

Our first task was to develop an epidemiological field team that could carry out case-finding, research, and treatment-intervention functions. We found it convenient to develop this field team structure by recruiting methadone-supported ex-addict fieldworkers to serve in neighborhoods where they were already known and trusted by the majority of active addicts. Professional researchers, working in partnership with the fieldworkers, made additional observations and supervised data collection. The feasibility of this field team structure for carrying out research and intervention functions was tested in four neighborhoods on Chicago's predominantly black South Side (Hughes, Crawford, & Barker, 1971). By administering survey cards in the field, we were able to identify addicts who had not yet been identified by the Illinois Drug Abuse Program and to collect basic demographic and drug-use data on the majority of active addicts in these neighborhoods. Using intensive outreach techniques, the field team also was able to involve many of these cases in treatment.

Developing Operational Field Concepts for Projects to Monitor and Reduce Prevalence

To assess the impact of intervention programs, we wished to determine if the field team could monitor prevalence of heroin addiction in target communities. The major problem here is that because heroin use is illegal, addicts go to great lengths to avoid being identified by official agencies. Therefore, conventional case-finding and survey techniques are unlikely to identify the majority of heroin users in a given neighborhood.

The field team began to analyze the social and spatial dynamics of the so-called "heroin subculture" in search of operational field concepts that would locate the addict as a member of a definable social system. After careful observation of the association patterns of active addicts in various Chicago neighborhoods, it was found that the majority of addicts in the Chicago area are organized for purposes of heroin distribution into neighborhood "copping communities" (Hughes & Jaffe, 1971). In other words, they are required to make daily visits to stable drug distribution sites or "copping areas" to obtain heroin and relieve the discomfort of withdrawal distress. By stationing the field teams at these sites, we were able to monitor prevalence by maintaining a simple census of the active heroin addicts who regularly visited these locations.

After monitoring prevalence of active heroin addicts at one copping area over a 5-month period, we launched an outreach project that offered immediate admission to treatment to selected visitors to the site. We found that 58% (16 of the 28 offered treatment) could be involved even though the project required their presence at two home visits for approximately 8 hours of interviews and questionnaire administration. Their response to this outreach project was even more striking since the only treatment incentive for their cooperation was a 50% chance to bypass the treatment program's 4-month waiting list on completion of the work-up. By removing 16 members of this copping community, we were able to test our framework for measuring the impact of a treatment outreach program, i.e., a quantitative reduction in local copping area prevalence. This study also permitted us to observe the natural events affecting copping area size and viability. For example, we witnessed the dispersal of members of several copping communities when their regular meeting places were brought under intensive police or delinquent gang pressure. Once the pressure was removed, however, the copping areas again flourished and the original membership returned.

Because the choice of our initial study community was fortuitous, i.e., dependent on the unusual competence of our fieldworker from that area, we wished to replicate our intervention approach in other Chicago neighborhoods. Heroin-distribution sites were selected in a black West Side neighborhood, a Puerto Rican neighborhood on the city's North Side, and a center-city Mexican neighborhood (Hughes, Sanders, & Schaps, 1972). Following selection of these neighborhoods, highly competent ex-addict staff were recruited to serve as fieldworkers. This project demonstrated our ability to monitor copping area prevalence and to replicate our intervention approach in neighborhoods of our choice. Findings suggested that approximately three-fourths of the chronic street addict population might be converted rapidly to methadone outpatients if offered immediate treatment by outreach teams. By observing these areas during the postintervention period, however, we found that copping area prevalence returned to the preintervention level after 6 months. These data suggested that intensive, short-term outreach projects might reduce the number of addicts at local heroin distribution sites, but the reduction is likely to be short lived in areas where addiction is endemic. A long-term reduction in prevalence would require that treatment services be convenient and attractive to the target population and that outreach activities be persistent.

A Field Methodology for Monitoring and Reducing Incidence

We next turned our attention to designing projects to measure the incidence of new cases of heroin addiction. Incidence, usually defined as date of first heroin use, is a measure of the rate of spread of the disorder to new populations. Whereas prevalence of active addicts can be observed at any time of the day and in many parts of the city, incidence occurs only once for each addict and is almost impossible to observe. Consequently, one must rely on retrospective accounts of this event.

One of our earliest projects in this area was a retrospective study designed to clarify several parameters of a massive heroin epidemic among Chicago's black youth following World War II (Hughes, Barker, Crawford, & Jaffe, 1972). Incidence data obtained from Illinois Drug Abuse Program admission questionnaires and field surveys showed that the epidemic reached a peak in 1949 and declined during the early 1950s. In an effort to explain the sudden decline in the number of new cases, we interviewed addicts and enforcement personnel involved in the epidemic and reviewed court and police records, newspaper accounts, and legislative hearings from that period. It was found that the decline of this epidemic was closely associated with decreased quality and increased cost of heroin available to Chicago addicts.

Perhaps the most important finding to emerge from this study was that the incidence of first heroin use had begun to decline at least a year before the community became aware of its addiction problem and took steps to control it. These data, and our observations of recent outbreaks in various Chicago neighborhoods, suggested that the community's failure to respond effectively during the early stages of heroin spread may be a characteristic feature of heroin epidemics and that this should be a prime consideration in designing addiction-control programs. Finally, this study provided empirical support for the notion that incidence of heroin addiction can follow the course of contagious diseases, fluctuating from periods of epidemic spread on the one hand to periods of relative quiescence on the other.

Another project was designed to study the process of heroin spread in Chicago during recent years (Hughes & Crawford, 1972). Some Chicago neighborhoods have produced 50 or more new addicts in the short span of several years—these are called "macroepidemics." In other neighborhoods the outbreaks appear to produce fewer than 50 new addicts, perhaps only 5 to 15—we refer to these as "microepidemics." In still other neighborhoods addiction apparently does not spread beyond one or two individuals—these are called "isolated cases."

On the basis of epidemiological field observations, patient interviews, and Illinois Drug Abuse Program admission data, 11 macroepidemics were identified in Chicago between 1967 and 1971 (Figure 1). Nine were in black neighborhoods; two were in mixed Puerto Rican-white neighborhoods. We also identified 28 microepidemics; 14 were in black neighborhoods, 12 in white neighborhoods and suburban areas, and 2 in Puerto Rican-white neighborhoods.

Between January and October 1971, 365 heroin addicts admitted to treatment reported first heroin use between 1967 and 1971. Based on their community areas of residence at the time of initial heroin use (Kitagawa & Taueber, 1967), we determined the proportions of subjects whose first use occurred in macroepidemic, microepidemic, and isolated-case neighborhoods. It was found that 204 (56%) appeared to be produced in macroepidemic neighborhoods and 137 (37%) in microepidemic neighborhoods; only 24 (7%) were isolated cases. The data suggested that the majority of addicts are produced by macroepidemics that occur in a relatively small number of neighborhoods. The largest outbreaks continue to occur in underprivileged neighborhoods that have experienced large population shifts, frequently an influx of welfare and "multiproblem" families. Furthermore, several of these communities have been extremely hostile to local police in recent years, making it difficult for narcotics agents to identify and penetrate new groups of heroin users.

Through interviews with recent heroin addicts and their nonaddicted friends, we have examined the dynamics of heroin spread, including the specific interpersonal routes of heroin transmission, the characteristics of

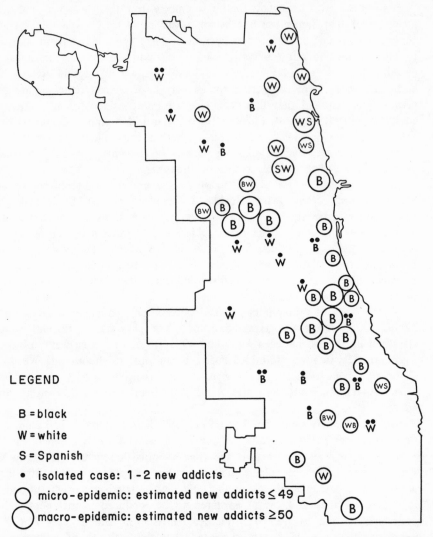

FIG. 1. Distribution of macroepidemics, microepidemics, and isolated cases in Chicago, 1967–71.

"disease" spreaders, and the circumstances surrounding initiation to heroin use. We modified the approach developed by deAlarcon (1969) to portray the spread of heroin use in a London suburb for our own study of multiple outbreaks of addiction in a large urban area. In examining the circumstances preceding localized heroin outbreaks in Chicago, we found that the polydrug using friendship group provides the fertile soil for the growth of heroin addiction. Young heroin users were not simply occasional marijuana smokers prior to their initiation to heroin. Rather, they tend to have been heavy polydrug users who spent much of their leisure time getting high. These young people were likely to have been introduced to heroin, not by a sinister dope dealer, but by their best friends who wished to share a new high. The most "contagious" individuals tended to be in the early stages of heroin experimentation or addiction.

These findings suggested that an effective control strategy must include early detection of these localized epidemics and rapid involvement of all new heroin users in treatment. This intervention strategy was successfully tested in a white middle-class neighborhood that had experienced a small outbreak of heroin addiction (Hughes & Crawford, 1972). The initial case contact was used to identify and lead us to other young people involved, a standard case-finding principle for some contagious diseases. After several weeks of intensive outreach efforts, we were able to involve 11 of the 14 active heroin addicts in a nearby treatment facility. Of the three who did not respond, two were shortly arrested and the other left the neighborhood. Of the seven heroin experimenters identified for outreach, five were involved in treatment and two were reported to have discontinued their heroin use. We are continuing to monitor the area to determine whether our intervention efforts will be followed by a decline in the number of new cases in the coming months. Some of the occasional experimenters who were not included in the project may eventually become addicted so that it will be necessary to continue outreach efforts to keep the neighborhood free of heroin addiction.

We have also tested our case-finding and intervention approach in an underprivileged black neighborhood on Chicago's far South Side which has recently experienced a much larger outbreak of heroin addiction (Figure 2). The model developed to control heroin addiction in that community can be described in terms of the following four phases (Hughes, Senay, & Parker, 1972):

Phase 1: Epidemiological field investigation. Upon contact with the first case in the outbreak, an epidemiological field team was assigned to the neighborhood to carry out intensive case-finding efforts and assess the size and other parameters of the epidemic. By maintaining a weekly census of all active heroin users identified, we were able to monitor incidence and prevalence of addiction in the community.

Phase 2: Pilot outreach and treatment. The field team succeeded in involving in treatment a sample of those involved, both to establish itself in a helping role and to explore the most appropriate modalities and location for treatment services. For example, we found that many of those admitted to treatment during this phase quickly dropped out because of the difficulties and expense of obtaining transportation to existing facilities. It became apparent that to achieve maximal impact we would be required to develop treatment services in a location readily accessible to the target population.

Phase 3: Intensive outreach and treatment. Attractive and convenient treatment services were provided to meet the needs of the local addict

96

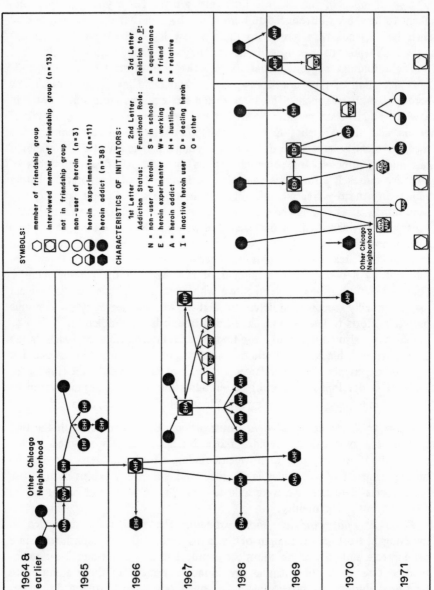

FIG. 2. Heroin spread in a macroepidemic neighborhood.

population, and efforts were made to involve those who did not actively seek treatment. Special outreach efforts were directed at high-status young heroin users because they seemed the most likely to spread the disorder to others.

Phase 4: Continued outreach and prevention. Community leaders met with clinical and epidemiological staff to develop approaches to involve those addicts who continued to resist outreach efforts. There is a rapid outreach response when new cases develop and when treated cases relapse. To the extent possible, the local community is involved in ongoing prevention programs.

In this project we chose a rather isolated community and recruited clinical and field staff from community residents, thereby maximizing our opportunity to identify and treat the total addict population of the neighborhood. While we are continuing to monitor the community to observe the long-term effects of intervention, the project appears to have been highly successful in reducing the prevalence of addiction, which in turn might be expected to reduce the incidence of future cases. Thus, as the pool of active heroin addicts and, presumably, the viability and stability of the local drug distribution system have been reduced, vulnerable individuals will be less likely to be exposed to active users and to the drug itself. Furthermore, the project has shifted the community's sizable population of young heroin addicts into treatment so that the peer group that previously promoted heroin spread now discourages it.

This study has, of course, left a number of questions unanswered. For example, would the model have been effective without the support of a relatively strong community organization? Would the model be equally effective in suburban and inner-city areas? Was the model successful because of the fortuitous timing of our intervention efforts—in other words, had the epidemic already run its course? How does an epidemiological field team determine the stage of an epidemic and measure the natural fluctuations in incidence trends? At what stage is intervention most effective?

Social Dynamics of Heroin Using Subcultures

We have carried out several projects directed at a more basic understanding of the structure and dynamics of heroin using subcultures. Our initial inquiry into this area (Hughes, Crawford, Barker, Schumann, & Jaffe, 1971) employed the analytic framework developed by Preble and Casey (1969) to describe the role structure of heroin-distribution systems from international to neighborhood levels. This permitted us to describe the role structure elaborated by the membership of one black South Side copping community that was observed for 1 year. Because of the heavy police pressure directed at heroin-distribution sites in Chicago, the roles elaborated by these drug-distribution networks are substantially more complex than the usual dichotomy of "user" and "dealer." In the black copping community chosen for intensive study, we identified 125 heroin addicts and two nonusers who regularly visited the area to buy or sell drugs during the year of observation. Six percent of the membership occupied the role of "big dealer" or local wholesaler; 6% were "street dealers" who sold drugs directly to consumers; 15% were "part-time dealers" who usually sold only enough heroin to support their own habits; 3% were "bag followers" who attached themselves to dealers to support their drug habits; 3% were "touts" who carried out liaison functions to protect dealers from direct exposure to consumers and risk of arrest. Thus, a third of the membership of this copping community maintained their heroin habits by performing dealership functions. It was interesting to note that only two of those who occupied dealer roles were nonaddicts, motivated purely by profit. Of the remaining two-thirds, 38% were "hustlers" who supported their habits through some kind of illegal activity; and 28% were "workers" who held at least part-time legitimate jobs.

The treatment outreach project in this copping area permitted us to assess the relative treatability of the occupants of these subcultural roles (Hughes, Crawford, Barker, Schumann, & Jaffe, 1971). For example, we found that addicts occupying dealership roles were difficult to involve in treatment and, if involved, were unlikely to remain over time. Working addicts, on the other hand, were found to be the most favorable rehabilitation prospects; the majority remained in treatment after 6 months. Finally, hustling addicts held an intermediate position in terms of their likelihood of entering treatment and remaining involved over time.

These findings raise the question of how treatment approaches might be modified so as to attract and hold different categories of addicts. Our impression that higher-level dealership roles were associated with lower motivation for treatment and higher dropout rates suggests that voluntary community programs might consider special approaches for involving and holding these groups. For example, one might obtain better results with high-level dealers through immediate hospitalization, thereby removing them from the temptation to continue dealing purely for profit. Alternatively, the demand for immediate behavioral change among drug dealers might be postponed until they have worked through their initial difficulties in accepting the lower prestige of the patient role.

Outreach projects subsequently carried out in three other copping areas produced additional data on the treatability characteristics of various role occupants (Hughes, Sanders, & Schaps, 1972). Although these data are still being analyzed, our initial impression is that the findings generally support the trends observed in the pilot study.

In another study (Hughes, Parker, & Senay, 1974), we examined more closely the question of a community's awareness of and interactions with its heroin addict subculture. For this inquiry we selected a copping area that had been serving Puerto Rican and white addicts during the previous 4 years. We interviewed samples of local residents, businessmen, community organization representatives, and district police. The data indicated that the majority of residents and community agency representatives were not aware of the neighborhood's heroin copping area, even though most lived or worked less than a block away. Those persons in the resident, business, and community agency samples who were aware of the local "drug scene" generally revealed a desire to help narcotic addicts but felt that they lacked channels for expressing their concern. Some also voiced the opinion that local police were not really doing their job. Interviews with narcotics officers, however, suggested that their most effective enforcement activity was carried on in secret and was not visible to the public. In sum, the findings indicated that respondents were not apathetic to the heroin addict subculture nor were they secretly profiting from it. Most were simply not aware of its existence and had very limited interactions with it. Although respondents agreed that treatment was desirable for addicts, they were generally burdened with too many other responsibilities to commit themselves to a course of concerted action.

DISCUSSION

In the history of the control of any disorder, the development of effective low-cost treatment and prevention techniques marks the introduction of a new era. This is the era of practical application of epidemiological knowledge and techniques to the design of program elements which can eventually be tested in controlled field trials. Although current treatment techniques for heroin addiction have serious limitations, they are sufficiently effective and attractive to the target population to permit exploration of tentative program structures for addiction control. This report has reviewed efforts in this area and has described a voluntary medically oriented program structure for neighborhood level addiction control. This framework evolved from careful epidemiological study of the dynamics of heroin spread among new users and the characteristics of heroin subcultures in communities with high prevalence of adult chronic addicts. A series of exploratory projects in a number of Chicago neighborhoods has permitted refinements of this research-intervention model so that it can be tested in more systematic fashion. The ultimate test of the efficacy of the model requires multiple field trials in experimental and control communities; we currently are designing such studies.

In our epidemiological research-intervention framework the community is viewed as a natural "laboratory." We have attempted to develop clear operational definitions and to assure that the key elements in this system are relatively simple and reproduceable. These elements are consistent with established public health practices that have been used to control certain infectious diseases. This evolving model has been tested in six Chicago neighborhoods that differed in ethnic makeup and chronicity of addiction.

Even if this research-intervention model is found to be successful in further field trials, the specific structure of the model is not intended to be definitive. We see a need for continued experimentation with case-finding, monitoring, and outreach strategies; with the type of personnel selected as fieldworkers; and with different legal frameworks and treatment modalities. Furthermore, the current model is based on intervening in heroin spread at a late stage, for we are able to identify outbreaks only after they occur.

There are signs that epidemiologically oriented program evaluations are being conducted elsewhere. For example, DuPont and Katon (1971) point to declining crime rates in Washington, D.C., associated with the expansion of methadone treatment services. Judd, Deitch, and de Giacomo (1972) in San Diego selected a heroin copping area for a treatment program site and reported a subsequent decline in the availability of heroin in the area. With the rapid expansion of addiction treatment systems in a number of communities, researchers are increasingly presented with opportunities for experimentation in program design.

PROBLEMS ACCOMPANYING EPIDEMIOLOGICAL INTERVENTION EXPERIMENTS

This report has emphasized positive findings and has not dwelt on the numerous methodological and human problems involved in carrying out intervention experiments. At this point, then, it might be useful to review some of the major problems which center on relations with (a) ex-addict field staff, (b) clinical staff, (c) police, and (d) the community, and on (e) conducting research in the addict's natural setting.

Ex-addict field staff. The ex-addict fieldworker plays a key role in our system by facilitating access to our target population. His knowledge of street codes and subcultural dynamics provides an important source of learning for the researcher and protects against program designs that might be offensive to untreated addicts. Early in our work we erred in choosing several methadone-supported patients and abstinent ex-addict staff who had not previously been drug dealers. We found that they did not understand the intimate workings of the local heroin-using subculture as did their ex-dealer coworkers. Since then we have been careful to select fieldworkers who were high-status ex-drug dealers, known and respected by addicts in the target area. We prefer that fieldworkers be methadone supported; the abstinent ex-addict tends to minimize the time he spends at local distribution sites because of his anxiety about relapse.

A significant source of motivation for the fieldworker is his genuine wish to help his friends obtain treatment; therefore, he is frustrated by research design requirements that delay outreach activities or that choose only selected samples for outreach. Thus, it is essential that he be convinced at an early stage of the importance of the research beyond the problem of heroin addiction in his own community. To deal with these problems we have placed fieldworkers under the joint supervision of an experienced ex-addict and a professional researcher. The ex-addict supervisor is a highly respected individual with a responsible administrative position in the treatment system. He is better able to socialize the fieldworker into his research role and to protect the research staff from "manipulation" by fieldworkers. The cosupervisor, a professional researcher, is thereby able to focus primarily on the data collection and research dimensions of fieldwork activities. Periodic visits to the field site for observations and interviews by both supervisors and by other research staff permit us to check the accuracy of fieldworkers' reports.

Clinical staff. Clinicians are sometimes disturbed by our special efforts to involve poorly motivated street addicts when treatment services for highly motivated patients remain inadequate. Following admission, outreach subjects may continue to be poorly motivated, but we discourage clinicians from discharging them lest they return to active addict status in target communities. The notion of making intensive efforts to recruit and hold poorly motivated patients is a public health concept that runs counter to those clinical traditions that view treatment as a highly prized commodity that should be withdrawn for nonconforming behavior. Certainly, we are tampering with the basic levers of social control in clinical programs by attempting to modify certain key rules of the treatment game, and we should expect resistance.

Another serious clinical issue that must be considered is the high cost of treatment services. Admission of a large number of heroin addicts from a target community may require establishment of a new clinic or expansion of existing services. This accounts for the frequently hidden costs of this type of research, particularly when we recognize that most patients will require rehabilitation for a considerable period. For these reasons it is necessary to have the active support of high-level administrators and experienced clinicians who can spot and correct problems and maintain liaisons with clinical facilities during intensive outreach phases. The clinician understands the workings and limitations of the treatment system and determines its overall effectiveness. Furthermore, he has the skills and "legitimacy" necessary to manipulate this system in any intervention program.

Police. A common fear is that a field researcher found in the presence of illegal drugs or in the company of known addicts or criminals may be arrested. A parallel fear is that police will go to great lengths to obtain confidential research data. Although these may be realistic concerns for researchers in some communities, we have encountered no such problems.

To guard against difficulties with local police, each fieldworker carries a letter explaining that his work may require contact with drug users, delinquents, alcoholics, and other deviant populations and listing the telephone numbers of supervisory research staff. We have also found it helpful to visit local police precincts to explain the aims of our research. Although our field staff have frequently been stopped and on occasion "picked up," these incidents have been quickly resolved by a confirming telephone call. An additional reason for our lack of problems with local police stems from our research base in a large and respected university medical center and in the official state agency for drug treatment programs. In general, local police avoid interfering with the legitimate activities of other governmental agencies. The epidemiological researcher may find this an added reason for association with a large, centralized treatment agency in his particular community.

Community. Initially we approached community leaders in target neighborhoods and generally found them to be responsive to treatment approaches for local addicts; however, they rarely had concrete information about the local addict street scene. Those who were knowledgeable tended to maintain a healthy distance from addicts for reasons of personal safety. We found that our epidemiological fieldworkers have better access to a community's addict population than do local leaders in the same neighborhood. When intervention requires that treatment facilities be established in the target neighborhood, however, the active support of community leaders is essential to mediate with residents who may fear the establishment of a drug treatment facility in the immediate vicinity.

Research in the addict's natural setting. The most serious problems confronting the researcher who conducts field studies in the addict's natural setting center on the researcher's personal safety and the instability of the local drug-distribution system. Street copping areas are frequently located in the most dangerous sections of any city. The close guidance of the fieldworker and the researcher's identification with a drug treatment program help assure his personal security among the addict population. Even so there are other groups over which the fieldworker has no control, such as alcoholics and delinquent gangs; and the researcher must take his cues from the fieldworker.

The unstable features inherent in research in the natural setting can cause difficulties in data collection and intervention. For example, copping area prevalence trends can be dramatically affected by factors other than outreach efforts. Intensive and prolonged pressure from police or delinquent gangs can lead to the closing down of a heroin distribution site and the dispersal of its membership. This is particularly discouraging if considerable time and effort have been spent preparatory to launching an intervention project. The occurrence of such confounding variables, however, can sometimes be converted into a "natural experiment," providing that the target community was appropriately monitored before and during these nonmedical interventions.[3]

---

[3]Note: Figure 1 is reprinted with permission from "A Contagious Disease Model for Researching and Intervening in Heroin Epidemics," *Archives of General Psychiatry* 27, pp. 149–155, August 1972, Copyright 1972, American Medical Association.

REFERENCES

Ball, J. C. Two patterns of opiate addiction. In J. C. Ball & C. D. Chambers (Eds.), *The epidemiology of opiate addiction in the United States*. Springfield, Ill.: Charles C Thomas, 1970.

Ball, J. C., Chambers, C. D., & Ball, M. J. The association of marihuana smoking with opiate addiction. In J. C. Ball & C. D. Chambers (Eds.), *The epidemiology of opiate addiction in the United States*. Springfield, Ill.: Charles C Thomas, 1970.

Ball, J. C., Englander, D. M., & Chambers, C. D. The incidence and prevalence of opiate addiction in the United States. In J. C. Ball & C. D. Chambers (Eds.), *The epidemiology of opiate addiction in the United States*. Springfield, Ill.: Charles C Thomas, 1970.

Chein, I., Gerard, D. L., Lee, R. S., & Rosenfeld, E. *The road to H.* New York: Basic Books, 1964.

Cherubin, C., McCusker, J., Baden, M., Kavaler, F., & Amsel, Z. The epidemiology of death in narcotic addicts. *American Journal of Epidemiology*, 1972, 96, 11–22.

Dai, B. *Opium addiction in Chicago.* Shanghai, China: Commercial Press, Ltd., 1937.

deAlarcon, R. The spread of heroin abuse in a community. *Bulletin on Narcotics*, 1969, 21, 17–22.

DuPont, R. L., & Katon, R. N. Development of a heroin addiction treatment program: Effect on urban crime. *Journal of the American Medical Association*, 1971, 216, 1320–1324.

Feldman, H. W. Ideological supports to becoming and remaining a heroin addict. *Journal of Health and Social Behavior*, 1968, 9, 131–139.

Finestone, H. Cats, kicks, and color. *Social Problems*, 1957, 5(1), 3–13.

Hughes, P. H., Barker, N. W., Crawford, G. A., & Jaffe, J. H. The natural history of a heroin epidemic. *American Journal of Public Health*, 1972, 62(7), 995–1001.

Hughes, P. H., & Crawford, G. A. A contagious disease model for researching and intervening in heroin epidemics. *Archives of General Psychiatry*, 1972, 27(2), 149–155.

Hughes, P. H., Crawford, G. A., & Barker, N. W. Developing an epidemiologic field team for drug dependence. *Archives of General Psychiatry*, 1971, 24, 389–393.

Hughes, P. H., Crawford, G. A., Barker, N. W., Schumann, S., & Jaffe, J. H. The social structure of a heroin copping community. *American Journal of Psychiatry*, 1971, 128(5), 551–558.

Hughes, P. H., & Jaffe, J. H. The heroin copping area: A location for epidemiologic study and intervention activity. *Archives of General Psychiatry*, 1971, 24, 394–400.

Hughes, P. H., Parker, R., & Senay, E. C. Heroin addiction and the neighborhood social system. *American Journal of Orthopsychiatry*, 1974, 44(1), 129–141.

Hughes, P. H., Sanders, C. R., & Schaps, E. Medical intervention in three heroin copping areas. *Proceedings of the Fourth National Conference on Methadone Treatment.* New York: National Association for the Prevention of Addiction to Narcotics, 1972.

Hughes, P. H., Senay, E. C., Parker, R. The medical management of a heroin epidemic. *Archives of General Psychiatry*, 1972, 27(5), 585–591.

Judd, L., Deitch, D. A., deGiacomo, E. E. The elimination of a heroin "copping" zone: A preliminary report of a treatment strategy. *Proceedings of the Fourth National Conference on Methadone Treatment.* New York: National Association for the Prevention of Addiction to Narcotics, 1972.

Kavaler, F., Denson, P. M., & Krug, D. C. The narcotics register project: Early development. *British Journal of the Addictions*, 1968, 63, 75–81.

Kitagawa, E. M., & Taueber, K. E. (Eds.) *Local Community Fact Book Chicago Metropolitan Area 1960.* Prepared by the Chicago Community Inventory, University of Chicago, 1967.

Kobrin, S., & Finestone, H. Drug addiction among young persons in Chicago. In J. F. Short (Ed.), *Gang delinquency and delinquent subcultures.* New York: Harper & Row, 1965.

MacMahon, B., & Pugh, T. F. *Epidemiology principles and methods.* Boston: Little, Brown, 1970.

Morris, J. N. *Uses of epidemiology.* London: E. S. Livingstone, 1957.

Preble, E., & Casey, J. J. Taking care of business—The heroin user's life on the street. *International Journal of the Addictions,* 1969, 4, 1–24.

Robins, L. N., & Murphy, G. E. Drug use in a normal population of young Negro men. *American Journal of Public Health,* 1967, 57, 1580–1596.

Sapira, J. D., Ball, J. C., & Penn, H. Causes of death among institutionalized narcotic addicts. In J. C. Ball & C. D. Chambers (Eds.), *The epidemiology of opiate addiction in the United States.* Springfield, Ill.: Charles C Thomas, 1970.

Sheppard, C. W., Smith, D. E., & Gay, G. R. The changing face of heroin addiction in the Haight-Ashbury. *International Journal of the Addictions,* 1972, 7(1), 109–122.

Sutter, A. G. The world of the righteous dope fiend. *Issues in Criminology,* 1966, 2(2), 177–222.

Terry, C. E., & Pellens, M. *The opium problem.* New York: Committee on Drug Addictions and the Bureau of Social Hygiene, 1928.

Vaillant, G. E. A twelve-year follow-up of New York narcotic addicts: II. The natural history of a chronic disease. *New England Journal of Medicine,* 1966, 275, 1282–1288.

Winick, C. The life cycle of the narcotic addict and of addiction. *Bulletin on Narcotics,* 1964, 16, 1–11.

World Health Organization Technical Report Series: *Expert Committee on Drug Dependence, Nineteenth Report.* Geneva: World Health Organization, in press.

7
SOME ASPECTS OF CAREERS OF CHRONIC HEROIN USERS

Charles Winick
City College and Graduate Center
City University of New York

Benjamin Disraeli, whose name has recently been evoked paradigmatically by the highest federal officials, is sometimes cited by historians for his efforts to bring reality into policy decisions. On one occasion, when joining with the Cabinet to discuss education, he had an urchin brought off the street and into the meeting to bring home to the assembled ministers a notion of what the subject of the debate was really like.

Let us assume that we were to get a chronic heroin user to talk about the subject of careers of heroin users. What kind of user should make the presentation? A masochist, counterphobic personality, or an oral passive type? Someone with an emotional conflict? A Chicago cool cat, an Oakland mellow dude? A person with endocrine dysfunction? Someone who is medicating himself? A proponent of the hang-loose ethic? A head or a freak? A double retreatist or someone else suffering from anomie? One who lacks impulse control? An extremely intelligent person, making an astute adaptation to the realities of ghetto life? A victim of the knowledge of how to alleviate withdrawal distress? Or a risk discounter?

Obviously, the manner in which we defined a heroin user and, therefore, the kind of person we asked to give the talk, would substantially affect what we would hear about careers. Each of the putative speakers refers to one of the many types of heroin users described in the abundant literature. Each would see the path of chronic heroin use differently and likely would expect different benchmarks along the way. Although many discussions setting forth these various types describe them as "addicts," the term has many complex connotations. Therefore, this report uses the term "chronic heroin users."

The term "career" refers to a relatively orderly sequence of events in a person's life, such that he or she starts at a specific point and ends at a predictable place. The term is often found in descriptions of work, especially the professions; but it is also used to identify employment with a recognizable pattern, where we know enough about the events and phenomena, or career contingencies, that produce the patterns and determine their probability (Gross, 1964).

One of the immediately obvious problems in applying the concept of career to the chronic heroin user is that he or she may enter the cycle at different places, is not usually seen over time, and it is not at all clear that ending at a predictable outcome is probable. Among the other problems in studying heroin careers is the lack of large-scale data on nonclinical and noninstitutionalized populations; the uncertain reliability of information obtained from self-reporting of users; a lack of cheap, simple, and reliable biochemical tests for assessing the quality of drugs used; ambiguities in the definition of chronic use; and the increasing importance of mixed dependencies (Kaprio & May, 1972). These difficulties exist although prevalence of heroin use is relatively rare, even in the population at risk, when compared with other major problems in public health.

Along what dimensions or patterns can a career trajectory be followed? One approach is to divide user characteristics into status and "dynamic" approaches (O'Donnell, 1969). Ten status attributes of opiate users (sex, color, region, residence, hospital status, marital status, religion, education, number of admissions, and minority group status) and seven "dynamic" attributes (age at arrest, marijuana history, occupation, drug source, age at admission for treatment, arrest record, and first arrest) have been identified, with the latter group most likely to be productive in defining typologies.

Almost a half century ago, Terry and Pellens (1928) classified types of users by various status attributes: age, constitutional makeup, intellectual status, mental balance, moral character, nervous balance, and sex and social status. They noted, however, that ". . . this condition is not restricted to any . . . age . . . . There is no type which may be called the habitual user of opium . . . . All types are actually or potentially users [p. 516]."

In terms of heroin use in the United States today, generalizations are most productively ideographic, relevant to a specific cultural and geographic setting. When Terry and Pellens were reporting, despite their disclaimer, generalizations about opiate users more reasonably could be expected to be nomothetic or applicable to the whole country. In the 1920s the population of opiate users was relatively homogeneous, but it probably is more heterogeneous today.

Not too long ago, it was possible to identify two narcotics patterns: (a) the young heroin users, mainly in metropolitan centers, engaging in illegal activities and (b) the middle-aged Southern white, on morphine or paregoric, getting the drug by legal or quasi-legal means (Ball, 1965). The second group of users is doubtless growing smaller, and the number of such persons newly entering the heroin population is comparatively low. It is unlikely that there are two basic patterns today, or if there were, that they would remain dominant in the next few years.

Even on the basis of reports from persons undergoing treatment, who are not necessarily representative of the total population, there seem to be significant differences among groups of heroin users. The most obvious range is geographic and can be easily suggested by some findings from a large-scale study of 6,678 narcotics users receiving drug-free treatment in seven cities (U.S. Office of Economic Opportunity, 1971). Over half the clients represented voluntary admissions, so that extrapolation to the total use population may be hazardous. The study, however, includes locations in three states (New York, Illinois, and California) that probably include over three-fourths of the country's users.

The patients receiving help reflect an enormous range in key variables. Thus, the mean age of patients in New York City is 23.2 years, but it is 32.3 years in Chicago. San Antonio clients had been arrested an average of 12.9 times, compared with 5.4 in New Jersey. Average earnings during the previous 4 weeks varied from $42 in New York to $112 in Washington, D.C. Although 11.3% in Washington were Caucasian, they accounted for 94.1% in Los Angeles. Some 59.2% in Chicago but only 21.7% in New Jersey were engaging in illegal activities. The average longest time off drugs ranged from 35 months in Los Angeles to 7 months in Tacoma.

Estimated cost of the heroin habit per day averaged $13.08 in New York City but $69.10 in Washington, D.C. Some variables manifested a narrower range, e.g., an average of 66.3% of all patients "shot" intravenously, with a range from 59.1% (New York City) to 80.7% (Chicago). On a substantial number of variables studied, however, the population in treatment in each of three areas differed from that in the other areas. Even within one city, the persons using heroin may differ substantially from those in another area only a short distance away.

In terms of many dimensions relevant to the study of careers of heroin users, it is probably fair to say that they frequently reflect local conditions and life chances. As a result, it is often difficult to formulate generalizations that help us to understand more than one geographic area.

For example, we might wish to know, in terms of intervening variables, about important life intersections such as induction to heroin use, entrance into criminal behavior, first withdrawal, and first full-time job. Induction would reflect access to heroin and to competing satisfactions and the opportunity structure, all of which will differ from one area to the next. Criminal behavior involves the nature of any criminal subculture and is certainly a partial function of the degree of police activity. Initial withdrawal could reflect access to treatment and declining ease of access to drugs, as well as more profound factors. A user's first full-time job must be related to jobs that are available. All four benchmarks therefore must be interpreted in terms of larger social circumstances rather than as reflections of psychodynamics or the inevitable course of chronic heroin use.

Although culture-free theories of the genesis and cycle of chronic heroin use have the appeal of tidiness, the wide range of groups that appear to be using the drug suggests that relatively cautious explanations are probably most appropriate at the current state of knowledge. An explanation of the course of heroin use valid in the 1950s or even late 1960s simply may not be relevant today, over and above regional and population differences. It may be useful to consider what can be said about chronic heroin use in terms of the cycle, onset, age of onset, and outcomes developing identity as a user, work, criminal activity, arrest, abstention, patienthood, older users, deaths, and careers.

THE CYCLE

Central to the concept of careers is some consideration of the sequence of events—in what often involves spurts, reverses, periods of quiescence, and lateral movement—from starting drug use to stopping to starting again and stopping, a sequence that may occur many times. Sometimes the sequence is relatively fast, and at other times it may be relatively slow or involve no movement.

Most efforts to plot the cycle include some discussion of the user's ability to relate to conventional social roles independent of the world of drugs. Without such a capacity, the user will be less able to deal with abstinence. The first exploration of the interaction between the roles of the user and abstainer suggested how shared interpersonal and institutional experiences provide users with perspectives about themselves and others (Ray, 1961). After withdrawal, the user tries to live out a new identity as an abstainer, for which he seeks ratification from others. When socially disjunctive experiences lead to questions about the merit of an abstainer identity, the former user may realign his values with the user world. But then, recall of the period of abstinence may lead to efforts to reestablish it. The user is seen to be relating intermittently to the drug subculture and the process of straight socialization.

A later explication of the life cycle suggested four major stages in the user's movement from an identity as user to one as abstainer (Alksne, Lieberman, & Brill, 1967):

1. Experimentation, adaptation to regular use, chronic use; tolerance for potential chronic use.
2. Individual and sociocultural interaction system of chronic use.
3. Moving into abstinence, including recidivism, drug substitution, drug free with supports; tolerance for potential abstinence.
4. Nondrug use with no need of supports; tolerance of abstinence.

This sequence assumes that the heroin user is probably in some correctional or treatment situation, which is central to the third stage.

An early formulation of the drug-use cycle presented a schematic analysis of the making and unmaking of a chronic heroin user in relation to the peer group and the group to him (Scher, 1961):

1. Introduction—acceptance of available narcotic; usually two or more persons participate.
2. Continuity—may be periodic, usually two or more persons, in a group activity.
3. Narrowing—reduction in number of friends and contacts, often a progressively isolated activity.
4. Isolation—a period of anomie, maximum narrowing.
5. Realignment—on reentry into group experience, with reorganization of goals and relationships.

Another view of the process by which a person's heroin use leads to modification of his self-concept draws on the concept of crystallization. It suggests that, in time, a drug user accumulates an identity and associated habits and values that label his overall life at any moment (Fiddle, Mayfield, & Green, 1971). Countercrystallization is a turning away from this identity; and decrystallization is the breakdown, by the treatment process, of the person's subjective and objective status as a user.

Four stages in adolescents' degrees of involvement with drugs were identified in one study: experimentation, occasional use, regular or habitual use, and efforts to break the habit (Chein, Gerard, Lee, & Rosenfeld, 1964). A user might progress through all four stages or stop at any one.

Another formulation of the sequence of steps involved in assumption of an identity as a heroin user also involves four steps, in terms of social functioning: experimenting, social recreational using, involved using, and dysfunctional abusing (Chambers, 1972). This conceptualization classifies the first two categories of "users" as engaging in what is now almost a normal maturational activity. Society would probably regard the "seekers" in the third and fourth categories as persons participating in an ultimately destructive activity.

ONSET

One of the nodal elements in the concept of a career in heroin use is how it begins. Under what circumstances is a person likely to start using the drug? There would appear to be at least one condition for onset: access to the drug.

Other circumstances and particulars would be described by adherents of every viewpoint and theory in different ways, reflecting models from such approaches as psychiatry, psychoanalysis, and collective behavior. Even if an explanation of onset seems atheoretical, e.g., saying that curiosity is the major determinant, it is likely to involve such underlying questions as why a person was curious about the drug at the time and felt motivated enough to translate the curiosity into action, rather than pursue competing satisfactions.

A multifactorial model of onset, considering psychological, demographic, cultural, economic, and sociological factors, is probably most in accord with current knowledge. Such a model is only emerging on the basis of the formulations of proponents of one or another extreme position, each of which may ultimately contribute to a theory not yet in existence.

There is general agreement on relatively few aspects of onset. One of the few features of onset about which there was consensus, up to fairly recently, was the probability that the neophyte heroin user had previously experimented with marijuana.

This relationship between marijuana and subsequent heroin use has been clarified, at least historically, by a study of a large group of persons (2,213) admitted to federal hospitals in 1965 (Ball, Chambers, & Ball, 1968). Several relationships between marijuana use and subsequent opiate use were found. In 16 states, Puerto Rico, and the District of Columbia, over half the subjects had used first marijuana and then opiates. Most opiate users in 12 other states, largely in the South, had not used marijuana. In 22 states, there was little opiate use, with or without marijuana use. In the 16 high-association states, an illicit drug culture exists. Interviews with a sample of the patients determined that the primary sequence of events was marijuana smoking (at 17), arrest (at 19), and heroin onset (at 20).

The heroin user in the United States typically "chippies" for some time before becoming a regular user. A dramatically different pattern of onset has emerged among servicemen in Vietnam. When a group of soldiers from Thailand visited South Vietnam in 1968 to help American forces, they introduced the first substantial amounts of heroin to the latter (Bentel & Smith, 1972). The drugs seemingly helped many Americans to deal with what they perceived as an unendurable reality in Southeast Asia. By 1970, 95%–97% pure heroin was available cheaply, either as a powder or a "soap ball." The novice military user could develop a habit relatively quickly, because of the strength of the drug. Others smoked an "opium joint." Heroin became a social drug in Vietnam, much like marijuana in the United States. The returning serviceman who had become a heroin user had to develop a whole new series of relationships to sustain his habit.

On the basis of a study of the persons seeking help at the Haight-Ashbury Free Clinic, a typology was suggested based on the first year of onset of heroin use (Gay, Newmeyer, & Winkler, 1972):

1. The New Junkie, whose first use postdates January 1967, during the end of the hippie movement and at a time of disillusionment in the counter culture.

2. The Transition Junkie, whose first use occurred from 1964 through 1966, the psychedelic era.

3. The Old Style Junkie, whose first use was prior to 1964, and who is likely to be an economically deprived person.

The Transition Junkie typically participated in a fairly lengthy experimentation with many drugs before heroin. He also often used heroin as a downer after a substantial speed run or an LSD "bummer." The New Junkie found heroin more directly, knowing the unpleasant aspects of speed and LSD. The Old Style Junkie typically was ghetto bred.

The sample studied at the Haight-Ashbury Clinic is about 30% minority group, or somewhat less than half the minority representation in the Bay Area's known opiate-user population of about 15,000. Of the whites in the group, there appears to be a substantial overrepresentation of youths from working-class Catholic backgrounds. It is therefore difficult to say how representative Clinic patients are of area heroin users and how typical the typology is of other areas.

It is possible to concentrate on the substances involved in onset and not pay enough attention to the attractions of the "hustle" or involvement with the subculture of heroin. One typology of onset that tried to integrate personal and social factors, even though developed on juvenile users in New York City in the 1950s, may still be valid (Chein, 1965):

1. Strongly influenced by craving but with relatively little personal involvement.

2. Strongly influenced by personal involvement but with relatively little craving.

3. Strongly influenced by both craving and personal involvement.

4. Neither strong craving nor personal involvement, but with histories of personal dependency.

There is a substantial literature on onset of heroin use, but relatively few reports seek to integrate psychological and sociological considerations, as was done in the typology above. Another approach focused on the circumstances of first use of heroin, using the critical incident technique (Brown, Gauvey, Meyers, & Stark, 1971). Curiosity and influence of friends were the most important factors cited by patients in treatment in Washington, D.C. Other considerations included influence of relatives, relief of personal disturbance, and seeking a high.

Except for Vietnam veterans, it seems plausible to suggest that onset of heroin use is mediated by significant others and that it usually involves some previous experience with other psychoactive substances. Other dimensions of onset may be difficult to document, except as they apply to special populations.

OUTCOMES AND AGE OF ONSET

Several kinds of data suggest a relationship between age at onset of heroin use and various possible outcomes. From criminology, there is evidence that the earlier a person enters into criminal behavior patterns, the longer is such behavior likely to continue (Glaser, 1964).

Various studies suggest that the lower the age of onset of heroin use, the longer it is likely to continue (Winick, 1964). The person involved in the drug scene at a relatively early age presumably has had fewer success experiences in conventional socialization and thus little opportunity to try nondrug roles.

Patients in a Brooklyn methadone maintenance program who became heroin users at a relatively early age were less likely to have worked at one job for more than 3 years and somewhat less likely to have married than were patients who began using later (Sardell, 1972). An analysis of the 30 best outcomes in a followup study of former Lexington patients concluded that late onset was correlated with an intact home until age 6, a prior ability to hold a job, and eventual abstinence (Vaillant, 1966).

A followup study of 108 Puerto Rican males previously treated at the Lexington hospital concluded that the one-fifth who had been successfully rehabilitated had begun drug use at a later age than had patients who had not done as well (Zahn & Ball, 1972).

Heroin use also began at a later age in a group of 53 male Puerto Rican patients at Lexington, in the subgroup that had been steadily employed, in contrast to the subgroup following sporadically criminal careers and those following permanent criminal careers (Defleur, Ball, & Snarr, 1969).

A comparison in New York City of heroin using and nonusing siblings in a slum area concluded that the former were more involved in early marijuana use and delinquency, as a result of which they had less employment and schooling and more arrests and incarceration (Glaser, Lander, & Abbott, 1971).

Thus, the available evidence strongly suggests that age at onset is inversely related to successful social functioning and to subsequent abstinence. In terms of considerations of public policy, this relationship is crucial because of the fairly consistent evidence that the age of onset has been declining fairly steadily and is positively correlated with mixed dependencies and earlier criminal involvement in a broader range of offenses.

DEVELOPING IDENTITY AS A USER

If we define a chronic heroin user as someone who averages one dose of heroin or more on a daily basis for a month or more, it would be surprising if he or she were not significantly affected by such a recurrent and cathected activity. The user is likely to develop some changes in identity as a result of this continual process.

There are as many ways of conceptualizing identities and social histories of chronic heroin users as there are reasons cited for onset. It ought to be possible to develop a series of paradigms or schematic progressions that would include most users, as has been done in complex fields such as value orientations and family constellations (Morris, 1956; Toman, 1961).

Such formulations of different approaches to user identity may emerge during the next few years. For the present, the most elaborately described identity is what may be called action-seeking, young "stand up cats" (Feldman, 1968). The ability of a "cat" to succeed on the street has been said to depend on a feeling of omnipotence, access to the initial shot, experiencing a flash, learning how to be a successful drug consumer, disengagement from nonusers and movement into a drug-using subculture.

Furthermore, to be a chronic heroin user, it is necessary to work at it (Rubington, 1967). The user develops an identity as participant in a deviant career. He must relate to institutions, participate in a range of informal relationships, and develop various roles, in a relatively orderly manner. The drug subculture blunts the impact of harsh laws while permitting the user to assume a new deviant identity—via language, ideal self image, skills involved in getting and using drugs, and new norms and world view. The young user who may not have been able to deal with the conventional social system derives a new ideology in the user subculture.

A street user's commitment to subculture values provides him with a status and identity within it (Sutter, 1966). The user culture offers not only an ideology of justification but also ritualistic and magical patterns. There is a class system within the chronic heroin user's world, which has the same kind of success symbols as does conventional society. The heroin user may get status not only for achieving something but for not doing so; e.g., it could be honorific not only to avoid arrest but also to be arrested very frequently. At the top of the prestige hierarchy is the "righteous dope fiend."

It is possible to document other dimensions of heroin-user identity, even within the variable of activity, which is the one most frequently used. Six essential relationships to activity-passivity have been suggested, based on users in East Harlem in New York (Fiddle, 1967):

1. Pseudo—hinging on the pretense and "phoniness" in the manipulation of reality.
2. Passive—apathetic, desirous of being moved along with the world.
3. Obsessional—compulsively oriented around rituals and codes.
4. Paranoid—vigilantly full of stress and strain.
5. Depressed—preoccupied with failure, gray.
6. Retreatist—expressing dividedness, constriction, alienation.

Similar subgroups and types can probably be identified in any large population of users. They suggest that the socialization of chronic heroin users into a new identity does not proceed in a uniform way, and that even fairly homogeneous population in terms of age and ethnicity actually consists of a number of subgroups. The assumption of a new identity as a chronic heroin user will not be equally salient to all users, and its intensity will reflect their relationship to the conventional social system.

WORK

One of the key ways in which a chronic heroin user relates to society is by working. If he was working before onset of heroin use and continued on the job after development of a habit, the job will have one kind of significance. If, however, a chronic heroin user who has little vocational experience starts a job during a period of abstention, it probably has a different impact on his life space. A job may reflect a desire to support a heroin habit or a step out of the drug subculture. The age of the user at the time he assumes the job is obviously important in terms of what it means to him. Whether he is referred to the job by a probation officer or counselor or finds it without institutional help can also be central to his attitudes toward the work situation.

Working at a conventional job was long believed to be very difficult for the heroin user. He was presumably either "on the nod," unable to keep regular hours, or otherwise incapacitated. Of a sample of 1,352 male patients admitted to the Lexington hospital in 1965, however, one-third claimed regular employment in the 6 months prior to admission (Ball & Chambers, 1970). That one-third had regular employment is perhaps surprising because Lexington patients probably represented a relatively unsuccessful group of users.

Of the 6,678 persons receiving drug-free treatment in seven cities, only a minority (26.7%) were unemployed and unskilled (U.S. Office of Economic Opportunity, 1971). Over two-fifths had worked for more than 6 months at one job. In a survey (Winick, unpublished study) of 1,300 chronic heroin users in the metropolitan New York area who were not known to treatment or correctional institutions, 81% had worked for more than 6 months at one job.

Among a sample of regular heroin users in New York State, where jobs are relatively difficult to get because of the economy, unemployed males constituted 34.4% and employed females represented 18.7%, so that a total of 53.1% of the heroin users were working (Chambers, 1971). Over a fourth (28.1%) used heroin while on the job.

The ability of a user to get and hold a job is a function of variables such as age of onset, criminal involvement, personality, education, habit, degree of mixed dependency, possession of specific skills and mobility. It is also a function of jobs available and employer attitudes, if the employee is known to be a former or current user.

In conventional society, a person's occupation contributes perhaps 85% of the variation in his lifestyle. For many a chronic heroin user, the kind of job he has is probably far less important, especially if the drug has become the overwhelming center of his life.

A number of heroin users have a habit that is more or less controlled, usually because of money limitations. Such persons can integrate both their drug use and work adjustment into their larger definitions of the social reality with which they must cope.

The user's adaptation to a job situation will reflect factors such as his degree of isolation and other relationships with coworkers. An employee who is the only user in his place of employment might "play it cool." Or, he might be a member of a significant minority of users. The population of users will clearly influence the manner and extent to which the worker's drug use will be salient in terms of the interpersonal relations on the job (Fiddle, 1971). A heroin-using worker may "put shades on" himself and derive satisfaction from knowing that his colleagues are unaware of his situation.

A user not known as such could be a superemployee, in anticipation of and seeking to postpone being discovered and fired. He also may develop a repertory of excuses for not being on time, such as imaginary family crises or cars breaking down.

Someone working together with other users will probably cooperate with them in covering up latenesses, buying drugs on a group basis, and sometimes engaging in thefts. One employee of a plumbing supply firm stole so much material that he was able to open his own shop. Drug users may seek work where it is relatively easy either to steal, such as the garment industry, or to derive extra income, like a resort hotel.

A substantial proportion of heroin users are clearly able to function in a regular work situation. For some, the drug may actually improve their level of functioning, or at least do so until their need for higher dosages asserts itself. Heroin may maintain a high level of motivation for people who are ambivalent about their work or dislike it. A number of prostitutes take heroin as a way of bringing themselves to conduct their business, which they otherwise find most unpleasant (Winick & Kinsie, 1972). Many rock musicians, like the jazz musicians of the previous generation, take heroin to make themselves more sensitive to their colleagues and audiences.

Leaving a job may have the same multiplicity of meanings for the user as does its start. Its connotations include whether the departure was voluntary; the employee's age and the salience of his heroin use; what would replace the income from the job, if the job was left in order for the user to become more actively involved in a heroin or criminal subculture; and similar considerations.

CRIMINAL ACTIVITY

The chronic heroin user must have some contact with a criminal subculture, if only because the drug can be obtained only by contact with an illegal distribution system. It is possible to identify four different kinds of user relationship to criminal life (Brotman & Freedman, 1969).

1. Conformist—a person highly involved in conventional life and not significantly in criminal life.
2. Hustler—a person highly involved in criminal life and not significantly involved in conventional life.
3. Two worlder—a person highly involved in both areas of life.
4. Uninvolved—a person not significantly involved in either area.

It is also possible to observe several attitudes of chronic heroin users toward the risks involved in their activities, and the outcome (Fiddle, 1967):

1. Good hustler—takes risks, profits from them.
2. Into something—minimal risks, gets reward.
3. Fool—takes larger risks, profits little.
4. Creep—takes few risks, gets little reward.

Such considerations of typology must be applied before interpreting the statistics of criminal activity often cited to shed light on the cost of heroin abuse. In terms of male heroin users known to the authorities, several studies have concluded that at least until the mid-1960s, users tended to be involved in antisocial and frequently criminal activities that antedated their heroin use (Winick, 1967). The users were more likely to engage in criminal behavior after onset than before, but their offenses tended to be an extension of behavior that preceded drug use.

Females are far less likely than are male heroin users to engage in criminal activity, for several reasons, one of which is their generally lesser habit. Older users are more likely than younger ones to have participated in criminal activity.

The distinction between work and criminal activity is sometimes unrealistic to some heroin users. Among users, to be a "real hustling dope fiend," or successful criminal, can be a mark of status. The major criminal occupations found in a sample of New York City chronic heroin users were: burglar (23%), generalized ("flat footed") hustler (12%), shoplifter (12%), and robber (9%) (Preble, & Casey, 1969). There are some unusual specialties, like the "cattle rustler," who steals meat from supermarkets.

The user escapes from monotony, uses criminal activity to turn the tables on a society that rejects him, and can justify doing so on the ground of the need to handle his sickness. Not only does his round of activities provide a rationale and keep him busy, but he may also have a role in the street distribution system for heroin. For some users, to become a dealer is to assume a subcareer that is profitable, offers emotional gratification and reinforcement of their importance to the group. Other users may be afraid of any extended stint as sellers for fear of winding up with a "dealer's Jones"[1] because they could not resist using what they started out selling.

By stealing and reselling other merchandise, the user contributes to the economic life of the slums. Jail may punctuate his arduous life—and it often *is*

---

[1] A heavy habit.

arduous—a user may be out 12 or 15 hours a day "taking care of business," often "working" 7 days a week.

As users drift out of or otherwise stop heroin use, or enter treatment, they tend to leave criminal activity in an intermittent rather than dramatic way, much as they leave heroin use.

ARREST

A chronic heroin user may be arrested as one consequence of buying or selling the drug or of participation in other criminal activity. The arrest may have different meanings for different users, depending on its circumstances and outcomes. It may be shrugged off or, at the other extreme, be cautionary. It may lead a person into treatment or incarceration, along with more experienced users, and the whole process of imprisonment.

An arrest may also bring the user into contact with social casework in an authoritarian setting, as represented by probation or parole. In some states, the user may find himself in a criminal commitment situation, in which he must receive residential treatment for a minimum period of time and then serve out the rest of his sentence in the community, under parole supervision.

Arrest is a reflection of many things: visibility of the illegal activity, size and quality of the police effort, degree of user involvement in a criminal subculture, place of residence, ethnicity, alertness, and luck. As a general rule, a user who is arrested once stands a good chance of being rearrested. In a study of 6,678 patients in drug-free treatment in seven communities throughout the country, the average number of times arrested was 5.5 (U.S. Office of Economic Opportunity, 1971).

Not only the likelihood of arrest but also the severity of sentencing vary from one community to the other. The average longest uninterrupted time served in prison in months reflected a large range:

Los Angeles	30.3
Chicago	24.9
Washington, D.C.	17.3
San Antonio	16.1
New Jersey	11.6
New York City	9.6
Tacoma	7.9

How an arrest is perceived and experienced by a heroin user will be related to many factors, including his place on the continuum of use from beginner to seasoned user, attitude to police, whether it leads to a prison term or to treatment, and the like. Whether it is the first or just another in a long series also is relevant.

Chronic heroin users who are not arrested tend to have mixed dependencies; be careful about their "works"; interact with fewer people; sustain fewer peer relationships; learn from "close calls"; avoid "dumb busts"; be less heavily "strung out"; avoid overconfidence; be very sensitive to and wary of police activities; have ties to the straight world; and engage in illegal activities where the likelihood of arrest is slight, e.g., numbers runners.

It seems much easier for female users to avoid arrest than for men. Women can earn substantial amounts of money working as prostitutes without having to run the risks involved in burglary and robbery. Even in female nonprostitute chronic heroin users, their sociometric range is relatively more constricted than that of men.

ABSTENTION

One feature of the life of many chronic heroin users is the existence of periods in which they do not use the drug, or any drugs. When it is voluntary, the noncontinuation of drug use is almost always multifactorial and overdetermined. The reasons for the cessation are likely to be reciprocally and complementarily related to those for the genesis of drug use.

There are perhaps five basic kinds of reasons for temporary or permanent abstinence from heroin use:

1. External circumstances—drug not available, lack of money, court pressure, leave community, job, response to threat.

2. Relationships jeopardized by continued drug use—loss of a significant relationship, friends, family difficulties.

3. Weariness—hassle exceeds user's threshold, reaching a nadir or "existential moment," high not achievable.

4. Personality and insight—sense of maladaptiveness of drug, decline in counterphobic pressures, a sense of movement into psychosis, insight into destructive aspects of use, desire to change life.

5. Physical problem—symptoms of illness that are incapacitating.

Many users seek to achieve a reduction in the strength of their habits by entering treatment. They may not have the money to sustain a habit, need to deal with a temporary external situation, or be moving toward a goal of improved adaptation without the outside support needed for achieving such a goal. Seven-tenths of a sample of 253 male patients at New York's Metropolitan Hospital said their major goal was getting off drugs, 20% mentioned staying off, and 10% sought social or psychiatric change. The basic reason of the majority clearly did not include the goal of ending the habit (Brotman & Freedman, 1969).

Although little attention has been paid to the neophyte heroin user who decides not to continue with the substance, there is reason to believe that some make such a decision because of their response to the realization that they might be in an irreversible situation, friends' difficulties, arrest, or social pressure (Schasre, 1966). Those who stop using without a specific decision to do so either move to another community or their suppliers are no longer available.

No matter what the reasons for abstention, the user, whether neophyte or seasoned, must experience withdrawal before he can stop using. Even though the decreasing purity of street heroin makes some withdrawal almost subclinical, it can be very unpleasant. How it is experienced and its attendant circumstances could substantially affect the user and his attitudes toward subsequent involvement with heroin.

Almost all users have had varying periods of abstention. Two-fifths of a sample of 422 New York men receiving treatment had abstained voluntarily from heroin for at least 3 months (Waldorf, 1973). The longer they had used heroin, the more likely were they to have had at least one substantial abstention. During their time of nonuse, the majority worked, did not drink, got along with their family, did not associate with other users, were usually happy, and were not bored with their social life. More than two-thirds of the group had not engaged in criminal activity while off heroin. Education and compatibility with one's family were positively correlated with the ability to sustain abstinence, suggesting that a person who has been reasonably able to deal with his immediate social world is better able to adjust to life without heroin.

Abstention from heroin may become permanent. Some of the reasons for abstention noted previously may, in combination, develop into a process of maturing out. It was originally speculated that perhaps two-thirds of the users known to federal authorities in 1955 had not resumed heroin use 5 years later (Winick, 1962). One explanation was that by a process of emotional homeostasis, the stresses and strains faced by the former users, at a mean age of 35, had become sufficiently stabilized so that these stresses could be faced without drugs. It was also noted that there were differences in the rate of maturing out in different communities, suggesting the importance of local factors.

De-addiction over time could be analogized to the role of maturation in the derecidivism of criminals (Winick, 1964). In analysis of the sequence of heroin users' movement into and out of the criminality-convention dimension, it has been suggested that the sequence is likely to be as follows: conformist, two worlder, hustler, uninvolved, and back to conformist (Brotman & Freedman, 1969). At this last stage, we can speculate, the maturing-out phenomenon may manifest itself.

Various studies sought to determine what proportion of an original population of heroin users seem to have become permanently abstinent, using the criteria of a user's appearance on official records of death, entrance into treatment, or involvement with an agency of the criminal justice system. One study concluded that over four-fifths of the heroin users studied in St. Louis had ceased using the substance (Robins & Murphy, 1967).

In an effort to explore the extent of the maturing-out phenomenon, interviews were conducted with a sample of 242 former patients at Lexington who were residents of Puerto Rico. It was concluded that perhaps one-third, with a mean age of 33, had become productive citizens and had not used drugs for a period of at least 3 years (Ball & Snarr, 1969).

Another study was based on a sample of 3,655 cases, or every other person originally reported to the New York City Narcotics Register in 1964 (Snow, 1974). These cases were followed through 1968, and those not reappearing at all during the 5-year period were classified as inactive and presumed to have matured out. Twenty-three percent did not reappear on official records from 1964 through 1968; their average age was 33.8 years. They were more likely to be white, older, and female than were members of the original population subsequently rereported to the Register for drug use.

The under-28-year inactive group tended to be white, male, doing clerical or factory work, not in Manhattan, and living in medium or low drug use areas.

The over-38-year inactive group tended to be black, male, working at a service job, and living in Manhattan and in a high drug use area.

It would seem that the inactive group consists of a number of subgroups, differentiated by factors such as age, ethnicity, sex, and area of residence. As a result, it is plausible to speculate that there are different routes out of heroin use, in varied circumstances and for different reasons, just as there are different routes to chronic heroin use. It is possible that the maturing-out phenomenon is more likely to occur among younger persons if they are in a more advantaged life situation, such as whites in a medium or low use area. On the contrary, it probably occurs at later ages for persons with less access to other options, such as blacks living in high use areas. The most likely generalization is that maturing out or any other avenue to permanent abstention is likely to occur where access to non-heroin-user roles is plausible, encouraged, and reinforced. The substantial proportion of Vietnam veterans who, after their return to this country, ceased using heroin with minimal therapeutic assistance, suggests the importance of role change and access.

PATIENTHOOD

A chronic heroin user may become a patient on one or more occasions during his period of relationship to the substance. Various authoritarian forces, such as court or probation or parole, may affect the nature and salience of the user's self-definition as a patient.

Becoming a patient is a process, an ambiguous state in which a person oscillates until he comes to terms with what is involved in patienthood. There are enormous differences in what is expected of a patient in a drug-free therapeutic community, a methadone maintenance program, or an outpatient counseling program. If a patient does not internalize the norms communicated by the specific modality, usually more on the basis of cues and informal means rather than explicit formulations, he is not likely to do well.

Treatment groups tend to be aware of the importance of identity and the self-concept. A therapeutic community may require its residents to call themselves "dope fiends" as a way of reinforcing a specific self-concept, just as a methadone maintenance center may insist on referring to its participants as "drug dependents" who are "members of a program," rather than "patients" at a "clinic." In both cases, there is recognition of the central relationship between internalization of patienthood and therapeutic progress.

Just as non-drug-using patients seek out psychotherapy of a specific kind because they think they have the "right" kind of problem, chronic heroin users in a position to choose their treatment modality go to a situation they believe to be consonant with their needs. Their needs may not be the same as those favored by the modality, e.g., a methadone client may want to substitute one drug for another and keep two identities, one as a chronic heroin user and another as a methadone patient. Such an incompatibility will probably be resolved, by the person's either assuming a new identity as a methadone maintenance patient or his resumption of chronic heroin use.

Some patients may alternate, circling from status as a patient to user and return to patienthood. Others may "dib and dab" in contact with a number of treatment agencies because of their need to belong to a larger group.

Partial patienthood may be sought by the user whose motivation for treatment is weak or other defined, often under coercion. Full or partial patienthood can be found at almost any place in the chronic user's career.

Success at patienthood is often positively correlated with what might be a significant benchmark in the user's career: moving out of the neighborhood or area that was associated with heroin use. Moving to a new area could also be correlated with success as a worker or in sustaining abstinence.

OLDER USERS

The concentration on juvenile heroin users, because of a community's desire to maximize the productive involvement of its young people and its concern about street crime, has led to a lack of interest in what was happening at the other end of the age spectrum. A substantial proportion of the 1300 metropolitan New York heroin users not known to the authorities (studied by Winick, unpublished study) gave every indication of indefinitely continuing drug use. For some, heroin use had replaced interactions with other people and institutions and provided a relationship with continuity and meaning. They adapted their drug habits to changing realities of income and availability of drugs.

Other "unknown" older users could be found in almost any city. For example, a group of 38 heroin users in New Orleans, largely unknown to public agencies, ranged in age from 48 to 72 years, with a mean of 58.9 and a habit averaging 35.4 years (Capel, Goldsmith, Waddell, & Stewart, 1972). By recognizing the virtue of moderation, they had learned how to get drugs of reliable quality at minimum risk of arrest. These "old pros" preferred Dilaudid, heroin, and morphine, obtained from pushers or friends. Two-thirds had legitimate jobs, 16% received welfare or pensions, and the rest hustled. All but two were single, divorced, or separated.

Some older users of advancing years have surfaced recently because of their desire to enter methadone maintenance programs rather than continue with illegal drugs. At Roosevelt Hospital in New York, from 15% to 20% of the initial methadone maintenance patients were over 60 years (Pascarelli, 1972). These older patients, who used to "shoot" three or four times daily, preferred heroin but generally reduced their habit as they grew older, for economic reasons. Mixed dependencies were very common, with Dilaudid and short acting barbiturates especially popular. These senior users dug into the community and maintained a low profile to avoid harassment and attention. Some of them "shot up" cocaine as an occasional indulgence. Most were unmarried. Long-term users tend to acquire more satisfactions from their drugs as they grow older.

For such older users, heroin use can become a routinized aspect of daily life. The ordinary benchmarks of the career of users known to the authorities become irrelevant because these users are unlikely to seek treatment or be arrested. They have comparatively few friendship ties and instead can interact with the drug.

DEATH

One possible outcome of a chronic opiate user's career is death related in some way to drug use. Considerable publicity has been given to heroin-related deaths stemming from hepatitis, infections, and circulatory disorders. Even more attention has been given to deaths from heroin or (illegally acquired) methadone overdoses, which have also been used to extrapolate to the incidence and prevalence of heroin use in the community or even in the United States, much as death from cirrhosis of the liver has been used to estimate the total population of alcoholics.

The ratio between a dose that will give someone a high and one that can kill is perhaps on the order of magnitude of 1 to 15. This high ratio, and the relatively small proportion of a minute within which a user may get a massive dose into his bloodstream, help to explain some overdose deaths. On the one hand, an annual death rate of 1% to 5%, much of it from overdoses, has been suggested. On the other hand, it has been proposed that there are few genuinely authenticated deaths from overdoses among chronic heroin users and that the deaths actually reflect a factor that has not been fully identified (Brecher and the editors of Consumers Union, 1972). This factor may involve considerations like concomitant use of alcohol or barbiturates, effects of the quinine that may be mixed with heroin, and other yet unknown considerations.

Because information on deaths of chronic users, like statistics on crime waves, possibly may be used for bureaucratic or political purposes, such information must be approached cautiously. An analogy may be drawn to the many elaborate conclusions that were drawn by social scientists, on the basis of official statistics on suicide ever since the publication of Emile Durkheim's famous monograph on the subject. Various revisionist scholars have pointed out that the studies of suicide were often conducted by officials using common-sense definitions of the subject, but that these definitions tended to be vague and inconsistent, especially on the part of coroners and medical examiners (Douglas, 1967). Also, the commitment of officials to specific ideologies, it was noted, could militate against the objectivity of their findings. Similar factors could be relevant to heroin overdose reports, where the data are much more ambiguous than in the case of suicide.

It is unlikely that deaths among heroin users will occur on a random basis. One study of New York City deaths, using the Narcotics Register, concluded that they were most likely to occur in the age group over 29 years in males, and in blacks. The persons who died tended to reside in areas of high rate of chronic heroin use. Although there was substantial representation of white deaths, they tended to be of persons residing in all sections, but particularly in medium and low use areas (Snow, 1974). Some 2.17% of the total population of 3,242, originally reported to the Narcotics Register in 1964, had died by 1968. It is possible that a higher death rate would obtain today. In view of the ultimate nature of death as an outcome of a heroin user's career, it seems important to apply some of the insights that were applied by revisionist sociology to the study of suicide. We can also adapt the notion of the psychological autopsy from the field of suicidology, for intensive study of deaths related to heroin use.

Whatever its effect on deaths, long-term use of opiates has never been related to any significant medical condition. In fact, a study of the 31 patients most frequently hospitalized over a 32-year period at Lexington concluded that 28 were in average or fair health (Ball & Urbaitis, 1970). Since it would seem to be the secondary effects of opiate use that probably lead to illness or death, and since such effects may be expected among subgroups in the heroin-user population, extensive studies of the subgroups are needed before reasonable generalizations can be made. As the use of contaminated needles and syringes increases among persons who inject heroin, the proportion of heart, liver, and other infections will probably increase among both mainliners and skin poppers.

CAREERS THEN, NOW, AND IN THE FUTURE

Much information on careers of heroin users comes from large-scale studies of patients at Lexington or from intensive studies of specific populations in the past. Although the accessibility of the Lexington population was ideal from the view point of the researcher, we cannot be sure that it was representative of the total of chronic heroin users in the United States. Changing social conditions, variations in the groups at risk, new importance of political factors, the emergence of methadone and other chemotherapies, and similar developments intimately related to the onset and sustenance and abandonment of chronic heroin use require us to update our data on a regular basis.

It may be useful to summarize one kind of chronic heroin user's career by some benchmarks in the life of Alberto, a Puerto Rican user in New York (Kron & Brown, 1967):

1. Arrived in New York from Puerto Rico, age 6, reunited with mother; father absent.
2. Baby sister born when Alberto is 10.
3. Impotent, at 15, with a "bad girl."
4. Joined a gang, in rumble; engaged in sexual intercourse.
5. Marijuana smoking, occasionally and then daily, after being given reefer by older schoolmate John.
6. Experience of sexual confusion, in interaction with both males and females; homosexual prostitution.
7. Restless, asked John for "something more."
8. Heroin introduction at 16; snorting, skin popping, mainlining.
9. Regular use of heroin, four bags a day, financed by thefts.
10. Arrest en route to a burglary; suspended sentence.
11. Small time pushing; six shots a day.
12. Unconscious from overdose.
13. Hospitalization; abstinence.
14. Begging, stealing, and prostitution.
15. Counseling treatment; moderate drug use.
16. Hospitalization to reduce habit.
17. Counseling; job at gas station; abstinence.
18. Marriage and fatherhood.
19. Stronger habit, more stealing; arrested for possession and burglary.
20. Three months in prison.
21. Return to Puerto Rico to meet father.
22. Return to New York.
23. Cooperation with parole officer; abstinence; factory trainee.
24. Death attributed to overdose; age 23.

Alberto would be identified as an Old Style Junkie, in terms of the typology of the San Francisco studies. His voluntary induction by peers, movement in and out of the chronic heroin user's culture, periods of abstentions, participation in increasing criminal activity as he became more "strung out," intermittent contacts with the world of "square" work, sporadic participation in treatment, and processing by the criminal justice system, are representative of one kind of New York user career, with the exception of the sad reality of his death.

But even in New York, such a sequence of events may be less likely than it was in the 1960s, or may be less relevant for many kinds of the "newer" users. Perhaps the single most significant difference between the old and the "new" population of users is the widespread prevalence of mixed dependencies, including even alcohol, among the latter. As a result, they are less likely to be "addicts" in the traditional sense because their lives are less singlemindedly organized around the pursuit of a heavily mythologized "H." Their needs, drug-related satisfactions, behavior and goals are likely to be differently focused. Their participation in the de-addiction process is much more complicated and problematical (Brill, 1972).

Why has there been such a significant shift to mixed dependencies? They represent an adaptation of persons and groups to a variety of events, contingencies, and trends, such as the following:

1. Interaction, interpenetration, and blending of Vietnam veteran experience and the cultures of youth, colleges, ghettos, and the counterculture.

2. Reassertion of ghetto gangs and other informal groups, often claiming to be antidrug and with new incentives and viewpoints on drug use.

3. The emergence of methadone as a competitive substance and one that can, for some people, allay anxiety about a heroin "panic," and indirectly, help to legitimize psychoactive drug use, while its use by persons in treatment frees the heroin formerly bought by the patients.

4. New connotations for heroin because of its comparative scarcity, and partial decathection.

5. Significant changes in some social institutions: variations in access to employment; shifts in mass media content and emphases.

6. The direction and nature of the massive government intervention in both law enforcement and treatment of "drug abuse" since 1970, which has led to the ready availability of most kinds of treatment and competition among treatment agencies for clients, especially those referred by the criminal justice system.

7. Democratization of drug dealing.

8. The enormous publicity generated by and about various aspects of "drug abuse."

9. Rapidly changing notions of what constitutes gender identity.

10. Substantial and progressive erosion of mechanisms of social control; extreme pluralism, sometimes near-anarchic.

As a result of the development of mixed dependencies, many resocialization and other agencies may be providing services that are not fully in touch with the realities of the "new" drug scene, and our need to optimize impact and resources makes it incumbent on us to adapt our programs and institutional structures to a changing situation.

The ability of our institutions to understand and ultimately cope with chronic heroin use will only be enhanced as we develop (*a*) contemporary detailed social histories like that of Alberto and of the users who are not known to either treatment or criminal justice resources and (*b*) a heuristic career typology. Detailed information from many different parts of the country is necessary before we can have confidence in our understanding of the careers of chronic heroin users.

REFERENCES

Alksne, H., Lieberman, L., & Brill, L. A conceptual model of the life cycle of addiction. *International Journal of the Addictions*, 1967, **2**, 221–240.

Ball, J. C. Two patterns of opiate addiction. *Journal of Criminal Law, Criminology, and Police Science*, 1965, **56**, 203–211.

Ball, J. C., & Chambers, C. D. Overview of the problem. In J. C. Ball & C. D. Chambers (Eds.), *Epidemiology of opiate addiction in the United States*. Springfield, Ill.: Charles C Thomas, 1970.

Ball, J. C. Chambers, C. D., & Ball, M. J. Association of Marihuana smoking with opiate addiction. *Journal of Criminal Law, Criminology, and Police Science*, 1968, **59**, 171–182.

Ball, J. C., & Snarr, R. W. A test of the maturation hypothesis with respect to opiate addiction. *UN Bulletin on Narcotics*, 1969, **21**, 9–13.

Ball, J. C., & Urbaitis, J. C. Absence of major medical complications among chronic opiate addicts. In J. C. Ball & C. D. Chambers (Eds.), *The epidemiology of opiate addiction in the United States*. Springfield, Ill.: Charles C Thomas, 1970.

Bentel, D., & Smith, D. E. Drug abuse in combat. In D. E. Smith & G. R. Gay (Eds.), *It's so good, don't even try it once: Heroin in perspective*. Englewood Cliffs, N. J.: Prentice-Hall, 1972.

Brecher, E. M., and the editors of Consumers Union. *Licit and illicit .drugs*. Boston: Little, Brown, 1972.

Brill, L. *The de-addiction process: Studies in the de-addiction of confirmed heroin addicts*. Springfield, Ill.: Charles C Thomas, 1972.

Brotman, R., & Freedman, A. M. A community mental health approach to drug addiction. Juvenile Delinquency Publication 9005. Washington, D.C.: U.S. Government Printing Office, 1969.

Brown, B. S., Gauvey, S. K., Meyers, M. B., & Stark, S. D. In their own words. *International Journal of the Addictions*, 1971, **6**, 635–646.

Capel, W. C., Goldsmith, B. G., Waddell, K. J., & Stewart, G. T. The aging narcotic addict: An increasing problem for the next decades. *Journal of Gerontology*, 1972, **27**, 102–106.

Chambers, C. D. An assessment of drug use in the general population. New York: Narcotic Addiction Control Commission, 1971.

Chambers, C. D. A behavioral progression typology of drug users. Paper Presented at Tarrytown Conference Center, Nov. 20, 1972. Tarrytown, N.Y.

Chein, I. The use of narcotics as a personal and social problem. In D. M. Wilner & G. G. Kassebaum (Eds.), *Narcotics*. New York: McGraw-Hill, 1965.

Chein, I., Gerard, D. F., Lee, R. S., & Rosenfeld, E. *The road to H.* New York: Basic Books, 1964.

DeFleur, L. B., Ball, J. C., & Snarr, R. W. The long term correlates of opiate addiction. *Social Problems*, 1969, 17, 225-233.

Douglas, J. D. *The social meanings of suicide*. Princeton, N. J.: Princeton University Press, 1967.

Feldman, H. W.: Ideological supports to becoming and remaining a heroin addict. *Journal of Health and Social Behavior*, 1968, 9, 131-139.

Fiddle, S. *Portraits from a shooting gallery*. New York: Harper & Row, 1967.

Fiddle, S. *Drug taking and work organization*. New York: Exodus House, 1971.

Fiddle, S., Mayfield, L., & Green, M. *Annual report of Exodus House, 1970*. New York: Exodus House, 1971.

Gay, G. R., Newmeyer, J. A., & Winkler, J. J. The Haight-Ashbury Free Medical Clinic. In D. E. Smith & G. R. Gay (Eds.), *It's so good, don't even try it once: Heroin in perspective*. Englewood Cliffs, N. J.: Prentice-Hall, 1972.

Glaser, D. *The effectiveness of a prison and parole system*. Indianapolis: Bobbs-Merrill, 1964.

Glaser, D., Lander, B., & Abbott, W. Opiate addicted and non-addicted siblings in a slum area. *Social Problems*, 1971, 18, 511-521.

Gross, E. *Work and society*. New York: Crowell, 1964.

Kaprio, L. A., & May, A. R. *Drug dependence.* Document COP/23. Copenhagen: World Health Organization, 1972.

Kron, Y. J., & Brown, E. M. *Mainline to nowhere: The makings of a heroin addict*. New York: Meridian, 1967.

Morris, C. W. *Varieties of human value*. Chicago: University of Chicago Press, 1956.

O'Donnell, J. A. Patterns of drug abuse and their social consequences. In J. R. Wittenborn, H. Brill, J. P. Smith, & S. Wittenborn, (Eds.), *Drugs and youth*. Springfield, Ill.: Charles C Thomas, 1969.

Pascarelli, E. Old drug addicts do not die, nor do they just fade away. *Geriatric Focus*, 1972, 11(1), 1-5.

Preble, E., & Casey, J. J. Taking care of business—The heroin user's life on the street. *International Journal of the Addictions*, 1969, 4, 1-24.

Ray, M. B. The cycle of abstinence and relapse among heroin addicts. *Social Problems*, 1961, 9, 132-140.

Robins, L. N., & Murphy, G. E. Drug use in a normal population of young Negro men. *American Journal of Public Health*, 1967, 57, 1580-1596.

Rubington, E. Drug addiction as a deviant career. *International Journal of the Addictions*, 1967, 2, 3-21.

Sardell, A. Age of addiction as a predictor of conventional behavior in heroin addicts. Paper presented to annual meeting of Society for Study of Social Problems, New York, N. Y., Aug. 1972.

Schasre, R. Cessation patterns among neophyte heroin users. *International Journal of the Addictions*, 1966, 1, 23-32.

Scher, J. Group structure and narcotic addiction: Notes for a natural history. *International Journal of Group Psychotherapy*, 1961, 11, 88-93.

Snow, M. Maturing out of narcotic addiction in New York City. *International Journal of the Addictions*, 1974, 8, 917-933.

Sutter, A. G. The world of the righteous dope fiend. *Issues in Criminology*, 1966, 2, 177-222.

Terry C. E., & Pellens, M. *The opium problem*. New York: Bureau of Social Hygiene, 1928.

Toman, W. *Family constellation*. New York: Springer, 1961.

U.S. Office of Economic Opportunity. *Uniform evaluation of programs to combat narcotic addiction*. Washington, D.C.: U.S. Government Printing Office, 1971.

Vaillant, G. E. A twelve year follow-up of New York narcotic addicts. *American Journal of Psychiatry*, 1966, **123**, 573–585.

Waldorf, D. *Careers in dope.* Englewood Cliffs, N. J.: Prentice-Hall, 1973.

Winick, C. Maturing out of narcotic addiction. *UN Bulletin on Narcotics*, 1962, **14**, 1–7.

Winick, C. The life cycle of the narcotic addict and of addiction. *UN Bulletin on Narcotics*, 1964, **16**, 1–11.

Winick, C. Drug addiction and crime. *Current History*, 1967, **52**, 349–354.

Winick, C. A survey of chronic heroin users unknown to treatment or correctional institutions. Unpublished study.

Winick, C., & Kinsie, P. M. *The lively commerce: Prostitution in the United States.* New York: New American Library, 1972.

Zahn, M. A., & Ball, J. C. Factors related to cure of opiate addiction among Puerto Rican addicts. *International Journal of the Addictions*, 1972, **7**, 237–245.

8
ISSUES IN THE EVALUATION
OF HEROIN TREATMENT[1,2]

Irving F. Lukoff
Addiction Research and Treatment
Corporation Evaluation Team
Columbia University School of Social Work

INTRODUCTION

This chapter considers several questions that arise in the effort to assess the outcomes of heroin treatment programs. The issues addressed here have to do with the impact of current treatment systems in two important problem areas. First, will there be a significant abatement in crime as current programs (primarily methadone maintenance) expand? Second, will the rapid expansion of treatment facilities curtail the recruitment of individuals into the drug scene?

There is a paucity of data with which to deal with either issue in an altogether satisfactory way. For the most part the data here come from a few programs where some information has been made available and from studies already completed as part of the research program conducted by the Addiction Research and Treatment Corporation Evaluation Team at the Columbia University School of Social Work.

A variety of program objectives can be specified. Most would agree that there should be a cessation of heroin use without the substitution of another

[1] The research on which this paper is based is supported by grants NI–71–046–G and NI–72–008–G from the U.S. Department of Justice, Law Enforcement Assistance Administration, to the Addiction Research and Treatment Corporation Evaluation Team at Columbia University School of Social Work, through the Vera Institute of Justice. Additional funds come from the Addiction Research and Treatment Corporation. We gratefully acknowledge their support.

[2] Reprinted from *Principles of Criminology*, (7th edition) by E. H. Sutherland and D. R. Cressey, with permission of J. B. Lippincott Company. © 1966.

addiction, such as barbiturates, amphetamines, or alcohol to excess. There is, of course, an implicit bias because any detection of, say, barbiturates, in the urine of an addict in treatment is generally looked at askance and might be a cause for counselor intervention or even program dismissal. Yet, the moderate use of alcohol is perfectly acceptable. Methadone programs, of course, exclude methadone from the proscribed list of drugs.

The elimination of criminal behavior is also a program objective, in most cases. At least one program administrator, however, has raised the question, if only rhetorically, whether this is not imposing middle-class values on people from backgrounds where many types of illicit activities are commonplace, and generally acceptable, such as policy numbers, dealing in stolen goods, and pimping (Newman, 1970). But such caveats are the exception because the primary motivation in the expansion of drug treatment programs, whatever other laudatory objectives may also be identified, is the concern with crime, much of it attributed to addicts.

Increasingly, the major source of funds and the aegis for the expansion of treatment programs throughout the United States are programs closely integrated with the criminal justice system in various court-diversion schemes. These come primarily from the U.S. Department of Justice, and their primary focus is clear: expand treatment in order to contribute to the reduction of crime.

Other types of conventional behavior are also specified: employment, or equivalent socially productive activities; stable family patterns; and, for at least one set of guidelines issued by the Special Action Office for Drug Abuse and Prevention (SAODAP), improved mental health!

The reduction of crime is discussed first, because it is in fact the main objective, if not always exactly formulated that way. Certainly, we are all acquainted with the familiar equation that drug addiction creates a dependency that can only be sated by obtaining large sums of money with which to purchase drugs. Therefore, the increase in heroin addiction has, as a byproduct, the increase in crime in our urban communities.

CRIME AND HEROIN

When heroin use began to be studied in its contemporary form, the emphasis was on the nature of the drug response, the euphoria and attendant withdrawal from one's immediate surroundings. The thesis was advanced, first by Chein, Gerard, Lee, and Rosenfeld (1964) and elaborated by Cloward and Ohlin (1960), that drug use was retreatist and attracted those who could not make it in the rougher bopping gangs of the era or who were unable to commit illegal acts or inept at crime. Because of the drug response and its attendant physiological and psychological effects, heroin use was distinguished from other forms of deviance. Its use was assumed, first, to attract different kinds of people and, second, to be the result of a process different from the one that led to other kinds of illegitimate activities in the ghettos where most heroin users were located.

Although heroin addiction is no longer confined to the ghetto communities, it is still concentrated there. Whatever is known about persons who become addicts, the mechanisms for induction are indeed similar to other types of youthful deviance (Lukoff, 1972; Preble, 1966). Many addicts are well ensconced in other forms of illegitimate activity even before they become addicted, and many are integrated into a much more complex delinquent pattern. There may be different clusters of addicts, some of whom may indeed conform to the pattern described by Chein et al. (1964) and others. Even in a ghetto-based program that mainly attracts long-term addicts, a fair portion have no criminal records at all and except for drug use avoid most of the other criminal activities associated with addiction. Preble and Casey (1969) have also raised important questions about the "retreatist" aspects of heroin addiction by noting the extraordinary activity that occupies the addict's routines wherein he has only brief moments to enjoy his reverie. He is kept frantically busy obtaining money, looking for drugs, and avoiding the police.

A typology of drug addicts will not be developed here, as some aspects of this thesis will be documented later. Many, if not all, addicts, however, are socialized into deviant activities at about the same time that they begin to experiment with drugs. They are committed to a lifestyle and values associated with other types of deviant behavior often found in their communities and are not a group that is set apart, isolated from the communities they inhabit.

If heroin addiction is, for some segment of the addict population, only an aspect of a more coherent pattern of deviance, then there are very important consequences. First, doubt is cast on the assumption that the crime associated with addiction is necessarily a function of the addicts' desperate need for funds to purchase drugs. In addition, although many addicts do indeed commit crimes and a large portion of their booty is spent on drugs, one may find that supplying drugs to addicts—whether methadone, heroin or narcotic antagonists—may not produce a dramatic reduction in overall crime that can be attributed to the methadone treatment system.

Second, the technologies available for transforming deviants of almost any type into useful and productive citizens—or, at the least, into persons who do not harm anyone else—are severely limited. The psychological therapies and the various group-living arrangements employed in drug treatment, even if there are some notable individual exceptions, have not been successful in altering lifestyles for significant numbers of addicts (for summaries of what is publicly known about therapeutic communities, see Brecher, 1972; DeLong, 1972).

Third, there is the question of whether the treatment system that has emerged will not only transform the behavior of addicts, but contribute to the decline in new recruits to the drug scene. Aside from some modest and inadequate educational programs, almost all moneys are invested in treating people already addicted. Will this have any impact on the incidence of new heroin addicts? Only bits and pieces of the answers to the puzzling question are known, but it is important to address the question and bring whatever information is available to this issue.

The question to be examined first, however, is: How indeed do we account for the high success rates reported for some methadone maintenance programs? This type of program is one of the few large-scale program expansions developed after some careful study and evaluation. No other national effort has been preceded by an assessment of a fairly large group of the target population for a particular service. The reports have been widely distributed and serve as a testimonial to the purported success of methadone maintenance. Other reports lend further credence to many findings first reported by Gearing (1970, 1972).

A PARADIGM FOR ASSESSMENT

Any treatment system assumes resources and a technology that can make desirable modifications or even alterations in some disability or behavior that is dysfunctional to the person or to others in his environment. But all individuals who are potential targets for a treatment system are never alike. Schizophrenia or cancer may be difficult to cure, but there are variants of both disabilities with which a great deal of success may be anticipated with current technologies.

Thus, any evaluation must also be assessed in the context of the differences or similarities in crucial variables that are associated with remission. This may seem an obvious requirement, but it is one difficult to implement. One usually studies particular programs; thus, it is difficult altogether to visualize a successful strategy for sampling patients from some target population. Even looking closely at patient characteristics to gain some insight into how they may contribute to success is not altogether simple. It is not completely understood what contributes to success or failure or what is the precise distribution of important characteristics of patients who are susceptible to treatment.

The intervention system also must be assessed in a thorough evaluation, even if we dwell on the predisposition of some individuals to change as a crucial element in success. The treatment system is a hodgepodge of different modalities sponsored by every layer of government, as well as private endeavors, some started by concerned and committed individuals and groups, and others by entrepreneurs. Different programs, even within the same modality, may have different results even if everything else is constant.

The drug-free programs, while exciting and innovative, have not yet demonstrated any significant potential for completing the process they attempt to establish; i.e., the resocialization of addicts. There are indeed individuals who have undergone impressive personal transformations. But the experience of places like Synanon, Daytop Village, Phoenix House, and other similar programs all add up to the same story. First, they are quite selective in the patients they accept. Second, there is a rapid rate of withdrawal from these programs. Third, those who remain are primarily involved in helping to run the programs; those who leave after completing the long course of treatment, (these tend to be few in number) are likely to return to the use of drugs (Brecher, 1972).

This study, therefore, examined the experience of methadone programs, because they have been more successful in holding addicts in treatment. There is an increasing acceptance, even in communities where the early reception was hostile. If the current course of program expansion continues, then it will become the dominant modality, as it has already become in New York City, with almost 33,000 patients (Methadone Maintenance and Detox Census in New York City, 1973).

Finally, to understand the nature of any decline in criminal activity and the other parameters of "success," an attempt must be made to link the patients to their communities. It is obvious that if addicts are unacceptable to employers then there can be little improvement in this area. But even the criminal behavior of addicts must be studied to understand how it is integrated into the fabric of the communities from which many addicts come. Only in this way will there be some basis for understanding what may be taking place.

SOME FACTORS ASSOCIATED WITH SUCCESS

Several themes were briefly developed in the present study:

1. Early onset of drug use is associated with a truncated socialization that impedes accommodation to the demands of a treatment program.

2. Adherence to program requirements sufficiently to remain in treatment is a function of advancing age.

3. A disproportionate share of crime is associated with early onset of drug use.

4. Patient attrition is a substantial element in the improvement that takes place through time.

5. Criminal behavior is not always a simple function of the need for funds to finance drug use but for many addicts is a part of a cohesive deviant pattern.

Data in this and subsequent sections were derived from an ongoing evaluation of the Addiction Research and Treatment Corporation (ARTC)

Center located in the heart of a ghetto community with an extremely high rate of heroin addiction (Narcotics Register, 1969). These data come from a series of staff papers prepared by the Addiction Research and Treatment Corporation Evaluation Team (Hayim, 1973; Lukoff, 1972a, 1972b; Lukoff & Vorenberg, 1972; Lukoff & Quatrone, 1973; Sardell, 1972; Quatrone, 1972).

The area served by the program contains all but one of the health areas with the highest addiction rates in Brooklyn. Admission to the program is limited to persons 21 years of age or older who have been heroin addicts for at least 2 years. No effort is made to screen patients; and, except for gross contrary medical indications, the program accepts all those who apply from the catchment area who conform to the provisions of age and duration of addiction.

The Addiction Research and Treatment Corporation accepted the first group of patients in October 1969. Since then, the Center has added successive clinics to accommodate additional patients until it reached its present size of about 1,300 active individuals.

The program, from its inception, was guided by a strong commitment to a multimodality approach to the treatment and rehabilitation of heroin addicts. Almost all patients are given methadone, although the quantity of methadone may vary. Counselors are assigned small caseloads to assist each patient in the process of resocialization and to provide him with the necessary support to cope with his environment without reliance on heroin. Various forms of group therapy are also available to assist patients. There is an extensive program of medical services, job development, education, and legal services. In addition, there is a community education program that provides speakers and conducts programs in the community with the aim of preventing youngsters from experimenting with drugs.

The typical patient was 31.7 years old when accepted in the program (Table 1). He started using heroin on a daily basis when he was 21.5 years, and thus had been addicted to heroin for 10.2 years when he entered the program. The average number of years of schooling completed is 10.5 years. About four-fifths of the patients are male; and, reflecting the ethnic character of the community where the ARTC Center is located, 77.4% of the patients are black, 10.4% white, and 11.7% Puerto Rican. Less than 1% are from Oriental and other racial backgrounds.

When entering the program, only 18% reported that their major source of income was from gainful employment; 19% were on welfare; and 7%, mainly females, reported that they were supported by their spouse or kin. Almost half (48%) reported that their major sources if income were from illegal activities (see Table 1).

The patient group investigated in this report, then, was primarily black, of whom fewer than one-fifth were gainfully employed, and who typically had less than a high school education. Almost half derived their major income from illegal activities. This patient group, therefore, was heavily weighted with

TABLE 1
Patient Characteristics

Characteristic	Percent
Marital status:	
Single	37
Married	33
Separated/divorced	29
Widowed	1
Primary source of income	
at admission:	
Legitimate job	18
Welfare	19
Spouse/kin	7
Illegal	48
Other	7
Ethnic classification:	
Black	77.4
White	10.4
Puerto Rican	11.7
Other	0.4
Sex:	
Male	81.5
Female	18.5
Average age	31.7[a]
Age regular drug use	21.5[a]
Average years of schooling	10.5[a]

[a]In years.

long-term drug users who presented a profile of characteristics that was most likely to be recalcitrant to rehabilitative efforts.

ONSET OF DRUG USE AND CONVENTIONAL BEHAVIOR

Table 2 shows the relation between age of onset of addiction and longest job held prior to admission within chronological age categories. Note the persistence through time of early onset with less employment experience, an element crucial to the likelihood of subsequent employment. But once individuals pass 35 years of age, there is some mitigation of the impact of age of onset. With advanced age, addicts are increasingly able to cope with the world of work. This is particularly significant because it precedes admission to treatment, although many have been in a variety of treatment programs,

TABLE 2
Length of Time on Longest Held Job by Age at Addiction and Age at Admission (Percent)

Time on longest held job	21-25 Age at addiction				26-30 Age at addiction				31-35 Age at addiction				36+ Age at addiction			
	11-17	18-21	22-25	26+	11-17	18-21	22-25	26+	11-17	18-21	22-25	26+	11-17	18-21	22-25	26+
0-12 months	60	47	35	—	38	28	27	21	42	29	19	18	28	36	29	16
13-36 months	28	44	34	—	43	44	42	25	42	40	22	23	47	29	40	27
37 months and over	12	9	31	—	19	28	31	54	16	31	59	59	25	35	31	57
Total	100	100	100	—	100	100	100	100	100	100	100	100	100	100	100	100
N	(67)	(121)	(32)	—	(42)	(76)	(59)	(28)	(31)	(52)	(36)	(40)	(32)	(66)	(59)	(79)

particularly the older patients. Similar interactions have been found to exist between chronological age and onset of regular drug use for other forms of conventional behavior that predispose toward successful outcomes, such as education and marriage. These findings lend credence to the thesis that early onset is indeed associated with a truncated socialization that complicates the problem of rehabilitation.

Table 3 shows a similar relationship regarding program terminations. Indeed, those patients who were less likely to have completed their education, to have stable employment experiences, and to be married were precisely the ones who had the highest rates of terminations. Again, those over 36 years of age are able to overcome the deficits associated with early onset of addiction.[2]

Table 4 shows that earlier onset is associated with higher levels of criminal activity before admission to the program. That is, those who started earlier had higher *rates* of arrests. As might be expected, this did not vary as a function of chronological age since these rates were based on the arrest histories of the patients. As documented in the section, "The Pattern of Addict Crime," it is the patients with higher arrest rates who are also most likely to terminate.

Table 5 shows that while onset of drug addiction retains its importance in program retention, especially for those who began drug use before they were 21, the patients who were able to combine early onset with higher educational achievement were more likely to remain in treatment.

There are many interesting and important aspects of the data just reviewed that are not examined here. This study presented findings that programs tend to prune themselves of younger addicts whose whole configuration is likely to

[2] These tables are derived from reports prepared at different times when the patient cohort differed; therefore, the number of cases is not the same in this series of tables.

TABLE 3

Relationship between Program Retention, Age at Admission, and Age of Onset
(Percent)

Program status	Age of Onset					
	11–17		18–20		21+	
	Age at Admission					
	21–35	36+	21–35	36+	21–35	36+
Active	45	74	60	65	67	70
Terminated	55	26	40	35	33	30
Total	100	100	100	100	100	100
N	(62)	(35)	(95)	(34)	(105)	(94)

TABLE 4

Level of Criminal Activity by Age at Admission and Age of Onset (Percent)

Level of criminal activity[a]	Age at admission					
	21-35			36+		
	Age of onset					
	11-17	18-20	21+	11-17	18-20	21+
Low	15	17	27	13	14	35
Medium	34	40	40	30	36	44
High	51	43	33	57	50	21
Total	100	100	100	100	100	100
N	(53)	(81)	(78)	(30)	(28)	(82)

[a]"Low" is no arrests since the onset of regular drug use; "medium" is up to 1 arrest every 3 years; and "high" is more than 1 arrest every 3 years.

contribute to poorer outcomes. But the same forces also increase the age of the surviving treatment population, and as addicts become older, there is an increasing proportion who enter treatment having somehow overcome at least some of the deficits that would make them more likely to terminate. It appears as if they somehow have to achieve the level of socialization ordinarily achieved by younger persons, and especially is this necessary for those who began drug use at a young age.

Sutherland and Cressey's (1966) findings from a study of persons released from federal prison are useful in elucidating some of the implications of these findings for the reduction of criminal behavior. (See Table 6.) Recidivism rates are first analyzed by age at release from prison and the number of felony-like offenses committed by the discharged inmates. Here there is an almost perfect progression. If the number of offenses is controlled, there is a substantial decline in recidivism as age increases. In turn, persons with more extensive criminal careers are more likely to be rearrested, although this is attenuated by increasing age. In addition, Table 6 shows the influence of early criminal careers. As with age of onset of drug use, earlier onset is associated with higher rates of recidivism within chronological age groups.

It seems, then, that the discharged prisoner who is not involved in drugs tends to follow similar patterns to those patterns operating in drug treatment programs.[3] It is, of course, a conjecture without considerably more evidence. But it does seem to conform to the general observation that patterns begun when young are likely to persist and tend to attenuate only with increasing age. That is, recidivism for criminal activity in general is similar to the

[3] This is also true for postadmission criminal behavior.

patterns of criminal behavior for those addicts examined at the Center. Just as many forms of deviance unrelated to addiction tend to become less frequent with advancing age, the addict is also likely to come to terms with conventional society.

There are many observations in the literature that suggest that the patterns described are not unique to either one program or to any particular modality. Nash, in a 2-year follow-up of Phoenix House patients, states: "When success is measured in terms of remaining in or graduating from the program ... younger people, as mentioned above, do substantially worse than older people [Nash, Waldorf, Foster, & Kyllingstad, 1971, pp. 8-9]." A study of Lexington patients (Bowden & Langenauer, 1972) in a special aftercare unit observed five significant variables differentiating the modest number of successful patients: "Successful patients were more likely to have graduated from high school, began using opiates later in their lives, more frequently began work during their first month in aftercare, and had much better vocational records over the six month period [p. 854]." Many other observations (Sardell, 1972; Vaillant, 1966; Winick, 1964) confirm the same pattern.

It is suggested, then, that successful outcomes may be substantially a function of processes that select those who come into treatment and remain independent of the program input. It is impossible, without an experimental design, altogether to assess the independent thrust that treatment programs may have in the transformation of addicts into more conventional individuals. The age of patients in most methadone programs is skewed toward older addicts: In ARTC the average is almost 32 years, and in the series of programs studied by Gearing (1970, 1972) it is 33. Goldstein (1970) noted that the favorable results in Santa Clara were influenced " ... by the predominance of better motivated, older, and more stable patients." Methadone, then, is substantially a way station for the addict who is maturing out of the heroin street scene. It is necessary to entertain the view that much of the improvement

TABLE 5

Program Status by Level of Education Achieved and by Age of Onset for Patients Ages 21-35 (Percent)

Program status	Age of onset, by education					
	1-11th grade			12th grade and over		
	11-17	18-20	21+	11-17	18-20	21+
Active	40	52	67	59	74	67
Terminated	60	48	33	41	26	33
Total	100	100	100	100	100	100
N	(45)	(60)	(57)	(17)	(35)	(48)

TABLE 6

Percent of Postrelease Failures among 1956 Federal Releases of Various Ages,
by Prior Involvements in Crime (Percent)

Number of prior sentences for felony-like offenses and age	Age at release from prison				
	18-21	22-25	26-35	36 and over	All cases
Number of sentences:					
None	44 (78)	31 (98)	21 (151)	11 (96)	25 (423)
One	52 (31)	46 (37)	34 (105)	25 (48)	37 (221)
Two	57 (23)	52 (27)	45 (64)	28 (40)	44 (154)
Three or more	45 (11)	63 (16)	48 (86)	42 (104)	46 (217)
Age at first arrest:					
16 and under	53 (94)	43 (68)	43 (106)	40 (36)	46 (304)
17-20	37 (49)	45 (73)	41 (116)	28 (78)	38 (316)
21 and over	–	24 (37)	24 (184)	24 (174)	24 (395)

Note: Figures in parentheses represent number of persons.

Source: Adapted from E. H. Sutherland & D. R. Cressey. *Principles of Criminology*, 7th ed. (1966) p. 545 (Reprinted by permission of J. P. Lippincott Co.)

is a function of age, with the changes wrought by maturation playing a significant role.

The impact of methadone treatment on the reduction of criminal behavior was examined to see if maturation and age of onset appeared to be operative here also.

TREATMENT AND CRIME REDUCTION

Many programs have reported a diminution in crime not only for those who remain in treatment but even for those who withdraw, although the decline for the latter group is attenuated. If there is a substantial reduction in crime and it is possible to get a healthy portion of addicts into treatment, then there should be a marked decline in the types of crime associated with addiction.

First, a review was conducted of some findings that have had such a substantial influence on our assessment of the impact of treatment on crime reduction. Another program then was examined where the data have been more carefully scrutinized. At this point, some tentative conclusions were attempted on just what appears to be happening in this sphere.

The various reports from the Beth Israel program all show an abrupt drop in criminal behavior (Gearing, 1970, 1972). In fact, it is this experience that has had the most extensive coverage and has been the basis for the very rapid expansion of methadone programs throughout the United States. Ninety-six percent of the Methadone Maintenance Treatment Program (MMTP) patients had been arrested at least once in the 3 years prior to admission. After only 1 year of treatment only 6% had been arrested, and in each succeeding year this percentage declines still farther. The rates presented in 1970 were 115 arrests per 100 patient years prior to admission and only 4.3 per 100 patient years only 1 year after treatment.[4] This must be considered the most remarkably successful intervention program ever devised to alter patterns of conduct that have always been extremely recalcitrant to efforts at modification. No program effort in criminology or any other area of social service and rehabilitation has ever been able to demonstrate such a substantial rate of success.

Three observations will set these findings in context. First, it must be determined how the patient population was assembled; as already noted, some concatenation of background factors and age may be operating to reduce crime irrespective of the nature of the intervention. Second, it must be determined how the data were obtained in order to assess their validity. Third, how the data are aggregated through time must be noted, since this may seriously affect the results.

The patient population in 1970 had a median age of 33.3 years, and for blacks it was 35.6 years. This population, of course, is much older than the general population of addicts and is a significant figure for comprehending the decline of arrests, as noted earlier. In 1970 the treatment group was 40% white, 40% black, 19% Spanish, and 1% Oriental. Precise figures on the ethnic distribution of addicts do not exist, but it is clear that the treatment group is substantially overrepresented with white addicts and a corresponding under-representation of black and Spanish (mainly Puerto Rican) patients. Moreover, there was careful screening, especially in the first several years, of patients who were accepted in the program. This selection has been amply documented by Perkins and Bloch (1970a, 1970b), who compared applicants with those who were accepted, and demonsrates a tendency to select those who had more job experience, who exhibited less severe criminal

---

[4]These rates were contrasted with a group who only underwent detoxification. There was no reason, however, to suspect they were even remotely comparable; therefore, the contrast group was not examined here.

histories, who were better educated, and who were "whiter" than the applicants.

The significance of such selectivity can best be appreciated by citing a reanalysis of the data used by Gearing (Chambers, Babst, & Warner, 1970). The authors found that a juxtaposition of the types of characteristics on which intake tended to select could have a serious impact on program retention. For example, addicts who were generally law-abiding before admission and had no alcohol problem were retained at a rate of 95.8%. On the other hand, those with extensive criminal records and no marketable employment skills were retained at a rate of 55.6%. We observe, therefore, that the selection procedures were, indeed, in the direction that tended to exaggerate success. Further, as the information on retention illustrates, it is precisely those who would most likely be recidivists who terminated or withdrew from the program.

Now we come to a more difficult issue because the various reports have not always been clear on this point. The official arrest information obtained on patients when they entered treatment provide the basis for the arrest rate used in the MMTP studies. The postadmission arrest rates were apparently not based on official records. Instead, they were compiled from counselor reports, legal representatives at the clinics, and any information that may have filtered to the Narcotics Register. Therefore, the rates were subject to many uncontrollable errors. It is a simple matter to be thorough in compiling data in interviews at intake and for counselors to be less thorough, and patients more secretive, after they entered treatment. At another program, when counselors' knowledge of patients' arrests was compared to the official police records, the counselors were found to know about one-third of the charges encountered by the patients.[5] The counselors knew only of those arrests that resulted in the patient being detained, which simply does not occur in most cases, even for many felonies. It must be concluded that there is some underrepresentation in these figures for the postadmission period, although the precise extent cannot be estimated.

Finally, as data are presented for varying periods of retention in treatment the same cohorts are not followed. Patients who were discharged after one time span, say 1 year, were included in the figures for the first year but excluded from the second year. But those who withdrew always include a disproportionate share of recidivists; i.e., those who are arrested, return to drugs, etc. As noted previously, those who were less likely to find jobs and had more extensive criminal histories were much more likely to terminate. All programs, of course, go through a "self-cleansing," and any outcome measures

---

[5]A comparison was made of rates based on counselor reports for the National Institute of Mental Health, Texas Christian University (form 68–R1086) and rates based on official police records from the New York City Police Department.

will tend constantly to improve by this process alone. While the retention rates at MMTP are impressive for a program treating heroin addicts in the community, there is a constant attrition through time so that by the end of 4 years almost 40% of the original group are no longer in treatment.

The findings in this area, therefore, are relevant primarily to older addicts; and the methods of data collection and analysis all contribute to at least an exaggeration of the impact of the treatment, even if many hundreds of individuals have been helped. Similar observations may also be made about the increases in "social productivity" noted in the Gearing reports.

THE PATTERN OF ADDICT CRIME

Still another program, the Addiction Research and Treatment Corporation, has provided data. This program is located within a ghetto community. The ARTC is different from some other methadone programs in that most patients are maintained on lower dosages of methadone, a factor that has not been demonstrated to be significantly related to program retention or other parameters of program outcomes (Goldstein, 1970; Jaffe, 1970).

The following discussion presents data in a sequence that will provide some insight into the problem of comprehending the relationship between program outcomes and the crime problem in general. Although the data derive from only one program, the way the information is disassembled may be instructive.

Figure 1 shows the arrest rates for patients, following them through for 2 years after entering treatment. These arrests were based on official police records so that the inevitable differences that arise between official arrest rates and actual level of criminal activity probably influence all the rates, although there may have been some tendency for the police to treat registered patients somewhat differently. Figure 1 shows data for active patients, those who withdrew, and finally, all patients.

It is apparent that there was a substantial decline in arrests, although the rate did not vanish even for those who remained in treatment. But the rate of 78 the year before admission declined to 44 in the first year and to 32 by the end of two years, a decline of 59%. Even those who withdrew or dropped out had a much higher rate of arrests before they came into treatment, although even for this group there was a significant decline. Combining all patients, whether or not they remained in treatment, the impact appeared to be substantial, with less than half the arrest rate for all who were admitted within 2 years.

But arrest rates, even if they are accurate because they were obtained from official records, do not tell the full story. It has been noted that older parolees are much less likely to be recidivists. The impact of other crucial variables in the criminal picture must be deciphered to fully evaluate the impact of treatment.

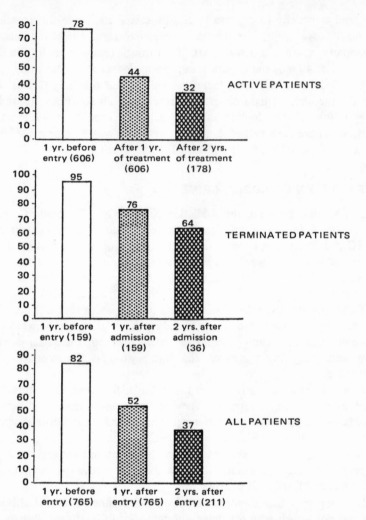

FIG. 1. Arrest rates for Addiction Research and Treatment Corporation patients 1 year before treatment, after 1 year of treatment, and after 2 years of treatment for all patients, active patients, and terminated patients.

First, the arrest records were re-analyzed. Rather than simply considering the number of arrests, the charges for which patients had been arrested were examined. What may seem like a fairly effective reduction in crime may then appear to be somewhat less dramatic.

In Figure 2 several rates are computed. The rate designated "Onset to entry in program" is the annual charge rate for all patients in the program from the date they began to use heroin regularly until they entered the program. The second rate is the charge rate in the year prior to entrance in the program.

This is followed by charges in the first year in the program, and then the rate for those in the program for 2 years.[6]

The top portion of Figure 2 shows rates for all 765 patients who were in the program for at least 1 year and the 216 who were in the program for 2

[6] Charge Index $= \dfrac{\text{total number arrests}}{\text{number patient months}}\; k/(.833)$

For the Onset-Entry indices the denominator is the total number of months from first regular drug use to the date of admission. For the remaining indices it is simply 12 times the number of patients. The constant (.833) adjusts the rate so that one arrest/year would result in an index value of 100, to facilitate interpretation. For the specific indices the numerator includes only the designated charges.

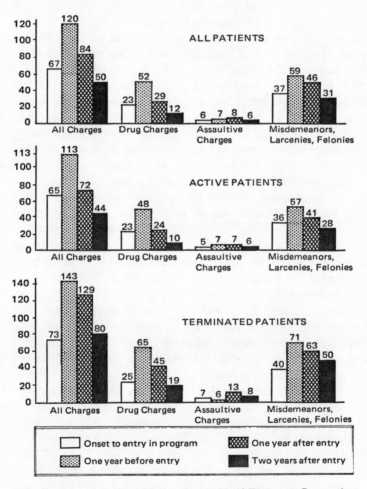

FIG. 2. Charge rates for Addiction Research and Treatment Corporation patients from onset to entry in program, 1 year before entry, 1 year after entry, and 2 years after entry.

years. This chart assesses the impact of the program on all who entered treatment, even though some were discharged or withdrew in the intervening timespan.

The middle portion of Figure 2 is limited to those who remained in treatment during the designated period. This chart shows whether their rates differed from those shown in the bottom portion, where rates for terminated patients are presented. A comparison of these charts aids in determining whether those who remain in treatment differed initially in their criminal behavior from those who left the program and whether the criminal behavior of those who stayed in treatment was altered more dramatically. It can also be observed, if only crudely, whether the program impact resulted in substantially different arrest experiences for patients who remained than for those who withdrew in the intervening periods.

There are four rates in each timespan: the overall rate and the arrest rates for charges classified as assaultive; drug related; and misdemeanors, felonies, and petty larcenies. The overall rate is the annual number of charges for the designated timespan. "Assaultive" includes all charges where there were weapons or where the patient was accused of inflicting physical injury on the victims. Drug arrests are those charges that are related to possession of drugs or "works." or for selling drugs. The balance, and the largest category, includes felonies, misdemeanors, and larcenies where there were no weapons or any indication that there was violence. Most charges were for shoplifting, forgery, pursesnatching, burglary, and similar crimes.

The onset-entry index measures the volume of crime in the patient group since they became addicted to heroin until the time of their admission to the program. Figure 2 shows that the typical patient had about two-thirds of an arrest per year since he had been using heroin, or seven arrests in a 10-year span.

The year just before the patients were admitted to the program, however, was a peak year for criminal activity: the rate for this time span was 120 for all patients (top of Figure 2), compared with 67 for the entire period since they became addicted. There was little change in Assaultive crimes (six compared to seven for the year prior to admission). Both drug arrests and those for misdemeanors, felonies, and petty larceny showed a steep rise.

The overall crime index for the first year in the program declined relative to the year prior to their admission in the program from 120 to 84, although it was still higher than the rate based on their arrest histories over the full timespan of their drug addiction. There was a slight, although negligible, increase in assaultive crimes. Petty misdemeanors, felony, and larceny charges decreased from 59 to 46. The largest decline, however, was for drug-related charges. These showed a steep drop from 52 to 29 per annum. Thus, it is apparent that the decline in criminal activity in the first year of the program was primarily attributable to the sharp drop in drug charges. This was accompanied by a smaller decline in misdemeanors and petty larceny charges. This decline is to be expected since patients were using much less heroin, some none at all, and therefore were less likely to be arrested for possession.

Analysis of the overall crime index for 216 patients who were in the program for two years shows considerable improvement in reduction of criminal activity in the second year. The overall index declined from 84 at the end of the first year to 50 in the second year. As was observed in the discussion of the decline of specific charge rates from the year prior to the year after admission, the most significant decline occurred in the drug-related charge category (from 29 to 12). There was a minimal decline in the assaultive crime index in the second year (from 7 to 6). However, the decline in the index of felonies, petty misdemeanors and petty larceny was somewhat more significant in the second year than in the first. This index was 31 in the second year as compared with 46 in the first year. Although the picture markedly improved, the overall index remained fairly high relative to the overall Onset-Entry index (50 and 67, respectively).

The middle and bottom portions of Figure 2 separate patients who remained in treatment from those who terminated in the particular timespan. Several important trends emerge. First, terminated patients had higher charge rates prior to their entering treatment than did patients who remained in treatment, demonstrating that those who are retained tend to be less "criminal" to begin with. In the year preceding entrance, active patients had a rate of 113, compared with 143 for terminated patients. Despite this generally higher level of preprogram criminal activity, however, addicts who terminated also showed an apparent decline in criminal activity, although it was markedly smaller than for active patients.

On examination of the particular charges for which patients have been arrested, it is seen that only the treated group show reduced arrest rates in the felony, larceny, and misdemeanor category below the rates that prevailed over their entire period as addicts (onset to entry). This does not occur, however, until after 2 years of treatment. The rates for felony, misdemeanor and larceny charges for those patients who remained in treatment declined from 36 to 28 after 2 years, a 22% decline in such charges. Their drug arrests, on the other hand, declined 57% over the same 2 years, from 23 to 10. When the rates during treatment are contrasted to rates reported during the year prior to entrance, a more rapid decline appears; but, as noted earlier, this year was a peak period for arrests among this group of patients.[7]

Although a comparison of the year prior to treatment and successive time period for terminated patients also showed a decline in arrest rates, for those charges that are most directly related to crime on the streets, there was little change. Assaultive charges after 2 years approximated the rate that characterized this group over most of their period as addicts. A similar observation was made for felony, misdemeanor, and larceny charges. Only drug charges

[7]A similar observation was documented in a study of patients in the New York City Methadone Maintenance Treatment Program (Gearing, 1972).

showed a drop, but these patients were in the program receiving methadone during at least part of the period.

In summary, when arrests were studied by types of charges for active and terminated patients it was observed that

1. Patients who remained in treatment differed from patients who were terminated by having fewer arrests prior to entrance in treatment.

2. A substantial proportion of the decline was attributable to fewer arrests directly associated with the purchase, possession, and sale of drugs.

3. The year prior to treatment provided a base that exaggerated the decline in criminal activity.

4. The decline in the crimes that most concern the community required a prolonged investment in treatment before they began to decline relative to crime rates based on their full period of drug-use.

AGE OF ONSET OF DRUG
USE AND ARRESTS

Some perspective on the issue of the persistence of criminal behavior may be gained by looking simultaneously at two variables: age of onset of daily drug use and whether there is an arrest on the police records that antedates drug use. Those who began drug use at an early age are underrepresented because juvenile records were not available.[8] At least 44% of the patients were involved with the criminal justice system even before they used heroin regularly. For those whose addiction did not begin until after 22 years of age, 60% had been arrested on a variety of charges before daily heroin use, and 32% of those whose drug use began when they were still young. This, of course, lends credence to the thesis that drug use, for a substantial portion of ghetto addicts, is preceded by other forms of deviant behavior. These figures, moreover, are undoubtedly an underestimate.

Table 7 shows the preprogram arrest patterns. Note that those with charges that antedate heroin use, irrespective of age of onset, tended to have higher rates on all charges. When only larcenies, felonies, and misdemeanors are examined, to the exclusion of drug charges, the differences associated with arrests prior to drug use are even more substantial. Youthful onset is also generally associated with higher rates of criminality when contrasted to those whose drug use began later, but who are in the same category of preheroin use arrests.

It should also be noted that a substantial portion of those who have no preheroin arrests managed to avoid being arrested at all: 19% of those who began drug use at 21 years of age or earlier and 43% whose drug use began

[8] Self-reports on juvenile crime that may refine this classification will be examined at a later date.

TABLE 7

Age of Onset of Daily Heroin Use; Arrests Prior to Drug Use and Charge Pattern
Before Treatment (Percent)

Charge[a]	Preaddiction charges, by age of onset regular heroin use			
	21 and under		22 and above	
	Yes	No	Yes	No
All charges, onset of drug use to program entry:[b]				
None	4.1	19.2	15.5	42.7
Low	11.6	17.3	17.6	15.3
High	84.3	63.5	66.9	42.0
Total	100.0	100.0	100.0	100.0
Larcenies, felonies, and misdemeanors:[b]				
None	10.8	30.0	32.6	57.3
Low	27.9	32.2	27.3	23.4
High	61.3	37.8	40.1	19.3
Total	100.0	100.0	100.0	100.0
Never arrested	–	19.2	–	42.7
Number of cases	(147)	(307)	(187)	(124)

[a]Low are those with charge rate less than .33 per year; high are those with higher rates.
[b]Excludes drug-specific charges and assaultive charges.

when they were at least 22 years old. Thus, for some heroin addicts criminal
behavior is at a much lower level, and the kinds of crimes that the community
finds most offensive are less often committed by this group.

More careful analysis must take place before all factors can be unravelled.
However, even so crude an index as the one used here distinguishes different criminal patterns and identifies a substantial number with no criminal records at all.

Table 8 shows that these patterns generally persisted after patients entered
treatment. The information is restricted to the first year of treatment. Again,
those who began drug use earlier were more likely to be arrested as well as
those who were arrested before heroin use became a daily affair. Another
control, chronological age, needs to be introduced that will undoubtedly
strengthen the patterns observed here.[9]

[9]Older patients have fewer larcenies, felonies, and misdemeanors. Those who began
drug use earlier are, on the whole, a younger group of patients. The typical patient was
using heroin for 10 years before he began treatment; therefore, younger patients tend to
have started drug use at an earlier age.

TABLE 8

Age of Onset of Daily Heroin Use; Arrests Prior to Drug Use and Arrests: First
Year in Treatment (Percent)

| Arrests and charges | Preaddiction charges, by age at onset of regular heroin use | | | |
| | 21 and under | | 22 and above | |
	Yes	No	Yes	No
Number of arrests:				
None	59.2	68.8	63.7	80.7
1-2	23.8	17.0	25.6	15.3
3 or more	17.0	14.2	10.7	4.0
Total	100.0	100.0	100.0	100.0
Charges:				
Assaultive charges	11.6	5.9	4.3	2.4
Drug charges	18.7	18.6	18.2	9.7
Misdemeanors, larcenies, and felonies	26.4	22.1	24.0	10.5
Number of cases	(147)	(307)	(187)	(124)

Observe, also, that assaultive charges, those that involve violence to the person or the use of dangerous weapons, occur considerably more often in the younger onset group where arrests antedate drug use.

The present analysis is necessarily incomplete because there was detailed access to only one program. References to other studies, while they suggest that there be an exaggeration in the crime reduction that has been reported, do not preclude the very real impact this program has had for many patients. But to develop the thesis of this report further, some conclusions might be drawn in relation to the impact of ambulatory methadone programs on criminal behavior and the consequences of an extension of similar treatment modalities on the epidemiology of drug use, more particularly the recruitment of new addicts. These conclusions are as follows:

1. Arrest rates alone tend to exaggerate the decline in criminal behavior.

2. The decline in criminal behavior—in fact any conformist behavior—is contingent on increasing chronological age.

3. More conventional socialization, as reflected by education, family status, and employment, are linked to age of onset of drug use and have consequences for the retention of patients as well as continuous deviant behavior.

4. Programs are attracting patients who are older than most heroin addicts; these programs succeed in retaining the older patients and those who were less deviant in other respects.

5. Program mortality, although impressively low for methadone patients when compared with other treatment modalities, does appear continuous and unrelenting even for those who have been in treatment for several years.

6. A large part of the decline in crime is a function of the unusually high rates in the period preceding entrance and possibly is the reason why many enter treatment. The largest part of the decline is attributable to fewer arrests for drug charges.

7. Those with arrests preceding heroin use tend to persist in criminal behavior; and where they began drug use when young, these persons are responsible for a high proportion of assaultive crimes.

COMMUNITY PARAMETERS

The forms of deviant conduct and the magnitude observed for its many varieties are never random events. Whether suicide or alcoholism or murder or drug abuse, such conduct is invariably located in some societies and not in others, and more often in particular groups than in others located in the same society. This, of course, is the point of departure for the sociological analysis of deviance. The theories that exist, however inadequate they may be, endeavor to unravel the social and cultural forces that account for the prevalence of certain forms of deviance in particular social contexts.

Drug abuse with attendant crime, whether conceived as moving from drug use to crime, or as emerging from very similar mechanisms, is concentrated in particular communities. Heroin use is primarily found in black, Puerto Rican, and Chicano communities. White addicts generally have to carry on many of their activities where addicts congregate, which is in the ghettoes.

We have been suggesting—perhaps urging is more apt—that drug addiction must be examined in much the same way as are other forms of deviance and that the processes are integrated into the very fabric of communities. This thesis is only suggested because it would be a more complex analysis to demonstrate this in an altogether satisfactory way. Data are presented from a community survey carried out in the catchment area of the Addiction Research and Treatment Corporation. The description of the sample and additional data relevant to the thesis may be found in Lukoff (1972b).

Despite the fear addicts create in the communities they inhabit and the direct suffering they often inflict, there is an important sense in which addicts are significant members of their communities. They carry out activities for established segments of the nonaddicted population who support and maintain them. Indeed, unless there were such an integration of the addict in his community, he could not survive as well as he does.

Heroin addicts are intimately linked to a complex market system in which they can dispose of stolen goods through highly organized channels, well described by Tardola (1970) and Cartey (1970). Behind this important market system are merchants, brokers, and customers who provide the necessary mechanisms for marketing the stolen goods; and these persons finally bring the addict and his customer together, if not always directly then through intermediaries. How extensive this system is cannot be accurately gauged because by its very nature firm information is unobtainable.

The community survey obtained information on whether respondents had friends or acquaintances who were heroin users,[10] whether they had been offered stolen goods, and if they knew a place where they could purchase stolen goods. Table 9 shows that as one's acquaintance with heroin users is more extensive, the likelihood of admitting having been offered stolen goods and knowing where to find them increases.

The addict is not an isolated member of the community in another fundamental sense, not simply as a provider of important economic services. Forty-seven percent of respondents under 30 stated that they had friends who used heroin. A substantial proportion (21%) of those over 30 acknowledged friends who have used heroin.

Table 10 shows that increasing contiguity[11] with drug users is both a function of age and length of residence in the community. For persons under 30, 40% knew addicts; this increases to 68% for respondents who have resided in the community over 5 years. Older persons, on the other hand, appear to be less likely to become acquainted with addicts even after an extended residence in the community.

[10]These "users" are not necessarily addicts: the question concerned only persons who used heroin.

[11]"High on contiguity" means reporting that a friend or a family member has used heroin.

TABLE 9

Deviant Network and Reporting Offers of Stolen Goods and Knowledge of Places to Purchase Stolen Goods (Percent)

Statement	Acquaintance with heroin users[a]		
	None	One	Two
Offered stolen goods	25	39	50
Know place to buy stolen goods	4	5	15
Number of cases	(329)	(115)	(143)

[a]Count on whether respondent reports acquaintance or friends have used heroin.

TABLE 10

Age, Length of Time in Community, and Reporting Friends or Family Members
Who Have Used Heroin

| Age | High on contiguity with drug users[a] | | | |
| | Less than 5 years in community | | 5 years or more in community | |
	Percent	Number	Percent	Number
Under 30	40	(104)	68	(46)
30 and cover	20	(149)	21	(267)

[a]"High on contiguity" means reporting that a friend or family member has used heroin.

The issues are complex. They have been explored in more detail in other papers, and still more has to be learned. It has been noted that in treatment centers, whether isolated facilities (like Lexington) or community-based programs, the focus is on patients (and sometimes families). However, a very complex social system exists that is often at cross-purposes with the objectives of treatment programs. The very structure of the community facilitates and stabilizes the addicts' lifestyle in numerous ways. The present study has cited the way in which only one form of illicit activity important to the addict is a major economic force in the community. It has also been demonstrated how a large segment of the nonaddict population is on intimate terms with addicts and how younger people, especially as they remain in the community, are more often on intimate enough terms with addicts to identify them as friends than is the converse. Addicts are part of the community and not merely an isolated segment inhabiting empty tenements.

The treatment system may also unwittingly help to stabilize the addicts' adaptation without necessarily contributing to any significant alteration in illicit activities. For example, ambulatory methadone programs are anxious to accept patients and will accept anyone who is identified as an addict. Moreover, for many patients the program serves as a basic source of supply for narcotics which they can supplement with preferred drugs whenever it is possible, and if they are careful, with impunity. Although the experience reported by different programs on continuous drug use of methadone patients is variable, it is clear that many patients still consume heroin and other drugs (Lukoff & Quatrone, 1973). Becoming a member of a program is also a way to obtain financial support, since addicts are accepted for welfare if they are registered in a treatment program. Twenty-seven thousand addicts affiliated with treatment programs, mainly methadone maintenance, are receiving welfare in New York City. In January 1973 there were, at the same time, 32,551 patients in the various methadone programs in the city. It is not altogether clear that this effort is making any significant dent in crime or other forms of deviant activity. The programs may be helping the older addict make his transition to some accommodation to the straight world. Certainly, a substantial segment of the population in treatment are using the programs as a buffer that does not rehabilitate them but only serves to make their lives more bearable.

SOME EPIDEMIOLOGICAL IMPLICATIONS

As already stated, it would be desirable to draw implications concerning the possible impact the treatment system might have in reducing the recruitment of new addicts. Necessarily, our analysis is confined to some publicly available data; this, perforce, places limits on the generalizability of any conclusions drawn thus far. There is more information on other programs, but programs studied thus far provided data that essentially conform to the findings cited in the present study (Brecher, 1972; DeLong, 1972).

Despite these limitations, it is important to scrutinize the treatment system more carefully than has been done previously. But as already indicated, addicts who are being helped are those who are about ready to change either because they were more conventional all the time, as indicated by a variety of indicators, or because the maturing-out hypothesis (Winick, 1962) is probably more viable than many have thought.

What follows is a rough schema of the "Heroin System." It is not a complete model nor does it attempt to specify all the possible directions people may take as they move through the various segments identified in Figure 3.

The treatment system is at the left side of Figure 3. Addicts can move in and out of the active addict population, and the route between the treatment system to the criminal justice system is also a two-way street. Insofar as addicts are imprisoned (on the right side) or in treatment facilities that are removed from the community, then there is little movement into the other subsystems.

Almost all programs, however, are now ambulatory or community based. It has been observed that treatment systems now functioning are successful primarily with older addicts who have been addicted for long periods of time. Those who are younger or only recently addicted flow back into the addict population in the manner of a revolving door. This is true for drug-free and methadone programs. Those younger addicts who are rehabilitated are generally those who were less deviant to begin with and who have the background and personal resources to make it in the straight world. They are few in number.

But who is recruited into the addict culture? It is primarily younger addicts, although it should be noted that blacks in ARTC are more often inducted into the heroin scene at somewhat older ages, even if most are still in their teens and early 20s.

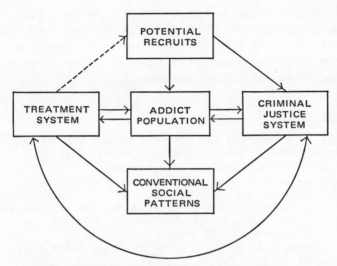

FIG. 3. Simplified schema of heroin addiction system.

Who recruits the potential addict? The experience of ARTC patients and reports from all other programs that inquire into the circumstances in which persons were first offered heroin indicate it is almost always peers. But it is precisely the peers of potential addicts who stay away from treatment programs; or, if they do enter treatment, are more likely to withdraw and return to the streets.

The conclusion of the present study, some of it conjecture, but using the only information available, is that the expansion of treatment programs can have only a negligible impact on the recruitment of new addicts, unless they can succeed in attracting and successfully working with large numbers of younger addicts.

Given the current state of the art, a strategy that mobilizes resources and energy on treatment systems alone is one that essentially does not intrude on the continuous supply of new addicts. Addiction is not simply crime on the streets and the personal destruction it inflicts on thousands of young men and women, but it must also be understood as a functional element in some communities—certainly for some segments of the nonaddicted inhabitants.

This chapter has raised some questions concerning the dramatic reports that have been presented concerning methadone. It is useful to have mechanisms to help even older addicts get their bearings. But such programs probably will not interfere with the crime wave because the addicts who continue to commit crimes are not likely to remain in treatment.

Moreover, the market for methadone may have been saturated by the rapid expansion that has been underway. All methadone programs in New York City, whether run by the Health Services Administration, other publicly supported programs, or the large number of private programs, have facilities for over 40,000 addicts. In January 1973, however, there were only 32,551 persons in treatment. No one suggests that there are only 32,000 heroin addicts in New York City. The current treatment system is under-utilized, suggesting that many addicts prefer the accommodations they have made to the prospect of abandoning the heroin scene.

REFERENCES

Bowden, C. L., & Langenauer, B. J. Success and failure in the NARA addiction program. *American Journal of Psychiatry*, 1972, 128(7), 853–856.

Brecher, E. M. *Licit and illicit drugs.* Boston: Little, Brown, 1972.

Cartey, D. How black enterprises do their thing: An odyssey through ghetto capitalism. In G. Jacobs (Ed.), *The participant observer.* New York: George Braziller, 1970.

Chambers, C. D., Babst, D. V., & Warner, A. Characteristics predicting long-term retention in a methadone program. *Proceedings of the Third National Conference on Methadone Treatment,* 1970, 140–143.

Chein, I., Gerard, D. L., Lee, R. S., & Rosenfeld, E. *The road to H.* New York: Basic Books, 1964.

Cloward, R. A., & Ohlin, L. E. *Delinquency and opportunity.* New York: The Free Press, 1960.

DeLong, J. V. Treatment and rehabilitation. In *Dealing with drug abuse,* a report to the Ford Foundation.: Praeger, 1972.

Gearing, F. R. Success and failures in methadone maintenance treatment of heroin addictions in New York City. *Proceedings of the Third National Conference on Methadone Treatment,* 1970, 2–16.

Gearing, F. R. Road back from heroin addiction. *Proceedings of the Fourth National Conference on Methadone Treatment,* 1972, 157–158.

Goldstein, A. Dosage, duration, side effects. *Proceedings of the Third National Conference on Methadone Treatment,* 1970, 31–37.

Hayim, G. J. Changes in the criminal behavior of heroin addicts under treatment in the Addiction Research and Treatment Corporation: Interim report of the first year of treatment. In U.S. Department of Justice, Law Enforcement Assistance Administration, *Heroin use and crime in a methadone maintenance program: An interim report.* Washington, D.C.: U.S. Government Printing Office, 1973.

Jaffe, J. H. Methadone maintenance: Variation in outcome criteria as a function of dose. *Proceedings of the Third National Conference on Methadone Treatment,* 1970, 31–37.

Lukoff, I. F. Social and ethnic patterns of reported heroin use and contiguity with drug users. In U.S. Department of Justice, Law Enforcement Assistance Administration, *Some aspects of the epidemiology of heroin use in a ghetto community: A preliminary report.* Washington, D.C.: U.S. Government Printing Office, 1972. (a)

Lukoff, I. F. The vicious circle: Drug use, illicit activities and victimization. Unpublished manuscript, Addiction Research and Treatment Corporation Evaluation Team, Columbia University School of Social Work, 1972. (b)

Lukoff, I. F., & Quatrone, D. A two-year follow-up of the Addiction Research and Treatment Corporation, In U. S. Department of Justice, Law Enforcement Assistance Administration, *Heroin use and crime in a methadone maintenance program: An interim report.* Washington, D.C.: U.S. Government Printing Office, 1973.

Lukoff, I. F., & Vorenberg, J. Methadone maintenance evaluation studies: Some unresolved issues on crime and drug use. *Proceedings of the Fourth National Conference on Methadone Treatment,* 1972, 489–492.

Methadone Maintenance and Detox Census in New York City. New York: Health Services Administration, Jan. 24, 1973.

Nash, G., Waldorf, D., Foster, K., & Kyllingstad, A. The Phoenix House Program—The results of a two-year follow-up. Unpublished manuscript, (none), 1973.

Newman, R. G. *Proceedings of the Third National Conference on Methadone Treatment,* 1970, 123.

New York City Department of Health, *Narcotics Register,* 1969 (Mimeograph).

Perkins, N. E., & Bloch, H. J. Evaluation of methadone maintenance treatment program. *International Journal of the Addictions,* 1970, 5(3), 517–543. (a)

Perkins, N. E., & Bloch, H. J. Survey of a methadone maintenance treatment program. *American Journal of Psychiatry,* 1970, 126(10), 33–40. (b)

Preble, E. Social and cultural factors related to narcotic use among Puerto Ricans in New York City. *International Journal of the Addictions,* 1966, 1(1), 30–41.

Preble, E., & Casey, J. J., Jr. Taking care of business—The heroin user's life on the street. *Interntional Journal of the Addictions,* 1969, 4(1), 1–24.

Quatrone, D. Profile of active and terminated patients in a methadone maintenance program. Unpublished manuscript, Addiction Research and Treatment Corporation Evaluation Team, Columbia University School of Social Work, 1972.

Sardell, A. Age of addiction as a predictor of conventional behavior in heroin addicts. Unpublished manuscript, Addiction Research and Treatment Corporation Evaluation Team, Columbia University School of Social Work, 1972.

Sutherland, E. H., & Cressey, D. R. *Principles of criminology,* 7th ed. Philadelphia: Lippincott, 1966.

Tardola, H. The needle scene. In G. Jacobs (Ed.), *The participant observer.* New York: George Braziller, 1970.

Vaillant, G. E. A twelve-year follow-up of New York addicts. IV. Some characteristics and determinants of abstinence. *American Journal of Psychiatry,* 1966, 123(9), 573–584.

Winick, C. Maturing out of narcotic addiction. *UN Bulletin on Narcotics,* 1962, 14(1), 1–7.

Winick, C. The life cycle of the narcotic addict and of addiction. *UN Bulletin on Narcotics,* 1964, 16, 1–11.

9

METHODOLOGICAL CONSIDERATIONS FOR A MODEL REPORTING SYSTEM OF DRUG DEATHS

Dan J. Lettieri and Michael S. Backenheimer
National Institute on Drug Abuse

INTRODUCTION

The task of initiating and carrying out a systematic collecting and reporting of drug-related deaths has never been done satisfactorily despite much reporting of statistics (and their implications) on the topic. For most purposes of classifying death, the 8th revision of the *International Classification of Diseases, Adapted* (1968) (ICDA) is viewed as a model to be implemented. The classifications in the ICDA are used to report mortality statistics in the United States by the National Center for Health Statistics. For purposes of extensively examining drug-related deaths, this system of reporting has several weaknesses. The system does have the virtue of separating out intentional (suicide), unintentional (accidents and homicide), and undetermined intentional deaths due to drugs; but the drug classifications used are too omnibus when viewed as a means of measuring the nature and extent of the drug abuse problem. For example, a classification generally referred to as "morphine and other derivatives" includes heroin, morphine, methadone, and other opiates such as demerol. The illegal drugs of abuse are thus classified with drugs that can be abused but that also have a place in the legitimate medical treatment model. It is quite difficult to separate out deaths due to specific drugs or even to separate out those drug deaths resulting from a therapeutic misadventure (and thus occuring in a legitimate medical context). Using this same ICD model it is possible to overlook or miss some drug-related deaths by coding them in such categories as "pulmonary edema," "pending toxicology," etc. New York City, using its own reporting system of drug deaths, reports as many drug deaths as the rest of the nation combined. Standardization of criteria, definitions, and tests have yet to be established; moreover, the need for such data is both obvious and pressing. As a final indicator of drug abuse and addiction, drug-related death statistics are critical.

OBJECTIVES AND AIMS

This study presents a reporting model for drug-related deaths using statistics from diverse sources. The focus is the reporting model rather than the data presented. After presenting available data in a suggested reporting scheme, the discussion shifts to confounding considerations of why the data cannot be construed to mean what they appear to demonstrate. As a final aim, a model reporting scheme is presented. This model does not address itself to all issues but, on balance, suggests a workable model that answers some of the more pressing questions about drug-related deaths.

SOURCES AND AVAILABILITY OF DATA

Available data on drug-related deaths are limited in many ways. There are really three systems through which drug-related deaths are reported, with very little consistency prevailing between systems. These systems can be thought of as a medical examiner system, a coroner system, and some combination of the two.

Medical Examiner System

Of the three systems, more validity and reliability can be attributed to data furnished by a medical examiner than to data furnished by the other two sources. A medical examiner is both a physician and a pathologist and is usually an expert in forensic pathology. He holds office as an appointed official and functions at the state (not local) level. The medical examiner thus is freed from pressures of local elections and politics and he can be objective. The resources of states employing a medical examiner system are usually highly centralized; thus, lab reports, autopsy findings, etc. emanate from the same source rather than from several sources of varying degrees of competence.

Coroner System

Although data provided by a coroner system is generally quite valid and reliable, there is, nevertheless, more room for error in the coroner system than in the medical examiner model. Coroners are autonomous in that their jurisdiction is precisely spelled out and is never statewide. Thus there is no centralization of authority or decision-making in states employing this system, and the number of coroners in any given state may vary from a few to several hundred. Coroners are not shielded from local pressures. Because they are elected officials they cannot avoid local pressures and politics. What may happen in the coroner system is that the data provided by such systems serve as a comparison of different coroners rather than as a compilation of data on cause and mode of death. The education and training of coroners can be extensive or quite minimal. Many, but not all, are physicians. Some are full-time workers, others part-time. Some are pathologists, but many are not; and a few may be lawyers as well as physicians. There are localities where the local justice of the peace is also the coroner. In such cases the justice of the peace need not have any medical or legal training. Such diversity serves to introduce much error into the mortality reporting system.

Combination System

While this model has many variations, often a medical examiner model exists within a central city of a state while a coroner model exists in other parts of the state, or perhaps several medical examiners have split responsibility for a state. This system, no matter how effective, lacks the centralization concept of a pure medical examiner system.

Other Considerations

Considerations other than the type of death collection system need mention. These can be conceptualized as cross-cut variables since they can introduce bias and error into any system.

1. Quality of relationships. A reporting model of drug-related deaths (particularly when couched in a drug abuse and drug addiction context) must at least note that the quality of relationship which the coroner or medical examiner has with the hospitals, police, physicians, undertakers, etc. will play a role in what deaths are brought to his attention. The poorer his relationship with the people who first see death, the more likely some deaths will not be brought to his attention and hence missed.

2. The economic factor. All death collection systems operate within a fixed budget. This economic variable functionally determines which deaths are examined, which are autopsied, and which undergo toxicologic study. Most bodies undergoing autopsy are not toxicologically examined. This means that at least some drug-related deaths are not recorded as such. Further, the justification for classifying a death as drug-related requires rather extensive and expensive investigation on the part of the medical examiner or coroner; and conceivably there exists the enhanced temptation to opt to a "cheaper" but still acceptable "other" cause of death.

3. The problem of definition. Many drug-related deaths are not counted in the present system because the toxic substances in and of themselves do not singularly cause death. Many drug-related deaths do not have a pharmacologic potential for death per se; rather it is the consequent actions of the drug or drugged state that may actually cause death. Such deaths are often misrecorded. Deaths due to drug intoxication (e.g., committing suicide while

on LSD) generally do not find their way into the existing classification scheme. Other types of drug-related deaths such as homicide while on drugs, accidents while drug intoxicated, and hepatitis from dirty needles are often missed.

THE CURRENT MODEL

Given that the available data on drug-related deaths are flawed in many ways, how can they best be used? The following model is presented as one scheme of how drug data might be analyzed to give immediate emphasis to the drug abuse and addiction problem.

Conceptual Frame

For this model, drug death data are seen as a measure of excess mortality. Excess mortality refers to the extent to which drug addicts are more likely to die than other population groups. In essence, the goal is analogous to the "high risk estimates" currently made with respect to cigarette smokers, viz., that smokers are at risk to a much higher (and known) extent than are nonsmokers.

Methodology

To carry out the concept several pieces of information were obtained. Some estimate of the live addict population was necessary as well as some estimate of the number of deaths occurring within this population. This allowed a mortality rate to be computed for the addict population. The same kinds of information were necessary for the comparison population. The resulting mortality rates were then compared and conclusions drawn. One correction factor in estimating deaths which has been used is the number of "man years at risk." Essentially, such a statistic controls for differential time periods of exposure to and use of drugs; moreover, this statistic, when available, serves much the same function as age-adjusted corrections applied to the calculation of death rates. While such a correction factor is desirable, availability of data parameters to establish such a correction are rarely available.

In the example demonstrated, 1970 population estimates were obtained on eight selected areas, each encompassing as a main component a large city and each making up the major portion of a standard metropolitan statistical area (SMSA). Mortality data were then obtained. Two mortality rates were computed, that for the general population of each area, all ages, all causes, and that for the general population of each area, all causes but limited in age to persons aged 15-44. The age-limited mortality rate was computed since it was felt that most addicts and therefore most drug-related deaths would be in the age range 15-44. The general population and mortality estimates for these areas are shown in Table 1.

TABLE 1

Death Rate Estimates for 1969 by Selected Areas

Area	1970 Population estimate (all ages)	Actual number of deaths, 1969, all ages, all causes	Death rate per 1,000 population, all ages, all causes	1970 population estimate, ages 15–44	Actual number of deaths, 1969, ages 15–44, all causes	Death rate per 1,000 population, ages 15–44, all causes	Major city within area
Allegheny County	1,605,016	17,567	11	617,718	1,018	2	Pittsburgh
Baltimore City	905,759	11,567	13	357,662	1,199	3	–
Cook County	5,492,369	57,248	10	2,230,844	5,216	2	Chicago
Dallas County	1,327,321	9,653	7	596,066	1,174	2	Dallas
Los Angeles County	7,032,075	62,865	9	2,996,720	6,072	2	Los Angeles
Marion County	792,299	7,281	9	327,722	620	2	Indianapolis
Philadelphia City	1,948,609	24,932	13	761,494	1,904	3	–
Wayne County	2,666,751	26,900	10	1,063,073	2,672	3	Detroit

Note.–The actual death figures have been furnished by the National Center for Health Statistics, Division of Vital Statistics (unpublished data).

Obtaining estimates of addict populations and addict deaths was a more difficult task than getting comparison (general) population estimates. Table 2 presents estimates of live addict populations within selected areas. Eventually it was decided to err on the conservative side and use the Bureau of Narcotic and Dangerous Drugs (BNDD) 1972 estimates. Estimates given by police, drug experts, and health departments were really guesses rather than counts. The BNDD figures reflect an actual count of the already identified addict population. While recognizing the many difficulties inherent in such a count, it was still thought to be better than the other estimates.

Obtaining drug death data for the selected areas was a most unrewarding task. Such drug death data as were available were not collected by any

TABLE 2

Number of Active Addicts in Selected Areas as Estimated by Different Sources, 1972

Area	BNDD[a] estimate	Local police	Local drug expert	Local health department
Allegheny County	371	NA[b]	NA	10,000–12,000[c]
Baltimore City	1,257	NA	8,000[c,d]	12,000–14,000[c,d]
Cook County	3,479	NA	30,000[c,d]	30,000[c]
Dallas County	175	NA	2,000	3,000 (City)
Los Angeles County	1,368	2,000–5,000[c]	61,000[c,d]	5,000[c]
Marion County	115	4,000[e]	4,000–7,000[c]	5,000–7,000[c]
Philadelphia City	2,185	NA	20,000–30,000[c,d]	20,000–25,000[c,d]
Wayne County	6,144[f]	10,000[c,f]	30,000–35,000[f,g]	29,000–40,000[c]

[a]BNDD = Bureau of Narcotics and Dangerous Drugs.
[b]NA = not available.
[c]Heroin addicts.
[d]Figures for the entire state.
[e]Indianapolis.
[f]Detroit.
[g]Opiate addicts.

uniform geographic or political boundaries, some data being by county, some by city, and some by SMSA. The areas selected for study overcame this problem as much as possible; but, even so, the final product was somewhat of a mix of city, county, and SMSA. While there was no way to accurately assess the error thus introduced, the comparison, for purposes of demonstration, was still felt to be useful, both in terms of the excess mortality concept and in terms of highlighting the difficulty of collecting comparable data.

Two estimates of drug deaths were available, one from BNDD and one from Kirschner Associates (unpublished data). Table 3 shows these data as they were available. The differences between the two estimates are in some cases striking. The lower drug death mortality estimates (Kirschner) were chosen for incorporation into a summary table (Table 4) since these estimates would be conservative and thus not overstate the problem.

Table 4 shows that addicts are indeed at risk of death—to a much greater extent than is the population in general. The predicted death rate for addicts aged 15–44 is predicated on that age range accounting for 80% of all addict deaths. This is a most conservative estimate in light of available data. (For example, of 105 drug deaths in Maryland in 1971, 91 percent were between ages of 16 and 30.) While much error and slippage exists in the presented data, they nevertheless serve to point up the risk of drug taking.

The problem of defining drug death is clearly evidenced by the wide variations between areas and in particular by Detroit, which reported only one drug-related death in a 3-year period. It would be most worthwhile to examine the classification schemes within each system and arrive at uniform definitions.

In summary, the data presented should serve only as a model as to how existing drug death data may be used fruitfully. The wide discrepancy between cities, the various kinds of drug death collection systems, and other variables only serve to emphasize the need for careful reporting of drug-related deaths.

PRELIMINARY ISSUES AND DEFINITIONS IN A MODEL SYSTEM

Overdose

This is a term that obfuscates more than it clarifies. It would seem to imply an adverse reaction that needs treatment. Certainly it does not necessarily imply lethality, although its shorthand notation OD has come to mean death from drugs. Forensic pathologists (*Medical World News*, 1973) have recently argued against the widespread use of the word "overdose" on death certificates primarily because there appear to be no consistent toxicologic standards for evaluation of what in fact constitutes a lethal dosage. *The Consumers Union Report on Licit and Illicit Drugs* (1972) challenges the

TABLE 3
Addict Death Rates for Selected Areas per 1,000 Population

Area	Kirschner Associates estimates (unpublished data)					BNDD[a] estimates				
	Total live addicts, 1972	Addict death rate per 1,000, 1971	Total addict deaths			Total live addicts, 1972	Addict death rate per 1,000, 1971	Total addict deaths		
			1969	1970	1971			1969	1970	1971
Allegheny County	371	173	17	37	64	371	173	17	37	64
Baltimore City	1,257	68	57	57	85	1,257	111	72	70	139
Cook County	3,479	NA[b]	NA	NA	NA	3,479	89	202	277	310
Dallas County	175	57	2	8	10	175	126	NA	13	22
Los Angeles County	1,368	353	NA	359	483[c]	1,368	246	NA[d]	NA[d]	336[d]
Marion County	115	165	5	23	19	115	165	NA[e]	19[e]	19[e]
Philadelphia City	2,185	125	114	184	274	2,185	124	110	189	271
Wayne County	6,144[f]	0	0	0	1	6,144[f]	32	65[f]	133[f]	199[f]

[a] BNDD = Bureau of Narcotics and Dangerous Drugs.
[b] NA = not available.
[c] Fiscal year.
[d] Los Angeles City.
[e] Indianapolis.
[f] Detroit.

TABLE 4

Death Rates per 1,000 Population for Selected Populations and Areas

Area	Death rate, all causes, all ages, per 1,000, 1969	Death rate, drug addicts, all causes, all ages (Kirschner Associates estimate), per 1,000	Addict excess mortality per 1,000, all ages	Death rate, all causes, ages 15–44, 1969	Predicted death rate, drug addicts, ages 15–44 (80% of all addicts)	Addict excess mortality per 1,000, ages 15–44
Allegheny County	11	173	15.73	2	138	69.0
Baltimore County	9	68	7.56	3	54	18.0
Cook County	10	89[a]	8.90	2	71	35.5
Dallas County	7	57	8.14	2	46	23.0
Los Angeles County	10	353	35.30	2	282	141.0
Marion County	7	165	23.57	2	132	66.0
Philadelphia City	10	125	12.50	3	100	33.3
Wayne County	9	0	0	3	0	0

[a]Estimate by Bureau of Narcotics and Dangerous Drugs.

notion that any death of a confirmed, opiate-tolerant addict was caused by a pharmacologic overdose. The report postulates "Syndrome X," an unexplained, swiftly fatal reaction to the combination of heroin with other substances, such as alcohol, barbiturates, or the quinine used as a diluent. Medical examiners quickly concede that many deaths of addicts after "shooting up" show no evidence of larger-than-usual dosages. Part of the difficulty rests with the fact that tolerance is both relative and highly subject to change, and it is now believed that addicts can easily lose their tolerance in just several days.

Drug-related Deaths

There are two main classes of drug-related deaths: directly related drug deaths and indirectly related drug deaths.

A death is a directly related drug death if it can be shown that were the drug not present, the death would not have occurred. Thus the drug is a sufficient and necessary condition of the death. This type of definition eliminates some of the issues inherent in the use of the term "overdose" (what is an overdose, and for whom) as well as some, but certainly not all problems associated with differentiating between primary and secondary causes of death. In summary, a directly related drug death is one in which the drug is a sufficient and necessary condition or cause of the death. For instance, consider the case of an addict who uses an unsterile needle which in turn causes hepatitis and then death. The primary cause of death is the dirty needle and not the drug; however, drug-taking behavior is an auxiliary cause. If one applies the "sufficient and necessary" test to this case, clearly the death could have occurred with no drug in the syringe—the drug is clearly not a sufficient cause of death while it may or may not be a necessary cause. Such deaths, in this schema, are classed as indirectly related drug deaths.

A death is an indirectly related drug death when the drug may be a necessary but not sufficient condition to explain the death in question. For example, an addict who, under the influence of drugs, falls out a window and dies of massive contusions can be classed as an indirectly related drug death. The drug in this instance acts as a catalyst or triggering agent. In short, the drug alone is not sufficient cause (i.e., not pharmacologically toxic) for death, but it is a necessary contributor to the death in conjunction with some other drug, condition, or agent.

Issues in Defining Causes of Death

In 1968, an eighth revision of causes of death was published for coding various causes of death along international standards. This volume, referred to as the ICDA, 8th Revision (*International Causes of Death, Adapted,* 1968) vastly improved on the preceding coding scheme, and introduced two categories of importance to researchers in the field of narcotic and drug abuse. First, the category "drug dependence" (coded 304) was accepted as a cause of death and replaced the more limited notion of drug addiction. Second, the omnibus category "undetermined intentionality in the mode of death" (coded 980) was introduced to add flexibility and greater accuracy in the coding system. As yet, there is no inclusive category coding for drug-related deaths, partly because of the controversy surrounding what should be defined as a cause for a drug-related death. A very conservative estimate (see Table 5) would include only four basic categories: drug dependence, accidental poisonings by drugs and medicaments, suicide poisoning by solid and liquid substances, and poisoning by solid or liquid substances in which it is undetermined whether accidentally or purposely inflicted. Currently D. Greenberg from the National Center for Health Statistics, Mortality Statistics Branch, (unpublished data) has suggested using the four-category estimate, fully aware of its conservative, underestimating nature. It is here suggested that many drug-related deaths are buried in more general categories. Tables 6 and 7 list those categories.

A future task is to choose those other categories which should be counted in these estimations, and moreover to develop techniques to parcel out those deaths that are truly drug-related from those that are only apparently drug-related. The first, and perhaps the most feasible place to start is with the homicide mode of death. Much of the information necessary is readily available in police files.

Defining the Decedent or Agent of Death

Clearly one needs to clarify the distinction between the general conception of deaths that have a drug-related cause and the causes of death among addicts. The death rate for addicts is both empirically and conceptually

TABLE 5

Drug-related Death Schema

Category	Code
Drug dependence	304
Accidental poisoning by drug and other medicaments	850–859
Suicide and self-inflicted poisoning by solid and liquid substances (specified as drugs)	950.0–950.3
Poisoning by solid or liquid substances, undetermined whether accidentally or purposefully inflicted (specified as drugs)	980.0–980.3

Note.—Schema used by D. Greenberg, National Center for Health Statistics (unpublished data) based on *International Classification of Diseases Adapted* (1968). This system is highly conservative and clearly excludes drug deaths from therapeutic misadventure, alcohol deaths, narcotic related homicides, and the bulk of categories listed in Table 6.

TABLE 6

Causes of Death Currently Classified by the 8th ICDA Which may be Drug-related

ICDA code	Description
	Health conditions and complications
011.9	Pulmonary tuberculosis
269.9	Malnutrition (see also child neglect 994.9)
450	Embolic pneumonia
514	Pulmonary edema (see also 429; 519.1; 782.4)
517	Pulmonary fibrosis
686.1	Granulomatosis
785.2	Cholemia
No code	Decreased capacity for diffusion of carbon monoxide
	Unsterile conditions
037	Tetanus
038.1	Staphylococcal septicemia
424.9	Endocarditis
573.0	Hepatitis (viral and serum); see also 572; 573.9; 931.9
692.3	Dermatitis due to drugs
709.1	Diseases of skin due to tattoo
995.0	Air embolism
	Alcohol
571	Cirrhosis (see also 571.0; 571.8; 571.9)
291	Alcoholic psychoses (see especially 291.0; 291.1; 291.2; 291.3 and 291.9)
303	Alcoholism
	Mental health
297	Paranoid states
298	Other psychoses
299	Unspecified psychosis
	Drugs
304	Drug dependence[a]
761.7	Addicted infants (see also 778.9)
850–859	Accidental poisonings due to drugs and other medicaments
	Undetermined intentionality in poisoning by
980.0	Barbituric acid and derivatives
980.1	Salicylates and congeners
980.2	Psychotherapeutic agents
980.3	Other and unspecified drugs
	Suicide by
950.0	Barbituric acid and derivatives
950.1	Salicylates and congeners
950.2	Psychotherapeutic agents
950.3	Other and unspecified drugs
	Homicide
960–969	Homicide all causes
962	Homicide by poisoning

Source:—International Classification of Diseases, Adapted (1968).
[a]For clarification, see Table 7.

TABLE 7

ICDA Causes of Death Listed Under the Drug Dependence Category

Code	Description
304	Drug dependence
304.0	Opium, opium alkaloids, and their derivatives
304.1	Synthetic analgesics with morphinelike effects
304.2	Barbiturates
304.3	Other hypnotics and sedatives and tranquilizers
304.4	Cocaine
304.5	Cannabis sativa
304.6	Other psychostimulants
304.7	Hallucinogenics
304.8	Other
304.9	Unspecified

Source: –International Classification of Diseases, Adapted (1968).

different from the general population rates of death caused directly or indirectly by drugs. A model scheme must separate drug deaths in addicts from drug deaths in nonaddicts. In short the nature of the decedent must be specified along the following minimal characteristics: (1) Addict versus nonaddict versus victim of addict; (2) age; (3) sex; (4) race of decedent; (5) geographic location of death; (6) mode of death (natural, accidental, suicidal, homicidal, or undetermined mode); and (7) whether directly or indirectly drug-related versus nondrug related. In the section "Drug-related Homicides," some attention is given to the special problems relating to the drug-related homicide.

The model reporting system schematic. There are many ways to conceptualize an improved model reporting system. At the current state of inquiry it is sufficient to introduce a tentative scheme that attempts to specify those parameters that should be examined and along which lines data should be collected and stored. The schematic is presented in Table 8.

Drug-related homicides. A drug-related homicidal death is defined as one that involves, as a significant motivational or triggering factor, various kinds of drug-dealing, -seeking, or -taking behaviors. This rubric includes the death of innocent bystanders killed by an addict in the pursuit of funds to purchase narcotics, as well as those deaths perpetrated by individuals under the psychotogenic influence (e.g., paranoid reactions) of various drugs. As various investigators have noted, certain dealers will purposefully kill a troublesome addict by supplying him with an unusually potent supply. The complete matrix would be a 360×360 cell matrix in which the following $(2 \times 8 \times 3 \times 5 \times 3)$ subheadings would appear:

Person involved:
    A. 1. Perpetrator
       2. Victim

TABLE 8
Summarized Schematic of Model Reporting System

Decedent[a]	All deaths			
	Drug-related deaths			Non-drug-related deaths
	Directly related deaths	Indirectly related deaths	Undetermined relation (direct and/or indirect)	
Addict Current			Tentatively includes all causes of death listed in Table 6 when applicable	Tentatively includes all causes other than those listed in Table 6
Former				
Nonaddict				
Addiction unknown				
Victim of addict Decedent is addicted				
Is not addicted				
Addicted infant				

[a]It is understood that each class in the "Decedent" column would be further broken down in terms of age, sex, race, geography, and specific ICDA causes, especially the major drug involved.

Race:
    B. 1. White
       2. Black
       3. Puerto Rican, Cuban
       4. Mexican American (Chicano)
       5. American Indian
       6. Asian American
       7. Other
       8. Unknown
Addiction:
    C. 1. Addict
       2. Nonaddict (may include addicted infants)
       3. Addiction unknown
Age:
    D. 1. 0-14

2. 14-24
3. 25-44
4. 44+
5. Age unknown

Sex:

E. 1. Male
2. Female
3. Unknown

DIRECTIONS FOR THE FUTURE

Several recommendations and resolutions related to the format for collecting various kinds of death data already have been discussed. There is, however, one final issue for researchers to consider; i.e., the manner in which future projects should be focused. In simplistic terms, a research director can conceive of two alternative research pathways. The first would be to implement some of the methodological schema here presented in a total, comprehensive, city or statewide data collection system. Doubtless this is the ideal solution; regrettably such a large statewide system is costly in time, effort, and money. Moreover, the lead time needed for implementation would not be responsive to other research and social needs, as well as program planning needs. A second alternative, favored in this discussion, would be to apply a public health model of estimation to the phenomena of drug-related deaths. In particular, it is suggested that certain key cities be studied with the aim of arriving at correction factors or indexes, which could then be applied to the currently collected statistical data and statistically correct the available data so that it most nearly approximates the true incidence of the phenomena. For example, it is suggested that we attempt to calculate what percentage of serum hepatitis deaths occurring within one city can be attributed to drug-related deaths. If it were found that 25% of such hepatitis cases were related to drug-related deaths, then one could assume, with some certainty, that this percentage or correction factor could be applied to the state level statistics on hepatitis cases, and hence extrapolate what the state level drug-related death incidence would be. Other correction factors could be calculated for all causes of death listed in Table 6, and these could serve to estimate, in a more comprehensive and geographically larger area, approximately to what extent drug-related deaths were a problem.

REFERENCES

Consumers Union Report on Licit and Illicit Drugs. Mount Vernon, N.Y.: Consumers Union, 1972.
International Classification of Diseases, Adapted. 8th rev. National Center for Health Statistics, Public Health Service (PHS Pub. No. 1693). Washington, D.C.: U.S. Government Printing Office, 1968.
Medical World News, 1973, 14(3), 15-17.

PART III
YOUTH AND DRUGS

10
TRENDS IN ADOLESCENT MARIJUANA USE [1]

Eric Josephson
School of Public Health
Columbia University

THE PROBLEM

Known and used all over the world for centuries, marijuana has recently become popular with increasingly large numbers of young people in many countries. How and why youthful interest in the drug grew so quickly is a study in itself; but marijuana's future is a matter of more than academic interest. Has it become a permanent part of the drug scene, or is its use a passing fad? Answers to this question depend in part on its legal status; they will also help to determine that status. If marijuana use increases, one alternative will be to legalize the drug; another will be to attempt much more vigorously than heretofore to prohibit its use. If marijuana use stabilizes at present levels or declines, there may be little inclination on the part of governments to change the drug's current ambiguous status—not legally obtainable, yet so widely used that prohibition is almost impossible to enforce.

With regard to the first of these possible futures, i.e., marijuana's permanence, Blum (1971) has remarked that an

> outstanding feature of drug use to be learned from history or the study of other societies is that new drugs once introduced and found not to be unacceptably

[1] Portions of the material in this chapter have appeared in *Addictive Diseases*, 1974, 1(10), 55–72, and are used with permission of the publisher. The original data presented here were collected as part of a national study of teenage drug behavior being conducted at the Columbia University School of Public Health and supported by NIDA grant R01-DA00043. The principal investigator is Jack Elinson; the coinvestigators, Anne Zanes and the author. Acknowledgments are due Paul Haberman, who has been chiefly responsible for the compilations of national adolescent survey data presented.

dangerous—within whatever limits of tolerance for destruction a society has—continue to be used. Furthermore, over time they come to be used by more and more people.

On the other hand, the very speed with which marijuana use has spread at least in the United States suggests to McGlothlin (1971b) the "characteristics of a fad" that presumably will pass.

Both of these possibilities are considered by Newitt and her fellow futurologists at the Hudson Institute. They write:

> We would expect that youthful drug use will be a permanent problem and that no marvels of law enforcement and drug education are going to turn the clock back to 1955. But this does not mean either that drug use will retain its present fascination for the young or that today's young people will carry through life the conviction that marijuana is a groovier intoxicant than beer or scotch. One uncertainty here is the legal status of marijuana, but . . . rapid changes in this area seem unlikely. Probably marijuana will continue to be available to people who are willing to defy the law to get it . . . In this situation, marijuana use may well come to be thought of . . . primarily as a "kid thing" or a tired fad [Newitt, Singer, & Kahn, 1971, p. 113].

In its 1972 report, the National Commission on Marihuana and Drug Abuse also peered into a crystal ball:

> The data [available] . . . suggest that American society may not witness a significant increase in the use of marijuana in the future. Instead, the data suggest that we may have reached or be nearing a plateau and that in time what may be the fashion of the present generation may cease to be in the future [*Marihuana: A signal of misunderstanding*, 1972b, Appendix, Vol. 1, pp. 264-265].

In its 1973 report, the National Commission repeated its earlier prediction that marijuana use was stabilizing and may decline. However, in a critique of the Commission's forecast, Johnson (1973) charged it with bearing "a heavy responsibility for misleading the public. Marijuana use seems to be here to stay."

Speculating about the future of marijuana is at best a hazardous business. But if that speculation is to be reasonably well informed and not merely the product of wishful thinking, certain questions need to be answered. What data are available on trends in marijuana use, and how reliable are those data? Will recent rates of increase continue into the future? Are people starting to experiment with the drug at earlier ages? How many of these who have used it will continue to do so as they grow older, and if so, for how long?

Both the National Institute of Mental Health [in its annual reports to the U.S. Congress (*Marihuana and health*, 1971, 1972)] and the National Commission on Marihuana and Drug Abuse (in its 1972 and 1973 reports) have reviewed much of the data at hand for the United States and addressed themselves to trends in the drug's use as well as to factors associated with those trends. However, many of the questions asked here have not been adequately answered. If they are to be answered, a number of conceptual and methodological problems need to be resolved. One major problem has to do with defining marijuana "use" itself, another with measuring levels of use and changes in those levels.

This chapter also addresses itself to such questions and particuarly to trends in adolescent marijuana use in the United States. It is based partly on data collected from more than 30,000 students in 1971 in the first stage of a two-wave trend and longitudinal study of drug behavior in 22 selected junior and senior high schools in four regions of the United States. Because the schools were selected purposively and are not representative of the nation as a whole, three consecutive national household sample surveys of marijuana use in smaller but more representative samples of adolescents 12-17 years of age were conducted in 1971, 1972, and 1973. This chapter is based largely on findings from these surveys.

First, the problem of defining and measuring marijuana use is considered, and a review is presented of data available from other sources on general trends in experience with the drug.

CONCEPTUAL AND METHODOLOGICAL ISSUES

What is meant by marijuana "use" and how is it measured? A problem that presents itself at the very outset is that the drug can be consumed in a variety of forms and apparently often in a shared way, which makes measurement difficult. Liquor can be consumed in only one way—by drinking it; but marijuana can be eaten and drunk as well as smoked. Drinkers of alcoholic beverages may share bottles, but they do not usually share glasses. In the case of marijuana, however, should a "communal" joint be given equal weight to an unshared one? Like alcoholic drinks, marijuana varies in strength; but again there are few if any measures available to determine that variety, at least in social surveys.

Then, of course, the reliable production and per capita consumption data available for liquor and tobacco are unavailable for marijuana, as for any other illicit drug. This has not stopped some intrepid U.S. agencies from trying to calculate marijuana consumption rates. For example, the National Commission estimated that consumption of marijuana in the United States rose from just over 50,000 kilograms in 1965 to nearly 2,300,000 kilograms by 1970 (*Marihuana: A signal of misunderstanding*, 1972b, Appendix, Vol. 1, p. 600). This estimate was based in part on another estimate by the Bureau of Narcotics and Dangerous Drugs that seizures of marijuana at ports and borders represent approximately 10% of the total amount entering the U.S. market. Perhaps no less far fetched is a British proposal to measure marijuana consumption by determining the number of packets of cigarette papers needed to wrap the hand-rolled tobacco sold each year and then subtracting the actual number of such packets of tobacco sold—the difference presumably indicating how much marijuana was used (Grass rolls up, Jan. 11, 1973).

But however ingenious or reliable such estimates are, they do not tell us how many people are doing what with marijuana. To find out, as in the case of drinking and smoking practices, we usually rely on surveys in which respondents are asked about their experiences with and intentions regarding the drug. What should they be asked?

In principle, as the National Commission suggests in its 1972 and 1973 reports, marijuana use has several dimensions. One has to with the frequency or level of use, i.e., the number of times the drug has been used "ever" or within a given period of time. Second is the intensity of use, i.e., how often one uses marijuana within any particular time period. A third dimension has to do with the amount of the drug used, either in toto or on any one occasion. Fourth is the duration of use, i.e., how long one uses the drug. There is nothing esoteric about such a multidimensional approach to drug use; it is often employed in studies of cigarette smoking or drinking behavior.

However, in practice epidemiological and sociological research on marijuana use has tended to be unidimensional and confusing with regard to the terms employed. Many investigators have limited themselves to the first dimension, the total number of times the drug has reportedly been used "ever" or within a given period of time. Marijuana "users" are then sorted into various nominal groupings: e.g., some are called "experimenters"; others "infrequent," "occasional," "casual" or "moderate" users; and still others "frequent" or "heavy" users. These terms suggest intensity of use, although they are really based on frequency-of-use measures. But more confusion reigns, since there is wide variation in the definition of such terms; thus an experimenter in one study may be regarded as a non-user in another—which of course makes it difficult if not impossible to compare them. Indeed, marijuana use, as well as other drug use categories, is often determined on an ad hoc basis rather than empirically, which means that the number reporting some particular frequency of use in a survey become the determining factor in the definition of use.

One problem with defining marijuana use in terms of frequency is that it combines those who have tried it once or twice and then no more with those who have used it hundreds of times and continue to use it. Schofield (1971) notes:

> It is plainly absurd to think of [experimenters] as pot smokers, yet some researchers ask their subjects if they have ever taken cannabis. Thus people whose only experience is three or four drags at a communal joint are included in the total number of cannabis users.

The figures this kind of inclusiveness yields can be very large indeed; e.g., it has been estimated that between 15 and 25 million persons in the United States had tried marijuana by 1971 (*Marihuana and Health*, 1972; *Marihuana: A signal of misunderstanding*, 1972a).

Sociologically, and whatever their reliability, such figures are not without significance; at issue is behavior—much of it by children in the eyes of the law—which is disapproved by most adults as well as behavior in violation of the law itself. Moreover, data from various studies (including the present one) show fairly sharp behavioral as well as attitudinal differences between those who have "ever" and those who have never used marijuana. Becoming a marijuana experimenter, it has been suggested, may be regarded as one of a number of *rites de passage* between puberty and adulthood, such as the loss of virginity with which it is apparently closely associated (Jessor, Jessor, & Finney, 1973). This is not to suggest that all those who have tried marijuana are alike; on the contrary, experimenters who remain such differ in many social characteristics from frequent marijuana users with their unique subcultures (Goode, 1970).

Epidemiologically, however, the problem is that these data are "experiential" and hence cumulative; they indicate how many people have "ever" tried marijuana, or how many times they have done so in the past. Consequently, the numbers derived cannot reflect discontinued use or declines in usage, although there is evidence from several studies that appreciable numbers of persons who have tried marijuana stop after a few experiences. Thus, in surveys of youth and adults conducted in 1972 for the National Commission on Marihuana and Drug Abuse, among those who reportedly had ever tried marijuana, the number who had subsequently stopped was as large as the number continuing to use it (*Drug abuse in America: Problem in perspective*, 1973, p. 64). Preliminary data from the present study of over 30,000 high school students in 1971 show that approximately 1 in 10 of those with marijuana experiences had not used the drug during the previous year; and, of these, two-thirds in turn said they had never used it more than twice.

The use of other drugs is not usually treated this way. To illustrate, some people apparently "try" alcoholic beverages and then stop drinking; according to a recent national survey of drinking behavior in the United States, one-third of the abstainers said they once used to drink—but they are not called "drinkers" (Cahalan, Cisin, & Crossley, 1969). In other words, from an epidemiological point of view, the data available on the number of people who have ever used marijuana are of little value in determining how many are using the drug at any one point in time (which would provide a measure of prevalence) or how many have started to use it within a given period of time (which would yield a measure of incidence). Perhaps we need a new category of "ex-users" of marijuana. Of course, like ex-drinkers and ex-smokers, they may start again.

With regard to the prevalence of marijuana use, there is no insurmountable conceptual problem here; the difficulty is that researchers fail to agree on the definition of "current" use. When they do, we will be able to obtain this important measure. Similar considerations apply to the question of incidence, i.e., how many people have started to use the drug during any given period of time. Again, the difficulty lies in failure by researchers to use the same time periods.

As for the other dimensions of marijuana use, amount and duration, relatively little systematic research has been done on large populations over an extended period of time. One of the many problems here has to do with the irregular or episodic nature of its use by many who have tried the drug. To be sure, there are "regular" and "heavy" marijuana users—the potheads—but apparently they are a small fraction of the total number with some marijuana experience. McGlothlin (1971a) has estimated that in the United States, among all those who have ever used marijuana, only 3% use it daily and among "current" users only 5%. In the present study of 22 schools in 1971— some of them selected precisely because they were assumed to be "high" in drug use—only 2% of all senior high school respondents and approximately twice that proportion of all those who had "ever" tried marijuana reported daily use, meaning that they had reportedly used it 60 times or more during the previous 2 months. In the distribution of "users" by the amount of the drug they consume, marijuana differs quantitatively as well as qualitatively from the use of cigarettes or alcoholic beverages, with their numerous regular and heavy consumers.

In short, our definitions of marijuana use remain fairly primitive. Whether more refined concepts of use can be made operational in social surveys remains to be seen. Progress in measuring trends in this as well as other kinds of drug behavior will only be achieved when researchers begin to employ uniform and therefore comparable terms.

On the methodological side, another problem in the study of marijuana use is that the drug can only be obtained illicitly. How many survey respondents are reluctant to report its use for this reason is not known, particularly since researchers in all but a few states in the United States enjoy no more protection from being forced to identify their informants than do journalists. In the future, under a new federal law, this may change; both researchers and respondents may be given the protection they have so far lacked (Marihuana and Health, 1972). Meanwhile, it would be hazardous to assume that the survey data available on marijuana use, as well as on the use of other illicit drugs, do not reflect understandable inhibitions about reporting such behavior, although with increasing use and acceptability this is less likely to be true. Of course, the opposite effect is also possible; that is, some people may falsely claim to have used the drug precisely because it is prohibited. How much overreporting or underreporting exists because of its illegality remains unknown.

In any case, data from several studies suggest that the promise of anonymity may be less important as a factor in drug use reporting than some researchers believe (Luetgert & Armstrong, 1973). This is illustrated by findings from the present study of schools. Thus, in two U.S. East Coast high schools in 1971 with more than 1,100 respondents, matched groups of students were asked either for no identifying information whatsoever about themselves or to provide their names on a separate card; no significant differences in reported drug use were found (Haberman, Josephson, Zanes, & Elinson, 1972). In another experiment in 1973 with matched samples of 530 eleventh graders, half were administered anonymous questionnaires in classroom settings and the other half in their homes (where, although no names were requested, their identity could hardly be secret); again there was no significant difference in reported levels of drug use.

Equally important, considering that most drug surveys depend on recalled frequency of use, is the reliability of such reports. As yet, relatively little research has been done in this area. One of the few studies reported so far, conducted in Canada, found adolescents generally reliable in reporting drug use (Whitehead & Smart, 1972). Another methodological study was conducted in the course of the present study. To assess the general reliability of answers to questions about drug use, 205 students in an East Coast high school were requestioned 2 weeks after the initial administration of questionnaires; the proportions reporting either nonuse or varying amounts of marijuana use were almost identical on the two occasions. Further evidence of reliability was provided by analysis of responses to two different series of questions about the same drugs; students were consistent in their reported use (Haberman et al., 1972). But 2 weeks is not a very long period of time, and whether respondents are equally reliable in self-reported drug use over a considerably longer period of time—e.g., the 2-year interval between first and second waves in the present study of schools—remains to be determined.

Strictly speaking, there is no practicable way to validate reported past use, or non-use, of marijuana in surveys and to distinguish between false positives and false negatives, as can be done, for example, in studies of heroin use relying both on self-reports and on urinalysis (Robins, 1973). What several investigators have done, therefore, is ask respondents whether they have used a fictitious drug (Whitehead & Smart, 1972). Most respondents reply negatively. In the first wave of the present school study, students were asked whether they had ever tried a fictitious drug; preliminary findings indicate that no more than 5% in any school reported that they had ever tried it; internal evidence suggests further that most of those reportedly using it were unaware of its fictitious nature. But while such findings may increase our confidence in self-reported drug use, they still fall short of validating these reports.

These are just some of the conceptual and methodological problems that present themselves in studying marijuana use at any one moment in time. These problems multiply when attempting to determine trends in such behavior since the data available are not only limited by inconsistencies in defining and measuring use; they also reflect wide variation in the populations studied, the methods employed for studying them, and the periods of time covered.

GENERAL TRENDS IN MARIJUANA USE

In approaching the trend data available, one feature of marijuana use in particular needs to be stressed: the age distribution of marijuana users themselves, probably the single most distinctive characteristic of those interested in the drug. In the countries where it has recently made the greatest impact, it is a drug favored by youth, although not yet by any means their drug of choice. At least in the United States at present, marijuana experiences begin for some people during adolescence or the high school years; but for most who have ever tried, experiences begin at college age, i.e., during the late teens and early twenties. Hence the greatest use has been reported by college students and their contemporaries. After the age of 25, reported use drops sharply with increasing age. In this respect as in several others, the users of marijuana differ from the consumers of alcoholic beverages and cigarettes. Whether the age curve of marijuana users is shifting downward or upward—i.e., whether people are starting to use it earlier or later in life and continuing to use it longer—is of course a critical question in measuring trends in marijuana use and one that is discussed in a later section of this report.

What do the available data show regarding trends in marijuana use? Studies conducted in selected U.S. high schools and colleges during the late 1960s and 1970s show widely varying levels of use and rates of change. Averaging data from "approximately 200 [selected] surveys of American secondary school and college students conducted in all parts of the country from 1967 to 1972," the National Commission on Marihuana and Drug Abuse reports an increase from 10% to 16% in the proportion of junior high school students who had ever used marijuana between 1969 and 1972, a corresponding increase from 15% to 40% among senior high school students between 1967 and 1972, and an increase from 22% to 50% among college students with marijuana experience during the same period (*Drug use in America: Problem in perspective*, 1973, pp. 81-83). As the Commission was aware, averaging data from hundreds of diverse studies conducted at different times in different ways is fraught with danger. Nevertheless, even allowing for considerable error, these figures indicate a dramatic increase in the numbers of secondary school and college students with at least some marijuana experience.

The question is whether these rates of increase will continue. The National Commission's claim that, except for college students, such rates of increase may be declining, is based in part on its interpretation of such school trends; it is also based on two consecutive national cross-section surveys of adolescents and adults conducted for it in 1971 and 1972, in which respondents were asked not only about their past experiences with marijuana but also about their future intentions regarding its use.

Thus, regarding the future use of marijuana in the United States, the National Commission (in its 1972 report) noted that most non-users of the drug say they do not intend to try it and that

> a fairly substantial proportion [of users] report reasonably firm expectations of decreasing or discontinuing use in the future. If these [forecasts] are accurate, as only time can tell, society may witness a stabilization, and possibly a decrease, in marijuana use in future generations.

The Commission predicted that the greatest future increase in use among those who have not yet tried it would be among college students and persons over 25 years of age although

> this increase may be of a considerably smaller magnitude than that witnessed within this age group in recent years. The data give no indication that the proportion of early adolescents who might try marijuana can be expected to increase in any significant manner in the future.

Even if the drug were to become legally obtainable and more readily available than at present, the Commission's report suggests that there would be no significant increase in use among those who have not yet tried it (*Marihuana: A signal of misunderstanding*, 1972b Appendix, Vol. 1, pp. 261-262). In its 1973 report, the National Commission stated that marijuana "use may have reached its peak and begun levelling off" and "that the proportion of students who may be expected to experiment with and to continue use of marijuana will stabilize and possibly decline within the foreseeable future [*Drug use in America: Problem in perspective*, 1973, pp. 64, 78]."

The National Commission's hypothesis that marijuana use in the United States is beginning to reach a plateau is challenged by Johnson (1973). His critique is based partly on justifiable skepticism regarding the Commission's averaging of findings from assorted school studies but mainly on trend data collected in one area, San Mateo County, California. In this county secondary school students have been questioned about their use of marijuana and other drugs each year since 1968 yielding annual data an trends for the longest period yet covered in any U.S. study of adolescents. These data show an increase in the proportion of senior high school students reporting having used marijuana during the past year from 32% in 1968 to 55% in 1973, an increase in the number reporting having used it 10 times or more during the past year from 18% in 1968 to 36% in 1973, and an increase in the proportions admitting having used it 50 times or more during the past year from 16% in 1970 to 24% in 1973. Except for the last category of users, these are sizable increases. However, data from San Mateo County also show a leveling off in each category of use between 1971 and 1973, which of course provides support for the National Commission's hypothesis (San Matio County, California Surveillance of student drug use, 1973).

The problem here is whether San Mateo County is representative of the United States as a whole. Very likely it is not. To further illustrate the danger of generalizing from localized data on marijuana use, in the present study of selected U.S. senior high schools, an extremely wide range of reported marijuana use was found in 1971, from a low of 23% in an all-black school in a Southeastern city who said they had ever tried the drug to a high of 58% in an ethnically mixed school in a West Coast university town. There was also a fairly wide range in the proportion of "current" marijuana users—defined as those who had used it three times or more during the previous 2 months—from a low of 7% in one senior high school to a high of 30% in another. But no more than San Mateo County are these schools representative of the United States as a whole.

Whether the National Commission was correct in its hypothesis regarding trends in marijuana use remains to be seen. To test that hypothesis, comparable national data over time are required. Many studies have been conducted in selected schools or communities, but relatively few have been done repeatedly with presumably representative national populations. Findings from the few such surveys regarding the proportions in different age groups who have "ever" tried marijuana between 1967 and 1973 are shown in Figure 1. As can be seen, trend data are missing for certain years, i.e., for college students between 1967 and 1969 and for persons aged 18

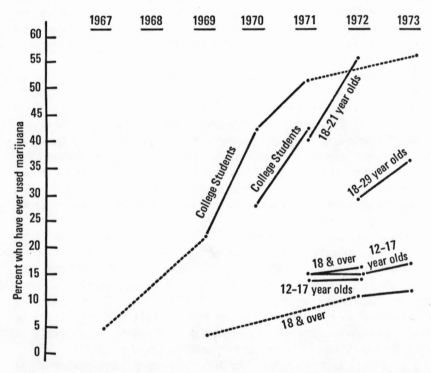

FIG. 1. National sample survey data on marijuana use in the United States, 1967–73. Dotted lines indicate no data available for intervening years. Sources: For college students, 1967–73; persons 18–29 years of age, 1972–73; and persons aged 18 years and over, 1969–73: The Gallup Poll, Releases of Feb. 6, 1972, Feb. 22, 1973, and May 12, 1974. For College students, 1970–71: Groves, E., Patterns of college student drug use and lifestyles, this volume. For 18–21-year-olds, 1971–72; persons aged 18 years and over, 1971–72; and 12–17-year-olds, 1971–72: Abelson, H., Cohen, R., Schrayer, D., & Rappaport, M. *Drug experience, attitudes, and related behavior among adolescents and adults.* Part 1 of a Nationwide Study for the National Commission on Marijuana and Drug Abuse. Response Analysis Corporation, Princeton, N.J., Jan. 1973. For 12–17-year-olds, 1971–73: The present study.

years and over between 1969 and 1972. Furthermore, different periods of time are covered; thus, there are no national survey data on adolescents prior to 1971. What we have therefore are bits and pieces of trend data for different segments of the U.S. population over varying periods of time.

What do these data show? Regarding the adult population (i.e., persons 18 years and over) successive national sample surveys conducted by the Gallup Poll show an increase in the proportion reporting "ever" having tried marijuana from 4% in 1969 to 11% in 1972 and then to 12% in early 1973 (The Gallup Poll, 1973). Survey data collected by Response Analysis for the National Commission in 1971 and 1972 found use at about the same level and also little change in the proportion of adults who had ever tried the drug: in 1971 the figure was 15% and a year later it was 16% (Abelson, Cohen, Schrayer, & Rappaport, 1973). At least among adults, the Gallup and Response Analysis data suggest relatively little variation between 1971 and 1972. Younger adults (i.e., those 18-29 years of age) present a different picture: in this group, according to Gallup, marijuana use rose from 29% in 1972 to 36% in 1973.

Among college students or those of college age, the picture is quite different. At least in the United States, this is the age in which marijuana use begins for most who ever try the drug, and it is college students who have shown the most dramatic increase in such behavior. To illustrate, successive national sample surveys of college students conducted by the Gallup Poll show an increase in the proportion who had ever tried marijuana from 5% in 1967 to 22% in 1969 and 42% in 1970—an eight-fold rise in 3 years—and then a further increase to 51% in 1972 (The Gallup Poll, 1972).

Data collected by Johns Hopkins University in 1970 and 1971 as part of a national longitudinal study of drug use in a matched sample of college students show an increase of somewhat greater magnitude in the proportion ever having tried the drug, from 28% in 1970 to 42% in 1971 (Groves, this volume). So too, national survey data on subsamples of persons 18-21 years of age, not all in college, collected by Response Analysis for the National Commission in 1971 and 1972 show an increase from 40% to 55% in the proportions admitting experience with marijuana (Abelson et al., 1973).

However, a subsequent Gallup survey indicates a declining rate of growth in marijuana use among college students. As noted, in 1971 the figure was 51%; but more than 2 years later, in early 1974, it had only risen to 55% (The Gallup Poll, 1974). Extending over a period of nearly 7 years, the Gallup data provide the best evidence so far that college-age marijuana use has begun to stabilize in the United States.[2]

---

[2]Trend data collected from 1968 to 1972 on the graduating class of 1972 at Carnegie-Mellon University also show a leveling of interest in marijuana. The proportion

(Footnote continued)

As for adolescents (defined here as those between 12 and 17 years of age), so far there have been two national trend surveys, one in 1971 and 1972 and the other covering the period 1971–73. The first of these surveys, conducted by Response Analysis for the National Commission, found no change in the proportion (14%) reporting ever having used marijuana (Abelson et al., 1973). In another sequence of national surveys of this age group, conducted in 1971, 1972, and 1973 for Columbia University, there was no significant change in the proportion reporting ever having tried marijuana; the figure was 15% the first 2 years and 17% the third year. Detailed findings from the Columbia surveys are presented in the following section.

Such then are the available national trend data for the United States on the proportions in different age groups who have "ever" tried marijuana. In considering their significance, a number of conceptual as well as methodological problems present themselves. For one thing, while the Gallup Poll has conducted repeated surveys of college students and of adults over a 7-year period, most of the other surveys cover no more than 2 years; this may be an insufficient time to measure national trends in drug use. Then too, the surveys have been conducted in different ways with different populations, making comparison between them difficult. Some of the differences between surveys of the same age group conducted at approximately the same time may be attributed to sampling variability between them or to differences in the wording of questions. Repeated studies of one population segment, such as the Gallup surveys of college students between 1967 and 1974, may well reflect increasing marijuana usage during this period; but they may also reflect a growing readiness to admit such behavior in an interview (Abelson et al., 1973).

Another problem, noted earlier, is that such data are "experiential" and hence cumulative; they do not provide measures of prevalence, which in this case means the number of people using the drug at any one moment in time. To be sure, several national surveys have attempted to collect data on "current" marijuana use, although unfortunately they vary in their definitions of what is current. Thus, Gallup found little change between 1970 and 1971 in the proportions of college students who had used the drug within the past 30 days: the first year it was 28%, the next year 30% (The Gallup Poll, 1972). Similarly, two successive surveys conducted by Response Analysis for the National Commission found little change in the proportions reporting that they "use [marijuana] now": among adults the figures were 5% in 1971 and

---

reporting ever having used the drug rose from 18% in 1968 to 52% in 1970 and then to 63% in the weeks just prior to graduation in 1972. However, by 1972 the proportion intending to increase their use of marijuana dropped in comparison with their own intentions 4 years earlier as well as in comparison with the seniors of 1968; interest in the drug among non-users also fell during this 4-year period (Goldstein, 1973). But Carnegie-Mellon may be no more representative of all universities in the United States than San Mateo County high schools are of all high schools in the nation.

8% in 1972; and among youth 12-17 years of age, the corresponding figures were 6% and 7% (Abelson et al., 1973). On the other hand, the national longitudinal study of college students conducted by Johns Hopkins University found an increase in the proportions who had "used this year" from 24% in the 1969-70 academic year to 37% 1 year later and among those who were using it "regularly" (at least every week or two) from 12% to 20% during the same period (Groves, this volume).

As for national trends in the incidence of marijuana use, little information is available. The difference between annual "experiential" rates (where they are available) does not provide a reliable measure of incidence. To illustrate, the 9-point increase reported by Gallup in the proportion of college students who had tried marijuana between 1970 and 1971 is not necessarily an indicator of how many began to use it in that period since some who had used it by 1970 may subsequently have stopped.

Indeed, repeated cross-section surveys are unlikely to provide incidence data unless they determine just when marijuana use began, and this has rarely been done. Prospective longitudinal studies are best designed for this purpose; but only one national survey of this kind has been reported so far, the Johns Hopkins University study of college students. In this study 14% of the students in the matched subsample had initiated marijuana use between 1970 and 1971 (Groves, this volume).

In short, the national trend data collected in the United States so far suggest that, marijuana use may have leveled off by 1973, thereby providing support for the National Commission's hypothesis. However, given the methodological problems in research on such behavior as well as rapid change in the drug scene, this interpretation must be treated with caution.

ADOLESCENT MARIJUANA USE, 1971-73

The data reported here were collected as part of a longitudinal study of drug behavior and its correlates in selected junior and senior high schools in four regions of the United States. Because the panel of schools in this study is not representative of the nation as a whole and because an objective was to measure national trends in drug use, three successive cross-section surveys of adolescent marijuana use were undertaken. Most of the findings presented here derive from these surveys. However, where appropriate, comparable data from the much larger although selective study of schools in 1971 also is presented.

The first of the three surveys was conducted by Opinion Research Corporation in May 1971 with a national household sample of 498 persons 12-17 years of age; findings from it have been reported earlier (Josephson, Haberman, Zanes, & Elinson, 1972). The second survey was performed by Response Analysis in April 1972 with another national household sample of 779 youngsters the same age; findings from the first two of these surveys have also been reported elsewhere (Josephson, 1974). The third survey was conducted by Opinion Research Corporation in September–October 1973 with still another national household sample of 493 persons 12–17 years of age.

Although small, the three samples of adolescents were nearly identical in age, sex, and regional distribution; they were also representative of the total U.S. population 12–17 years of age (Table 1). However, certain subgroups were underrepresented—particularly blacks and other minority groups, youngsters with low educational attainment, and those rarely at home.

Insofar as possible, methods of data collection were identical in the three surveys. To maximize cooperation, youngsters were asked to fill out a short, anonymous questionnaire and place it in an envelope which they themselves sealed. Questions about drugs dealt chiefly with the number of times marijuana had "ever" been used and in 1971 and 1972, more briefly, experimentation with a number of other drugs: amphetamines, barbiturates,

TABLE 1

Selected Demographic Characteristics of National Survey Respondents, 1971, 1972, and 1973 Compared with U.S. Census Estimates for 1972

| | Samples | | | Census |
| Characteristic | 1971 (1,701)[a] | 1972 (778) | 1973 (983)[b] | 1972[c] |
	%	%	%	%
Region:				
South	32	35	34	31
North Central	27	28	27	28
Northeast	25	21	23	23
West	16	16	16	17
Total	100	100	100	99
Age:				
12–13 years	34	32	35	33
14–15 years	35	35	34	34
16–17 years	31	33	31	33
Total	100	100	100	100
Sex:				
Girls	50	49	48	49
Boys	50	51	52	51
Total	100	100	100	100

[a]This is based on a weighted sample (the actual number interviewed was 498).
[b]This is based on a weighted sample (the actual number interviewed was 493).
[c]*Source*: U.S. Bureau of the Census, *Current Population Reports*, series P. 25, Nos. 490 and 500, 1972.

glue, LSD (asked about only in 1971), and heroin. Also included were questions dealing with drinking outside the family setting and cigarette smoking. In the 1972 survey a few additional questions were included about the drug behavior of friends, school attendance, and attitudes regarding the legalization of marijuana. Data on the social characteristics of adolescent respondents were obtained from adults in their families.

What do the three consecutive national surveys show? First, let us consider overall patterns of drug use, including liquor and cigarettes. Half the youngsters in the three annual samples said they had drunk alcoholic beverages outside family settings, the older ones more than the younger; unfortunately, no data are available on the amount of liquor consumed. In 1971, nearly one-quarter reported that they were currently smoking cigarettes and nearly one-tenth said that they had stopped smoking; in 1972, almost one-fifth said they were currently smoking and nearly one-eighth claimed they had stopped; in 1973, one-fifth said they were currently smoking cigarettes and less than one-tenth said they had stopped. Alcoholic beverages and cigarettes remained the drugs of choice in these three samples of adolescents.

As noted earlier, there was no significant change between 1971 and 1973 in the proportions of adolescents who said they had tried marijuana at least once. The figures were 15% in 1971 and 1972 and 17% in 1973 (Table 2). Nor was there any significant change between 1971 and 1973 in the proportions of "experimenters" (defined here as those who had used it no more than 9 times), "occasional" users (those who had used it 10-59 times), and "frequent" users (those who had tried marijuana 60 times or more). The proportion of nonusers who said they were interested in trying the drug fell from 12% in 1971 to 7% in 1973. Three-quarters of the 1971 sample, four-fifths of the 1972 sample, and three-quarters of the 1973 sample claimed that they had never used marijuana and were not interested in doing so.

Few of the youngsters in either of the first two survey years, no more than 10%, said they had ever experimented with the other drugs about which they were questioned—amphetamines, barbiturates, LSD, glue, or heroin—and the proportions reporting such experiences varied only slightly between the 2 years. Thus in 1971, 1% of the total sample said they had "tried" heroin; in 1972 the figure was 2%.[3] (No comparable data are available from the 1973 survey.)

Who then were the relatively few marijuana users in these three consecutive surveys of U.S. adolescents? Their regional, age, and sex

---

[3] "Trying" heroin is as much in need of improved definition as the "use" of marijuana. What it means here is not entirely clear. However, it should not be confused with heroin addiction; relatively few heroin addicts are likely to turn up in household samples or in school studies. In our 1971 study of 30,000 high school students, 5% reported that they had "tried" heroin, but only 1% claimed that they had used it more than twice.

TABLE 2

Adolescent Marijuana Use, 1971, 1972, and 1973

Level of use	1971 (1,701)[a] %	1972 (778) %	1973 (983)[b] %
Non-users; not interested in trying	74	80	76
Non-users; interested in trying	10	5	6
Experimenters (used 1-9 times)	9	6	11
Occasional users (used 10-59 times)	3	5	2
Frequent users (60 times or more)	3	4	4
No answer	1	([c])	1
Total	100	100	100
Proportion of non-users who would like to try it	12	6	7

[a]This is based on a weighted sample (the actual number interviewed was 498).
[b]This is based on a weighted sample (the actual number interviewed was 493).
[c]Less than 1%.

characteristics are shown in Tables 3 and 4. In all 3 survey years youngsters in the West were more likely to have tried the drug and reported more use than their contemporaries in other regions of the country. Thus the proportion of adolescents in the West who said they had tried marijuana at least once fluctuated between 23% the first survey year and 27% the third. However, interest in trying the drug among non-users in the West fell from 14% in 1971 to only 1% in 1973, suggesting that the saturation point of interest may have been reached at least in this region. In the North Central and Northeastern regions there were also declines (although of lesser magnitude) in the proportions of non-users who said they were interested in trying the drug. Only in the South was there a slight increase in the amount of interest in marijuana reported by non-users. In the Northeast there was little fluctuation in the proportion of adolescents with at least some marijuana experiences: in 1971 the figure was 20%, in 1973 it was 23%. The two other regions also showed little significant change in the proportions of youngsters with marijuana experiences. For all 3 years, adolescents in the South were chiefly experimental or occasional users, while youngsters in the West were more likely to have proceeded beyond the experimental stage of use.

According to these surveys, the age distribution of adolescent marijuana users did not change in any significant way between 1971 and 1973; nor was there any appreciable shift by age in the frequency of use. In all three surveys older adolescents were considerably more likely to have tried

TABLE 3

Marijuana Users and Non-users by Region, 1971, 1972, and 1973

Level of use[a]	South			North Central			Northeast			West		
	1971 (545) %	1972 (267) %	1973 (333) %	1971 (448) %	1972 (219) %	1973 (266) %	1971 (417) %	1972 (165) %	1973 (222) %	1971 (275) %	1972 (124) %	1973 (152) %
Non-users (not interested in trying)	84	86	79	77	83	80	68	80	70	63	63	72
Non-users (interested in trying)	5	3	8	10	4	5	12	7	7	14	4	1
Experimenters	9	5	8	7	5	8	13	8	15	10	12	18
Occasional users	2	3	2	3	6	3	3	4	4	6	11	3
Frequent users	(b)	3	3	3	2	4	4	1	4	7	10	6
Total	100	100	100	100	100	100	100	100	100	100	100	100

Note: Percentage bases exclude respondents who did not answer question about marijuana use. 1971 figures are based on a weighted sample of 1,701 (the actual number interviewed was 498). 1973 figures are based on a weighted sample of 983 (the actual number interviewed was 493).

  [a]Experimenters were those who had used marijuana 1–9 times; occasional users those who had used it 10–59 times; and frequent users those who had used it 60 times or more.
  [b]Less than 1%.

TABLE 4

Marijuana Users and Non-users by Age and Sex, 1971, 1972, and 1973

Age

Level of use[a]	12–13 years			14–15 years			16–17 years		
	1971 (571) %	1972 (250) %	1973 (339) %	1971 (594) %	1972 (271) %	1973 (328) %	1971 (520) %	1972 (254) %	1973 (306) %
Non-users (not interested in trying)	87	91	89	74	85	74	64	64	64
Non-users (interested in trying)	10	5	7	11	4	8	8	5	4
Experimenters	3	2	3	11	7	11	14	11	18
Occasional users	(b)	1	(b)	3	3	3	5	12	6
Frequent users	0	1	1	1	1	4	9	8	8
Total	100	100	100	100	100	100	100	100	100

Sex

Level of use[a]	Girls			Boys		
	1971 (839) %	1972 (380) %	1973 (463) %	1971 (846) %	1972 (395) %	1973 (510) %
Non-users (not interested in trying)	78	84	83	72	77	70
Non-users (interested in trying)	8	4	5	11	5	7
Experimenters	8	7	8	11	6	13
Occasional users	4	4	3	2	6	3
Frequent users	2	1	1	4	6	7
Total	100	100	100	100	100	100

Note: Percentage bases exclude respondents who did not answer question about marijuana use. 1971 figures are based on a weighted sample of 1,701 (the actual number interviewed was 498). 1973 figures are based on a weighted sample of 983 (the actual number interviewed was 493).
[a]Experimenters were those who had used marijuana 1–9 times; occasional users those who had used it 10–59 times; and frequent users those who had used it 60 times or more.
[b]Less than 1%.

marijuana than the younger ones; the older youths were also more likely to be frequent users of the drug. No more than 1 in 20 of the 12- and 13-year olds had tried the drug any one year; but among 16- and 17-year olds, the proportion was approximately 3 out of 10. Furthermore, younger adolescents were chiefly experimenters, while among the 16- and 17-year-olds at least 1 in 7 reported occasional or frequent use of marijuana in each of the 3 survey years. Nearly identical age distributions of marijuana use were reported in the two surveys of 12- to 17-year-olds conducted in 1971 and 1972 by Response Analysis for the National Commission (Abelson et al, 1973).

The importance of age differences in marijuana use is underscored by a comparison of the oldest and youngest respondents in the larger and more detailed 1972 sample survey. Two-fifths of the 17-year-olds in 1972 said they had tried the drug, but only 1% of the 12-year-olds reported such behavior. But otherwise, the 17-year-olds (14% of the total sample interviewed in 1972) accounted for 39% of all marijuana users and 59% of the frequent users; on the other hand; the 12-year-olds (15% of the sample) accounted for only 1% of all marijuana users, none of them reporting as many as 10 experiences with the drug.

In all 3 survey years, we found similar and major age differences in reported experiences with marijuana, but relatively little variation by age in the proportions of non-users who said they would like to try the drug, possibly because as many older youths who wanted to use it were already doing so while the younger ones had not yet satisfied their curiosity. Although the differences are relatively small, in each age group in 1973 there was less interest in trying it on the part of non-users than had been reported in 1971.

One of the surprising findings in the 1971 survey was the relatively modest difference in reported marijuana use between boys and girls. The 1972 survey yielded similar results. To be sure, girls were somewhat less likely to report having tried the drug than boys and less likely to report frequent use; but if they had not already tried it, they were just as interested in doing so. However in 1973 boys reported nearly twice as much experience with and interest in marijuana.

In all 3 survey years marijuana use also varied according to the type of community in which youngsters lived and by family income. Adolescents residing in metropolitan areas were more likely to have used the drug than those living outside such areas; they were also more likely to report frequent use. As for the relationship between family income (reported by and adult in the household) and marijuana use, among youngsters in families with a reported annual income under $10,000, 6% had tried it in 1971, 10% in 1972, and 12% in 1973; but among those in families with an income of $15,000 and over 19% had tried the drug in 1971, 16% in 1972, and 25% in 1973.

In none of the three surveys was there an opportunity to explore the major social-psychological correlates of marijuana use. However, youngsters were asked several questions which, it was hoped, would provide at least crude measures of the hedonism and willingness to take risks presumably associated with marijuana use. One such question put to youthful respondents in each survey was whether the statement "I am afraid of new experiences" described them well or not. Each year there were fairly sharp differences between non-users (who also said they were not interested in trying the drug) and the combined group of occasional and frequent marijuana users: each year approximately one-third of the non-users indicated that they were afraid of new experiences, but among occasional and frequent users no more than about 1 in 10 said that the statement described them at all. Such responses are only suggestive of the motivational differences between youngsters who try marijuana and those who do not.

We turn next to the relationship between adolescent marijuana use and other kinds of drug behavior, including cigarette smoking and drinking outside family settings; relevant data appear in Table 5. On the whole, the 1971 findings were replicated in the two succeeding surveys. For example, regarding cigarette smoking and marijuana use, no more than 7% of the nonsmokers in any of the three surveys had ever reportedly tried marijuana. However, the proportion of marijuana users among current cigarette smokers was at least half in each of the 3 survey years. This close association berween cigarette smoking and marijuana experience works both ways: among the non-users of marijuana, no more than one in eight were currently smoking cigarettes in any of the 3 survey years, while among marijuana users the proportion of current cigarettes smokers ranged from approximately three-quarters in 1971 to three-fifths 2 years later. (Similar findings were produced by the study of 30,000 students in selected high schools in 1971. In that study, as in others, cigarette smoking was one of the strongest predictors of marijuana use. Thus, among students who had never smoked cigarettes, only one-fifth had ever used marijuana; but among current cigarette smokers, 7 out of 10 reported experience with marijuana. Looking at the relationship the other way, among students who had never tried marijuana approximately one in seven were currently smoking cigarettes while among marijuana users the corresponding proportion was one-half.)

As for drinking alcoholic beverages outside family settings, while no more than 2% of the nondrinkers in any of the three surveys had ever tried marijuana, the proportion among drinkers was more than one-quarter in 1971 and 1972 and one-third in 1973. Analyzing the relationship the other way, less than half of the non-users had ever drunk liquor outside family settings in any survey year; but among marijuana users the proportion was more than nine-tenths. The association between nonfamilial drinking and marijuana use is therefore not as strong as in the case of cigarette smoking. Furthermore, it is not clear from these cross-sectional data whether drinking is likely to precede,

TABLE 5

Smoking, Drinking, and Experimentation with Other Drugs Among Marijuana Users and Non-users, 1971, 1972, and 1973

Percentage who...	Non-users of marijuana			Experimenters			Occasional and frequent users		
	1971 (1,424) %	1972 (655) %	1973 (801) %	1971 (158) %	1972 (50) %	1973 (105) %	1971 (103) %	1972 (66) %	1973 (72) %
Have ever smoked cigarettes	22	22	17	91	76	60	78	79	87
Smoke cigarettes currently	13	9	11	83	52	48	70	77	77
Have drunk liquor apart from family	45	41	43	91	96	90	93	98	98
Have tried other drugs:[a]									
Heroin	1	1	NA	0	0	NA	12	14	NA
LSD	1	NA	NA	0	NA	NA	55	NA	NA
Glue	3	2	NA	10	26	NA	37	27	NA
Barbiturates	1	(b)	NA	18	18	NA	71	42	NA
Amphetamines	1	1	NA	38	26	NA	74	45	NA

Note: Experimenters were those who had used marijuana 1–9 times; occasional and frequent users those who had used it 10 times or more. Subtotals may not add to totals because not all respondents provided all information. 1971 figures are based on a weighted sample of 1,701 (the actual number interviewed was 498). 1973 figures are based on a weighted sample of 983 (the actual number interviewed was 493).

[a] In the 1971 survey 18% of the occasional and frequent marijuana users did not answer the question about heroin use and 12% did not answer the question about use of glue; the proportion who did not answer questions about other drugs was no more than 6%. In the 1972 survey no more than 3% in any marijuana use category—from non-users to occasional and frequent users—failed to answer questions about the use of other drugs.

[b] Less than 1%.

NA = Not available.

follow, or accompany the use of marijuana. (The much larger 1971 study of high school students produced similar findings. Among the nondrinkers, only one in eight said they had tried marijuana, among the drinkers half. Looking at the relationship the other way, nearly half the non-users of marijuana had ever drunk liquor outside family settings, but among marijuana users nearly 9 out of 10 reported such experiences).

No less striking in the national surveys is the relationship between adolescent marijuana use and experimentation with other mood-changing drugs. To illustrate, among non-users of marijuana the first 2 survey years (no comparable data are available for 1973), less than 3% had reportedly ever tried any one of the other drugs about which they were questioned: glue, LSD (asked only in 1971), barbiturates, amphetamines, and heroin. However, marijuana users in 1971 and 1972 were far more likely to report experiences with each one of these drugs, with occasional and frequent users reporting by far the greatest use of any of them. Within this combined group of users, three-quarters in 1971 and nearly half in 1972 said they had tried amphetamines; 7 out of 10 in 1971 and 4 out of 10 in 1972 had reportedly tried barbiturates; more than a third in 1971 and approximately one-quarter in 1972 said they had used glue; and 1 in 8 both years said they had tried heroin.

The apparent decline in the use of barbiturates and amphetamines by occasional and frequent marijuana users between 1971 and 1972 may be attributed to the variability associated with subsamples of this size. (In the 1972 survey, with the largest of the samples, there were only 29 occasional and frequent marijuana users who said they had also tried amphetamines.) In both survey years, however, the association between marijuana experience and the use of other drugs ran in the expected and same direction: as interest in marijuana increased, so did experimentation with other drugs. (Similar findings emerge from the larger study of selected high school students in 1971. In that study, among nonmarijuana users, few had reportedly used any of these drugs; but among those who had used marijuana 60 times or more, nearly three-fifths had also tried amphetamines, two-thirds had used barbiturates, one-third had tried glue, almost half had used LSD, and nearly one-fifth had tried heroin.) Since the national survey data are cross sectional rather than longitudinal, no inferences may be drawn regarding the sequence of drug experiences, i.e., whether marijuana use "escalates" to the use of other, presumably more dangerous, drugs.

The 1972 and 1973 surveys included a number of questions which had not been asked in 1971. One accomplishment of the second and third survey years was to compare marijuana use among black and white respondents.[4] This comparison revealed that black adolescents were somewhat less likely to have

---

[4] In the 1972 sample, 104 adolescents identified themselves as black; but in the smaller 1973 sample, only 48 identified themselves as nonwhite.

tried the drug than their white contemporaries: among the former the proportion of users was 10% in 1972 and 7% in 1973; among the latter the proportion was 16% in 1972 and 20% in 1973. Furthermore, in neither of the two survey years did more than 1% of the black respondents report frequent marijuana use.

The 1972 survey also included questions asked neither in the preceding nor in the following years, and responses to them are presented in Table 6. One question that year had to do with the relationship between adolescents' own marijuana experiences and what they reported about their close friends' use of the drug—one of the strongest predictors of marijuana behavior. As expected, a strong relationship was found between the two variables: as interest in the drug increased, so did the proportion reporting that their close friends used marijuana. To illustrate, among those who had never tried the drug and said they did not want to, only 1 in 10 reported that some or most of their close friends had done so; but among occasional and frequent users the proportion was 9 out of 10. Looked at the other way, among those reporting that most of their close friends had used marijuana, nearly 9 out of 10 had used it

TABLE 6

Selected Characteristics of Marijuana Users and Non-users, 1972

	Non-users		Users	
Percentage who...	Never used; would not like to try it (621) %	Never used; would like to try it (34) %	Experimenters (50) %	Occasional and frequent users (66) %
Say that "none" or "few" of their close friends use marijuana	91	71	32	9
Say that "some" or "most" of their close friends use marijuana	9	29	68	91
	100	100	100	100
Were absent from school 11 days or more during previous term	11	6	28	30
Are not attending school	2	0	4	11
Are favorable regarding legalization of marijuana[a]	35	88	92	86

Note: Experimenters were those who had used marijuana 1–9 times; occasional and frequent users were those who had used it 10 times or more.

[a]The question was, "As you may know, one thing that the [National] Commission recommended is that small amounts of marijuana used in private should not be against the law. Do you feel that this recommendation is in the right direction or not?"

themselves. (Nearly identical results were obtained in the much larger study of 30,000 high school students in 1971: in that study, 15% of the non-users who were uninterested in trying the drug said that some or most of their close friends used it, but among occasional and frequent users the proportion was 93%.)

The case of the non-users of marijuana who said they would like to try it is worth special attention. In the 1972 survey nearly one out of three among them reported that some or most of their close friends were using the drug. (To be sure, the number in this category is small; but comparable data from our larger school study in 1971 show the same result—i.e., 4 out of 10 senior high school students who had never used marijuana but said they would like to reported that some or most of their close friends had done so.)

Another new question in the 1972 household survey dealt with school attendance. While this was not as strong a predictor of interest in marijuana as the behavior of close friends, the differences between marijuana users and non-users ran in the expected direction. Thus, occasional and frequent users of the drug reported nearly three times as many absences from school during the previous term as the non-users and were more likely not to be attending school at all. (Comparable data from the 1971 school study show nearly four times as many absences among frequent marijuana users than among non-users. Furthermore, a special study in 1972 of nearly 600 habitual absentees in one East and one West Coast high school with extremely high absenteeism and drug use rates showed that absentees were twice as likely to report current marijuana use or to report having tried heroin than those present in school at the time the initial 1971 study was conducted.)

Finally, in 1972 a question was asked about the legalization of marijuana. The question was, "As you may know [it has been recommended] that small amounts of marijuana used in private should not be against the law. Do you feel that this recommendation is in the right direction or not?" Adolescents who had never used the drug but said they would like to try it were just as favorably inclined toward legalization as the experimental, occasional, and frequent users: in all three groups the proportion so inclined was approximately 9 out of 10. But among those who had never used marijuana and said they would not like to do so, little more than a third were favorably disposed toward the idea of legalization. (Comparable data from the 1971 school study show this relationship even more strongly: non-users who said they would like to try it were more favorably disposed toward repeal of marijuana prohibition than were experimenters, which is not surprising. Nor is it surprising that among 7th and 8th graders—almost all probably under the age of 16—the proportion of non-users who wanted to try it and wanted it legal for everyone was nearly twice that among the corresponding group of 9th to 12th graders. What would youngsters do if marijuana were legal? Perhaps most striking in the 1971 school study is that while 86% of the interested non-users said they would try it under these hypothetical circumstances, half the senior high school experimenters and 60% of the junior high school experimenters indicated that they would stop using the drug. This finding suggests that prohibition provides at least some of the incentive to experiment with the drug.)

INTERPRETATION

Apart from conceptual and methodological considerations, the substantive issue to which this chapter has been addressed is whether, as the National Commission on Marihuana and Drug Abuse hypothesized, marijuana use in the United States is leveling off. Three successive national sample surveys of 12–17-year-olds conducted in the United States between 1971 and 1973 suggest that at least in this period adolescent marijuana use had stabilized, thus providing support for the National Commission's hypothesis. Considering the small size of the three samples, the consistency of findings in the three surveys is perhaps one of the most remarkable results of all. Between 1971 and 1972 there was no change in the proportion of adolescents (15%) who reportedly had "ever" tried marijuana. (Nearly identical findings have been reported by Response Analysis in successive surveys of youths 12–17 years which were conducted for the National Commission the same 2 years.) The figure for 1973 (17%) is not appreciably higher than in the previous 2 years. Nor were there any significant changes from 1971 to 1973 in the reported frequency of marijuana use, i.e., the number of times it had been tried, or in the characteristics of marijuana users which cannot be attributed to sampling variability in study populations this size. Declining interest in trying the drug on the part of non-users in the West suggests that a saturation point may have been reached in this region, where levels of use have been higher than in other parts of the country.

However, before drawing any conclusions regarding trends in adolescent marijuana use, the limitations of these surveys should be noted. Samples of the size studied here may be adequate for determining aggregate rates, but they are too small for reliable measurement of differences within the samples; thus, in the 1972 sample survey (the largest of the three) there were only 12 marijuana users among the 12- and 13-year-olds. As a consequence, certain subgroups in the population were under-represented—perhaps most notably members of minority groups and youngsters not at home after a minimum number of call-backs by household interviewers. But the similarity of the three samples as well as of the survey procedures suggests that such biases remained constant between 1971 and 1973, which is one possible explanation of the findings.

Another and major limitation of these surveys is that they provide data on only one dimension of marijuana use: the frequency with which the drug has ever been used. Missing therefore are data on the other dimensions discussed earlier—levels of current use; the age at which such experiences begin; and the intensity, duration, and amount of use.

Can these findings—i.e., no significant change in reported marijuana use between 1971 and 1973—be attributed to the reluctance of youngsters the second and third survey years to admit such behavior? There is no evidence from the last two surveys that adolescents in 1972 and 1973 were more inhibited about reporting marijuana use than in 1971. On the contrary, in none of the surveys did more than 1% of all respondents fail to answer the question about marijuana use; and the proportion of marijuana users who did not answer questions about their use of other drugs actually fell between 1971 and 1972 (no such questions were asked in 1973). In other words, there is apparently no survey artifact which explains the major finding of these three surveys.

How then can one explain the difference between these findings and what has been reported in other studies of adolescent drug use in the United States? There have been many selected school studies, including the present one, that report considerably higher levels of marijuana use and different patterns of change in use. The very process of selection may be a determining factor in such differences. Another explanation offered for such differences is that adolescents are less inhibited about admitting marijuana—or any other illicit drug—use in school settings where they are anonymous and in the company of their peers than in households, where their identity cannot be concealed. However, as noted earlier, in an experiment conducted to test this hypothesis with matched samples of 11th graders, half questioned in school settings and half at home, there was no significant difference in reported levels of drug use.

A more plausible hypothesis to explain such differences. is that the 12–17-year age group excludes some older youths who are still in high school and precisely because of their age more likely to be experimenting with drugs. In the senior high schools studied in 1971, 8% of the students participating were over age 17. In the 1972 household survey, 41% of the 17-year-olds said they had tried marijuana; and data from other studies show a significant increase in such behavior after age 17.

Hence, when considering the different age groups included, comparable studies of drug use in representative rather than selected high school populations conducted at approximately the same time have produced findings that do not differ radically from what has been reported here. To illustrate, in Kandel's 1971 sample survey of senior high school students in New York State, 29% reported having tried marijuana, (Kandel, 1973); this figure is not much higher than what was reported here for a younger age group in the Northeast the same year, 20%. In addition, according to a national sample survey of 10th-12th-grade senior high school students conducted late in 1972, 36% reported having tried marijuana at least once (The Purdue Opinion Panel, 1973); this may be compared with findings presented here regarding 16- and

17-year-olds in the 1972 national household survey. Thirty-one percent in this age group reported such experiences.

However, even if the trend data produced by the three surveys discussed here are representative of what was taking place in the United States between 1971 and 1973, other problems remain to be considered. One, noted earlier, has to do with the cumulative nature of "experiential" marijuana use data. In principle, such rates cannot decrease unless incidence or initiation rates fall to zero and appreciable numbers who have had the experience disappear or die—an unlikely event as a result of youthful marijuana use. Experiential rates may of course increase, if incidence or initiation rates also increase; but at least in these three samples we found no evidence that this was happening. A third possibility is that experiential rates may remain constant in repeated samples of those the same age at different points in time if there is no change in initiation rates among those coming of age (the 12- and 13-year-olds of 1972 and 1973) as well as those remaining in it—which is suggested by our findings. Thus, between 1971 and 1973 there was no significant change by age in the proportions with marijuana experiences or (possibly excepting the West) in future intentions regarding use of the drug.

Perhaps the major limitation of such cross-sectional data on drug use is that they cannot provide measures of changes in either prevalence or incidence rates, let alone explain the processes of change; but for such purposes prospective longitudinal research (such as the Johns Hopkins University study of college students, Kandel's panel study of high school students in New York State, and the present panel study of high school students in four regions) is more appropriate.

In short, marijuana use as defined here apparently stabilized among adolescents, at least between 1971 and 1973. Here still another problem, also noted earlier, presents itself: the drug scene may change quickly in our volatile youth culture, but even so it is doubtful whether an interval of 2 years is long enough to measure national trends in the use of marijuana or any other drug for that matter. To determine whether the findings reported in this chapter reflect long-range or merely short term trends, similar studies, with larger samples and more sophisticated measures of marijuana use, should be extended into the future.

REFERENCES

Abelson, H., Cohen, R., Schrayer, D., & Rappeport, M. *Drug experience, attitudes, and related behavior among adolescents and adults.* Part 1 of a Nationwide Study for the National Commission on Marijuana and Drug Abuse. Response Analysis Corporation, Princeton, N.J., Jan. 1973.
Blum, R. H. To wear a Nostradamus hat: Drugs and America. *The Journal of Social Issues,* 1971, 27(3), 89–106.

Cahalan, D., Cisin, I. H., & Crossley, H. M. *American drinking practices: A national survey of behavior and attitudes.* Monograph No. 6. New Brunswick: Rutgers Center of Alcohol Studies, 1969.

Drug use in America: Problem in perspective. Second Report of the National Commission on Marihuana and Drug Abuse. Washington, D.C.: U.S. Government Printing Office, Mar. 1973.

The Gallup Poll. Releases of Feb. 6, 1972, Feb. 22, 1973, and May 12, 1974.

Goldstein, J. W. & Gleason, T. C. Significance of increasing student marijuana use for intended use of other drugs. *Proceedings, 81st Annual Convention of the American Psychological Association,* 1973, 305–306.

Goode, E. *The marijuana smokers.* New York: Basic Books, 1970.

Grass rolls up. *New Society,* Jan. 11, 1973.

Groves, E. Patterns of college student drug use and lifestyles. This volume.

Haberman, P. W., Josephson, E., Zanes, A., & Elinson, J. High school drug behavior: A methodological report on pilot studies. In S. Einstein and S. Allen (Eds.), *Proceedings of the 1st International Conference on Student Drug Surveys.* Farmingdale, N.Y.: Baywood Publishing Co., 1972.

Jessor, R., Jessor, S. L., & Finney, J. A social psychology of marijuana use: Longitudinal studies of high school and college youth. *Journal of Personality and Social Psychology,* 1973, 26(1), 1–15.

Johnson, B. D. Sense and nonsense in the "scientific" study of drugs: An anti-commission report. *Society,* May/June 1973, 53–58.

Josephson, E., Haberman, P. W., Zanes, A., & Elinson, J. Adolescent marihuana use: Report on a national survey. In S. Einstein and S. Allen (Eds.), *Proceedings of the 1st International Conference on Student Drug Surveys.* Farmingdale, N.Y.: Baywood Publishing Co., 1972.

Josephson, E. Adolescent marijuana use, 1971–1972: Findings from two national surveys. *Addictive Diseases,* 1974, 1(10), 55–72.

Kandel, D. Adolescent marihuana use: Role of parents and peers. *Science,* 1973, 181, 1067–1070.

Luetgert, M. J., & Armstrong, A. H. Methodological issues in drug usage surveys: Anonymity, recency, and frequency. *The International Journal of the Addictions,* 1973, 8(4), 683–689.

Marihuana: A signal of misunderstanding. First Report of the National Commission on Marihuana and Drug Abuse. Washington, D.C.: U.S. Government Printing Office, Mar. 1972.(a)

Marihuana: A signal of misunderstanding. The technical papers of the first report of the National Commission on Marihuana and Drug Abuse. Appendix, Vol. 1. Washington, D.C.: U.S. Government Printing Office, Mar. 1972.(b)

Marihuana and health: A Report to Congress from the Secretary, U.S. Department of Health, Education, and Welfare. Washington, D.C.: Subcommittee on Alcoholism and Narcotics of the Committee on Labor and Public Welfare, U.S. Senate, Mar. 1971.

Marihuana and health: Second Annual Report to Congress from the Secretary of Health, Education, and Welfare. Washington, D.C.: Subcommittee on Alcoholism and Narcotics of the Committee on Labor and Public Welfare, U.S. Senate, May 1972.

McGlothlin, W. H. *Marihuana: An analysis of use, distribution and control.* U.S. Bureau of Narcotics and Dangerous Drugs, SCID-TR-2. Washington, D.C.: U.S. Government Printing Office, 1971.(a)

McGlothlin, W. H. Introduction. *The Journal of Social Issues,* 1971, 12(3), 1–6.(b)

Newitt, J., Singer, M., & Kahn, H. Some speculations on U.S. drug use. *The Journal of Social Issues,* 1971, 27(3), 107–122.

The Purdue Opinion Panel. *Report of Poll No. 97. Incidence of drug use and issues of prevention.* Measurement and Research Center, Purdue University, West Lafayette, Ind., Mar. 1973.

Robins, L. N. *A follow-up of Vietnam drug users.* Special Action Office Monograph, Series A, No. 1. Executive Office of the President, Special Action Office for Drug Abuse Prevention. Washington, D.C.: U.S. Government Printing Office, Apr. 1973.

San Mateo County, California, Surveillance of student drug use. *Preliminary Summary, 1973.* San Mateo County Department of Public Health and Welfare, 1973.

Schofield, M. *The strange case of pot.* Harmondsworth: Penguin Books, 1971.

Whitehead, P. C., & Smart, R. G. Validity and reliability of self-reported drug use. *Canadian Journal of Criminology and Corrections,* 1972, 14(1), 1–8.

11
INTERPERSONAL INFLUENCES ON ADOLESCENT ILLEGAL DRUG USE[1]

Denise Kandel
Biometrics Research
New York State Department of Mental Hygiene
and
School of Public Health
Columbia University

A number of approaches have been followed to determine why young people use drugs. One approach stresses the personal attributes of drug users. It sees drug use as resulting from certain adolescent personality characteristics such as anxiety, depression, impulsiveness, or a need to be unconventional (National Commission on Marihuana and Drug Abuse, 1972, Appendix, Vol. 1, pp. 309–311). These traits are often assumed to reflect poor social adjustments, and drugs are seen as providing relief and escape from problems.

A second approach, considered here, emphasizes the role of the social context. It sees drug use as a behavior that develops in response to the social situation of the individual and the interpersonal influences to which he is exposed. For adolescents, the important interpersonal influences can emanate from peers and from parents. But sociologists disagree as to which influence is critical for drug use. Those who tend to see peer influences as critical stress the importance of the adolescent subculture. Those who see parental influence as critical emphasize the family context. According to the adolescent subculture view, drug use is a "sociogenic" phenomenon (Goode, 1969) that depends entirely on the nature of one's social network of friends. "It is out of special milieus that marijuana use grows—making and having friends within those milieus will encourage one to try the drug oneself [Goode, 1972, p. 39]." Friends introduce one to the drug and teach one how to recognize and

[1] Portions of this chapter appear in "Inter- and intra-generational influences on adolescent marihuana use," *Journal of Social Issues*, 1974, and are used with permission of the publisher. This investigation is supported by NIDA research grant DA 00064.

to enjoy its effects. Apparently simple physiological bodily reactions to the drug must be pointed out to the inexperienced drug user by those who initiate him to the drug (Becker, 1953, 1955). The experienced user also teaches the novice to recognize the symptoms of the "high" and to define the drug effects as pleasurable. There develops a subculture "in which users are more likely to identify and interact with other users than with someone who does not smoke marijuana [Goode, 1969, p. 54]."

These seminal interpretations on the role of friends derive from intensive interviews with a selected and limited group of heavy marijuana users, mainly musicians (Becker, 1953, 1955) or young adults in New York City (Goode, 1969, 1970). Additional support has now been seemingly provided by surveys based on larger adolescent samples that include nondrug users as well as users. In these surveys, respondents typically are asked to report their own use and that of their friends. Marijuana users report having many more marijuana-using friends than do nonusers of marijuana. Moreover, marijuana use increases in direct porportion to the reported number of friends who use marijuana. These findings are among the most consistently replicated empirical findings in drug research. They emerged from national surveys of adolescents and adults carried out by Abelson, Cohen, and Schrayer (1972), and Abelson, Cohen, Schrayer, and Rappaport (1973) for the National Commission on Marihuana and Drug Abuse, from a national sample of 25 schools (Haberman, Josephson, Zanes, & Elinson, 1972; Josephson, 1974); from more limited high school studies (Elseroad & Goodman, 1970; Lavenhar et al., 1972; Tec, 1972a, b; Wechsler & Thum, 1972a, b) and from college studies (Goldstein, Korn, Abel, & Morgan, 1970; Johnson, 1973) in the United States and abroad (World Health Organization, 1973). For example, Tec (1972a) found that 85% of the regular marijuana users among a sample of high school students reported that "many of my close friends use marijuana with regularity" as compared with only 4% of nonusers who did not want to try marijuana. Furthermore, most drug users report that they have been first introduced to the drug by a friend (National Commission on Marihuana and Drug Abuse, 1972, Appendix, Vol. 1, pp. 280–281). Marijuana use by one's friend may not only be an important variable in explaining adolescent drug use, it may be the critical variable. In a stepwise multiple regression analysis of factors associated with drug use, reported "drug use by close friends" was the single most important discriminating variable.[2] It accounted for 27% of variability in the use of marijuana as compared with 5% for the variable next in importance, cigarette smoking (Lavenhar, et al., 1972, p. 47). As stressed by the National

[2]The regression analysis was based on 54 variables covering a variety of demographic and social-psychological student characteristics. Five factors accounted for most of the explained variability in marijuana-use patterns: drug use by many close friends; current cigarette smoking; sibling use of drugs; participation in activist groups; and no current religious practice (Lavenhar, Wolfson, Sheffet, Einstein, & Louria, 1972, p. 47).

Commission on Marihuana and Drug Abuse, "Almost no one tries or uses marijuana without having marijuana using friends [Appendix, Vol. 1, p. 305]."

Underlying the subcultural interpretation is the presumed alienation of adolescents from adults. Because drug use is illegal and violates existing norms, such acts tend to be carried out secretly. They carry with them the notion of rebellion against adult norms and values, as embodied for the adolescent by his own parents. The young are thought to use drugs to signify their independence and separateness from parents.

Recently, in apparent antithesis to the subculture theory, another social interpretation of adolescent drug use was proposed. According to this view, drug use on the part of the young develops in response to parental drug use, namely parental consumption of psychoactive drugs, such as tranquilizers, barbiturates, or stimulants (Mellinger, 1971; Smart & Fejer, 1972a, b). The argument linking adolescent drug use to parental drug use is based on several interlocked assumptions. Ours is a pill-oriented society in which all problems, even interpersonal ones, are often thought to be solvable through drugs. Individuals evolve into a

> way of life in which the regulation of personal and interpersonal problems is accomplished through the ingestion of drugs ... relabeling as medical problems calling for drug intervention a wide range of human behavior, which in the past, have been viewed as falling within the bounds of normal trials and tribulations of human existence [Lennard, Epstein, Bernstein, & Ransom, 1971, pp. 23, 18].

A variety of legally prescribed medicines have been developed to affect changes in mood and psychological states. These psychotropic drugs have many obvious legitimate applications in psychiatric and medical practice (Klerman, 1971). However, there has been an increasing manufacture of these drugs by the pharmaceutical industry (Lennard et al., 1971); increasing prescription of these drugs by physicians (Mellinger, Balter, Parry, Manheimer, & Cisin, 1974); and an increasing demand and consumption of these drugs by adults[3] (Balter & Levine, 1971; Manheimer & Kleman, 1972). It is assumed that the young who are reared in this culture and who witness the use of psychotropic drugs by their parents come to share the cultural ethos and start

[3] Despite the obvious increase in the use of psychotherapeutic drugs, whether they are actually misused and overprescribed is open to question. Balter and his colleagues (Balter & Levine, 1971; Mellinger et al., 1974; Parry, Balter, Mellinger, Cisin, & Manheimer, 1973) are of the opinion that physicians are conservative in their prescribing behavior and that the American public is somewhat distrustful of these drugs. A very small proportion (6%) of adults have used any of these drugs on a regular daily basis for 6 months or more (Manheimer & Kleman, 1972; Parry et al., 1973). Furthermore, compared with the actual extent of psychic distress in the population, adults have underused psychotherapeutic drugs (Balter & Levine, 1971). In the present survey, a large number of adults used these drugs less than directed by their physicians. Thus, 38% of those mothers and fathers who used tranquilizers in the preceding month "took less than doctor prescribed or less than directed." Only 2% "took more than doctor prescribed or more often than directed."

using mood-changing drugs themselves. Since adolescence is a difficult period of intense psychological growth, it represents a stage in the life cycle in which the use of mood-changing drugs is particularly appealing. Rather than using medically prescribed drugs, however, the young turn toward the illegal drugs. Under these assumptions, drug use by children is but a juvenile manifestation of adult behavior.

This hypothesis recently received apparent support from reports in the United States (Blum & associates, 1972; Lavenhar et al., 1972; Lawrence & Vellerman, 1970) and in Canada (Smart & Fejer, 1972a, b) concluding that the use of illegal drugs by young people is strongly related to the use of psychoactive drugs by their parents. The studies included high school students in a Long Island school (Lawrence & Vellerman, 1970), six New Jersey schools (Lavenhar et al., 1972), and several schools in Southern Ontario (Smart, Fejer, & Alexander, 1970) and Toronto (Smart & Fejer, 1972a, b). Those adolescents who reported their parents as using tranquilizers, amphetamines, or barbiturates were more likely to use marijuana, LSD, or other hard drugs. In these families, parents were also more likely to be reported as smoking and using alcohol. Thus, what appears to be a mode of adolescent behavior may be, on closer scrutiny, only more vivid expressions among the young of values and behaviors exhibited by their parents. However, the empirical evidence is based primarily on perceptual data. Except for the anecdotal and impressionistic reports provided by Blum and associates (1972) on the basis of intensive family interviews, the available studies are based exclusively on data obtained from adolescents and rely for their assessment of parental drug use on the perceptions of the children.

The explanation in terms of parental influence represents a radical departure from the explanation in terms of peer influence considered earlier. The emphasis on peers implies rebellion of the young against their parents and discontinuity between the generations. The emphasis on parents implies continuity between the generations. According to the parental-influence theory, parents themselves would carry—paradoxically—the responsibility for generating the type of behavior that they explicitly condemn in their children. Use of legally prescribed drugs by adults would have as one unanticipated and clearly unwanted consequence the use of illegal, mood-changing drugs by their children.[4]

Thus, the same issues arise with respect to adolescent drug use as have arisen in regard to other aspects of youth behavior. To what extent are these patterns of behavior a signal of their rebellion against adults? And to what

---

[4] The question of parental role on children's drug use involves two issues. One concerns the extent to which the child's use of drugs represents an imitation of parental behavior. The second asks to what extent adolescent drug use develops in the context of, and in response to, particular child-rearing practices and parent-child interactions. Although the present study is concerned with these two aspects of parental influence, only the first one is dealt with here.

extent do they represent youthful manifestations of a continuity between children and their parents? In short, do they signal the existence or absence of a generation gap? These questions have been asked in connection with radical political activities where generational continuity rather than discontinuity has been found to exist (Braungart, 1969; Flacks, 1967; Keniston, 1968; Thomas, 1971, 1974). Generational continuity has also been found in religious behavior (Braun & Bengtson, 1972), general life values (Troll, Neugarten, & Kraines, 1969) and adolescents' future life goals (Kandel & Lesser, 1969). In fact, parental and peer influences may be complementary rather than antagonistic to each other (Kandel & Lesser, 1972). Parental drug use may help specify the conditions under which certain adolescents become involved in networks of illegal-drug-using peers and others do not.

Curiously, the question of the relative influence of parents and peers in adolescent drug use has not even been raised in existing studies. Investigators have tended to focus their attention exclusively on one or the other source of interpersonal influence, without concern for how they could be reconciled or interconnected with each other in the adolescent's life. Each interpersonal context has been discussed as if the adolescent lived in a disconnected world and as if this context, either peer or parent, were the only real one for the adolescent. In view of the traditional emphasis on the role of the peer group, it is all the more curious that the recent proponents of parental influences have made no attempt to reconcile their hypotheses with those that stress the importance of peers; nor do they even indicate a concern for the problem.

To understand the role of intergenerational and intragenerational interpersonal factors in the use of drugs by young people several interrelated questions must be answered:

1. To what extent are youth actually influenced in their drug use by their parents?
2. To what extent are they influenced by their peers?
3. What is the concomitant and relative influence of parents and peers?
4. Under what patterns of generational relationships do these interpersonal influences vary in importance?

Because of design and methodology, none of the existing studies has provided adequate answers to these questions. Indeed, the assessment of influences, whether from peers (Johnson, 1973; Tec, 1972a) or from parents (Lavenhar et al., 1972; Smart & Fejer, 1972), has been based exclusively on the adolescent's perceptions of friends' or parents' behaviors. As such the data have not provided the necessary evidence that is required to conclude that youth drug behavior is very much determined by parental or peer drug use. Information is needed from the parent or the friend himself, since associations based on perceptions may be inflated and may result from the fact that the adolescent's own patterns of drug use determine his perception of drug use by others around him, whether parent or peer. Matched relational samples of adolescents, parents, and peers are needed, so that the degree of similarity and/or differences in values and behaviors within and between generations can be assessed properly on the basis of self-reports rather than perceptions. Finally, a true assessment of interpersonal influence requires longitudinal data so as to identify the nature and direction of influence.

The present study was specifically designed to examine the respective role of parents and peers on adolescent drug use. Independent data were obtained, at two points in time, from adolescents, their parents, and their best schoolfriends, providing for a direct assessment of the relative influences of parents and peers on adolescent drug use.

In line with the argument presented earlier, this study explores four basic questions:

1. The relationship between adolescent and parental drug use.
2. The relationship between adolescent and friend's drug use.
3. The relative influence of parents and peers.
4. The conditions, particularly interactional factors, that affect the levels of interpersonal influences.

Regarding adolescent drug use, the discussion emphasizes marijuana, the most frequently used of the illegal drugs. Parental influence is examined not only with respect to parental use of psychotherapeutic drugs but also with respect to socially accepted substances, such as alcohol and tobacco. As noted by Nowlis (1971-72) the definition of a particular substance as a drug is very much determined by the value judgments placed upon it. Alcohol and tobacco, "which have eluded medical control . . . are not normally considered drugs [p. 6]." However, as is well recognized, alcohol and tobacco alter moods and can be used for many of the same reasons as the psychoactive drugs. Parents' influence may exert itself not only through their use of psychotherapeutic drugs, but also through their use of socially accepted substances.

To anticipate the conclusion of this report, it was found that the mother's use of psychotropic drugs has some impact on adolescent use of all types of illegal drugs; the mother's and father's use of alcohol have a greater impact, but solely on marijuana use. However, compared with the influence of peers, parental influence is small.

METHOD

Sample

A two-wave panel survey was carried out in 1971-72 on a multiphasic random sample of adolescents representative of public secondary school students in New York State,[5] their parents and their best schoolfriends. The present report is based on the first wave of data collected in fall and winter 1971. Structured self-administered questionnaires were given in a classroom situation to a random sample of homerooms in 13 schools and to the entire student body in 5 schools. The latter procedure made possible the collection of data from the student's best schoolfriend so as to obtain a relational sample of matched student-friend dyads. Within each school, all homerooms were surveyed simultaneously. A total of 8,206 student questionnaires were processed.

Two to 3 weeks after each of the 18 schools was surveyed, questionnaires were mailed to one of the student's parents, alternately mothers and fathers. A maximum of three follow-up contacts was involved. Parents did not sign their names, but indicated on a postcard, which they mailed separately, whether they had returned their questionnaires. Usable questionnaires were obtained from 5,574 parents, or 62% of the initial group contacted.[6]

When analyzed by themselves, student and parent samples were weighted to take into account the probabilities of selection for each school and for each homeroom and to correct for different absentee and nonparticipation rates among students in each school and nonresponse rates among parents in each community. The samples of matched dyads and triads were not weighted.

The Protection of Subjects' Rights

Two features of the methodology, which resulted directly from investigating illegal behavior among minors, require particular notice since they may have introduced a bias in the results. First, to protect the rights and privacy

[5] The universe for the study includes all public high schools in New York State, i.e., public schools with grades 7-12, 9-12, or 10-12. The two-stage sample selection involved (a) selection of sample schools throughout New York State and (b) selection of homerooms within the sample schools. The first stage included a sample of 18 high schools stratified on four criteria: geography (New York City; other cities over 200,000 or suburbs; rest of state); minority (black or Puerto Rican) enrollment; proportion of students going on to college; number of homerooms. The second stage included a sample of students clustered by homerooms and stratified to represent the different grades within a high school. Homerooms within each school were selected in relation to the probability of selection of the high school, with approximately 10-14 homerooms sampled in each school. Six of the 18 schools are located in New York City, 6 in the suburbs, and 6 in the rest of the state.

[6] The return rate varied in different parts of the state, being lowest in New York City. Whatever clues available tend to discredit the interpretation that parents who were heavy users failed to return their questionnaires and that the sample is biased in favor of adults with low psychotropic drug use. A traditional technique in mailed surveys is to infer the characteristics of nonrespondents from the attributes of participants who respond at various times in the mailing procedure. Nonparticipants are assumed to be more like late than early respondents. In the present survey, early parent respondents reported slightly *more* psychotropic drug use (41% having used one or more psychotropic drugs) than did late respondents (34%).

of the adolescents in the survey and to obtain informed consent for their participation, all parents in the sample homerooms were notified of the student survey prior to its administration in each school, via certified mail, return receipt requested. Parents were given an opportunity to refuse their child's participation, if they so desired. The refusal rate was generally low, averaging 3.6% for the state as a whole. However, in one New York City school, it was as high as 14%.

Second, no respondent signed any of the questionnaires. Identification and linkage of records between waves and within each wave between adolescent and parent and between adolescent and best schoolfriend was accomplished through the use of self-generated identification code numbers. Each adolescent constructed a code for himself, and each parent was asked to construct a number identical to the one the child constructed for himself. In the five schools surveyed in their entirety, each adolescent was also asked to construct a number for his best friend in school, which was identical to the number constructed by the friend for himself. Most adolescents (94%) and most parents (98%) were willing and able to construct such numbers for themselves; 82% of adolescents constructed a number for their friends. However, some numbers produced were incorrect, incomplete, or, in the case of friends, for someone not in the school sample. With these codes, 49% of all the students were matched to their parents, and 38% of the students in the five schools were matched to their best schoolfriends. In these five schools, 1,110 students (23% of those surveyed) could be matched to parents as well as to best schoolfriends and were incorporated into triads. The overall resulting number of dyads and triads is below that obtained when matching is done on the basis of names.[7] Clearly the procedure used for linking and matching questionnaires represents a compromise and is inferior to the use of names. Not only does it reduce the overall rate of matching, but it also introduces a bias in the resulting relational sample, since students who give no code number contain a higher proportion of drug users than those who provide a code. The proportion of marijuana users is 25% among adolescents matched with a parent and/or best friend versus 35% among those not matched to either. However, since these relational samples are used to analyze processes and interactions among variables, the loss of cases is less serious than it would have been if the samples had been used to estimate incidence or prevalence rates of drug use in the New York State adolescent population.

Measurement of Drug Use

The questionnaires included a wide variety of items about the use of legal and illegal drugs as well as about personal characteristics and behaviors.

---

[7] In a previous study not dealing with drugs (Kandel & Lesser, 1972) in which names were used, 93% of adolescents could be matched to their best schoolfriend. With an overall return rate of 70% to a mailed parental questionnaire, 59% of the initial student sample in that earlier study was matched to parents and 53% to parents and best schoolfriends (Kandel & Lesser, 1972, Appendix B, Table 1).

Adolescents were asked how many times they had (a) ever used for nonmedical reasons and (b) used in the past 30 days each of the following substances: alcohol, marijuana, hashish, LSD, other psychedelics, methedrine, "ups," "downs," tranquilizers, cocaine, heroin, other opiates, and inhalants. They were also asked whether their mothers or fathers had ever used any of the three major types of psychotropic drugs: tranquilizers, barbiturates, and stimulants (pep or diet pills); whether each parent had used each drug in the past 12 months and how frequently; and whether parents smoked, drank beer or wine, drank alcohol, or used marijuana. Parents were asked parallel questions about their patterns of use of these drugs and substances. In all instances, a category "never used" or "not used" was provided. Any respondent who gave a positive response in answer to either of the two use questions ("ever" and "past 30 days" or "past year") was considered a user.[8]

Among parents matched to a responding adolescent, the proportions using each drug or substance are presented in Table 1. The rates of use observed in the present sample are strikingly similar to those recently reported for comparable age groups by the most comprehensive and sophisticated national survey carried out to date (Parry et al., 1973). In that survey conducted in 1970 on a representative sample of the American population, 18% of men and 37% of women aged 30-59 years reported having used at least one psychotherapeutic drug during the previous year. In our sample, 21% of fathers and 34% of mothers report having used one or more such drugs in the past 12 months. In line with other surveys of adult psychotropic drug use (Balter & Levine, 1971; Chambers, 1971; Manheimer & Kleman, 1972; Manheimer et al., 1969; Mellinger et al., 1971; Parry, 1968; Parry et al., 1973), the men in this sample are less frequent users of psychotropic drugs than women.

Although this study examined a broad range of adolescent drug use, the emphasis in this report is on marijuana, the most frequently used of the illegal drugs in the sample and by young people in general. In this representative sample of New York State high school students, 29% report having ever used marijuana. It should be kept in mind that marijuana use overlaps with the use of other drugs. Marijuana users include a great variety of youths: the experimenters who have tried the drug only once or twice and have tried no

[8] Extensive analyses were conducted which establish the high reliability and validity of illegal drug reports in the samples. The small proportion of adolescent respondents who gave inconsistent answers were more like users than nonusers on a variety of criteria variables, and should be considered drug users. The majority of adolescents gave honest and valid answers (unpublished data). Parents who responded via mailed questionnaires, without the aid of charts depicting various pills, might have underreported their psychotropic drug use, especially sedatives and stimulants (Parry, Balter, & Cisin, 1970-71). However, self-reported rates of parental use were similar and, in some cases, even higher in this sample than in previous national surveys (Balter & Levine, 1971; Manheimer & Kleman, 1972; Mellinger et al., 1974; Parry, 1968; Parry et al., 1973), state surveys (Chambers, 1971; Manheimer, Mellinger, & Balter, 1969), and local surveys (Mellinger, Balter, & Manheimer, 1971) based on personal interviews.

TABLE 1

Self-Reported Use of Psychoactive Drugs, Alcohol, and
Smoking by Mothers and Fathers in Matched
Adolescent-Parent Dyads
(Adolescent-Parent Dyads—Wave I, Fall 1971)

Use of psychoactive drugs, alcohol, or smoking	Mothers (%)	Fathers (%)
Ever used:		
1 or more psychoactive drugs	50	31
Tranquilizers	38	23
Barbiturates	16	12
Diet pills, stimulants	20	8
Used in last 12 months:		
1 or more psychoactive drugs	34	21
Uses alcohol at least once a month[a]	36	53
Currently smoking	42	44
Total $N \geqslant$	(2,361)	(1,576)

[a]Restricted to hard liquor. Excludes beer and wine.

other drugs (23%) as well as extensive users who have used marijuana many
times (for instance, 33% have used it 40 times or more). The overwhelming
majority (90%) of the heavy marijuana users are polydrug users. It facilitates
the analysis of interpersonal processes to focus on this single drug and treat it
as if it were a simple behavioral entity.

FINDINGS

Adolescent and Parental Drug Use

In examining the potential link between adolescent illegal drug use and
parental behavior, a variety of parental drug uses were considered:

- Parental use of psychoactive drugs, i.e., tranquilizers, barbiturates, and
  stimulants at any time in their lives.
- Use of these drugs in the past 12 months.
- Use of marijuana.
- Use of alcohol, tobacco, beer, and wine.

For each of these drug-related behaviors, the child's perception of parental
use as well as the parent's self-reports were examined. The relationship
between parental behavior and child's drug use was examined for mothers and
fathers separately and among boys and girls. In the present report, all data are
presented for boys and girls together.

First, we present the relationships of perceived and self-reported parental psychoactive drug use to adolescent marijuana use; next, the relationship of self-reported parental psychoactive use to adolescent use of illegal drugs other than marijuana; finally, the relationship of self-reported parental use of other substances (for example, marijuana and alcohol) to adolescent illegal drug use.

Adolescent marijuana use and parental use of psychoactive substances. The present data confirm the previously reported associations (Lavenhar et al., 1972; Smart & Fejer, 1972a, b) between adolescents' drug use and *perceived* parental use of psychotropic drugs. Adolescents who report that their parents have ever used tranquilizers, barbiturates, or diet pills are more likely to be marijuana users than adolescents who do not report such parental use. For example, among adolescents who perceive their mothers to have used tranquilizers, 37% use marijuana, as compared with 24% among those who perceive their mothers never to have used tranquilizers (Table 2). Parallel percentages for fathers are 37% and 26%, respectively. Similar differences appear with respect to perceived parental use of stimulants or barbiturates. The association is stronger with perceived maternal than paternal use, as was reported by Smart and Fejer (1972a, b). The difference in favor of the mother persists even when the sex of the child is taken into account. Boys, as well as girls, are more responsive to perceived maternal behavior.

Furthermore, adolescent marijuana use is directly related to the *perceived* degree of parental drug involvement. Such involvement was inferred from several criteria: perceptions of the extent to which each drug had been used within the past year; the number of different drugs ever used by each parent; and whether each drug had been used by both parents, only by one, or by neither (see Table 2). As a minimum, there is a 50% increase in the rate of marijuana use among those youngsters who report their mothers to be consumers of psychoactive drugs as compared with those who do not report such parental use. Among adolescents who perceive their mothers to have used all three types of psychoactive drugs (tranquilizers, barbiturates, and stimulants), 46% use marijuana, as compared with only 22% among those who perceive their mothers to have used no psychoactive drugs (Table 2). Similarly, 54% of the youths use marijuana when they report that their mothers have used tranquilizers every day in the past year, versus 26% when they report her to have used them only a few times. When both parents are perceived to have ever used tranquilizers, 39% of the youths use marijuana, versus 23% when neither parent is perceived to have used. The associations are comparable in magnitude to those reported by Smart and Fejer (1972a), who indicated, for instance, that "mothers who were daily tranquilizer users were twice as likely to have children who were marijuana smokers [p. 156]."

In contrast to previous surveys, the present research provides information on the parents' self-reported use of psychotropic drugs and permits a more accurate assessment of the relationship between parental and child use within

TABLE 2

Adolescent Marijuana Use and Perceived Parental Ever Use of
Psychoactive Drugs
(Weighted New York State Student Sample—Wave I, Fall 1971)

Perceived use of	Adolescents having ever used marijuana					
	When mother is perceived to have used			When father is perceived to have used		
	%	N	Tau-beta	%	N	Tau-beta
Tranquilizers:						
No	24	(4,341)	.135	26	(5,224)	.089
Yes	37	(2,273)		37	(1,264)	
Barbiturates:						
No	25	(4,867)	.147	27	(5,387)	.066
Yes	40	(1,671)		35	(1,097)	
Diet pills, stimulants:						
No	25	(4,863)	.140	28	(5,844)	.038
Yes	39	(1,864)		33	(824)	
Number of psychoactive drugs used:						
None	22	(3,862)	.161	26	(5,008)	.092
One	32	(2,178)		36	(1,138)	
Two	40	(1,095)		40	(433)	
Three	46	(563)		30	(393)	
Parental use of tranquilizers:						
Neither parent uses	23	(3,585)	.128			
Mother only uses	34	(1,181)				
Father only uses	30	(429)				
Both parents use	39	(727)				

the same families. An examination of drug use in matched parent-adolescent dyads shows that the relationship between adolescent marijuana use and parental *self-reported* psychotropic drug use is small and appears only in relation to mothers (Table 3). The likelihood that an adolescent uses marijuana increases in direct proportion to the number of psychoactive drugs ever used by the mother. Thus, 26% of adolescents use marijuana when their mothers report never having used any psychoactive drugs as compared with 37% when mothers report having used all three types (Table 3).

The association between adolescent marijuana use and *self-reported* parental ever use of psychoactive drugs is low and much lower than the association with *perceived* parental use. (Compare Tables 2 and 3.) In this representative sample of New York State high school students, the association, as measured by tau-beta, between adolescents' marijuana use and *self-reported* maternal tranquilizer use is .057 [measured by tau-beta, a symmetric measure of association for ordinal data (Kendall, 1962)], as compared with .135 with *perceived* maternal use. Similar trends appear with respect to maternal self-reported use of other drugs. Associations based on the adolescents' perceptions of parental behavior are more than twice as high as the associations based on parental self-reports.[9,10]

When adolescent marijuana use is examined as a function both of perceived and self-reported drug use, perceptions are found to be the most strongly related. Among adolescents who perceive their parents to have used tranquilizers, the same proportion (35%) use marijuana whether or not the parents report having actually used tranquilizers. Among adolescents who perceive their parents to be nonusers, 25% use marijuana, irrespective of the parents' reports. An implicit assumption underlying analyses based on adolescent perceptions of parental drug use is that these perceptions accurately reflect acutal parental drug use and determine in turn the child's drug behavior. However, the causal sequence might be quite different. The child's use of drugs may bias his/her perception of parental drug use, as a justification for his/her own behavior, so that perceptions of parental behavior would vary as a function of the child's rather than the parent's drug behavior. Indeed, we find that adolescent drug users are more likely than nonusers to perceive that their parents use drugs when the parents actually report none.

Adolescent illegal drug use and parental psychoactive drug use. Parental use of psychoactive drugs has an impact, not only on the child's use of marijuana, but also on the child's use of other illegal drugs, such as psychedelics and pills. Again, the most influential parent is the mother.

When parental use is examined separately for each class of psychoactive drug, barbiturate use is the most crucial for adolescent use of illegal drugs other than marijuana. For fathers, this is the only self-reported use related to

---

[9] Table 3, which presents the data for boys and girls together, obscures certain relationships. The most important is the association that father's barbiturate use has to son's marijuana use. In addition, the influence of maternal use of psychotropic drugs is greater among daughters than sons. Thus, the association (as measured by tau-beta) between total number of psychoactive drugs ever used by mothers and their children's marijuana use is .109 for daughters but .050 for sons.

[10] Parental report of psychotropic drug use at any time in the parent's life may refer to use that took place a long time ago and may therefore have currently little visibility and potential influence on the children in the family. Parental report of recent use of these drugs, i.e., within the past year, may provide a more valid measure of influential parental drug behavior than use at any time in the past (see Parry, Balter, & Cisin, 1970–71). However, the correlations between adolescent marijuana use and parental self-reported uses of psychotropic drugs do not increase when use in the past 12 months is substituted for use at any time in the past.

TABLE 3
Adolescent Marijuana Use and Parental Self-Reported Ever Use
of Psychoactive Drugs
(Adolescent-Parent Dyads–Wave I, Fall 1971)

| Parental use of | Adolescents having ever used marijuana | | | | | |
| | When mother reports to have used | | | When father reports to have used | | |
	%	N	Tau-beta	%	N	Tau-beta
Tranquilizers:						
No	28	(1,446)	.057	26	(1,182)	.022
Yes	33	(848)		28	(353)	
Barbiturates:						
No	29	(1,926)	.043	26	(1,350)	.025
Yes	34	(361)		30	(186)	
Diet pills:						
No	28	(1,837)	.078	26	(1,410)	.019
Yes	37	(458)		29	(126)	
Total number of psychoactive drugs used:						
None	26	(1,164)	.083	25	(1,057)	.044
One	32	(707)		32	(321)	
Two	35	(315)		26	(133)	
Three	37	(110)		27	(26)	

adolescent's illegal drug use. For mothers, barbiturate use is more strongly related than use of other two types. This is in contrast to the use of marijuana, for which maternal use of diet pills or stimulants was the more relevant. At this time, it is unclear why these differences appear in connection with particular types of psychotropic drugs.

Adolescents' use of LSD, other psychedelics, methedrine, ups, downs and tranquilizers, opiates other than heroin, and inhalants increases in direct proportion to the number of psychoactive drugs used by mothers. No relationship appears between the total number of psychoactive drugs ever used by fathers and adolescent's use of illegal drugs.

Maternal use is particularly influential when more than one class of psychoactive drugs is involved (Figure 1). When mothers report using all three types of psychoactive drugs, the proportion of their children using one of the illegal drugs other than marijuana is at least twice as large as among mothers who report using none. For example, among mothers who report using no psychoactive drugs, 6% of the children report using psychedelics as compared

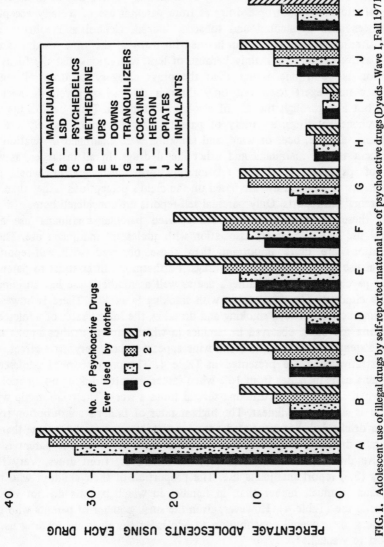

FIG. 1. Adolescent use of illegal drugs by self-reported maternal use of psychoactive drugs (Dyads—Wave I, Fall 1971).

Legend (within figure):

A — MARIJUANA
B — LSD
C — PSYCHEDELICS
D — METHEDRINE
E — UPS
F — DOWNS
G — TRANQUILIZERS
H — COCAINE
I — HEROIN
J — OPIATES
K — INHALANTS

No. of Psychoactive Drugs Ever Used by Mother
0 1 2 3

PERCENTAGE ADOLESCENTS USING EACH DRUG

with 15% among mothers who use all three types of drugs. Corresponding percentages for adolescent use of methedrine are 4% and 14%; for ups, 10% and 21%; for downs, 9% and 20%; for tranquilizers, 5% and 12%.

Adolescent illegal drug use and parental use of other substances. The link between parent and adolescent drug behavior may derive not as much from parental use of psychotropic drugs as from parental use of socially accepted substances such as alcohol and tobacco. Indeed, alcohol and tobacco are mood-altering substances and can be used for many of the same reasons as the psychoactive drugs. It is mainly because of legal restrictions that the focus of attention is upon one rather than the other category of drugs. Parental influence may exert itself not only through the use of psychotherapeutic drugs, but also through the use of alcohol and tobacco. Thus, besides the use of psychoactive drugs, a variety of parental drug behaviors, namely use of marijuana, alcohol, beer or wine, and smoking, were examined in relation to adolescent use of marijuana and other illegal drugs. In all instances, as was true of psychotropic drugs, relationships are much greater when the assessments of parental use are based on the child's perceptions rather than on the parents' self-reports. Only parental self-reports are considered here.

Of these parental behaviors, self-reported parental marijuana use and alcohol use have the largest association with adolescent marijuana use. These associations are more important than those observed with self-reported parental use of psychotherapeutic drugs. Furthermore, in contrast to parental use of psychoactive drugs, father's use as well as mother's use has an impact on the children. The relationship with smoking is weaker. There is however, some interaction between smoking and drinking, the lowest rates of adolescent marijuana use being observed in families in which parents neither smoke nor drink. Parental drinking of beer and wine appears to have very little effect.

Illustrative data are presented in Table 4. The proportion of adolescent marijuana users increases from 16% when fathers report drinking no alcohol to 38% when fathers report drinking several times a week. The relationship with alcohol is slightly curvilinear. The highest rates of father's consumption (one or two drinks daily) is associated with lower adolescent marijuana use than is moderate drinking, suggesting that in those cases in which the parent is an excessive drinker, the adolescent may be turned off from drugs. Very few parents (3%) report marijuana use. The proportion of their children who use marijuana is much higher than in families in which parents do not report marijuana use (Table 4). However, given the small number of parents who use marijuana, their overall contribution to adolescent involvement in drug use is at most very small.[11]

---

[11]Most theories of family socialization are based on an implicit unidirectional model in which influences are assumed to flow uniformly from parent to child. However, such a model may not reflect the fact that under certain circumstances children themselves may influence their parents and that certain parental attitudes and behaviors develop in response to their children's behaviors. Parental marijuana use may be such a case of "reversed" family influence in which influence flows from adolescent to parent.

TABLE 4

Adolescent Marijuana Use by Parental Self-Reported Marijuana,
Alcohol Use, and Smoking
(Adolescent-Parent Dyads—Wave I, Fall 1971)

| Parental use of | Adolescents having ever used marijuana | | | | | |
| | When mother reports to have used | | | When father reports to have used | | |
	%	N	Tau-beta	%	N	Tau-beta
Marijuana:						
No	29	(2,189)	.072	26	(1,467)	.066
Yes	49	(63)		41	(58)	
Alcohol:						
Never	23	(632)	.101	16	(219)	.116
Once a month or less	30	(831)		25	(513)	
1–3 times a month	28	(341)		26	(279)	
Once a week	37	(251)		32	(239)	
Several times a week	43	(135)		38	(182)	
1–2 drinks a day or more	39	(77)		29	(92)	
Smoking cigarettes:						
Never	24	(915)	.088	25	(355)	.051
Used to but stopped	32	(406)		24	(496)	
Occasionally	34	(166)		25	(102)	
Under a pack a day	34	(313)		26	(156)	
A pack a day or more	35	(469)		32	(412)	
Smoking or drinking:						
Neither	18	(435)	.100	10	(129)	.091
Smokes only	33	(189)		24	(89)	
Drinks only	31	(876)		27	(719)	
Smokes and drinks	34	(752)		30	(576)	

Parental use of marijuana and alcohol are related to adolescent use of other illegal drugs besides marijuana. Father's alcohol use appears to have a smaller relationship than mother's with adolescent use of these other illegal drugs (Table 5).

In summary, associations between parental and adolescent drug use are much lower when based on parental self-reports than on adolescents' perceptions of parental drug use. Parental self-reported drug behavior has a certain impact on adolescent's use of illegal drugs, an impact which varies with the drug involved—both on the parent's and the adolescent's side—and with the sex of the parent and of the adolescent. The following trends are the most important:

TABLE 5

Adolescent Use of Illegal Drugs by Parental Self-Reported Alcohol Use
(Adolescent-Parent Dyads—Wave 1, Fall 1971)

Type of drug used by adolescents by whether mother or father uses alcohol	Percent adolescents using each drug					
	Parental alcohol use					
	Never %	Once a month or less %	1-3 times a month %	About once a week %	Several times a week %	1-2 times a day or more %
LSD:						
Mother drinks	5	7	5	9	12	14
Father drinks	4	5	5	4	7	6
Psychedelics:						
Mother drinks	5	7	6	9	10	10
Father drinks	4	6	5	5	7	8
Methedrine:						
Mother drinks	5	5	2	7	8	6
Father drinks	3	3	3	4	4	4
Ups:						
Mother drinks	10	13	8	14	20	11
Father drinks	7	10	9	11	12	9
Downs:						
Mother drinks	9	12	8	14	17	8
Father drinks	5	8	6	10	8	6
Tranquilizers:						
Mother drinks	7	7	6	6	8	2
Father drinks	3	7	6	5	5	3
Cocaine:						
Mother drinks	3	3	1	5	4	5
Father drinks	1	2	2	2	4	3
Heroin:						
Mother drinks	2	1	1	2	2	—
Father drinks	—	1	1	—	1	1
Opiates:						
Mother drinks	6	7	5	7	14	8
Father drinks	4	5	4	7	5	5
Inhalants:						
Mother drinks	6	6	5	8	11	2
Father drinks	3	3	3	6	9	3
Total N (mothers)	(632)	(831)	(341)	(251)	(135)	(77)
Total N (fathers)	(219)	(513)	(279)	(239)	(182)	(29)

- Overall influence of parental drug behaviors on adolescent illegal drug use is small.
- Adolescent marijuana use is related to maternal use of psychoactive drugs and especially to maternal and paternal use of alcohol.
- Adolescent use of illegal drugs other than marijuana, and more particularly psychedelics and pills, is related to maternal use of all three classes of psychotherapeutic drugs, to paternal use of barbiturates, and to parental use of alcohol.
- Parental use of psychotropic drugs has a greater influence on adolescent use of pills than on use of marijuana, while the reverse is true for parental alcohol use. The effects of parental alcohol use are greater on the use of marijuana than on other illegal drugs.

As the next section shows, adolescent illegal drug use is predominantly responsive to the influence of peers.

Illegal Drug Use and Peer Influence

The most striking finding to emerge from this study is the crucial role that peers play in the use of drugs by other adolescents. Although previous surveys suggested the importance of peers in youth's drug use (Elseroad & Goodman, 1970; Johnson, 1973; Lavenhar et al., 1972; National Commission on Marihuana and Drug Abuse, 1972; Tec, 1972a), these findings were based on youths' perceptions of their friends' behavior. The independent data obtained from the student's best friend in school allows one to examine and establish the role of peers on the basis of the friend's self-reported drug behavior.[12] Involvement with other drug-using adolescents is the most important correlate of adolescent drug use.

First, the data indicate that an extremely strong relation exists between the adolescent's own drug use and his perception of his friends' use. When adolescents report that none of their close friends is a user, only 2% have used marijuana themselves, as compared with 92% when they report that all their close friends are users (Table 6). Similarly, adolescents are more likely to be users if their brothers and sisters are marijuana users themselves than if their siblings are nonusers (Table 6). The association with perceived peer use (.618 as measured by tau-beta) is much higher than the associations with perceived parental drug use (see Table 2).

The most dramatic demonstration of peer influence appears when adolescent illegal drug use is correlated with the *self-reported* drug-use patterns of their best schoolfriends, in the sample of *dyads*. Thus, adolescent's use of marijuana is directly related to the best friend's self-reported use (Table 7). Fifteen percent of adolescents have ever used marijuana when their friend

[12]Since in 79% of the cases the adolescent's best friend in school is also the best friend outside of school, the data permit inferences about the role of best friends in general.

TABLE 6

Adolescent Marijuana Use by Perceived Peers' Use of Marijuana
(Weighted New York State Student Sample—Wave I, Fall 1971)

Peers' perceived marijuana use	Percent of adolescents having ever used marijuana		
	%	N	Tau-beta
Number of close friends having used marijuana:			
None	2	(3,083)	
Few	17	(1,907)	.618
Some	50	(1,176)	
Most	83	(1,060)	
All	92	(472)	
Do siblings use marijuana?			
No	16	(4,530)	.508
Yes	69	(1,616)	

reports never having used the drug, as compared with 79% when their friend reports having used 60 times or more. Although the likelihood that the adolescent will be a user of the drug himself increases the greater number of times marijuana has been used by his friend, the increase does not progress at a constant rate. There seems to be a major threshold effect, such that if the friend has tried marijuana even only once, the adolescent is much more likely to try the drug himself. Correlatively, beyond a certain point (approximately 10 times), frequency of use by one friend does not appreciably increase the likelihood that the other friend will be a user himself. The overall association between marijuana use in friendship pairs is .477 as measured by tau-beta. The association is larger for girls than for boys.

TABLE 7

Adolescent Marijuana Use by Self-Reported Marijuana Use of
Best Schoolfriend
(Student-Best Schoolfriend Dyads—Wave I, Fall 1971)

Adolescent use	Best schoolfriend use of marijuana						
	Never	1–2 times	3–9 times	10–39 times	40–59 times	60 times or over	Tau-beta
Percent of adolescents having ever used marijuana	15	50	50	72	77	79	.477
Total N	(1,181)	(135)	(140)	(124)	(44)	(126)	

Having a friend who uses marijuana is related, as a minimum, to a four-fold increase in the number of adolescents who are themselves users of that drug. The increase with respect to drugs other than marijuana is at least as large, and sometimes even larger. For instance, the proportion of LSD users is 3% among adolescents whose friends did not use LSD, but 36% or more than 10 times as large, among those whose friends used LSD (Figure 2).

As noted in connection with parental drug use, self-reports of friends' drug use gives rise to lower associations with adolescent use than do perceptual data. In contrast to parents, however, self-reports of friend's behavior show very high correlations with adolescent's own use.

Whether on the basis of perceptions or of actual self-reports, friends have an extremely large influence on adolescent drug use, an influence much stronger than parents'.

Relative Influence of Parents and Peers

The greater importance of friends than parents on adolescent drug use is illustrated further when adolescent's drug use is examined simultaneously in relation to best schoolfriend's and parental drug behavior in the triads.

Table 8 presents the proportion of marijuana users, as a function of best schoolfriend's marijuana use and parent's use ever of psychoactive drugs, for mothers and fathers separately.

While parents and best friends both have an independent effect, the effect of peers is larger by far than the effect of parents. This is seen clearly in those triads in which parental and friends' behavior diverge, that is, when one uses drugs and the other does not, and the adolescent is exposed to conflicting role models. In those instances, adolescents are much more responsive to peers than to parents. In the mother dyads, 56% of adolescents use marijuana when the best schoolfriend has used marijuana and the parent has never used psychoactive drugs; but only 14% are marijuana users when mothers have used one or more psychoactive drugs but the friend has never used marijuana (Table 8). In the latter case, the rate of use is almost as low as when neither the parent nor the best schoolfriend are drug users. The highest rate of adolescent marijuana use (72%) appears when both friend and mother are drug users. There is thus a small synergestic effect in which both parents and peers reinforce each other's influence on the adolescent.

The same findings obtain when parental self-reported alcohol use is substituted for psychotropic drug use (Table 9).

The data also suggest that parental behavior has an impact especially when illegal drug use is present in the child's peer group. In the absence of peer use, parental behavior is not very influential. By contrast, peers' use of illegal drugs has a strong influence even in the absence of parental psychotropic or alcohol use.

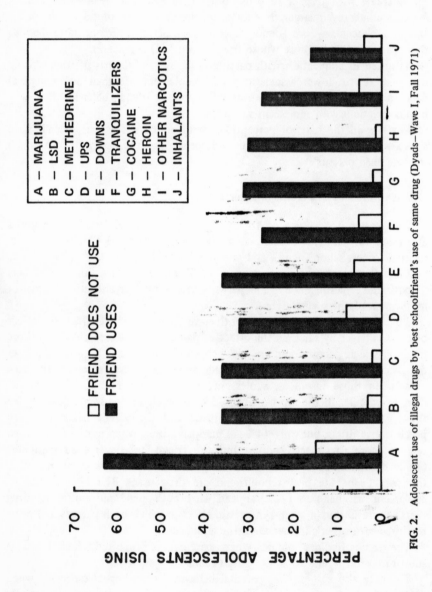

FIG. 2. Adolescent use of illegal drugs by best schoolfriend's use of same drug (Dyads—Wave I, Fall 1971)

TABLE 8

Adolescent Marijuana Use by Best Schoolfriend Marijuana Use and
Parental Self-Reported Ever Use of Psychoactive Drugs
(Triads—Wave I, Fall 1971)

Parental self-reported psychoactive drugs ever use	Percent of adolescents having ever used marijuana			
	Best schoolfriend never used marijuana	Best schoolfriend has used marijuana	Percent difference	Average percent difference
Mother dyads:				
Never used	10	56	46	
Total N	(200)	(89)		51
Used	14	72	56	
Total N	(213)	(111)		
Percent difference	4	16		
Average percent difference		10		
Father dyads:				
Never used	15	57	42	
Total N	(184)	(76)		32.5
Used	23	56	33	
Total N	(111)	(54)		
Percent difference	8	−1		
Average percent difference		3.5		

The relative importance of parents and peers may vary in different
communities and school contexts. In a pilot study conducted 6 months earlier
in a suburban school, the influence of parents, while still smaller than peers',
was greater than it appears to be in our total New York State sample
(Kandel, 1971). The reasons for this discrepancy are not yet clear. It does
suggest, however, that parental influence may vary in strength in different
social contexts.[13]

Adolescent Illegal Drug Use and Involvement with Peers

Clearly, adolescent drug use is very much under the influence of peers and
takes place in great part in response to peer pressures.

Other data from this study document the extent to which experience with
marijuana and with other drugs is a focus of interaction with peers and is
closely related to the extent of involvement with peers. The present data, in
fact, suggest that marijuana use is the single most important behavior which
friends share in common. Whether friendships develop as the result of

---

[13]Further analyses will explore the conditions under which the relative influence of
parents on adolescent drug use varies in importance.

TABLE 9

Adolescent Marijuana Use by Best Schoolfriend Marijuana Use and
Parental Self-Reported Use of Alcohol
(Triads—Wave I, Fall 1971)

Parental self-reported alcohol use	Percent of adolescents having ever used marijuana			
	Best schoolfriend never used marijuana	Best schoolfriend has used marijuana	Percent difference	Average percent difference
Mother dyads:				
Never used	10	62	52	
Total *N*	(334)	(158)		52
Used	22	74	52	
Total *N*	(78)	(38)		
Percent difference	12	12		
Average percent difference		12		
Father dyads:				
Never used	16	49	33	
Total *N*	(206)	(78)		43.5
Used	23	67	54	
Total *N*	(87)	(52)		
Percent difference	7	18		
Average percent difference		12.5		

similarity in values and behavior, or whether similarity develops as the result
of close association, friends generally have been found to share in common a
variety of attributes and characteristics (Kandel & Lesser, 1972; Lindzey &
Byrne, 1968; Newcomb, 1961). Excluding certain demographic characteristics,
the data in this study indicate that on no other activity or attitude is
similarity among friends as great as on marijuana use. We examined
similarity within friendship dyads on a variety of attributes, including
use of other drugs, attitudes toward school, school-related activities,
deviant behavior of various kinds, political attitudes, drug-related attitudes,
and attitudes toward parents (Table 10). Association between friends' use of
marijuana is greater than on any other item, except sociodemographic
characteristics such as sex, age, or race.

Furthermore, drug use is directly related to the frequency of contacts with
peers and to an orientation to peers away from parents. Table 11 indicates,
for example, that drug users are more likely to be found among students who
visit with their friends on a daily basis, among those who would continue to
see their friends over their parents' objections, or those who respect their
friends' opinions over their parents' when faced with a problem.

Adolescents who use marijuana move in peer groups in which drug use is
approved or, at least not a cause for disapproval, and in which drugs are an

TABLE 10

Similarity on Selected Demographic Characteristics, Behavior, and
Attitudes within Friendship Pairs
(Student-Best Schoolfriend Dyads—Wave I, Fall 1971)

Attributes	Tau-beta	Attributes	Tau-beta
Demographic characteristics:		School activities:	
Sex	.811	Overall grade average	.367
Age	.686	Educational expectations	.351
Ethnicity	.662.	Classes cut per week	.308
Program in school	.267	Time spent on homework	.282
Religion	.166	Days absent from school	.187
Father's education	.155	Peer activities:	
Use of illegal drugs:		Driving around with friends	.414
Marijuana	.487	Dating	.322
Psychedelics	.386	Hanging around with kids	.271
LSD	.383	Attending parties	.265
Methedrine	.366	Getting together with friends	.240
Downs	.318	Other activities:	
Heroin	.301	Attending religious services	.255
Cocaine	.290	Participating in political	
Ups	.255	activities	.239
Tranquilizers	.244	Listening to records	.229
Other narcotics	.219	Index of serious	
Inhalants	.134	delinquency	.193
Use of legal drugs:		Reading for pleasure	.166
Smoking	.360	Watching TV	.155
Drinking alcohol	.294	Other attitudes:	
Drinking beer or wine	.264	Political orientation	.175
Drug-related activities and		Who understands better:	
attitudes:		parents or friends	.142
No. of friends reported to		Importance of getting along	
use marijuana or hash	.463	with parents	.123
No. hard drugs purchased	.375	What would do if parents	
Regular use of marijuana		objected to friends	.119
can cause harm	.335	Important to be liked and	
Ever sold marijuana	.235	accepted by others	.108
Should marijuana be			
legalized	.119		

important part of the day-to-day interactions (Table 12). Thirty percent of nonmarijuana users report that they have been offered marijuana by their friends, as compared with 93% of the users. Or, when asked how frequently they talk to their friends about drugs, 32% of marijuana users versus 6% of nonusers report that they do so daily.

Sources of information about drugs are also revealing of the extent of peer influences. For drug users, information is channeled through contemporaries, and not adults. Drug users are much more likely than nonusers to say that they learned most of what they know about drugs from their friends or their

TABLE 11

Adolescent Marijuana Use by Involvement with Peers
(Weighted New York State Student Sample—Wave I, Fall 1971)

Involvement with peers	Adolescents having ever used marijuana		
	%	N	Tau-beta
Frequency of getting together with friends:			
1–2 times a month or less	15	(881)	.171
Once a week	18	(1,101)	
Several times a week	30	(2,764)	
Daily	38	(2,988)	
If parents objected to friend would:			
Stop seeing friends	9	(430)	.251
See friends less	14	(2,334)	
Continue to see friends	39	(4,896)	
Whose opinions respect more when has problems: parents' or best friends':			
Parents', much more	16	(2,382)	.204
Parents', a little more	28	(1,306)	
About equal	34	(2,390)	
Best friends', a little more	39	(917)	
Best friends', much more	49	(669)	

siblings, while nonusers are much more likely than users to rely on the mass media, the schools, or their parents as sources of information (Table 13). In addition, users rely extensively on their personal experience with drugs.

It is striking how, for both groups, parents are rarely relied on as sources of information and are apparently outside the flow of communication regarding drugs. When asked specifically how often they discuss drugs with their parents and their friends, 39% of the total student sample report that they talk at least once a week about drugs to their friends; only 17% do so with their parents.

Peer Influence and Interpersonal Factors

Even though the best friend's influence is extremely strong, it obviously is not the only influence on adolescent illegal drug use. Not all adolescents use marijuana even when their best schoolfriends do so. Table 7 indicates that 21% are nonusers even when their best schoolfriend has used marijuana more than 60 times. Correlatively, a small percentage of adolescents (15%) report using marijuana despite the fact that their friend is a nonuser. The question of further interest, therefore, is what are the conditions under which peer

TABLE 12

Peers' Attitudes Toward Drugs and Communications about Drugs by
Adolescent Marijuana Use
(Weighted New York State Student Sample—Wave I, Fall 1971)

Peers' attitudes and communications	Adolescent marijuana use		
	Has not used	Has used	Tau-beta
Friends' reactions to drug use:			
Approve	4%	25%	.407
Would not care	20	42	
Disapprove, still be friends	47	30	
Disapprove, no more friends	29	3	
Whether has been offered marijuana by friends:			
Yes	30%	93%	.573
No	70	7	
How often talks to friends about drugs:			
About every day	6%	32%	.372
Once or twice a week	21	36	
Once or twice a month	31	18	
Never or hardly ever	42	14	
Total $N \geqslant$	(5,288)	(2,187)	

TABLE 13

Most Important Sources of Information About Drugs
by Adolescent Marijuana Use
(Weighted New York State Student Sample—Wave I, Fall 1971)

Sources of information about drugs[a]	Adolescent marijuana use	
	Has not used	Has used
Siblings	6%	12%
Friends	26	51
Parents	16	4
School	47	21
Television	56	26
Own experience with drugs	([b])	41
Total N	(5,386)	(2,249)

[a]Percentages add up to more than 100% since adolescents could check the 2 most important sources.

[b]Less than 1%. This group includes a few students who have used illegal drugs, but not marijuana.

influence vary? Under what conditions is it strong? Under what conditions is it weak? Of particular interest are those interpersonal factors that characterize the quality of interactions adolescents have with their peers on the one hand, and with their parents on the other. It can be hypothesized that the closer the relationship to peers, the stronger their influence. Correlatively, the closer the relationship with parents, the lesser the influence of peers. The data support both hypotheses.

Best friend's influence is positively correlated with the current intensity of the friendship (Table 14). Concordance on marijuana use with friends is higher when the adolescent sees his friend frequently out of school, when the friendship choice is reciprocated, or when this best schoolfriend is also his best friend overall. Number of years the friend has been known does not affect concordance in drug use. This last finding suggests that certain friendships that revolve around the usage of drugs may have been formed

TABLE 14

Concordance Between Best Schoolfriends on Marijuana
Use by Closeness to Friend or to Parent
(Dyads—Wave I, Fall 1971)

Closeness to friend	Concordance on marijuana use	
	Tau-beta	N
Best schoolfriend is best friend overall:		
Yes	.516	(1,307)
No	.371	(342)
How often sees best schoolfriend out of school:		
Every day	.508	(934)
Less often	.454	(774)
Reciprocity of choice:		
Reciprocated	.538	(715)
Not reciprocated	.452	(1,035)
How many years has known best schoolfriend:		
1 year or less	.499	(192)
2 years	.466	(269)
3–4 years	.476	(462)
5 years and over	.496	(791)
How close feels to mother:		
Very close	.452	(1,036)
Not very close	.508	(700)

relatively recently, and perhaps specifically because of a common interest in drugs. Correlatively, adolescents are somewhat less receptive to their friend's influence if they are close to their parents.

However, the introduction of additional variables does not modify to any great extent the initial association between friend's and adolescent drug use. Regardless of degree of closeness to parents or intimacy of the friendship, the single most important factor is simply whether or not the best friend uses drugs himself.

DISCUSSION AND CONCLUSION

In reviewing the results presented in this report, several questions are addressed: (a) What is the extent of parental and peer influences on adolescent drug use? (b) What is the nature of parental influence? and (c) Why is drug use a focus of peer culture?

Parents, Friends, and Illegal Drug Use

The data indicate that the estimates of parental influence on adolescent use of illegal drugs, based on the child's perception of parental use of psychoactive drugs, greatly exaggerate the importance of parents. The relationships of adolescent illegal drug use with parental drug use are much smaller when based on the parents' self-reports than on the adolescents' perceptions. Parental self-reports of certain types of drug behavior—i.e., use of psychoactive drugs by mothers and, particularly, use of alcohol or marijuana by mothers or fathers—have some relationship to adolescent marijuana use. Use of all three psychoactive drugs (tranquilizers, barbiturates, and stimulants) by mothers and use of barbiturates by fathers have a stronger relationship to adolescents' use of psychedelics and pills. Parental influence varies with the parental drug involved, the illegal drug used by adolescents, the sex of the parent, and the sex of the child. Overall, mother's influence is larger than father's. But parental influence is relatively small, especially when compared with the influence of peers.

Furthermore, there is a suggestion that parental drug behavior is related to the child's use of illegal drugs especially when such illegal drug use exists in the peer group. A necessary condition for the appearance of adolescent illegal behavior may be the use of illegal drugs by friends. Parental use of psychoactive drugs, or alcohol, may be neither necessary nor sufficient for such adolescent behavior to develop. But given a situation in which peers use drugs, parental behavior becomes important in modulating peer influence. Certain parental drug-use patterns decrease, others potentiate peer influence. When their friends use illegal drugs, children of nondrug using parents are somewhat *less* likely to use drugs, whereas children of drug-using parents are *more* likely to use drugs. Moreover, there is a synergestic influence of parents and peers, so that the highest rates of adolescent illegal drug use appear in situations in which both parents and peers use drugs.

These findings on the relative influence of parents and peers on drug use fit a "cultural deviance" model of behavior and, in particular, the theory of differential association developed by Sutherland to explain delinquent behavior (Sutherland & Cressey, 1970). The crucial factor in the learning of delinquent roles by adolescents may be the availability of delinquent role models in the adolescent peer group. Sutherland advanced the notion that the family can potentially lead the child toward delinquent behavior, either because it engages in delinquent behavior that the child imitates, or because it creates a hostile climate from which the child seeks escape. While either or both factors may characterize the home, the child will not engage in delinquent acts unless such acts are present in the peer culture around him. This theory has been much debated since its formulation in 1939 and has often been held to be incorrect (for a recent critique, see Jensen, 1972). However, the present findings on illegal adolescent drug use appear to fit the model (see also Tec, 1972b). Peer behavior is the crucial determining factor in adolescent drug use, and parental behavior becomes important once such behavior exists in the peer group.

The Nature of Parental Influence

The question arises as to why certain parental drug uses, for example the use of psychoactive drugs by the mother, or alcohol by the father, are particularly influential. The answer may lie in part in the differential visibility of various types of parental behavior.

Certain types of parental behavior are more accurately perceived by children than others, most probably because they occur in social and public settings and are therefore more visible to the child. Parental drinking and smoking are more accurately perceived by adolescents than the use of psychoactive drugs (data not presented). In addition, because of differences in the amount of time each parent spends in the home, the behavior of one parent may be more accurately perceived than the behavior of the other. Probably because mothers spend more time at home than fathers, use of psychoactive drugs by mothers is more accurately perceived than fathers' use A number of children are actually *unaware* of their parents' use of psychotropic drugs. In this study, slightly over a third (36%) reported no parental use when mothers or fathers actually reported having used one or more drugs. And 26% of adolescents reported parental use in the absence of parental self-reported use. Misperceptions are consistently more frequent for fathers than for mothers. It is possible that the associations reported here between parental self-reported behaviors and adolescent illegal drug use represent minimum parental influence. Were the children correctly to perceive the extent of parental psychotropic drug use, parental influence potentially could be higher. However, inferences are difficult to make since adolescents' underreporting of parental use is offset by overreporting.

However, any contribution of parental drug use to their children's use of illegal drugs is a completely unanticipated consequence of such parental behavior. Indeed, that the use of illegal drugs by youth is typically disapproved of by adults (Abelson, Cohen, & Schrayer, 1972), while approved of by peers, is obvious and clearly documented by the responses of the two generations in the study. Although 94% of the parents say that they actively discourage or forbid the use of drugs by their child as best they can, only 21% of the adolescents report that their friends disapprove of drug use and would break up the friendship if they, the adolescents, used drugs. In fact, 48% have been offered marijuana by their friends. A family rule against using drugs appears to be almost universal: 83% of parents and 80% of adolescents report such a rule. While there generally exists a tendency for parents to report more rules than their children (see also Kandel & Lesser, 1972), this tendency does not apply to the rule against using drugs. Adolescents accurately perceive the existence of this rule, yet violate it and almost always without their parents' awareness: *19%* of adolescents report using marijuana within the past 30 days, but only *1%* of their parents acknowledge marijuana use by their children in that same period of time.

Thus there exists a somewhat paradoxical situation in which parents forbid and deny the use of illegal drugs by their children, but in which parental behavior influences, albeit weakly, the illegal use of drugs by adolescents. However, as noted previously, such parental influence appears mostly in contexts in which illegal drug use is current in the child's peer group.

Drug Use as a Focus of Peer Culture

The demonstration of the important role played by peers in the use of drugs by adolescents does not answer the basic question as to why such behavior becomes a focus of peer activities. Why is marijuana use the one characteristic that friendship pairs share in common more often than any other activity, attitude, or value? In some way, drugs represent the ideal behavior pattern to rally and organize the young. Many factors contribute to the appeal of drugs: Recognizing and experiencing their effects is learned from others; drugs are illegal; getting the drug depends on an informal network of buyers and sellers (Becker, 1963; Goode, 1970); drugs are believed to facilitate human interactions (Lennard et al., 1971); and drugs bring about physiological effects and changes in consciousness. Most basically, the exchange of drugs among the young acts as a cementing of social solidarity and may be the equivalent of the exchange of gifts in primitive societies (Dessi S., & Gaffney, C. The Lower East Side service center, Unpublished manuscript, 1970).

Stressing the fact that youths who use drugs associate together does not answer a basic question about the peer group: "How much feathering precedes how much flocking?" (Hirshi, 1969, p. 159). Which came first:

drug use or drug-using friends? Do adolescents seek out drug users after they themselves have become involved with drugs or do they start using drugs because they come to associate with other drug-using friends? Probably both processes are involved. Only longitudinal data can begin to provide an answer to this question. Hopefully, the panel data we obtained will enable one to determine which processes are predominantly involved and under what conditions.

Whatever one's social goals with respect to illegal drug use by the young, the single most irreducible fact is its dominance by the peer group. Parental influences come into play only secondarily.

REFERENCES

Abelson, H., Cohen, R., & Schrayer, D. *Public attitudes toward marihuana,* Part I. Princeton, N.J.: Response Analysis Corporation, 1972.

Abelson, H., Cohen, R., Schrayer, D., & Rappaport, M. *Drug experience, attitudes and related behavior among adolescents and adults.* Princeton, New Jersey: Response Analysis Corporation, 1973.

Balter, M. B., & Levine, J. Character and extent of psychotherapeutic drug usage in the United States. Paper presented at the 5th World Congress on Psychiatry in Mexico City, Nov. 30, 1971. *Excerpta Medica,* in press.

Becker, H. S., Becoming a marihuana user. *American Journal of Sociology,* 1953, 54, 235–242.

Becker, H. S. Marihuana use and the social context. *Social Problems,* 1955, 3, 35–44.

Becker, H. S. *Outsiders.* New York: MacMillan, 1963.

Blum, R. H., & associates. *Horatio Alger's children.* San Francisco: Jossey-Bass, 1972.

Braun, P., & Bengtson, U. Religious behavior in three generations: Cohort and lineage effects. Paper presented at the 25th Annual Meeting of the Gerontological Society, San Juan, Puerto Rico, Dec. 1972.

Braungart, R. G. Family status, socialization and student politics. Paper presented at the annual meeting of the American Sociological Association, San Francisco, Calif., 1969.

Chambers, C. D. An assessment of drug use in the general population. Unpublished study, Special Reprint No. 1, Drug Use in New York State. New York State Narcotic Addiction Commission, May, 1971.

Elseroad, H., & Goodman, S. A survey of secondary school students' perceptions of and attitudes toward use of drugs by teenagers, Parts II and III. Unpublished study, Montgomery County Public Schools, Jan. 1970.

Flacks, R., The liberated generation: An exploration of roots of student protest. *Journal of Social Issues,* 1967, 23, 52–75.

Goldstein, J. W., Korn, J., Abel, W. H., & Morgan, R. M. The social psychology and epidemiology of student drug usage: Report on phase one. Unpublished study, Report No. 70–18, Carnegie-Mellon University Drug Use Research Project, June 1970.

Goode, E. Multiple drug use among marihuana smokers. *Social Problems,* 1969, 17, 48–64.

Goode, E. *The marihuana smokers.* New York: Basic Books, 1970.

Goode, E. *Drugs in American society.* New York: Knopf, 1972.

Haberman, P. W., Josephson, E., Zanes, A., & Elinson, J. High school drug behavior: A methodological report on pilot studies. In S. Einstein & S. Allen (Eds.), *Student drug surveys.* Farmingdale, N.Y.: Baywood Publishing Co., 1972.

Hirshi, T. *Causes of delinquency.* Berkeley, Calif.: University of California Press, 1969.
Jensen, G. F. Parents, peers and delinquent action: A test of the differential association perspective. *American Journal of Sociology,* 1972, 78, 562–575.
Johnson, B. *Marihuana users and drug subcultures.* New York: Wiley, 1973.
Josephson, E. Trends in adolescent marihuana use. (This volume).
Kandel, D. Family processes in adolescent drug use. Unpublished study, Progress Report, Grant No. DA-00064, National Institute of Mental Health, Oct. 1971.
Kandel, D. Adolescent marihuana use: The role of parents and peers. *Science,* 1973, 181, 1067–1070.
Kandel, D., & Lesser, G. Parental and peer influences on adolescent educational plans. *American Sociological Review,* 1969, 34, 212–223.
Kandel, D., & Lesser, G. *Youth in two worlds.* San Francisco: Jossey-Bass, 1972.
Kendall, M. G. *Rank correlation methods.* New York: Hafner Publishing Co., 1962.
Keniston, K. *Young radicals.* New York: Harcourt, Brace, & World, 1968.
Klerman, G. L. A reaffirmation of the efficacy of psychoactive drugs. *Journal of Social Issues,* 1971, 1, 301–311.
Lavenhar, M., Wolfson, E. A., Sheffet, A., Einstein, S., & Louria, D. B. A survey of drug abuse in six suburban New Jersey high schools. II. Characteristics of drug users and nonusers. In S. Einstein & S. Allen (Eds.), *Student drug surveys.* Farmingdale, N.Y.: Baywood Publishing Co., 1972.
Lawrence, T., & Vellerman, J. Drugs/teens–alcohol/parents. *Science Digest,* Oct. 1970, 34, 47–56.
Lennard, H. S., Epstein, L. J., Bernstein, A., & Ransom, D. B. *Mystification and drug misuse.* San Francisco: Jossey-Bass, 1971.
Lindzey, G., & Byrne, D. Measurement of social choice and interpersonal attractiveness. In G. Lindzey & E. Aronson (Eds.), *The handbook of social psychology,* Vol. II, *Research Methods,* 2nd ed. Reading, Mass.: Addison-Wesley, 1968.
Manheimer, D. I., & Kleman, M. T. Use of mood changing drugs among American adults. Paper presented at the 30th International Congress on Alcoholism and Drug Dependence, Amsterdam, Sept. 6, 1972.
Manheimer, D. I., Mellinger, G. D., & Balter, M. B. Marihuana use among urban adults. *Science,* 1969, 166, 1544–1545.
Mellinger, G. H. Psychotherapeutic drug use among adults: A model for young drug users? *Journal of Drug Issues,* 1971, 1, 274–285.
Mellinger, G. D., Balter, M. B., & Manheimer, D. I. Patterns of psychotherapeutic drug use among adults in San Francisco. *Archives of General Psychiatry,* 1971, 25, 385–394.
Mellinger, G. D., Balter, M. B., Parry, H. J., Manheimer, D. I., & Cisin, I. H. An overview of psychotherapeutic drug use in the United States. In E. Josephson & E. Carroll (Eds.), *The epidemiology of drug abuse.* 1974. (This volume)
National Commission on Marihuana and Drug Abuse. *Marihuana: A signal of misunderstanding.* Appendix, Vols. I and II. Washington, D.C.: U.S. Government Printing Office, 1972.
Newcomb, T. H. *The acquaintance process.* New York: Holt, Rinehart & Winston, 1961.
Nowlis, H. H. Speaking of drugs and drug problems. *Contemporary Drug Problems,* 1971-72, 1, 3–14.
Parry, H. Use of psychotropic drugs by U.S. adults. *Public Health Reports,* 1968, 83, 799–810.
Parry, H., Balter, M. B., & Cisin, I. H. Primary levels of underreporting psychotropic drug use. *Public Opinion Quarterly,* 1970-71, 34, 582–592.
Parry, H., Balter, M. B., Mellinger, G. D., Cisin, I. H., & Manheimer, D. I. National patterns of psychotherapeutic drug use. *Archives of General Psychiatry,* 1973, 28, 769–783.

Smart, R., & Fejer, D. Drug use among adolescents and their parents: Closing the generation gap in mood modification. *Journal of Abnormal Psychology,* 1972, 79, 153–160. (a)

Smart, R., & Fejer, D. Relationship between parental and adolescent drug use. In W. Keup (Ed.), *Drug abuse.* Springfield, Ill.: Charles C Thomas, 1972. (b)

Smart, R. G., Fejer, D., & Alexander, E. *Drug use among high school students and their parents in Lincoln and Welland counties.* (Substudy 1–7 and J0-70). Toronto: Addiction Research Foundation, 1970.

Sutherland, E., & Cressey, D. *Criminology.* 8th ed. New York: Lippincott & Co., 1970.

Tec, N. Socio-cultural context of marihuana. In S. Einstein & S. Allen (Eds.), *Student drug surveys.* Farmingdale, N.Y.: Baywood Publishing Co., 1972. (a)

Tec, N. The peer group and marihuana use. *Crime and Delinquency,* 1972, 18(3), 298–309. (b)

Thomas, E. L. Political attitude congruence between politically active parents and college-age children. *Journal of Marriage and the Family,* 1971, 33, 375–386.

Thomas, G. Generational discontinuity in beliefs: An exploration of the gap. In V. Bengston & R. Laufer (eds.), special issue on Generations and Social Change. *Journal of Social Issues,* 1974, 30, in press.

Troll, L., Neugarten, B. J., & Kraines, R. L. Similarities in values and other personality characteristics in college students and their parents. *Merrill-Palmer Quarterly,* 1969, 15, 323–336.

Wechsler, H., & Thum, D. *Drug usage among high school youth in the town of Brookline.* Unpublished study, Medical Foundation Inc., Boston, Mass., Feb. 1972. (a)

Wechsler, H., & Thum, D. *Drug usage among high school youth in the town of Quincy.* Unpublished study, Medical Foundation Inc., Boston, Mass., Feb. 1972. (b)

World Health Organization, *Youth and drugs.* (Technical Report Series No. 516) Geneva: World Health Organization, 1973.

12
PATTERNS OF COLLEGE STUDENT DRUG USE AND LIFESTYLES

W. Eugene Groves
The Johns Hopkins University and
Institute for Research in Social Behavior
Berkeley, California

Broadly conceived, studies of college student drug use have addressed three types of questions. The first simply asks how much of which drugs are being used, how different drugs are associated in their use, and how usage is changing from year to year in selected populations. The second asks what characterizations of persons or subcultures best discriminate between users and nonusers of various drugs. The search here is for predictive power, as well as for correlates that give meaning to the individual's pattern of use. The third set of questions probes for causal patterns and mechanisms that best explain the causes or effects of drug use. With cross-sectional survey data, this type of analysis typically uses models with three or more variables to test causal hypotheses.

The present study primarily focused on first two sets of questions. Usage of a wide variety of drugs reported in early 1970 and 1971 by a sample of students on 48 college campuses was presented.[1] For selected drugs the changes over a year were examined further, and projections were made for the equilibrium point where use in a cohort will stabilize from one year to the next. Differences in the use of selected drugs across 12 types of colleges were discussed. In addition, the way in which the use of certain drugs is related to the use of other drugs was examined, and three general patterns of use were defined. Finally, the way in which these three patterns of use are associated with different student lifestyles were analyzed.

[1] This research was supported by grant MH16536 from the National Institute of Mental Health, Peter H. Rossi, principal investigator. Particular thanks are due to David Grafstein for his continual and invaluable assistance in most phases of this study.

SURVEY METHODOLOGY

College drug studies have measured usage in a variety of ways. The simplest common denominator is the question of whether a drug has ever been used by the respondent. The focus of a large number of studies has been on history of use—the total number of times used and the age of first use. Other research, including the present study, has focused primarily on measures of current use—over the last year, last semester, last month. Table 1 shows the five categories in which respondents were asked to classify their frequency of usage of all 17 drug types. From our perspective, the conceptualization of usage in recent-past time intervals has several advantages: recollection is probably much more accurate for recent past than for earlier time periods; current frequency of use readily corresponds to the way in which persons typically think of their own use; current use is more immediately related to other current activities, values, associations, friends, and institutional affiliations; and such measures more clearly define a social-chemical phenomenon at a given point in time, so that these behaviors can be more precisely related to other social, cultural, legal, and chemical factors in the society at that time.

On the other hand, history of drug use provides data on career patterns or stages through which persons have passed in arriving at their present state. It also gives some basis for discerning who has been involved in drug use over a long period of time and for assessing what effect such usage might have had on his or her present condition. Of course, long-term longitudinal data are much more valuable for this type of analysis than are retrospective reports.

Interests of some investigators are reflected in the varied definitions of drug categories. Distinctions in alcohol use, for example, are sometimes made between beer and hard liquor; sometimes various psychedelic drugs are listed separately, sometimes lumped together—the same with different narcotics. The importance of such distinctions depends entirely on what one is trying to discover. It has become fairly clear, for example, that regardless of how marijuana usage is defined, the correlates of use have been quite comparable across a number of studies. On the other hand, if an investigator is interested in potential habituation or addiction to various drugs (e.g., tobacco, alcohol, amphetamines, barbiturates, and narcotics), more precise measures of pharmacological potency, frequency of usage, and dosage would be rather important.

A particularly complex question arises in relation to the use of prescription drugs; i.e., amphetamines, barbiturates, tranquilizers, and some narcotics. Some studies have asked respondents to report only "nonmedical" usage; others have asked about all usage or have requested the respondent to distinguish his own use according to source or purpose. To add to the complexity, the purpose of using a particular drug is not necessarily determined by the source. One may obtain tranquilizers from friends to use for the same purpose as if the source were a physician or psychiatrist; or amphetamines or barbiturates obtained from a doctor may actually be used to

TABLE 1

Drug Use Ever and During Current Academic Year (1969–70)

Drug type	Ever used (percent of total, N = 7,948)	Frequency of use since school started in the fall (Percent of those who have ever used reporting each category)				
		Have not used	Once or twice	Every week or two	Several times a week	Several times a day
Caffeine	88	5	13	13	36	33
Tobacco	74	22	24	11	10	34
Alcohol (1–2 drinks)	89	5	32	47	16	0
Alcohol (several drinks)	69	6	43	42	9	0
Marijuana	31	11	44	28	15	2
Hashish	20	9	55	27	8	1
Methedrine	7	23	61	13	2	1
Other amphetamines	14	24	55	13	7	1
Barbiturates/sedatives	15	33	58	6	3	1
Tranquilizers	19	29	56	7	4	3
Cocaine	3	31	66	2	1	0
LSD	6	20	63	15	2	0
Other psychedelics	7	13	72	14	1	0
Opium	4	27	69	3	1	0
Heroin	1	46	52	1	0	0
Other narcotics	5	35	57	4	1	2
Narcotic cough syrups	38	37	60	2	0	0

get high. The present study inquired about use for any purpose. In addition, it inquired about the primary source as well as the purpose of use and whether the user had gotten "high" on each substance. Knowing the source predicts, in part, whether one has gotten high. With amphetamines, for example, of the students who had obtained them from a doctor, 14% had gotten high, while 56% of those who obtained them from friends or acquaintances reported having gotten high.

Another important difference is in the range of drugs included in the inquiry. Just as a number of studies of college drug use prior to the mid-1960s focused on alcohol use, the more recent ones have focused primarily on marijuana, psychedelics, and opiates. A few have inquired about the use of a broad range of substances.

The present survey attempted to give equal emphasis to the more widely used drugs like alcohol, tobacco, and caffeine and to the recently publicized "illicit" drugs. Our distinctions tried to reflect both predominant psycho-pharmacological effects and the social meanings and processes currently associated with different drugs by college students. The frequency categories listed in Table 1 gave both comparability across different substances and a reasonably ordered measure of current involvement with each type of drug. We have been interested primarily in finding current usage patterns at each of two points in time and relating these to other aspects of student lifestyle and culture. Table 1 presents the reported usage of all 17 drug categories in spring 1970. These results are generalizable to a large fraction of the 4-year undergraduate college population, and are weighted to be representative of the sampling frame.

The sampling frame consisted of those schools that the 1966 College Data Bank of the Bureau of Applied Social Research at Columbia University listed as predominantly white, nonspecialized, with 1970 projected undergraduate enrollment of over 1,000. A total of 603 institutions from the 1,144 listed in the Data Bank fit this description. The actual selection of schools was made from 566 of the 603 on which selectivity scores were available. [The index used was "estimated selectivity" listed by Astin (1965).] The 566 schools were stratified into two selectivity categories, two size categories, and three types of governance (public, private nonsectarian, and private affiliated). Institutions were sampled randomly from each of the 12 resultant cells, making a total of 48 colleges and universities on which the questionnaire was eventually administered. It was estimated that the colleges with more than 1,000 undergraduates contained between 85% and 90% of the 4-year college students in the United States. Excluding the specialized schools and those with insufficient information for adequate stratification, the universe probably represented between 70% and 80% of the 4-year student population. When students in 2-year colleges were included, the sampling frame represented about one-half of all college students in the country. Another limitation was that only full-time freshmen and juniors listed with the registrar at each institution for autumn 1969 were included. Students from the two classes were proportionately sampled at each institution. Sample sizes ranged from 180 to 260 per school, depending on the size of the undergraduate student body. Prospective respondents were selected from registrars' lists when available and from student directories in a few cases where registration printouts were not available. The actual selection was by interval sampling with an random start.

The initial sample to whom questionnaires were mailed totaled 10,596 students, but in the end at least one questionnaire was delivered to 10,599 students. In some fashion, 8,029 responded, with 81 questionnaires either blank or unusable. Initial nonrespondents were sent additional letters and questionnaires up to three times. Return of an indentifiable detachable postcard indicated response—a technique modeled after the study by Eells (1968) and used by several other investigators. The final result was 7,948 usable questionnaires, for an overall return rate of 75%. The return rate was above average for survey studies of college student drug use, especially the larger scale ones.[2]

Estimates of usage in the tables in this report should be interpreted with caution in several respects. First, sampling error is present in population estimates derived from sample responses. An estimated 31% had used marijuana, and 89% had used alcohol (one or two drinks), as of spring 1970. The standard errors of these weighted percentages were 1.2% for marijuana and about half that for alcohol. By confidence interval theory, there was about a two-thirds chance that the interval 31 ± 1.2% included the actual population use of marijuana.

Second, systematic response bias may have affected the results. About 25% of the students did not respond to the survey, and nothing certain was known of their identity. Goldstein, Korn, Abel, and Morgan (1970), in a similar survey, followed up nonrespondents with a few questions and concluded that their use of marijuana might be slightly but not significantly greater than that of respondents. From the present data, indirect evidence suggested that respondents were not, on the whole, greatly different from nonrespondents. Use of marijuana by those who responded after receiving reminders or new questionnaires was not markedly different from that by earlier respondents.[3] To the extent that we can extrapolate from late respondents to nonrespondents, there is little reason to believe that the prevalence of various drug experiences among nonrespondents varied from that among respondents by more than 1%–2%.

School response rates provided some indication of how marijuana usage was related to questionnaire response. If marijuana users were less likely than nonusers to respond to a drug questionnaire, then there should have been a negative relationship between school response rate and the percentage having used marijuana on each campus. Using reported marijuana use as an indicator of true use in each student body,[4] the correlation between percentage "ever used" and response rate across the 48 schools was slightly negative ($r = -.07$), but statistically insignificant. To the extent that the assumptions about indicators of true prevalence were valid, the hypothesis that marijuana users are less likely to respond than are nonusers was not confirmed.

---

[2] Response rate by school ranged from 56% to 92%. In a regression model using selectivity, number of undergraduates, percent residential, and type of governance as predictors of response rate, only selectivity shows a significant independent relationship to response rate. The more selective the school, the higher the response rate.

[3] This comparison was made after correcting for expected normal increase in use month by month.

[4] As long as the ratio of probabilities of response from users vs. nonusers remains fairly constant across schools, the reported usage rate will be a monotonically increasing function of the true rate, and will be similarly reflected in the covariation with response rate.

Another measure of response bias was derived by ascertaining who responded the first year but not the second year of the study. Addresses on only about 90% of the initial sample could be obtained the second year, and usable responses were received from 5,719 students. This was about 60% of those mailed a questionnaire in spring 1971, but only about 54% of the original sample, which was disappointingly low. Questionnaires were matched between one year and the next for as many persons as we could do so with confidence, as follows.

Each respondent was asked both years to generate a code consisting of two 3-digit numbers. One was the product of the digits representing the months of the respondent's birthday and his mother's birthday. The second number was the product of the days of the month of the two respective birthdays. All questionnaires for both years were stamped with the name of the school at which the respondent was registered the first year. The primary criteria used for matching were school, sex, and the birthday code. In some cases, other criteria were secondarily employed including age, class in school, father's and mother's education, intended major field, grade-point average, and hand-writing. These criteria established correspondences where multiple questionnaires were matched on the primary criteria, or where two questionnaires were consistent in almost all criteria, except for possible errors in multiplication in one of the birthday code numbers. Definite and possible matches were chosen by computer, and judges were employed when all criteria did not correspond. If doubt existed in any judge's mind that two questionnaires came from one individual, the questionnaires were not matched.

With this fairly conservative criterion, questionnaires from 2 years were finally matched for 3,961 respondents. These were 69% of the 1971 respondents, but only 37% of the initial sample sent questionnaires in the first year of the study. Between 10% and 15% of the 1971 respondents did not respond the previous year, and the remaining 15%–20% who could not be matched either did not generate a birthday code one year or the next (about 1% in 1970 and 3% in 1971) or made errors in generating the code—either in multiplication or in recall of mother's birthday.[5]

The relatively small fraction of the original sample who ended up in the matched subsample places limits on the conclusions drawn from the panel data. However, by establishing how this group differed from the larger sample in drug-use patterns and other relevant characteristics, one will have some idea what the biases might be in any conclusions. A least one can define a subpopulation of students to which the results are more appropriately generalizable. Furthermore, the differences between those who responded

---

[5] Where the mother or female guardian's birthday could not be remembered, respondents were asked to use the birthday of the person with whom "you most communicate—father, sister, etc." About 20% did not use mother's or female guardian's birthday in the 1970 questionnaire.

twice and those who responded once might reflect the same factors that distinguish the initial respondents from nonrespondents. To the extent this hypothesis is assumed, a comparison of the matched subgroup and the total 1970 respondents can give an indication of how respondents differed from the total initial sample.[6]

In Table 2 the changes in drug usage over the period of 1 year are shown for the respondents in the longitudinal panel. A comparison of reported "ever used" among the matched subgroup in 1970 with the same reports among the total respondents in 1970 (Table 1) shows the response bias in the panel. The matched subgroup differed by as much as 3% in reports of use of two types of drugs.[7] But interestingly, the differences were in opposite directions. The repeating respondents were more likely to have used caffeine (91% to 88%), and less likely to have used marijuana (28% to 31%). Among other drugs the pattern of smaller differences (1%–2%) suggests that the matched subgroup was more likely to have used some alcohol, barbiturates/sedatives, and tranquilizers, and less likely to have used the primarily "illicit" drugs—cannabis, psychedelics, amphetamines, opium—as well as alcohol in quantities of several drinks. Comparisons between the matched subgroup and the total respondents in spring 1971 exhibited a similar pattern of differences in drug use. Thus, the group of respondents on which conclusions are based for changes from 1970 to 1971 exhibited very slightly more "socially acceptable" drug use than did the total population. Likewise, by extrapolation, respondents to this type of questionnaire possibly were slightly more "conventional" than were nonrespondents. However, the differences were not large, and the relative proportions reporting usage of the different drug categories were similarly ordered in the smaller sample as in larger ones.

The third source of error that has seldom been considered with any rigor in drug studies is unreliability of response. Respondents may answer dishonestly or simply may commit an error in recall, interpretation, or in marking the questionnaire. To check on this type of error, one sometimes looks at inconsistencies in responses to the same item repeated, or to two or more similar items. While such inconsistencies may be taken as indicators of false reporting, they may also indicate genuine mistakes or varied interpretation of questions. In a few surveys, a nonexistent drug has been listed along with substances that might actually have been used. This technique may pick out those who exaggerate use, but not those who underrepresent their usage. There have been no reports of investigators throwing out a substantial number

---

[6] To be precise, the matched subgroup includes 80%–85% of those who responded both years (the others could not be definitely matched). Hence, of the total 1970 respondents ($N = 7,948$) who were not included in the panel, as many as one-fourth might have responded again the second year, but were unmatched. Comparisons between the matched subgroup and the total 1970 sample were thus only an approximate contrast between those who responded twice and those who responded once.

[7] The subgroup differed from the total group significantly (at $p = .01$) in both cases.

TABLE 2

Changes in Drug Usage Between Spring 1970 and Spring 1971

| Drug type | Percent of students in matched subsample (N = 3,961) | | | | | |
| | Ever used | | Used this year | | Used at least every week or two this year | |
	1970	1971	1969-70	1970-71	1969-70	1970-71
Caffeine	91	96	87	87	77	78
Tobacco	73	76	50	51	34	36
Alcohol (1-2 drinks)	90	94	80	87	50	63
Alcohol (several drinks)	67	76	60	67	30	35
Marijuana	28	42	24	37	11	20
Hashish	18	28	16	23	6	8
Methedrine	5	9	4	6	1	1
Other amphetamines	12	18	8	12	2	3
Barbiturates/sedatives	16	22	10	12	1	2
Tranquilizers	20	27	13	16	3	3
Cocaine	3	4	2	2	0	0
LSD	4	8	3	5	0	1
Other psychedelics	6	10	5	8	1	1
Opium	3	5	2	3	0	0
Heroin	0	1	0	1	0	0
Other narcotics	5	7	3	3	0	0
Narcotic cough syrups	38	44	23	19	1	1
Combined categories:						
Alcohol	91	94	83	87	54	66
Marijuana/hashish	28	44	24	37	12	20
Methedrine/amphetamines	15	25	10	16	3	4
LSD/psychedelics	7	13	6	9	1	1

of responses on these grounds. In the present study, about 15 questionnaires out of 8,029 were excluded on the basis of flagrant inconsistencies.

In addition to more subtle measurements of inconsistency, respondents were simply asked whether they felt "confident enough in this survey to answer the drug usage questions with complete honesty." Ten percent said they did not. Those who had used marijuana reported more confidence than those who had not used. The fraction indicating full confidence increased from 88% of the nonusers of marijuana to 98% of those using at least once a week. Most likely this indicates that users admitted their use only if they felt confident in the study. Hence, use was probably underreported. One cannot conclude from these data whether users who lacked confidence were more likely to report nonuse or not to respond at all. The one conclusion warranted is that those who reported extensive "illicit" drug use probably responded fairly honestly.

Unreliability of response also arises from more random errors of misreading, misinterpretation, selective recall, incorrectly marking answers, etc. This makes it particularly important to assess whether the changes reported at two points in time by individuals are significantly greater than might occur from random response error if there were no shifts in actual behavior. From data of the present study, two sources of estimating response uncertainty were available. First, in spring 1970, 90 respondents answered two identical questionnaires an average of about 1 month apart.[8] Assuming no real change for 1 month, one can obtain test-retest reliability estimates from these responses. The second method employed answers to more than one question measuring the same thing in the same questionnaire. In 1970, for example, respondents were asked in four different ways whether they had ever used marijuana. Each method of estimating reliability has its limitations, but both methods give some idea of how much confidence to place in reported switches from one year to the next.

Standard statistical measures of reliability are not discussed here; rather, simple percentage measures of inconsistencies are presented, which give approximations that can usefully be compared with reported changes in drug usage from one year to the next. For marijuana, the test-retest measures of reliability showed a total of 5% of the respondents switching their responses about ever having used—about an equal fraction shifted in either direction over a month's time. Between different questions in the same questionnaire, a maximum of 0.6% exhibited inconsistencies between any two questions. In answering "ever used" alcohol (one or two drinks), 6% changed from one month to the next, with a slightly higher fraction switching from "no" to "yes" than the reverse—consistent with a likely actual increase in experience with alcohol in a month's time. A maximum of 2.1% answered two alcohol-usage items inconsistently within the same questionnaire. By far the largest discrepancy was between a question listing the age of first use of alcohol (typically before college) and the other items asking about "ever used." About 1.5% more people gave an age of first use than said they had "ever used" in two later questions. The difference between alcohol and marijuana response inconsistencies leads one to believe that unreliability in reporting "current" behavior (most marijuana use began in college) is less than in reporting cumulative past behavior. In summary, probably somewhere between 0.5% and 5% of responses to drug-usage questions may change from time to time with no change in actual behavior.

PREVALENCE AND INCIDENCE FINDINGS

Most college students have ingested or inhaled one chemical or another, with alcohol being the most likely used—as well as the drug most used

---

[8] This was an unintended result of overlaps between receiving their first responses and mailing the second questionnaire to the list of nonrespondents.

illegally. As of spring 1970, students in the 48-college sample reported experience "ever" ranging from a low of less than 1% (0.6%) ever having used heroin, to a high of approximately 92% who had used at least some alcohol. Table 1 indicates the reported usage "ever" for 17 substances, as well as the current frequency of use among those who reported any use at all during their lives. A majority reported use of caffeine, tobacco, and alcohol. Over 31% claimed to have at least tried marijuana or hashish. Of the cannabis users, 89% used during the academic year 1969–70, and 45% used it at least every week or two. Less than 9% claimed to have used any of the psychedelic drugs (LSD, mescaline, DMT, psilocybin, etc.)

A sizable fraction indicated some kind of "pill" usage—amphetamines, barbiturates/sedatives, or tranquilizers. Though most of the more commonly used trade names of drugs in each of these three categories were provided to the respondent, there were probably significant errors in recollection or interpretation of what usage to include. A total of 17% reported having used methedrine or other amphetamines (combining two categories of Table 1), 15% reported barbiturate/sedative use, and 19% said they had used tranquilizers at some point in their lives. Combining these three drug types, a total of 35% said they had used at least one of these substances. If we distinguish "pill" use by source, a doctor was the primary source for 5% of methedrine users, 30% of users of other amphetamines, 65% of the barbiturate/sedative users, and 68% of the tranquilizer users.

Distinction by source further clarified the use of narcotics other than opium and heroin, and of cocaine. Seventy-six percent of the other narcotics users (5% of the sample reported any use) and 42% of the cocaine users (3% reported any use) claimed doctors as their primary source. For other narcotics, this includes prescriptions of codeine, Demerol, Percodan, etc. But for cocaine, the source distinction is less immediately apparent and most likely reflects administration of cocaine as a local anesthetic by dentists. The source distinction indicates that for both other narcotics and cocaine only about 2% of the sample population obtained these substances from nonmedical sources.

Opium was used by about 4% and heroin by less than 1%. However, only 22 out of 7,948 respondents indicated using opium at least every week or two, and only one person reported "regular" heroin use by this definition. Indeed, only about half those reporting ever use of heroin (59) claimed to have used it during that current year. Certainly, these usage reports give little grounds for suspecting a noticeable opiate addiction problem among college students during 1969–70. (Of course, it is quite possible that heavy users of opium or heroin would be less likely than others to answer the questionnaire.)

Drug usage changes over time have been examined in three ways. The Gallup and other national polling organizations, as well as several campus researchers (e.g., Blum and associates, 1969; McKenzie, 1970), have surveyed different samples representing the same age or college class distribution, or group membership, but at different points in time. These results give an indication of general social/cultural changes in successive college populations. Alternatively, the same group or people may be sampled at different points in time to indicate how people change through a combination of assimilation/maturation within a certain context and of changes in the campus culture as a whole from one year to the next. Goldstein and Korn (1972), for example, resurveyed the same freshmen cohort at two later points in time on one campus, providing data on overall usage changes in the group. Finally, a panel of individuals may be questioned at more than one point in time to assess how different individuals change. The third approach requires linking responses at two points in time from the same individual. The present 48-college survey attempted to follow up individual respondents 1 year after the initial survey. A number of similar drug-use questions are being asked in another longitudinal study on one campus. Manheimer, Mellinger, Somers, and Kleman (1972) conducted a study of changing lifestyles and values among undergraduate males at the University of California, Berkeley.

Successive national samples of college students, as well as several samples taken in different years on a number of campuses, have showed a marked rise in experience with "illicit" drugs—most noticeably with marijuana. In national surveys, the proportion of college students reporting having ever used marijuana has increased from about 5% in 1967 to over 50% in 1971-72. Use of other drugs is not increasing as noticeably, however, In fact, the use of some of the more prevalent drug types may even be decreasing. Goldstein and Korn (1972), for example, reported on one campus that while alcohol use increased appreciably over a 2-year period in the 1968 freshman cohort, its use in 1970 was less than that of the comparable junior class of 1968.

Regardless of overall trends among succeeding generations, one would expect the proportion of individuals in one cohort who have tried any substance to increase from one year to the next, on the grounds that some nonusers are almost certain to initiate use over an additional year of exposure. However, the incidence[9] of use in any given year, as well as the prevalence of regular use, might increase or decrease over time with changing trends. Data from the present study provide information on overall changes over a year in cohorts who were initially freshmen and juniors, as well as on individual switches that make up the aggregate group changes. First, aggregate changes between 1970 and 1971 are reported. Then an equilibrium level of use for the cohort is projected based on individual changes from one year to the next.

Table 2 compares reports of drug usage in 1970 and 1971 in three different categories: "ever used," "used this academic year," and "used at least every week or two this academic year." Some students initiated use of each of the drugs in the intervening year between the two surveys. These

---

[9] "Incidence" in this report indicates the proportion who use at least once during an academic year.

increases can be examined in different ways depending on the point of the analysis. Considering the change as a percent of the total sample population, the increases varied from 0.3% initiating heroin use to 14% initiating marijuana use over the year. Increases of several percentage points occurred in use of hashish, alcohol (several drinks), amphetamines, barbiturates/sedatives, tranquilizers, and narcotic cough syrups. If the proportion who had used by 1971 is compared with the proportion who had used by 1970, the largest fractional increase occurred for psychedelics—the percent having ever used psychedelics in 1971 almost doubled over 1970. The smallest increase, using this criterion, was in tobacco use (about 4%). Finally, considering the increase as a proportion of initial nonusers in 1970—i.e., the probability of a nonuser becoming a user— then 59% of the caffeine nonusers in 1970 had at least tried it by 1971, while only 0.3% of the heroin nonusers had tried that drug a year later. The drugs which initial nonusers were most likely to try over the course of 1 year were caffeine, alcohol, and marijuana, in descending probability. As expected in a diffusion process, the probability of initiating a new behavior is, in part, a function of exposure; and nonusers are presumably more likely to be exposed to those drugs used more prevalently.

In current use (used this academic year) marijuana showed the largest increase, as a percentage of the total panel (from 24% to 37%). On the other hand, fewer students used narcotic cough syrups the second year than the first. There were moderate increases in use of most "pills," especially amphetamines, and in psychedelics. Interestingly, most of those who had experience with psychedelics in 1970 had used them that year, while in 1971 only 9 out of every 13 users reported using during the current year. Some of the reported changes, for example in heroin use (from 0.3% to 0.6%), were so small that the differences might well have resulted from response uncertainty.

The only noticeable changes in "regular" use (at least every week or two) were in alcohol (from 54% to 66%) and in cannabis (from 12% to 20%). There were slight increases in frequent use of amphetamines and barbiturates/sedatives, but not enough to express confidence in any real changes. No one in the matched subgroup reported "regular" use of heroin either year, and only one or two reported such use of opium. The National Commission on Marihuana and Drug Abuse (1972) staff suggested that comparative institutional survey data indicated that the average frequency of use of marijuana increased with the proportion who had ever used. Data from the present study on changes over time indicated a slight increase in the proportion of regular users the second year compared with the first. Among those who have ever used, the proportion indicating "regular" use increased from .42 in 1970 to .45 in 1971. However, this change was small compared with the figure for alcohol. Regular alcohol users constituted .59 of those who had ever used in 1970, but .70 of those who had used by 1971. Tobacco, barbiturate/sedative, and psychedelic regular users constituted about the same proportion of those who had ever used in both years (about .47, .08, and .10, respectively). Decreases in the proportion of regular users occurred for methedrine/other amphetamines (from .20 to .14) and for tranquilizers (.14 to .11). Thus, while the experience with most drug types increased in the same cohort from one year to the next, the typical intensity of involvement increased only for alcohol and marijuana.

While repeated national surveys indicate changing usage patterns in comparable age groups at different times, the repeated measurements on individuals within a cohort can be used to project an equilibrium usage incidence for that cohort as they grow older in the same context. When approximately the same fraction of a population are users of a drug (such as tobacco) at two different points in time, the usage is at an equilibrium. Just as many people switch from use to nonuse as vice-versa over the time interval ("use" is defined here as use during a given academic year). For tobacco, approximately 50% of the panel reported usage in each of the 2 years of the study (see Table 2). For most of the other drugs, use was on the increase—more students began than ceased use from one year to the next. This is characteristic of a phenomenon which is either relatively new and diffusing throughout a population or to which inexperienced individuals are cumulatively exposed as they grow older. Assuming that the transition probabilities—the chances that individuals will change their user status in either direction from one year to the next—remain constant over time, one can project an equilibrium proportion of current users.

Table 3 summarizes the estimated transition rates across seven types of drugs. As well, the 1969-70 and the 1970-71 baseline usage incidence and the projected equilibrium usages are shown. To the extent that the estimated probabilities reflect true, unchanging, homogeneous population parameters, one should expect the observed incidence to change each year in the direction of the equilibrium value—at which point it will remain relatively constant over time. Nonusers of alcohol are most likely to become users from one year to the next (with probability .41), and users are least likely to stop ($p = .03$). Cannabis nonusers are about twice as likely to begin, as users are to stop, while tobacco use changes in either direction with about equal probability. Nonusing students are least likely to begin heroin use and are not likely to start psychedelics, amphetamines, or barbiturates/sedatives. Those who use barbiturates/sedatives are most likely to quit; and psychedelic, amphetamine, and heroin users are fairly likely to quit from one year to the next. The current use of tobacco, alcohol, psychedelic, barbiturates/sedatives, and heroin was fairly close to the projected equilibrium by 1971. Cannabis had the farthest to rise to achieve equilibrium—and, as previously noted, spread most rapidly during the year. Despite some recent alarm about heroin on the campus, no more than 2% of this cohort would be expected to try it in any given year. These calculations project that ultimately, in any given year, a majority of the sampled cohort will use tobacco, alcohol, and cannabis.

TABLE 3
Transition Probabilities for Changes in Drug Use 1969-70 to 1970-71
($N = 3,961$)

Drug type	Probability of use		Probability of changing		Projected equilibrium probability of use[a]
	1969-70	1970-71	From use to nonuse	From nonuse to use	
Tobacco	.50	.51	.18	.18	.50
Alcohol	.83	.87	.03	.41	.93
Marijuana/hashish	.24	.37	.11	.21	.66
Psychedelics	.06	.09	.39	.06	.13
Amphetamines	.10	.16	.34	.10	.23
Barbiturates/sedatives	.10	.12	.56	.08	.13
Heroin	.00	.01	.21	(.004)	.02

[a]The proportion of the sample who will use at least once in any given academic year when that proportion has reached a level that is constant from one year to the next.

Several factors are important in interpreting these equilibrium projections. First, projections are valid only for the cohort sampled. And this cohort will soon be in a different milieu after leaving college, so that the context may radically change before equilibrium is achieved. Second, changes in social and legal factors may alter the underlying transition probabilities from one time interval to the next—which will change the projected equilibrium values. Finally, if the transition probabilities are not relatively homogeneous, i.e., if they differ markedly for different kinds of individuals or on different types of college campuses, the projected equilibrium obtained from the average transition probabilities will not exactly equal the average of the projected equilibria across the respective colleges or population subgroups.[10] For drugs such as alcohol and tobacco, college students have presumably been exposed to the substance for a sufficient number of years, and the general social and legal attitudes of the culture have remained sufficiently constant over a few years that a relatively stable equilibrium of incidence can be estimated.

These projections cannot validly be applied to succeeding classes of college students. The observed changes in one cohort are a result both of acculturation and assimilation within a given collegiate subculture and of changing mores that pervade all age groups in college. For alcohol, the acculturation through cumulative constant exposure is probably the prodominant process, while for marijuana, both processes are probably important.

---

[10]Another assumption made in calculating the equilibrium incidence is that response unreliability is small compared to the actual changes as reflected in the reported shifts from one year to the next.

DRUG USE IN DIFFERENT SCHOOLS

The 48 schools in which students were surveyed were selected according to criteria that would maximize the contrasts in patterns of drug usage. Previous studies using the same instrument across a few colleges and universities suggested that intellectual orientation, affluence, and religiosity might be important distinguishing factors relevant particularly to "illicit" drug use. (See Barter, Mizner, & Werme, 1971; Blum and associates, 1969; Mizner, Barter, & Werme, 1970.) Kenniston (1968), in reviewing many studies of college student drug use, suggested that the more selective schools attract students who are more intellectually and more experimentally oriented. To counterbalance the dominant mode of postponed gratification entailed by the emphasis on academic achievement, the students develop an "experiential" counterculture, he suggested. Such a culture is conducive to the use of a variety of drugs to get high. A later study (Johnson, 1973) confirmed a strong positive association between marijuana use and selectivity among 20 colleges in the metropolitan New York area. Marijuana use was ordered in the same fashion as was selectivity except that the least selective schools had more usage than was expected.

For the present sampling, schools were stratified by high and low selectivity; it seemed that this factor would be importantly related to marijuana and psychedelic use. Colleges were also stratified by type of control: public, private nonsectarian, and private religious affiliated. This was, in part, a surrogate measure of the religiosity of the student body; it was assumed that religiously controlled institutions would attract a higher proportion of religiously oriented students than would other types of institutions. In addition, colleges were stratified by size of student body to increase the sampling fraction of the larger schools, which enroll more students, but which are far outnumbered by the smaller colleges in the United States.

Differences found among school types do not straightforwardly demonstrate any particular causal pattern. If, for example, students at more selective schools are more likely to use marijuana, the difference may be due to any combination of several factors. Some contrasts may arise from differences in the aggregate background characteristics associated with selectivity criteria, e.g., parents' socioeconomic status, students' IQ's or students' high school performances. Some of the contrasts may be due to compositional effects; i.e., being in a milieu of more affluent students may have an impact on a person's behavior above and beyond what might be predicted merely from his own background characteristics. And perhaps some differences may arise from contextual effects, i.e., faculty attitudes and behavior, school policies, or institutional traditions. Data from the present study are developed only to the extent of exhibiting the simple differences by school type.

Table 4 indicates the incidence (use or not during the 1969-70 academic year) of use of five different drug types across the 12 stratification cells. As well, the maximum and minimum incidence among the 48 schools is listed. While the incidence of alcohol ranged from 31% to 98%, most colleges clustered at the higher end. In only four schools did fewer than 75% report using alcohol during the year. Average incidence did not vary much across school types, with one exception. Small, low-selectivity, religious colleges

TABLE 4
Drug Use by Type of College

Type of college	Percent who used each drug during 1969-70 academic year				
	Alcohol	Cannabis	Amphetamines	Barbiturates/ sedatives	Heroin
Lowest incidence school	31	4	2	3	0.0
Highest incidence school	98	66	28	18	4.0
Small, public, low selectivity[a] (5,773)	87	14	10	8	0.3
Small, public, high selectivity (2,297)	88	48	22	12	0.7
Small, private, nonsectarian low selectivity (2,261)	88	28	17	15	0.3
Small, private, nonsectarian, high selectivity (5,865)	95	58	16	11	0.5
Small, private affiliated, low selectivity (7,1107)	66	13	7	10	0.2
Small, private affiliated, high selectivity (5,907)	92	30	12	13	0.0
Large, public, low selectivity (7,1202)	87	27	14	12	0.3
Large, public, high selectivity (5,956)	87	36	14	10	0.5
Large, private, nonsectarian, low selectivity (2,341)	89	42	22	15	0.6
Large, private, nonsectarian, high selectivity (3,478)	92	54	16	10	0.7
Large, private affiliated, low selectivity (3,464)	92	26	13	9	1.2
Large, private, affiliated, high selectivity (2,309)	96	30	8	7	0.8

[a]The figures in parenthesis indicate the number of schools sampled of each kind, and the total number of respondents in that type of school, respectively.

reported an incidence of only 66%. These were primarily small denominational colleges, which probably stress heavily an abstinent, religiously oriented student culture. Otherwise, religiosity made little difference; in fact, the school type in which the highest incidence was reported was the large, high-selectivity, religious colleges (primarily Roman Catholic.)

For cannabis (marijuana and hashish), the variation in incidence was more clearly associated with the stratification criteria than was true for alcohol. Incidence in private nonsectarian schools exceeded that in public or church-affiliated institutions across all combinations of size and selectivity. High-selectivity schools also in all cases exceeded low-selectivity schools in use, controlling for size and control. As with alcohol, the lowest incidence was found in the low-selectivity, small, religious colleges. The highest incidence was clearly among students at high-selectivity, private nonsectarian, small colleges. These are the high-status, affluent, intellectually oriented colleges that have been accorded considerable publicity as centers of countercultural activity. The relationships between selectivity of the school and the use of marijuana was even more impressive when the actual selectivity score, using the Astin (1965) index, was correlated with the percentage having used marijuana on each campus. Across the 48 schools the product moment correlation was .72—selectivity "explaining" about 52% of the variance from school to school. If one constructs a regression model predicting percentage marijuana use by selectivity and by type of control, a total of 76% of the variance (multiple R^2) is "explained." Knowing the selectivity of the school and how it is governed enables one to predict variation in marijuana use across student bodies with a rather high degree of accuracy.[11]

Methedrine and other amphetamine incidence ranged between 2% and 28%. As with cannabis and alcohol, the lowest incidence was in small, low-selectivity, church-affiliated colleges. Indeed, for all combinations of size and selectivity, the church-affiliated colleges had lower incidence than either public or private, nonsectarian institutions. Selectivity of the school did not exhibit a consistent relationship with incidence, however, Other than the relationship to religiosity, there appeared to be no clearly interpretable pattern to the variation in amphetamine usage.

Barbiturates and other sedatives showed a narrower range of incidence, from 3% to 18%, across the 48 schools. Variation across the 12 school types neither was wide nor exhibited any important interpretable pattern. Since

---

[11] From differences in marijuana use across schools, some investigators have suggested that location in, or near, a large metropolitan area increases the use of marijuana and other "illicit" drugs—due to greater availability. We found that location inside or outside a standard metropolitan statistical area (SMSA) "explained" about one-fourth as much variance in percentage having used marijuana across the 48 schools as did selectivity. More important, when location is added to selectivity and governance as predictors in a linear regression model, it increases the variance "explained" by only about 4%, which is rather small (though significant at $p = .01$).

these drugs are primarily medically prescribed, their usage should be less determined by those institutional factors associated with a drug-using counterculture.

Heroin use was generally quite low, with an exceptional 4% reporting at least trying it at one school. The variations among school types were too small to attribute any significance to a pattern; differences might have resulted from sampling error or response unreliability. It is rather interesting, though, to note that large, low-selectivity, church colleges had the highest reported incidence (1.2%). These are predominantly urban schools, and their location might be one factor contributing to the possible slightly higher use of heroin.

Comparing the five drug types, in all cases the lowest incidence was in religiously controlled institutions—mostly small, and a majority low-selectivity. Highest incidence occurred consistently among high-selectivity schools, except for heroin use. Marijuana use showed the highest variation across school types. This was consistent with the initial attempt to stratify schools to best reflect differences in "illicit" drug use. For marijuana, the prediction that usage is associated with high-selectivity, nonreligiously oriented college milieux was confirmed. Alcohol, which was also mostly used illegally by college students, also showed a slightly higher incidence in the more selective schools; but in contrast with marijuana, religiosity did not consistently diminish its use. Amphetamine and barbiturate/sedative use varied only moderately across types of schools, with the amphetamine incidence pattern exhibiting some similarity to that of marijuana. By and large, the prescription drugs did not vary in usage according to the same patterns as the social/personal drugs.

USAGE ASSOCIATIONS AMONG DIFFERENT DRUGS

Most college studies either analyzed the use of one drug, like marijuana, or combined several on an a priori basis. Some empirical relationships among usage of the various kinds of drugs have emerged, however. Unless the investigator has a special reason for observing only one kind of drug, it should prove much more fruitful to describe individuals in terms of related multiple-drug usage.

Among the "illicit" drugs, findings consistently agree that those who have used the less prevalent drugs are more likely to have used the more prevalent drugs. Thus Robbins, Robbins, Pearlman, and Philip (1970) suggested, from a pilot study on two campuses, that the use of LSD and other psychedelics implied the use of marijuana in one's life history. ("Imply" here means that the probability of use of one drug is significantly greater among users than among nonusers of the second drug.) Barter et al. (1971) similarly found that illicit use of psychedelics and amphetamines implied the use of marijuana. There exists a plethora of studies which have concluded that heroin users—in most populations—are much more likely than nonheroin users to have used marijuana. Surveys have also consistently found that the more frequent marijuana users are more likely to use other illicit substances, particularly psychedelics and narcotics (e.g., Goode, 1971; Johnson, 1973; McGlothlin, Jamison, & Rosenblatt, 1970; National Commission on Marihuana and Drug Abuse, 1972).

However, the emphasis on illicit drug use has tended to ignore the fact that users of one drug are more likely than nonusers to have at least tried almost any other substance. Robbins et al. (1970) found that users of illicit drugs (marijuana, LSD, cocaine, heroin, etc.) were more likely also to use other substances like coffee, amphetamines, antacids, etc. Barter et al. (1971) reported that those who had used other drugs (narcotics, other hallucinogens, barbiturates, and tranquilizers), with the exception of alcohol, were more likely to be amphetamine, marijuana, or LSD (AML) users. And Johnson (1973) found that tobacco use was one of the more important predictors of marijuana use.

One of the more comprehensive summaries of the interrelationship among the use of different kinds of substances has been provided by Blum and associates (1969). He found significant positive correlations across practically all sets among the lifetime cumulative history of use of nine types of drugs (tobacco, alcohol, amphetamines, sedatives, tranquilizers, hallucinogens, marijuana, illicit opiates, and "special substances"). Interestingly, the correlation between tobacco and marijuana usage ($r = .31$) exceeded that between marijuana and illicit opiates ($r = .24$).[12]

Data from the present 48-college study suggested similar positive interrelationships. Table 5 presents the current use of correlations among 14 different substances. The relative magnitudes of different correlation coefficients are quite comparable between the Blum's data and those presented here (where drug types are comparably defined) even though his was based on life history of usage and the present data dealt only with usage during the academic year 1969–70.

The different drugs clustered similarly when factor analyses were performed on the correlations matrices from the 5-college sample in 1966–67 (Blum and associates, 1969) and the 48-college sample in 1969–70. With a three-principal-component solution, orthogonally rotated, Blum and associates found marijuana, hallucinogens, "special substances," and amphetamines to load highest on one factor, which were labeled "illicit-exotic" use. Another factor had sedatives, tranquilizers, and illicit opiates loading highest, describing a desire for suppressive effects. The third factor featured the "social drugs," alcohol and tobacco. Findings of the present study are shown in Table 6. The first factor is characterized by high loadings of psychedelics, cannabis,

---

[12] The comparability of correlation coefficients across sets of variables which depart significantly from a normal distribution should be interpreted with caution because the magnitude is partially dependent on marginal distributions of the variables.

TABLE 5
Current Drug-use Frequency Correlation

Drug	(Pairwise product moment correlations (r)[a]												
	Cocaine	Opium	Other narcotics	Methedrine	Psychedelics	Other amphetamines	Barbiturates	Tranquilizers	Cannabis	Cough syrup	Tobacco	Caffeine	Alcohol
Heroin	.22	.20	.13	.24	.21	.10	.09	.04	.15	.02	.05	−.00	.01
Cocaine		.24	.10	.22	.22	.14	.12	.08	.18	.06	.07	.02	.03
Opium			.11	.38	.45	.23	.14	.09	.40	.05	.15	.01	.06
Other narcotics				.15	.11	.15	.12	.12	.11	.18	.08	.03	.05
Methedrine					.48	.34	.19	.13	.43	.05	.18	.04	.09
Psychedelics						.38	.17	.08	.60	.02	.21	.02	.08
Other amphetamines							.24	.19	.33	.09	.20	.09	.09
Barbiturates								.34	.16	.17	.10	.07	.08
Tranquilizers									.10	.16	.08	.06	.06
Cannabis										.02	.35	.07	.22
Cough syrup											.10	.12	.09
Tobacco												.20	.41
Caffeine													.12

Note.—The variables were scored 0 through 4 corresponding to the response categories for frequency of use during the 1969–70 academic year (see Table 1).
[a] A correlation coefficient of .033 is significantly greater than 0.0 at $p = .01$ ($N = 7,948$).

TABLE 6

Factor Analysis of Drug-use Frequency
(Factor Loading Matrix)[a]

Drug type	Factor 1	Factor 2	Factor 3
Psychedelics	0.775	0.109	−0.009
Cannabis	0.675	0.328	−0.008
Methedrine	0.624	0.085	−0.156
Opium	0.582	0.045	−0.075
Other amphetamines	0.398	0.148	−0.282
Cocaine	0.327	0.018	−0.138
Heroin	0.317	−0.044	−0.087
Tobacco	0.177	0.735	−0.066
Alcohol	0.051	0.527	−0.060
Caffeine	−0.012	0.248	−0.140
Barbiturates	0.183	0.057	−0.532
Tranquilizers	0.086	0.045	−0.522
Narcotic cough syrup	−0.004	0.118	−0.338
Other narcotics	0.156	0.044	−0.258

[a]After 3 principal components were subjected to Kaiser Varimax orthogonal rotation. Program used was the BMDX72. Input was a correlation matrix with R^2 along the diagonal.

methedrine, and opium and by moderate loadings of other amphetamines, cocaine, and heroin. The second factor consists primarily of tobacco and alcohol, and secondarily of caffeine and cannabis. The third factor is primarily defined by barbiturate/sedatives and tranquilizers, with narcotic cough syrups, other narcotics and other amphetamines having secondary importance. The only major difference occurs with opiates. Blum and associates listed all "illicit" opiates together, and they loaded most highly on the "suppressive effects" factor. Opiate use in the present study was obtained in four categories. Heroin and opium usage loaded highest on the "illicit-exotic" factor, while narcotic cough syrups and other narcotics (including both legal and illegal usage) were most highly associated with barbiturates and tranquilizers. This last factor in the present data could probably be characterized better as usage of medically prescribed substances than as desire for suppressive effects.[13] Similar findings were reported by Brehm and Back (1968) in a single-campus study of *willingness to use* 10 different substances.

[13] Other amphetamine usage loads moderately on this factor. If only medically prescribed usage (about one-fourth the use) were included, it would probably load much higher.

They extracted three factors: the first was "drugs," amphetamines, hallucinogens (presumably including marijuana), and opiates; the second was "social stimulants," coffee, tea, tobacco, and alcohol; and the third was "sedatives," analgesics, tranquilizers. Willingness to use opiates was most closely related to the "illicit-exotic" cluster, as was predominantly true in the present findings.

When interpretable factors emerge that are approximately replicable—even when the variables are measured in different ways—the drugs loading highly on each factor possibly share at least one important underlying dimension. To interpret the dimension(s), it is ideal to construct an index that clearly measures an ordered intensity. Such an index was constructed for the three sets of drugs defined by the factor analysis. They were labeled ALCTOB, MAPS, and DOWNS.

Both alcohol and tobacco were used by a majority of the sampled population—with a fairly broad distribution of current use frequency (see Table 1). To form an index, the two alcohol-use items were combined and scored as follows:

ALCTOB index	Percent of sample ($N = 7,948$)
0 = use no alcohol at all during the year.	13
1 = drink any quantity of alcohol only once or twice during the year.	26
2 = take one or two drinks at least every week or two, but several drinks no more than once or twice.	22
3 = take several drinks every week or two.	28
4 = take several drinks at least several times a week.	6

The current frequency of using tobacco was similarly scored from 0 to 4. The resultant variables were interrelated with $r = .41$, $\gamma = .48$. The sum of these measures of alcohol- and tobacco-use frequency define the ALCTOB index. A higher score on the index consistently implied a more frequent use of both alcohol and tobacco.

Marijuana, psychedelics, opium, and methedrine loaded most highly on the first factor. They are associated with intercorrelations or at least $r = .38$. However, the probability that these substances would be used during the academic year 1969–70 ranged from 38% for cannabis to 3% for opium, with psychedelics and methedrine lying between. The conditional probabilities of use of one drug given use of the other during the year are listed in Table 7. Clearly, among the drugs under consideration, almost all those who used psychedelics, methedrine, or opium also used marijuana or hashish. Three-fourths of the opium users and two-thirds of the methedrine users also used

TABLE 7
Conditional Probabilities of Drug Use During 1969-70

Drug	Heroin (.004)[a]	Opium (.03)	Methedrine (.05)	Psychedelics (.09)	Marijuana (.31)	Tobacco (.55)	Alcohol (.86)
Heroin	–	.64	.74	.84	1.00	.84	.97
Opium	.08	–	.50	.75	.97	.84	.97
Methedrine	.05	.32	–	.66	.94	.82	.96
Psychedelics	.04	.30	.41	–	.98	.78	.96
Marijuana	.01	.11	.16	.27	–	.77	.98
Tobacco	.01	.05	.08	.12	.44	–	.97
Alcohol	.005	.04	.06	.10	.36	.62	–

Note.–Probability of using column drug given use of row drug. These figures are based on 7,948 responses equally weighted, so they are slightly different than earlier probabilities based on differentially weighting individuals to better represent the entire sample population.

[a]Probability of use during year in total sample.

psychedelics. And a majority of opium users also used methedrine. The use of a less prevalent drug among this set quite strongly implies the use of a more prevalent drug. This suggests that the substances can be ordered in terms of intensity along a common dimension.

In forming an index, the users of opium and methedrine were combined so that there would be sufficient respondents in each category to assure that significant distinctions could be made. At the other end, marijuana use was trichotomized into nonusers, once or twice users, and those who used at least every week or two during the year. A MAPS (marijuana-psychedelic) index was formed according to these rules:

MAPS index	*Percent of sample* *(N = 7,948)*
4 = use of psychedelics and either methedrine or opium.	4
3 = use of psychedelics.	3
2 = use of marijuana at least every week or two.	7
1 = use of marijuana once or twice this year.	12
0 = none of the above.	72

Respondents were placed in the highest cateogry applicable. (The highest cateogry includes only those who have used both psychedelics *and* methedrine or opium. Thus some persons who have used methedrine or opium but not psychedelics may receive a relatively low score.)

"Intensity" as measured on this index reflects both the number of drugs used *and* the frequency of use of the more prevalent drug types. Psychedelics were used at least every week or two by 11% of those who scored 3 on the index, compared to 27% of those who also used methedrine or opium. Marijuana was used at least every week or two by 78% of those who scored 3 on the index, and by 96% of those who scored 4. Similarly, 31% of the psychedelic-only users and 61% of the psychedelic and methedrine/opium users reported smoking marijuana at least several times a week. Clearly the index score indicates frequency of marijuana use. Also, most (about 88%) of those who used psychedelics also used marijuana at least every week or two, while only about half of the "regular" marijuana users also used psychedelics. This further indicates that the categories of the MAPS index are appropriately ordered in "intensity."

Heroin use strongly implies use of all the drugs included in the MAPS index (see Table 7). However, it was not used to define an additional category of "intensity" primarily because so few people could be included. Moreover, over 90% of the heroin users scored at least 3 (psychedelic use) on the MAPS index.

The primary distinction in the frequency distribution of use of barbiturates/sedatives and tranquilizers is between nonuse and use once or twice during the academic year. A DOWNS index representing the common dimension they share, using three categories, is defined as follows:

DOWNS index	Percent of sample ($N = 7,948$)
2 = use of either barbiturates/sedatives or tranquilizers at least every week or two.	4
1 = use of either once or twice, but neither more frequently.	14
0 = use of neither during the academic year.	79

While these three indexes may reflect different dimensions of social-chemical experiences, they are not entirely independent of each other. Using the product moment correlation coefficient as a measure, the DOWNS index is only slightly related to the ALCTOB ($r = .12$) and MAPS ($r = .16$) indexes. However, a correlation of .33 between the ALCTOB index and the MAPS index suggests that these two types of drug usage share some qualities in common—as previously observed with the correlations among specific drugs like tobacco and marijuana. Almost the entire relationship between these two indexes, however, arises from the increased probability that a MAPS user, regardless of intensity, is more likely to be an ALCTOB user. Among those who use at least one drug in both indexes the correlation between indexes is .04 (which is not significant at $p = .01$). The relationship can be clearly seen in Table 8. While 83% of those who did not use marijuana, psychedelics, or psychedelics plus methedrine or opium used at least some alcohol or tobacco, almost 99% of the MAPS users used ALCTOB. While there is some small

TABLE 8

ALCTOB Collapsed Frequency by MAPS Index

MAPS index	ALCTOB index (percent in each collapsed category)					
	0	1-3	4-6	7,8	Total %	N
None	17	51	22	10	100	5,104
Marijuana:						
1 or 2 times	1	32	41	27	101	1,038
Several times	1	30	44	26	101	658
Psychedelics	3	30	50	18	101	308
Psychedelics +						
methedrine/opium	1	22	49	29	101	348

variation in frequency distribution of ALCTOB use across the four user categories of the MAPS index, there is no consistent increase or decrease in average frequency of use. The use of more illicit drugs certainly implies the use of alcohol and tobacco when the time framework for measuring use is an academic year. Beyond that, the actual intensity of use of either is relatively independent of the other.

Conceptually, the observed interrelationships among ALCTOB and MAPS may be represented as threshholds as well as intensities. Almost all marijuana/psychedelic users also used alcohol or tobacco in the same year. Hence, to be willing to use marijuana, a person must also have been willing to use alcohol and tobacco. ALCTOB usage perhaps represents a willingness to use drugs in a manner other than medically prescribed. One is either willing or not willing to do this. It is not a matter of intensity. The second threshhold consists of willingness to use marijuana or any other drug in the MAPS index. One aspect of this stage probably is taking the risk of being labeled a "criminal." Using marijuana is the primary indicator of breaking this threshhold. As Table 7 shows, the use of psychedelics, opium, and methedrine, as well as heroin, all imply the use of marijuana with almost certainty. "Intensity" along the MAPS index does not increase the probability of using marijuana (although it does increase the expected frequency of use).

Once the statistical relationships among various drugs are clarified, two sets of questions can be addressed. The first deals with why a particular set of drugs are used concurrently. The second asks why a person uses drugs within each set more or less "intensely." These two issues are certainly interrelated, but can be conceptually separated. It may be argued that different drugs are associated in their use because users experience effects that are similar, but which vary in intensity. Heroin users are almost certain to have used psychedelics within the same year; however, it would be difficult to claim that the typical effects of heroin are of the same quality, only more intense, than those of psychedelics. A common characteristic of the drugs included in the MAPS

Index is that they are frequently used to get some kind of "high." But, of course, so is alcohol. In addition to MAPS drugs enabling persons to get various kinds of highs, the one aspect they share is their legal status. A study by Johnson (1973) sheds light on the process by which heroin comes to be associated with frequent marijuana use.[14] He found that the statistical association between heroin use and the frequency of marijuana use largely disappeared when contact with heroin users was controlled. Engaging in dealing was the crucial process that tied the two drugs together. When frequent marijuana users became dealers, they came into contact with sources who used, or had available, heroin. The fact that marijuana and heroin are treated within the same legal framework places them together in the distribution channels, and it is essentially through communality of sources that the two drugs come to be associated. What "progression" there is from marijuana to heroin arises more from the effects of drug laws than from a desperate search for more intense experiences of the same kind. In addition to the effects on what drugs are marketed together, the legal status presumably influences social and cultural conceptions surrounding different drugs. Thus all "illicit" drugs have the common quality of "illicitness." Similarly, alcohol and tobacco share the quality of widespread social acceptability.

EXPLAINING DRUG USE

The myriad of studies of college student drug use over the last half decade have approached the second issue—why people use various drugs—in several ways. The simplest answer is that one learns from doctors, parents, and friends to use chemicals to alter one's internal state and/or to participate in a meaningful social ritual. Exposure to other drug users, in a setting of favorable usage norms, leads to experimentation (or prescribed use) which, if found rewarding, might turn into a more regular practice. Particularly for those drugs that play an integral part in social interactions, or that are obtained through trusted friends or acquaintances, the extent to which one associates with users is a major correlate of personal use (e.g., Blum and associates, 1969; Goldstein et al., 1970; Johnson, 1973).

The next logical step is to ask what will predict or "explain" who gets involved in a drug-using subculture of a given type. In practically all studies, users of "illicit" drugs have been found to come from families of higher socioeconomic status and from urban or suburban homes. They are more liberal or radical, less religious, more likely to engage in premarital sex, and more likely than nonusers to be social science or humanities majors. Several studies have attempted to contrast marijuana or other drug users on a variety

---

[14] The present data indicate that only 4% of those using marijuana several times a week also use any heroin, and 16% of those using marijuana several times a day also try heroin at least once during the year.

of personality or other inventories. Goldstein (1971) summarized these personality studies as indicating that

teenage cigarette smokers, college student marijuana users, college student amphetamine users, college student drinkers, and Haight-Ashbury multiple drug users all score lower than nonusers of these drugs on scales assessing satisfaction with self and higher on scales assessing flexibility.

Some background and personality characterizations distinguish between nonusers and users, or among users of different intensity, to a degree that is statistically significant, but of low predictive power. In the present study, for example, when an attempt was made to predict—using an analysis of variance regression model—the three drug-usage index scores using age, sex, college class, parents' education, parents' income, and rural, urban, or suburban background, all these variables together "explained" only 8% of the variance (multiple R^2) in MAPS use, 7% in ALCTOB use, and 2% in DOWNS use. Even where significant relationships between background variables or personality traits and different drug-use patterns have been established, interpretation of the observed associations has seldom been carried beyond a few impressions of possible causal mechanisms.

Since at least two drug-use patterns—ALCTOB and MAPS—clearly involve social interaction[15] around usage, the most fruitful approach to understanding them is through linking them with the larger set of social and cultural interactions that give meaning to the shared drug-taking behavior. Rather than drug-use patterns per se, the focus of inquiry should be lifestyles: sets of compatible attitudes, beliefs, activities, values, and modes of everyday living.

Although several items, such as religiosity, sexuality, and political beliefs, have been found to consistently and importantly predict "illicit" drug use, few investigators have attempted systematically to conceptualize and empirically investigate clusters of items that define a lifestyle. Even more, there has been no systematic attempt to relate such clusters to more than one type of drug use. The focus of recent studies has been primarily on predictors of "illicit" drug use. One of the earlier attempts to characterize a lifestyle cluster related to marijuana use was that by Suchman (1968), who defined the "hang loose" ethic in terms of several activity and belief items. A number of noncollege special youth population studies, primarily participant observational in nature, have made distinctions among types of drug users based, in part, on the kind of life a person leads (e.g., Carey, 1968; Davis & Munoz, 1968; Holmes & Holmes, 1971). For college students, one of the more frequently cited distinctions—that among "tasters," "seekers," and "heads"—was suggested by Kenniston (1968). More generally, for younger age groups, Fort (1969) has characterized drug use as part of a natural—but increasingly freely expressed—search for pleasurable activity.

---

[15] In a survey by Goode (1970), for example, 45% of the marijuana users said they had never smoked alone.

STUDENT LIFESTYLES

In an attempt to most parsimoniously describe the important distinctions among student lifestyles, a questionnaire included measures of most of the characterizations of lifestyles previously found to be related to marijuana use. As well, additional items were written that might be related to any major drug pattern. A total of 67 different items were finally used, measuring career values, social and recreational activities, religious participation, political and social values, interest in occult phenomena, approval of rock festivals and communes, etc. Six indexes characterized separable (but sometimes related) dimensions of lifestyles. The details will be described more fully in a future publication, but methodology and findings are summarized briefly here.

The correlation matrix among these 67 items was factor analyzed to reduce the data to a few significant and interpretable dimensions. This was done separately for males and females. The resultant six indexes seemed to most parsimoniously characterize both male and female lifestyle differences covered by the 67 items.[16] Each index is briefly described in the following discussion.

CONTCO (Counterculture): Consists of 16 items, paraphrased as follows:

> Money is not important in career choice
> Avoiding a high pressure job important
> Career preparation not important
> Community involvement important
> Engage in political activities
> Participate in demonstrations
> Approve rock festivals
> Approve communes
> Politically liberal or radical
> Making it is not a result of trying hard
> Breaking unjust laws is OK
> Saving for the future is not important
> Americans do not lead happy and useful lives
> Vietnam war part of U.S. imperialism
> Strict impulse control is not desirable
> Newspapers and magazines should not be censored on moral grounds

The common theme in these items is a politically active espousal of alternatives to the dominant "Protestant ethic" and the authority of associated social, political, and work institutions. The more "countercultural" define themselves more in terms of personal moral and experiential values than in terms of money, career, and the future rewards of working hard for someone else. They are more cynical about the "American dream" and are more likely to question the inherent rightness of government authority.

---

[16] Of course, the resultant dimensions are restricted by initial selection of questions. A few years later, one would give much more emphasis to emerging religious and mystical values and practices, for example.

USEFUL: This index consists of seven items, measuring the importance of the following:

Being useful to others
Being with others
Working with other people
Finding a purpose in life
Helping others
Building a better society
Sharing possessions

The common meaning in these items is a desire to be with and work with other people, out of social concern.

CREATIVE: The third index consists of only three items measuring an intellectual orientation:

Original/creative job is important
Living and working in the world of ideas important
Creatively expressing oneself is important

SOCIAL: This index primarily measures the sociability and social participation of the individual. It consists of six items:

Importance of being with others
Participate in sports
Participate in extracurricular activities
Attending parties
Self-rating as socially aggressive
Spend leisure time mostly with other people

MORALS: A seven-item index concerning sex, religion, and morality:

Unimportance of religious participation
Religious attendance low
Self-rating as not religious
Sexual activity
Attitudes toward premarital sex
Approve rock festivals like Woodstock
Against moral censorship of publications

Sexuality and nonreligiosity are frequently associated with the collegiate counterculture; and, as shown in Table 9, MORALS and CONTCO are signficantly correlated ($r = .43$). However, the two dimensions are separable—most clearly so for the males in the sample.

NOVEL: This consists of eight items:

Desire to discover new experiences
Listen to rock music
Approve rock festivals
Witchcraft is credible
Astrology is credible
ESP is credible
Approve communes
Work outside regular institutions to do anything rewarding

TABLE 9

Intercorrelation of Lifestyle Indexes and Correlations With Drug-use Indexes

Index	Lifestyle index					Drug-use index		
	USEFUL	SOCIAL	CREATIVE	MORALS	NOVEL	ALCTOB	MAPS	DOWNS
CONTCO	.17	.06	.25	.43	.46	.21	.51	.08
USEFUL		.35	.33	-.19	.22	-.04	.02	.05
SOCIAL			.11	-.15	.19	.20	.04	.01
CREATIVE				.08	.27	.05	.15	.06
MORALS					.21	.30	.35	.08
NOVEL						.24	.37	.11
Multiple R of all indexes with drug type						.42	.56	.13
Multiple R^2						.18	.31	.02
F ratio ($n_1 = 6, n_2 = 7,306$)						262.61	548.05	21.92

The factor NOVEL could just as easily have been labeled counterculture. But it reflects a rather different aspect of the counterculture than does CONTCO, even though the items on approval of rock festivals and communes are part of both indexes. NOVEL is a nonpolitical, more cultural dimension. Perhaps it reflects an openness to a reality not restricted to the "rational," scientific, and instrumental modes of dominant Western thought and interaction. Table 9 shows that NOVEL and CONTCO are the two most highly correlated indexes ($r = .46$).

LIFESTYLES AND DRUG USE

Different lifestyle dimensions are most highly associated with each of the three types of drug use (see Table 9). MORALS is the best single predictor of alcohol/tobacco use; CONTCO of marijuana/psychedelic use; and NOVEL of barbiturate/tranquilizer use (though the last correlation is rather small: $r = .11$). All the lifestyle dimensions together "explain" a sizable portion of the variance in MAPS and ALCTOB (31% and 18%, respectively),[17] but very little of the DOWNS usage (2%). This contrast in explanatory power supports the contention that MAPS and ALCTOB usage is much more social/cultural in nature than is DOWNS use, which is primarily medical. We have also "explained" more of the variance in MAPS than in ALCTOB, in part because we set out to devise a questionnaire that would measure lifestyles primarily associated with "illicit" drug use. But one of the typical characterizations of marijuana and psychedelic users—as nonreligious and sexually promiscuous—fits alcohol and tobacco users just about as well ($r = .35$ and .30, respectively).[18]

Another way to summarize the prediction of drug usage by lifestyle dimensions is that those who are more "countercultural," who are more open to novel experiences, and who more highly value being original and creative also score higher on both ALCTOB and MAPS usage indexes. The association is much stronger with MAPS than with ALCTOB in all cases. Those more liberal on sex and religion are about equally more likely to use ALCTOB and MAPS drugs. More "sociable" persons score higher on ALCTOB usage. Alcohol and tobacco are the drugs still most associated with the usual measures of participation in campus social life.

[17] As noted earlier, the standard background characteristics together "explained" much less variance—8% and 7%, respectively, for MAPS and ALCTOB.

[18] In fact, in a linear regression model, MORALS adds only about 2% to the "explained" variance in MAPS use once the effects of CONTCO and NOVEL are controlled (those two account for 28% of the variance in MAPS). Most of association between MORALS and MAPS can be viewed as arising because MORALS and CONTCO are so highly associated. Highly "countercultural" individuals tend also to be more liberal in sex and religion, but the variation explained in marijuana and psychedelic use is due largely to the CONTCO identification.

DISCUSSION

Three dimensions of drug use were defined in the college student population. Broadly conceived characterizations of lifestyles are important predictors of the two patterns of drug usage that can best be considered social/cultural in nature. What has been characterized as countercultural lifestyle is, as expected, the most important predictor of marijuana and psychedelic use. A person's stance on sex, religion, and morality is significantly related to MAPS use, but adds very little in predicting this kind of drug use once the CONTCO score is determined. On the other hand, moral stance, as well as sociability—two clusters of traits that have commonly been used to characterize different college students (as well as others)—are the most important predictors of alcohol and tobacco use. Those who engage more frequently, and more freely, in social interaction are more likely to use alcohol and tobacco, the common social lubricants. Marijuana and psychedelic use, on the other hand, is clearly part of a subcultural experience. The "counterculture" rejects the unquestioned authority of dominant legal, political, and social institutions; such an attitude is, to some degree, a prerequisite for using such highly proscribed substances. As well, the type of experience sought in these chemicals frequently stresses more intense, pleasurable highs—letting go of "rational" control of one's reactions and environment, being open to a variety of experiential modes.[19] This is part of the characterization of countercultural lifestyle, as measured in both the CONTCO and NOVEL indexes.

Lifestyle characterizations are important predictors of two kinds of drug use.[20] As well, they give meaning to that use, when we conceive of drug taking as one part of a thematically and statistically related cluster of social and cultural activities and interpretations of personal experience. In a sense, though, this is only a beginning. There seems always to be a demand in Western culture for more "explanation": an endless process of viewing one set of variables in terms of yet another set, and of conceptualizing mechanisms by which the sets affect each other.

To satisfy this demand—if we wish—there are several paths to pursue. In understanding the generation of the different clusters of lifestyles/drug-use patterns, it might prove fruitful to examine more fully the compositional and contextual effects across different educational institutions. The enormous variation in marijuana/psychedelic use from school to school, depending on

[19] An interesting study by Rouse and Ewing (1972) indicates that marijuana users desired, and were willing to take more risks to achieve, "altered" states of consciousness, such as "inner awareness" and "hallucinations."

[20] The lifestyle charcterizations as measured in our index do not "explain" all, or even a majority, of the variation in any kind of drug use. There are clearly many "traditional" students who smoke marijuana, just as there are many morally conservative or unsociable students who drink alcohol.

selectivity and religious affiliation, indicates that the counterculture has an important dynamic of its own. Where a large number of intellectually oriented, affluent students come together, the social exchange facilitates the development of a drug-using culture much more than we might expect from each person's background or personality alone. It may well be that the best predictor of an individual's marijuana use is simply what school he or she attends. The present study attempted to analyze, from data across 48 schools, the importance of such compositional effects relative to separate individual backgrounds, in predicting drug use and related lifestyle patterns.

Another set of questions arises from the possible impact of contextual factors—college drug policies, local police activity, geographical location, etc.—on drug use and related subcultural dynamics. This is not discussed here in any detail, except to emphasize that an inquiry into the deterrent effects of punitive legal sanctions will probably prove less fruitful than an inquiry into the social costs of such sanctions. (See particularly Kaplan (1971) for a discussion of this with respect to marijuana.) Social costs arise not only from the effects of being labeled criminal or immoral, but more generally from what one does to avoid such a label. As one example, 32% of the marijuana users in the present sample felt "not at all comfortable" discussing even their attitudes toward drug use in the presence of their doctor, compared with only 8% of the marijuana nonusers who felt such discomfort. Users even more frequently felt quite uncomfortable talking to parents, the college dean, and their faculty adviser about such issues. Clearly, labeling some drug use "illicit" tends to isolate users from many resources for medical, personal, and social support.

An inquiry into contextual effects, as well as an analysis of the causal interrelationships between drug usage and other factors on an individual level, has seldom been conducted with convincing rigor. While cross-sectional data are amenable to causal analysis (testing models with three or more variables), longitudinal measures are more appropriate for determining relative causal directions. This is especially true with phenomena whose prevalences in the population are rapidly changing. Although a panel analysis was not performed for the present study, it appears that causality frequently will operate in both directions—especially with factors that are part of the same meaningful cluster of attitudes and behavior.

Perhaps more useful than classical causal analysis is the framework of career contingencies. With measures at two or more points in time on the same person, the probability of changing from one state to another (e.g., from tobacco use to nonuse) can be determined for types of individuals in varying contexts, and at different drug-use stages. The problem, of course, is to find the most relevant characterizations to discriminate among persons and contexts. If the point of the analysis is to change individual outcomes, the focus, of course, would best be on contingencies that can be altered through intervention.

As an overview, it seems that drug use is neither a new, nor a particularly startling, phenomenon. Almost everyone uses some kind of chemical to alter internal states or to socialize with others around a shared ritual. Recently we have seen an increasingly widespread use of a particular set of substances—marijuana, psychedelics, etc.—within a youth subcultural milieu that stresses getting "high" in ways not understood, or not accepted, by the dominant culture. Such an openness to new psychic, social, and cultural experiences and ways of living may threaten many of the traditional patterns of authority and meaning that many people use as reference points in their lives. This is what much of the current drug-use controversy is about—a struggle over the kinds of experiences that will be treated as legitimate in this society, and over who has the right to interpret and control such experiences. Of course, as the use of marijuana, for example, becomes more prevalent, and legal and social attitudes toward its use more accepting, the association between its use and the particular cluster of countercultural lifestyles will probably diminsh.

REFERENCES

Astin, A. W. *Who goes where to college?* Chicago: Science Research Associates, 1965.

Barter, J. T., Mizner, G. L., & Werme, P. H. *Patterns of drug use among college students in the Denver-Boulder metropolitan area.* Washington, D.C.: U.S. Department of Justice, 1971.

Blum, R. H., and associates. *Students and drugs.* San Francisco: Jossey-Bass, 1969.

Brehm, M. L., & Back, K. W. Self image and attitudes toward drugs. *Journal of Personality,* 1968, 36(2), 299–314.

Carey, J. T. *The college drug scene.* Englewood Cliffs, N.J.: Prentice-Hall, 1968.

Davis, F., & Munoz, L. Heads and freaks: Patterns and meanings of drug use among hippies. *Journal of Health and Social Behaviour,* 1968, 9(2), 156–64.

Eells, K. Marijuana and LSD: A survey of one college campus. *Journal of Counseling Psychology,* 1968, 15(5), 459–67.

Fort, J. *The pleasure seekers.* New York: Bobbs-Merrill, 1969.

Goldstein, J. W., Korn, J. H., Abel, W. H., & Morgan, R. M. *The social psychology and epidemiology of student drug usage: A report on phase one.* Pittsburgh, Pa.: Department of Psychology, Carnegie-Mellon University, 1970.

Goldstein, J. W. *Motivations for psychoactive drug use among students.* Pittsburgh, Pa.: Department of Psychology, Carnegie-Mellon University, 1971.

Goldstein, J. W., & Korn, J. H. *Judging the shape of things to come: Lessons learned from comparisons of student drug users in 1968 and 1970.* Pittsburgh, Pa.: Department of Psychology, Carnegie-Mellon University, 1972.

Goode, E. *The marijuana smokers.* New York: Basic Books, 1970.

Goode, E. The use of marijuana and other illegal drugs on a college campus. *The British Journal of Addiction,* 1971, 66, 213–215.

Holmes, D., & Holmes, M. *Drug use in matched groups of hippies and nonhippies.* New York: Center for Community Research, 1971.

Johnson, B. D. *Marijuana users and drug subcultures.* New York: Wiley, 1973.

Kaplan, J. H. *Marijuana: The new prohibition.* New York: Pocket Books, 1971.

Kenniston, K. Heads and seekers. *American Scholar,* 1968, 38(1), 97–112.

Manheimer, D. I., Mellinger, G. D., Somers, R. H., & Kleman, M. T. Technical and ethical considerations in data collection. In S. Einstein & S. Allen (Eds.), *Proceedings of the 1st International Conference on Student Drug Surveys.* Farmingdale, N.Y.: Bagwood, 1972.

McGlothlin, W. H., Jamison, K., & Rosenblatt, S. Marijuana and the use of other drugs. *Nature,* 1970, 228, 1227–1229.

McKenzie, J. D. *Trends in marijuana use among undergraduate students at the University of Maryland.* Research Report No. 3–70. College Park, Md.: Counseling Center, University of Maryland, 1970.

Mizner, G. L., Barter, J. T., & Werme, P. H. Patterns of drug use among college students: A preliminary report. *American Journal of Psychiatry,* 1970, 127(1), 55–64.

National Commission on Marihuana and Drug Abuse. *Marihuana: A signal of misunderstanding.* Appendix, Vol. 1. Washington, D.C.: U.S. Government Printing Office, 1972.

Rouse, B. A., & Ewing, J. A. Marijuana and other drug use by graduate and professional students. *American Journal of Psychiatry,* 1972, 129(4), 75–80.

Robbins, L., Robbins, E., Pearlman, S., & Philip, A. College student drug use. *American Journal of Psychiatry,* 1970, 126, 1743–1751.

Suchman, E. A. The hang-loose ethic and the spirit of drug use. *Journal of Health and Social Behaviour,* 1968, 9(2), 146–155.

PART IV
HALLUCINOGENS AND STIMULANTS

13
THE EPIDEMIOLOGY OF HALLUCINOGENIC DRUG USE

William H. McGlothlin
University of California, Los Angeles

This report examines the use of hallucinogenic drugs in the United States during 1970-71.[1] An overview of the early history of LSD and other hallucinogens is presented. Characteristics of the user and the patterns and effects of use are examined; and the market for such drugs is described. The phenomena of the psychedelic movement and the drug subculture are explored with an eye to the future of hallucinogenic drug use.

AN OVERVIEW

Early History

The ritualistic use of hallucinogens by primitive tribes has a very long history. Schultes (1938, 1940) cites some evidence of the use of peyote and mushrooms in Mexico as early as 1000-300 B.C. Peyote use was introduced to the U.S. plains Indians around 1870 (Slotkin, 1956). It was primarily used in a formal ritual setting, and by 1930 peyotism had become the dominant religion of the American Indians (LaBarre, 1947; Mead, 1932). The Native American Church now claims to have some 200,000 members (Dustin, 1960).

[1] This report is based, in part, on a monograph prepared for the U.S. Bureau of Narcotics and Dangerous Drugs (BNDD) under Contract J-70-33 entitled: Amphetamines, Barbiturates and Hallucinogens: An Analysis of Use, Distribution and Control. Funding of this study by the BNDD does not necessarily imply their endorsement of the findings or conclusions. The work was also supported by a Research Scientist Award, No. K05-DA-70182 from the National Institute of Mental Health.

Peyote attracted medical attention around 1900 (Ellis, 1897; Mitchell, 1896), and later there were numerous warnings in the popular media concerning the dangers of its spread to the white population. Short-lived attempts to establish peyotism among the American Negro occurred around 1930 (Smith, 1934); and in 1933 a Swiss pharmaceutical firm advertised a patent medicine, "Peyotyl," as a means to "restore the individual's balance and calm and promote full expansion of his faculties [Anonymous, 1959, p. 25]." Mescaline, which produces the psychic effects of peyote without the unpleasant side effects, was isolated in 1896 and synthesized in 1919 (Anonymous, 1959). It was subsequently employed in psychiatric experimentation, and there is one early reference to its nonmedical use in Paris in 1931 (Critchley, 1931). A few students, artists, and members of the "beat" subculture experimented with peyote in the 1940-60 period; but, overall, its use was quite rare outside the American Indian population (*White House Conference on Narcotics and Drug Abuse*, 1963). This was true even though peyote could be legally ordered through the mail in most states during this period.

LSD

LSD was synthesized in 1938 and its hallucinogenic properties discovered by Hofmann in 1943 (Hofmann, 1970). Its discovery led to considerable scientific experimentation, and its use in psychotherapy was first reported by Busch and Johnson (1950). Limited nonmedical use began in California in the middle 1950's. Blum (1964) described informal usage among a small group of mental health professionals and others in the San Francisco area beginning in 1956. A similar group existed in Los Angeles during the same period. Access to the drug was through licit supplies provided for experimental purposes. Such nonmedical usage continued on a small scale until the early 1960s. Psilocybine and psilocin were synthesized in 1959 (Hofmann, 1970), and the former was also subjected to limited unauthorized use through diversion from experimental supplies.

The popularization of the hallucinogens began with Aldous Huxley's description of his mescaline experiences in *The Doors of Perception* (1954) and was greatly accelerated by the widespread notoriety given to Leary and Alpert's activities in 1963-64. The first LSD to be illicitly manufactured in the United States appeared in California in 1962. By 1964, clandestine manufacture of LSD was becoming more common and increasingly sophisticated.

Other Hallucinogens

As mentioned previously, a limited amount of diverted psilocybine was available for nonmedical use in the early 1960s; however, the synthesis is quite difficult, and very little has been clandestinely produced. Mescaline has occasionally been manufactured clandestinely, but its lengthy synthesis and the large dosages required (300–500 mg.) make it unprofitable to produce for sale on the illicit market.[2] LSD, mescaline, and psilocybin produce very similar psychic effects as well as cross tolerance. A large number of other drugs has been loosely categorized as hallucinogens. The psychic effects of dimethyltryptamine were discovered in 1957 (Szara, 1957), and it appeared on the illicit market from both legal and clandestine sources in the early 1960s. It is easily synthesized but is not generally available at present because of the lack of demand. STP or DOM (4-methyl-2, 5 dimethoxyamphetamine) was a new experimental drug manufactured by Dow Chemical Company. It first appeared on the illicit market in 1967 (U.S. Bureau of Narcotics and Dangerous Drugs, hereinafter cited as BNDD, 1967), was used quite widely for a brief period, and then became unpopular. It is still sold to some extent as alleged mescaline and other drugs. MDA (3, 4-methylenedioxyamphetamine) was also introduced on the illicit market in 1967 (BNDD, 1968b). It is an older drug, first studied by Alles in 1933 (Richards, 1971) and does not produce the characteristic perceptual changes of hallucinogenic drugs. Another pseudohallucinogen, phencyclidine (PCP, sernyl, peace pills), appeared on the illicit market in 1968 (BNDD, 1968a). It is used in veterinary medicine as an anesthetic. LSD, phencyclidine, and MDA are the only hallucinogens presently available on the illicit market with any regularity. Of those hallucinogens analyzed by BNDD laboratories in fiscal year (FY) 1971, 80% were LSD and another 10% were LSD and phencyclidine in combination (BNDD, 1971).

A number of other synthetic hallucinogens have made brief appearances on the illicit market in recent years. They include DET, DPT, DMA, TMA, DOET, MMDA, benactyzine, Ditran, scopolamine, N-methyl-3-piperidylbenzylate (JB-336), and nitrous oxide. In addition, the following organic hallucinogens are occasionally used: peyote, hallucinogenic mushrooms, morning glory seeds, Hawaiian wood rose seeds, and nutmeg. Other hallucinogens occurring in plants have rarely, if ever, been available on the illicit market, e.g., bufotenine, ibogaine, harmine, harmaline, *cohobo, yage',* and *yohimbine.*

Control Measures

There is a long history of legal efforts to control peyote use among the Indians,[3] but other hallucinogens were not federally regulated until the Drug Abuse Control Amendments of 1965, which was the same act that placed

[2] Street drugs are often sold as mescaline, but analyses show that they virtually always contain LSD or some other drug (Cheek, Stephens, & Joffe, 1970; Gunn, Johnson, & Butler, 1970; Marshman & Gibbins, 1969).

[3] Peyote was placed under the Liquor Suppression Act in 1923 and removed in 1935. The importation of peyote was prohibited in 1915 and once again allowed in 1937. The U.S. Post Office banned shipment of peyote through the mails in 1917, and rescinded the ban in 1940. Finally, peyote was included as a habit-forming drug in the Narcotic Farm Act of 1929. Slotkin (1956) lists a series of nine Congressional bills to prohibit peyote from 1916 to 1937, all of which were defeated.

amphetamines and barbiturates under control. Initially, LSD, mescaline, peyote, psilocybine, psilocin, and DMT were included. Bufotenine, ibogaine and DET were added in 1967, STP in 1968, and phencyclidine in 1969. The Controlled Substances Act of 1970 also included MDA, MMDA, TMA, and the piperidyl benzilate derivatives, as well as marijuana[4] and the tetrahydrocannabinols. Phencyclidine was placed in Schedule III because of its veterinary use. All other controlled hallucinogens were placed in Schedule I.

PATTERNS OF USE: PREVALENCE, FREQUENCY, AMOUNT, AND DURATION OF USE

Prevalence

Table 1 presents the prevalence of one or more uses of LSD or other hallucinogens in the United States as found in the major general population, college, and high school surveys conducted in 1970-71 (see Berg & Broecker, 1972). As mentioned previously, virtually all drugs currently sold on the illicit market as hallucinogens are LSD, phencyclidine, or MDA; however, these drugs often are now alleged to be mescaline, psilocybine, THC, or some other drug. As a consequence, current survey results often show mescaline or other non-LSD hallucinogens to be reported more frequently than is LSD. This is not a problem where survey respondents are asked to indicate the use of "any hallucinogen"; however, the percentage of use for those surveys that ask only about LSD use will likely be underestimated. Surveys reporting the results for "LSD" and "other hallucinogens" separately rarely indicate the extent of overlap; therefore, the total prevalence is unknown.

The only adult general-population data available on hallucinogen use are (a) a national survey on persons 18 years of age and over showing the percentage using marijuana that also reports use of LSD, mescaline, or peyote[5] and (b) the separate results for LSD and other hallucinogens for the New York State population aged 14 and over. The findings indicate the general population prevalence of one or more uses to be about 3%.

The 1971 Gallup national college survey found that 18% had used hallucinogens. The other college surveys shown in Table 1 indicate a somewhat lower prevalence. With the exception of California, the prevalence of one or more uses among high school students appears to be around 6% or 7%. The following composite estimates of nationwide student usage in 1971 are based on the survey results shown in Table 1:

---

[4] For the purposes of this report, marijuana is not included in the hallucinogen category.

[5] This is essentially identical with the overall prevalence of hallucinogen use, since very few persons have used these drugs without also using the more common marijuana.

TABLE 1
Prevalence of Hallucinogen Use: Survey Results

Source	Location	Year	1 or more users (percent)		
			LSD	Other hallucinogens	All hallucinogens
	General population				
National Marihuana Commission, 1972	National (age ⩾ 18)	1971	–	–	3[a]
Chambers, 1971	New York State (age ⩾ 14)	1970	2.4	2.2	–
	College				
Gallup Opinion Index, 1972	National	1971	–	–	18
Groves, Rossi, & Grafstein, 1970	National	1970	–	–	9
Gergen, Gergen, & Morris, 1972	National	1971	–	–	22
Chambers, 1971	New York State	1970	14	11	–
Center for Counseling and Psychological Services, 1970	University of Maine	1970	–	–	8
Brill, Christie, & Hochman, 1972	UCLA	1971	15	18[b]	–
	High school				
Josephson, Haberman, Zanes, & Elinson, 1971	National (age 12–17)[c]	1971	4	–	–
Chambers, 1971	New York State	1970	5	5	–
Hager, Vener, & Stewart	Michigan	1970	–	–	7
Coddington & Jacobsen, 1972	Ohio	1971	5	7	–
Brown, 1972	Fullerton, Calif.	1970	10	13[b]	–
Blackford, 1972	San Mateo County, Calif.	1971	15[d]	–	–

[a] Based on the percentage of persons having used marijuana who also report use of LSD, mescaline, or peyote.
[b] Alleged mescaline.
[c] This is a national household survey, age 12–17, not limited to high school students.
[d] Used 1 or more times during the preceding 12 months.

	Population (millions)	Percent ever used hallucinogens	Number having used hallucinogens (millions)
College	7.6	16	1.22
Grades 9-12	14.8	8	1.18
Grades 7-8	8.2	2	.16
Total			2.56

A general population (age 18 and over) estimate of 3% would yield, approximately 4 million. If the number under 18 years in grades 7-12 is added, the total number having used hallucinogens one or more times is around 5 million.

Frequency of Use

Unlike other psychoactive drugs, hallucinogens are rarely used on a daily basis. Tolerance to LSD occurs very rapidly, such that the effects are diminished on the second successive day of use, and largely are absent after three daily administrations (Cholden, Kurland, & Savage, 1955; Wolbach, Isbell, & Miner, 1962). A period of 4 to 6 days free of LSD must elapse before the full effects can again be experienced. The same rapid tolerance also exists for mescaline, psilocybine, and some other hallucinogens. Thus, for practical purposes, these drugs cannot be used more than twice a week without losing much of their impact. Other characteristics of the hallucinogen effects that tend to limit both the frequency and duration of use are discussed in a later section.

Table 2 shows the available survey data on frequency of hallucinogen use, expressed as a percentage of those having ever used the drugs. It appears that about one-half the college students and other adults who have used these drugs have either stopped, or have only taken them infrequently. Around 25% of the college students who have used the drugs indicate a frequency of one or more times per month, but weekly usage is rare. Among high school students, there is a tendency toward more frequent use, with about 15% of those having ever used indicating current usage of one or more times per week.

Amount

The LSD dosages used for experimental and psychotherapeutic purposes are normally in the 50-200 µg. range, although amounts up to 1,000 µg. have been administered occasionally. The alleged potency of LSD dosage units on the illicit market is typically 200-250 µg. although laboratory analyses show that the average amount is much less. BNDD (1971) laboratories listed quantitative evaluations for 999 samples of LSD as follows:

TABLE 2

Frequency of LSD or Other Hallucinogen Use Expressed as a Percentage of Those Having Ever Used the Drugs

Source	Location	Year	Percentage ever used	Frequency of current use expressed as a percentage of ever used[a]		
				Twice a year or less	Once a month or more	Once a week or more
General population						
Chambers, 1971	New York State (age ⩾ 14)	1970	2	39		13
College						
Gallup Opinion Index, 1972	National	1971	18		22	
Groves, Rossi, & Grafstein, 1970	National	1970	9		22	
Chambers, 1971	New York State	1970	14	49		2
Center for Counseling and Psychological Services, 1970	University of Maine	1970	8	47	37	4
Brill, Christie, & Hochman, 1972	UCLA	1971	15	70	10	
High school						
Chambers, 1971	New York State	1970	5	22		18
Blackford, 1972	San Mateo County, Calif.	1971	15[b]		32	14

[a]The various survey results are shown under these 3 frequency-of-use categories for comparative purposes. They approximate the categories used in the acutal surveys.

[b]Used 1 or more times during the preceding 12 months.

μg.	Percent
0-20	9
21-50	21
51-100	28
101-200	25
201-300	13
301-500	3
> 500	1
	100

The median potency was 83 μg. per dosage unit. This is a relatively small dose; of course, users may consume more than one unit per occasion. One study found the average reported dosage was around 400-500 "street micrograms" (Barron, Lowinger, & Ebner, 1970). This would translate to around 150-175 actual micrograms of LSD.

Duration of Use

The hallucinogens are unique among psychoactive drugs in that they appear to be self-limiting in terms of duration of use. In a 10-year followup of adults who initially received LSD under medical conditions and later self-administered the drug, the pattern of use was generally either discontinuance or declining frequency over a period of several years (McGlothlin & Arnold, 1971). Of the sample of 58, none showed an overall increasing frequency of use over the period of study. On the other hand, a pattern of increasing marijuana use over the same period was not uncommon. This sample was substantially older than the typical hallucinogen-using population; however, similar patterns are now emerging in the latter group (Barron et al., 1970; Salzman, Lieff, Kochansky, & Shader, 1972). These younger groups also generally continue to use marijuana after discontinuing the use of hallucinogens.

There are several reasons why the hallucinogens are not subject to long-term chronic use of the type frequently encountered with most other mind-altering drugs. First, of course, there is no physiological dependence of the type resulting from opiates, barbiturates, or long-term chronic use of alcohol. Second, at least for LSD and similar hallucinogens, the rapid buildup of tolerance discussed earlier precludes their use on a daily basis. A third reason why the hallucinogens appear unsuitable for chronic use is their lack of predictable effects. Habitual drug users seek to satisfy particular needs—e.g., escape, euphoria, anxiety relief, and relief from feelings of inadequacy. To qualify for chronic use, a drug must consistently produce the type of mood alteration desired. Hallucinogens are quite inconsistent in terms of mood alteration. The fourth and probably most important reason to expect persons to decrease rather than increase their use of hallucinogens over time is the diminishing utility of the experience as a function of continued use. The major attraction of these drugs is not mood change but the uniqueness of the experience. As the hallucinogen experience is repeated many times, what was initially unique becomes more commonplace; there is a process of diminishing returns. The effect of hallucinogens is indeed a "trip" and trips tend to lose their appeal when repeated too often.

Trends in Use

Although there is increasing evidence that hallucinogen users tend to discontinue after a few years, the available survey data do not as yet show a decline in overall usage. The Gallup Opinion Index (1972) showed college usage during the preceding 12 months to be 12% for both 1970 and 1971; use during the preceding 30 days was 6% in 1970 and 4% in 1971. The only long-term trend data is that for San Mateo County, California, high school students (Blackford, 1972). These data indicate that any use of LSD during the preceding 12 months has remained at about 15% from 1969 to 1972, and 10 or more usages per year at around 5%. Unfortunately, because this survey does not provide information on overall hallucinogen use, it is impossible to determine the additional usage of LSD under the name of mescaline or other drugs. Since other survey data show that reported "mescaline" usage often exceeded that for LSD in 1970-71 (Table 1), it seems likely that the *actual* use of LSD has continued to increase.

Thus the frequent assertion that the use of hallucinogens, and LSD in particular, have declined is not supported by the available evidence. Certainly the publicity and aggressive propagandizing of the hallucinogens are greatly diminished, and the reported LSD psychoses are also down. This decline in emphasis has apparently been mistaken for a decrease in use.

USER CHARACTERISTICS

Table 3 shows some of the characteristics of persons having ever used LSD in New York State. This survey shows the ratio of male-to-female use to be more than 2:1; however, most high school and college surveys have found a ratio of around 3:2 (Blackford, 1972; Gallup Opinion Index, 1972; McGlothlin, Jamison, & Rosenblatt, 1970). The male-female ratio is larger for more frequent use. Usage is heavily concentrated in the 14-24 age group; 91% of those reporting LSD use in the New York survey are under 35.

Aside from ritualistic peyote taking by the American Indians, hallucinogen use began among white upper-class and middle-class youth in the middle 1960s and is still most prevalent in this group. Substantial diffusion, however, to the minorities and lower socioeconomic group has now occurred (Table 3). Diffusion of other illicit drug use has generally been in the opposite direction: marijuana, barbiturates, opiates, and cocaine all had a history of use among the minorities before spreading to middle-class white users. Current hallucino-

TABLE 3

Percentage of New York State Residents, Age 14
and Over, Who Have Used LSD One or More Times

Characteristic	Percent ever used
Sex	
Male	3.7
Female	1.5
Age (in years)	
14–17	4.6
18–24	9.8
25–34	2.5
35–49	0.5
50 and over	0.2
Race	
White	2.6
Negro	1.2
Puerto Rican	2.2
Socioeconomic status	
Upper, upper middle	4.1
Middle	2.3
Lower middle	2.2
Lower	1.3

Source: Unpublished data that were collected in conjunction with the following study: Chambers, C. D. An
assessment of drug use in the general population. Special
Report No. 1, Drug use in New York State, Narcotic
Addiction Control Commission, May 1971.

gen use is highest in the urban areas of the West Coast and northeastern
states. It is lowest in the Southeast and rural locales.

Most of the published data show curiosity and self-exploration to be the
most frequent motivations for initial use (Barron et al., 1970; McGlothlin &
Arnold, 1971; Mizner, Barter, & Werme, 1970). Attempts to gain insight,
enhance creativity, and achieve mystical-religious experiences are among the
more common motivations given for continued use. Sensory enhancement and
pleasure, however, are often cited by the more frequent users and, with the
decline of the psychedelic movement and its associated philosophy, there
is evidence that these aspects are becoming the dominant motivation for
use.

Marijuana is the drug most closely associated with hallucinogen use.
Virtually 100% of hallucinogen users have also used marijuana. Only about
20%–25% of persons having tried marijuana have also taken the hallucinogens;

however, the percentage is around 70%–80% among persons using several times per week (Goode, 1970; Hochman & Brill, 1971; McGlothlin et al., 1970). Persons who have used the hallucinogens frequently also tend to experiment with the other available drugs, including the opiates; in most instances, however, marijuana is the only illicit drug habitually consumed. More extensive multidrug use has developed in some of the hippie communities. Progression from hallucinogens to intravenous methamphetamine use was common in some areas in the 1968-70 period. Sheppard, Gav, and Smith (1971) report that 40% of those addicted to heroin since 1967 in the Haight-Ashbury drug subculture of San Francisco were heavy users of psychedelics prior to using heroin. It is clear that heavy involvement in the use of psychedelic drugs may contribute to the progression to more dangerous drugs. The large majority, however, appear not to go beyond the experimental use of heroin and methamphetamine.

Because of the extensive overlap between hallucinogen and frequent marijuana use, the personality and behavioral correlates found in the numerous college marijuana studies are generally also applicable to hallucinogen users. As would be expected, marijuana/hallucinogen users are less conventional in attitudes and behavior than are nonusers. They are less likely to live at home, relate less well to parents, and exhibit a much more unstable lifestyle with respect to residence, work, school, and goals. They are less religious, belong to fewer organizations, and participate less in athletics. Users have sexual relations at an earlier age, more frequently, and with more partners. They exhibit much more liberal and leftist political views, see themselves as outside the larger society, have less respect for authority, and are more likely to be activists. Psychological test results show that users score higher on the psychopathic deviate scale of the Minnesota Multiphasic Inventory; have lower dogmatism scores (Rokeach Dogmatism Scale); are more susceptible to hypnosis and other nondrug regressive states (Aas Hypnotic Susceptibility Scale); believe more strongly in paranormal phenomena, e.g., astrology and extrasensory perception; demonstrate a strong preference for a casual, spontaneous style of life as opposed to one that is orderly and systematic, preferring intuition and ideas over conventional and factual approaches (Myers-Briggs Type Indicator); score high on esthetic and low on political and religious scales of the Allport-Vernon Value Scale; and low on the "Purpose of Life" test, i.e., less meaningful goals and integration to life. The California Personality Inventory shows users to be open to experience and concerned with the feelings of others, but also impulsive, pleasure seeking and rebellious. The only comprehensive prospective study (Haagen, 1970) of marijuana/hallucinogen use found that most of these traits antedated the drug involvement. In addition, it has been experimentally shown (McGlothlin, Cohen, & McGlothlin, 1967) that many of these variables are significantly related to the intensity of the response to LSD.

Persons making significant use of hallucinogens typically show larger deviations on these variables than do those restricting their usage to marijuana.

In particular, hallucinogen users are more often seeking to resolve personal problems through the drug experience and are more likely to have previously sought psychiatric counseling than are nonhallucinogen drug users (Walters, Goethals, & Pope, 1972). They also express greater sociocultural alienation (Walters et al., 1972). Marijuana and hallucinogen users generally score above average on risk-taking and sensation-seeking scales, and continuing hallucinogen users have been found to score significantly higher than have those discontinuing (Salzman et al., 1972). Frequent hallucinogen users consistently exhibit high unemployment and general underachievement (Barron et al., 1970; Blacker, Jones, Stone, & Pfefferbaum, 1968; Salzman et al., 1972). Another consistent finding among these groups is a strong tendency toward regressive magical thinking (Barron et al., 1970; Blacker et al., 1968).

EFFECTS OF HALLUCINOGEN USE

Psychoses and Suicides

On the basis of a 1960 survey of investigators using LSD in experiments or psychotherapy, Cohen (1960) found that the incidence of LSD-induced psychotic episodes lasting more than 48 hours was 0.8 per 1,000 persons for experimental subjects and 1.8 per 1,000 persons for those undergoing psychotherapy. The suicide rate was 0 per 1,000 persons among experimental subjects and 0.4 per 1,000 persons for psychotherapy patients. In 1968 Malleson (1971) conducted a similar survey among therapists utilizing LSD in England—the data covered some 4,300 patients receiving 49,000 LSD sessions. The incidence of psychosis lasting more than 48 hours was 9 per 1,000 patients, and suicides occurred at a rate of 0.7 per 1,000. There were 20 additional suicide attempts. Two deaths other than suicides were reported in this series: one from an acute asthma attack and a second from unknown causes. Bergman (1971), in a report on ritual use of peyote, estimated the incidence of psychotic reactions at only 1 per 70,000 ingestions.

Self-administration of hallucinogens poses a number of hazards not present under medical conditions. On the other hand, it is difficult to equate the predisposition for adverse reactions in the two populations. The so-called "bad trip" is quite common: probably 25% of the persons who have used hallucinogens as many as five times have experienced one or more such reactions. Several studies (Robbins, Frosch, & Stern, 1967; Smart & Bateman, 1967) have reported on samples of persons hospitalized for hallucinogenic-related psychotic reactions. In the large majority of these cases, the major symptoms subside within a few days, although occasionally they persist for several weeks or months. Most observers agree that the number of individuals hospitalized for hallucinogens has declined in the past few years. Since there has not been a comparable decrease in usage, the decrease is likely due to a greater familiarity with the phenomenon, both on the part of hospital person-nel and the drug subculture. Hospitals probably treat a larger portion on an outpatient basis with tranquilizers, and members of the drug subculture likely "talk down" or simply wait out such adverse reactions.

Flashbacks

Most of the literature on the incidence of flashbacks subsequent to hallucinogen usage is virtually meaningless because of the ill-defined nature of the reported phenomena. In the previously mentioned survey by Cohen (1960) no cases were reported among the 5,000 persons receiving LSD, although some instances were reported following the use of mescaline. Smart and Bateman's (1967) review of the literature lists only 11 such cases. By contrast, some current surveys (Blumenfield, 1971; Stanton & Bardoni, 1972) find up to 25% of LSD users reporting flashbacks. Using a definition of "repeated intrusions of frightening images in spite of volitional efforts to avoid them," Horowitz (1969, p. 147) estimates about 5% of the repeated hallucinogen users in the hippie culture have had flashbacks. In a 10-year followup of 247 persons receiving LSD under medical conditions (McGlothlin & Arnold, 1971), 15% reported experiencing a spontaneous LSD-like experi-ence without using drugs, but the descriptions indicated that the large majority were nothing more than the association of two events bearing certain similarities. Only one case would qualify under Horowitz's definition of "repeated intrusions." One likely explanation of the high incidence of reported flashbacks is the suggestible nature of today's hallucinogen-using population. These young people are prone to believe in all kinds of magical and fanciful phenomena, and they value perceptual changes and seek to induce them by various means in addition to drugs. It also appears likely that no more than a small fraction of the reported flashbacks could be causally related to hallucinogen use under a reasonably rigorous definition.

Chromosome Alterations

The literature on this subject is too extensive for review here. Briefly, the questions of LSD-related chromosome damage and teratogenic effects are still unresolved, although the weight of the evidence seems to be in the direction of no detectable effect for moderate doses in humans (Dishotsky, Loughman, Mogar, & Lipscomb, 1971). The early in vivo studies showing high rates of chromosome aberrations among persons from the drug subculture were not replicated in samples exposed only to pure LSD.

Organicity

Of the five published studies on LSD and organicity, none has found evidence of generalized brain damage (Barron et al., 1970; Blacker et al., 1968; Cohen & Edwards, 1969; McGlothlin, Arnold, & Freedman, 1971; Wright & Hogan, 1972). The Halstead-Reitan test battery used in three studies;

all examined relatively chronic users and employed a control group for comparison. Cohen and Edwards (1969) found that the LSD sample scored significantly lower on the trail-making-A and spacial orientation tests. McGlothlin et al. (1971) failed to replicate these findings, but showed significantly lower scores for the LSD group on the category test measuring abstract thinking abilities. Wright and Hogan (1972) did not replicate either of the previous findings. Two animal studies (Adey, 1966; Sharpe, Otis, & Schusterman, 1967) have found electroencephalographic and behavioral changes which persisted for several weeks or months after relatively large doses of LSD. The question of LSD-related organicity in humans could probably be resolved by pretests and posttests of LSD psychotherapy patients in England or other locales currently using this treatment.

Long-term Personality Change

The acute effect of hallucinogens is temporarily to suspend the mechanisms that normally provide structure and stability to perceiving, thinking, and valuing. This loosening of established associations and beliefs has been variously described as deactivation of perceptual filters, loosening of constancies, breaking down of ego boundaries, dehabituation, and deautomatization. The hallucinogenic drug effect is somewhat analogous to a catalyst in that it makes possible, but does not determine, the cognitive or emotional events experienced. This quality makes the hallucinogen experience fairly unpredictable and strongly dependent on the set and setting in which it is taken. This suspension of traditonal perspectives gives rise to the claims of beneficial personal insights and mystical-religious experiences. The reporting of long-term beneficial changes is unique to the hallucinogens. With exception of an occasional claim of such effects from the use of marijuana (which is itself a mild hallucinogen), no other class of drugs is considered by its users to produce more than acute effects. Such claims are not limited to the hippies and other youth using the drugs under illicit conditions. Many adults who took LSD under medical supervision some 10–15 years ago also reported lasting attitude and value changes that they regarded as beneficial (McGlothlin & Arnold, 1971; McGlothlin et al., 1967).

To the extent that it has been possible to obtain objective evidence to support or refute such subjective reports of hallucinogen effects, one conclusion (McGlothlin et al., 1967) seems clear: If the drugs are administered in a neutral setting to a more or less random sample of adults who are not self-selected on the basis of motivation to participate, the measurable lasting effect will be minimal.

On the other hand, it appears that the hallucinogens do create a condition in which rapid change *may* take place, given the presence of certain other factors. When the user is impressionable, e.g., the adolescent, or is predisposed to seek a new belief system, and especially when he continues to live and identify with a group committed to a particular philosophy, the hallucinogens can be a potent means of facilitating the rapid modification of beliefs and values. Whether such changes are beneficial or detrimental often depends on the frame of reference. It is clear, however, that the impact of hallucinogen use on adolescents is frequently harmful. Even without drugs, the adolescent is quite vulnerable to suggestions and pressure from his peers; with the addition of hallucinogens, his susceptibility to irrational beliefs and behavior is greatly increased. Regressive magical thinking is accentuated, and a general disregard for reality and the consequences of his behavior often follows. This unrealistic lack of concern may, in turn, result in poor judgment with respect to the use of other drugs and health practices in general.

THE ILLICIT MARKET

Amount Consumed

The annual consumption of hallucinogens may be estimated from the data in Table 2. If the prevalence of persons having ever used hallucinogens is assumed to be 5 million, and frequency of use is based on the New York State survey (age 14 and over), the estimated annual national consumption is as follows:

Uses per year	Percent of those having ever used	Number of persons	Annual number of doses (millions)
72	13	650,000	46.8
12	48	2,400,000	28.8
Total			75.6

It is assumed that the 13% using the drugs one or more times per week average six times per month, or 72 times per year; and it is assumed that the 43% using the drugs more than two times per year and less than one time per week average one time per month or 12 times per year. The 39% using two or less times per year contribute a negligible amount to the annual consumption.

If the frequency-of-use data from the college and high school surveys in Table 2 are treated in a similar manner, the following estimates are obtained:

College students: Ever used (N = 1.22 million)

Number of uses per year	Percent of those having ever used	Number of persons	Annual number of doses (millions)
72	3	37,000	2.7
20	22	268,000	5.4
6	25	305,000	1.8
Total			9.9

High school students: Ever used (N = 1.18 million)

Number of uses per year	Percent of those having ever used	Number of persons	Annual number of doses (millions)
72	15	177,000	12.7
20	15	177,000	3.5
6	45	531,000	3.2
Total			19.4

Although the number of students estimated to have used hallucinogens is about the same in colleges and high schools, the ratio of the annual consumption is 1:2 because of the higher frequency of use among high school students.

The combined annual consumption for high school and college students is 29 million doses, or 39% of the general population estimate made from the New York State survey. The survey results in Tables 1 and 2 do not reflect usage by persons in the drug subculture who are not at risk for household and student surveys. There is no means of estimating use by this group. If it is assumed that an additional 200,000 persons in the drug subculture use hallucinogens at a frequency of six times per month, 14.4 million doses would be added to the 75.6 million general population estimate, for a total of 90 million doses.

As indicated earlier, 80% of the hallucinogens analyzed by BNDD laboratories are LSD, and another 10% are LSD and phencyclidine. For the purpose of estimating overall hallucinogen consumption and economics, all usage will be assumed to be LSD. If the average dosage is assumed to be 150 μg., the estimated annual consumption of 90 million doses would represent 13.5 kg. of LSD. Assuming the median dosage unit on the illicit market contains 83 μg. of LSD, this would amount to 163 million dosage units.

Sources

Diversion of licit supplies was the source of the early nonmedical LSD use (1955-61) and similarly for psilocybine around 1961-64. When LSD use became widespread in 1962-64, however, the source became almost entirely clandestine manufacture.

The principal precursor currently used in the illicit manufacture of LSD is ergotamine tartrate. In the past, it has been purchased from U.S. chemical firms (U.S. Congress, 1970, pp. 282-304); in recent years, however, the main source is thought to be licit European suppliers. The synthesis of LSD requires a relatively high level of skill and equipment, especially if high yields are to be obtained. Clandestine manufacturers are currently reported to obtain about 200 g. LSD per kilogram ergotamine tartrate. With this yield, the estimated annual U.S. LSD consumption of 13.5 kg. would require only about 70 kg.

ergotamine tartrate. On the other hand, U.S. clandestine laboratories are reported to be a major source of the world LSD market; therefore, significant additional amounts are likely processed for export.

California was the site of the initial clandestine LSD laboratory in 1962 and has remained a major source to the present time. Numerous LSD laboratories have been discovered in other states (Gunn et al., 1970), and illicit manufacture is also reported in other countries. Most informants agree that the small LSD laboratories of the mid 1960s have now, for the most part, been replaced by relatively few large operations capable of producing 100 g. or more per week.

The key persons in the operation are the ergotamine tartrate supplier, the chemist, the bulk-form distributor, and the tableting operator. Arrangements differ, although the ergotamine tartrate dealer's role would normally end in the sale of the precursor. The chemist may be the central organizer; or he may simply receive the ergotamine tartrate from a second party, perform the synthesis, and return it in the form of LSD. The initial sale of the LSD is typically in crystalline form in lots up to 100 g. or more. These large-scale buyers then contact a tableting operator who either receives a flat fee or a share of the LSD.

The second most popular hallucinogen, phencyclidine, can be easily synthesized in large quantities from relatively common chemicals. The MDA synthesis is somewhat more difficult, requires large doses (100 mg.), and is usually produced in small quantities. As mentioned earlier, the clandestine manufacture of mescaline is a fairly long process, and the high doses required (300-500 mg.) make it economically unfeasible. The commercial price for mescaline is $7 per gram or about $3.50 per dose. A number of other hallucinogens can be produced clandestinely, some from easily available basic chemicals. Their absence on the illicit market is due to a lack of demand.

Finally, there are a few botanical sources of hallucinogens. The peyote cactus grows wild in southern Texas and northern Mexico and is occasionally available on the illicit market. The demand for morning glory seeds is not sufficient to require regulation of their commercial sale.

Economics of the Market

The LSD market is unique among illicit drugs in that the price has dropped sharply in the past few years. In 1967-68 the wholesale price per gram was $3,000-$4,000. In 1971 San Francisco prices fell to as low as $400-$450 per gram and are now around $500-$800 per gram in bulk form. Limited demand, increased availability of ergotamine tartrate, more efficient syntheses, and active competition probably all contributed to the decline in price. Marketing has been quite competitive, with dealers attempting to gain larger portions of the market by creating a good reputation for a tablet of a particular shape and color. Other dealers often copy a popular "brand"; thus frequent changes occur to maintain product identity. The selling of LSD as "mescaline" is another common means of increasing marketability.

At the current LSD prices ($650 per gram), a kilogram of ergotamine tartrate costing $7,000 and yielding 200 g. LSD would result in a profit of about $120,000. At the bulk-form level, the estimated annual U.S. consumption of 13.5 kg. would sell for about $9 million. After tableting, LSD sells for $600-$1,500 per 4,000 tablets. If the tablets contained the advertised 250 μg., this would be the price per gram; however, with the prevailing lower potencies, 4,000 tablets would typically contain less than 0.5 g. LSD. Prices are reported to be substantially higher after export to Canada or other foreign countries.

Retail prices in the East average around $2-$3 per tablet. On the West Coast the prices are $1-$2 per tablet and sometimes as low as 50 cents. Since even heavy LSD users generally take the drug only once or twice a week, the costs to the user are quite low. Similarly, retail dealing is not very profitable and is normally handled as a sideline to marijuana or other drugs. If the average retail price paid by the customer is assumed to be $1.50 per 83 μg. tablet, and doses average 150 μg. then the estimated 90 million annual doses would amount to $245 million in retail sales. This amount is relatively low in comparison with the estimated $1.2 billion illicit amphetamine-barbiturate market (McGlothlin, 1973) or the $1.4 billion estimate for marijuana-hashish retail sales (McGlothlin, 1972). The retail expenditures for heroin have been variously estimated at $2-$5 billion.

THE PSYCHEDELIC MOVEMENT AND ITS ROLE IN THE NEW DRUG SUBCULTURE

Although the hallucinogens represent only a very small part of the overall illicit drug market, they have had a disproportionate influence on the middle-class drug-taking phenomenon that began in the mid-1960s. The hippie movement was spawned around the use of the psychedelics; the movement, in turn, had a pronounced impact on the lifestyles and drug-using behavior of a generation of youth. It is difficult to envision the full development of the hippie movement without the LSD experiences that many, if not most, adherents cite as the essential affirmation of their particular belief systems. Even those who have discontinued hallucinogen use, but continue the hippie-type lifestyle, often point to the LSD experience as the turning point in their lives.

Why did the hippie and psychedelic movements occur in the last decade? Peyote and mescaline had been known for more than one-half century but made no headway among the white population. One answer is that social conditions permitted options not previously existing. When an adolescent grows up in a structured society that demands he assume adult responsibilities at a relatively early age, the alternative of turning on and dropping out is not available. An affluent society allowing prolonged periods of economic dependence and leisure greatly increases the possible choices as to lifestyles. Anything that leaves the individual without an established place in the social structure increases the likelihood for radical departures from the existing norms. Weakening of family and community groups, chronic social and technological change, and the lack of historical relatedness have been cited as contributors to the alienation among the younger generation. Others have suggested that the assassinations of the Kennedys added to the disillusionment, and undoubtedly the Vietnam war has played a major role. Whatever the explanations, it seems likely that if Leary's psychedelic philosophy had been propounded in the depression years of the 1930s or in the war years of the 1940s it would have gone unnoticed.

As Eric Hoffer (1966) has noted in his study of mass movements, such phenomena require a leader as well as the ripeness of the times. In the opinion of the author, Leary was an essential factor in the psychedelic movement. Peyote and other natural hallucinogens were known to be potent change agents in the hands of the shamans of primitive tribes. Leary used the mass media to (a) publicize and advocate the use of hallucinogens and (b) simultaneously propound a radical social philosophy. He wished to accomplish the shaman's results on a mass scale. Those who attempted to interpret Leary's claims on logical grounds either were perplexed or concluded he was irrational and an unfortunate embarrassment to the academic community. They failed to grasp Hoffer's point—that the very essence of a movement is the kindling of extravagant hope; that "it is futile to judge the viability of a new movement by the truth of its doctrine and the feasibility of its promises [p. 44]." Many hippies literally believed that if the world leaders could be introduced to take LSD a utopia could emerge. Hoffer outlines the requirements for an effective leader; "audacity and a joy in defiance; an iron will, . . . faith in his destiny and luck; contempt for the present; a cunning estimate of human nature; a delight in symbols (spectacles and ceremonials); unbounded brazeness [pp. 105-106]." Leary meets these specifications, and the ability of the hallucinogens to suspend the primacy of the habitual belief systems made them an ideal tool for facilitating rapid social change. When the validity of a heretofore unquestioned belief carries no more weight than does its opposite alternative, the conditions are clearly favorable for radical shifts in beliefs—especially among suggestible youth.

The underground press and popular music were strongly influenced by the psychedelic movement and, in turn, greatly aided in its growth. The advertising industry made "psychedelic" and "turn-on" household words. Children who had never heard of LSD learned what was "in" from their cereal boxes. In January 1967, 20,000 persons joined in the first "Human Be-In" in San Francisco, and a genuine movement took form. Similar large-scale gatherings became an almost weekly occurrence in various locales in California and soon spread throughout the country. The LSD trip provided a common ground on an experiential level which served as the unifying principle for hippie communities and for thousands of otherwise strangers at hippie gatherings. Hippie radio programs sprang up, and rock music effectively articulated the flower children's new ethic. A psychedelic subculture quickly formed, aided by the new underground press. It both suggested and sustained the new beliefs, and it acted as a buffer against the faith-eroding forces of the dominant culture.

The introduction of LSD as a formula for instant conversion was the catalyst that permitted a radical departure from the traditional culture in a short time. The hippie movement did not directly involve more than a small proportion of the youth; but it influenced the philosophy, music, dress, attitudes, and values of a much larger group. The widespread use of marijuana can be viewed as a marginal participation of the masses in the styles set by the psychedelic or hippie movement.

Future Hallucinogen Use

As discussed earlier, individual hallucinogen use tends to be self-limiting. Most persons either discontinue or sharply reduce their use of these drugs after a period of 2 or 3 years. If the initiation of new users were to cease, hallucinogen use could be expected largely to disappear within a few years. As yet there is no evidence of a decline in the incidence of new users, although the emphasis on the hallucinogens as an instrument of individual and social change has definitely decreased. It seems likely that this fading of the psychedelic movement will reduce the group identification and other attractions of hallucinogen use and eventually will result in a decline in their usage.

REFERENCES

Adey, W. R. Neurophysiological action of LSD. *Proceedings of the 5th Annual Meeting of the American College of Neuropharmacology,* San Juan, Puerto Rico, Dec. 7–9, 1966.

Anonymous. Peyotl. *Bulletin on Narcotics,* 1959, 11(2), 16–41.

Barron, S. P., Lowinger, P., & Ebner, E. A clinical examination of chronic LSD use in the community. *Comprehensive Psychiatry,* 1970, 11(1), 69–79.

Berg, D. F., & Broecker, L. P. *Illicit use of dangerous drugs in the United States: A compilation of studies, surveys, and polls.* U.S. Bureau of Narcotics and Dangerous Drugs, Washington, D.C.: U.S. Government Printing Office, June 1972.

Bergman, R. L. Navajo peyote use: Its apparent safety. *American Journal of Psychiatry,* 1971, 128(6), 695–699.

Blacker, K. H., Jones, R. T., Stone, G. C., & Pfefferbaum, D. Chronic users of LSD: The "acidheads." *American Journal of Psychiatry,* 1968, 125, 341–351.

Blackford, L. *San Mateo County, California: Surveillance of student drug use. Preliminary report.* County Department of Health and Welfare, San Mateo, Calif., 1972.

Blum, R. H. *Utopiates.* New York: Atherton, 1964.

Blumenfield, M. Flashback phenomena in basic trainees who enter the U. S. Air Force. *Military Medicine,* 1971, 136, 39–41.

Brill, N. Q., Christie, R. L., & Hochman, J. S. Changing patterns of marijuana use. Unpublished manuscript, University of California, Los Angeles, 1972.

Brown, M. Stability and change in drug use patterns among high school students: Fullerton, California (unpublished). In D. F. Berg & L. P. Broecker, *A compilation of studies, surveys, and polls.* U.S. Bureau of Narcotics and Dangerous Drugs. Washington, D.C.: U.S. Government Printing Office, June 1972.

Busch, A. K., & Johnson, W. C. Lysergic acid diethylamide (LSD-25) as an aid in psychotherapy. *Diseases of the Nervous System,* 1950, 11, 204.

Center for Counseling and Psychological Services. *Report No. 2, Survey of drug usage: Preliminary report.* University of Maine, Fall 1970.

Chambers, C. *An assessment of drug use in the general population: Special Report No. 1, Drug use in New York State.* Narcotics Addiction Control Commission, 1971.

Cheek, F. E., Stephens, N., & Joffe, M. Deceptions in the illicit drug market. *Science,* 1970, 167, 1276.

Cholden, L. W., Kurland, A., & Savage, C. Clinical reactions and tolerance to LSD in chronic schizophrenia. *Journal of Nervous and Mental Disorders,* 1955, 122, 211–221.

Coddington, R. D., & Jacobsen, R. Drug use by Ohio adolescents. *The Ohio State Medical Journal,* 1972, 68(5), 481–484.

Cohen, S. Lysergic acid diethylamide: Side Effects and complications. *Journal of Nervous and Mental Diseases,* 1960, 130, 30–40.

Cohen, S., & Edwards, A. E. LSD and organic brain damage. *Drug Dependence,* 1969, 5, 1–4.

Critchley, M. Some form of drug addiction: Mescalism. *The British Journal of Inebrity,* 1931, 28, 99–108.

Dishotsky, N. I., Loughman, W. D., Mogar, R. E., & Lipscomb, W. R. LSD and genetic damage. *Science,* 1971, 172(3982), 431–440.

Dustin, C. B. *Peyotism in New Mexico.* Santa Fe, N.M.: Vergara, 1960.

Ellis, H. A note on the phenomena of mescal intoxication. *Lancet,* 1897, 1, 1540–1542.

Gallup opinion index, No. 80. Princeton, N.J.: American Institute of Public Opinion, Feb. 1972.

Gergen, M. K., Gergen, K., & Morris, S. Correlates of marijuana use among college students (unpublished). In D. F. Berg & L. P. Broecker, *A compilation of studies, surveys, and polls.* U.S. Bureau of Narcotics and Dangerous Drugs. Washington, D.C.: U.S. Government Printing Office, June 1972.

Goode, E. *The marijuana smokers.* New York: Basic Books, 1970.

Groves, W. E., Rossi, P. H., & Grafstein, D. Preliminary results from national college study of life styles and campus communities. Unpublished manuscript, The Johns Hopkins University, Department of Social Relations, Baltimore, Md., Dec. 1970.

Gunn, J. W., Johnson, D. W., & Butler, W. P. Clandestine drug laboratories. *Journal of Forensic Sciences,* 1970, 15(1), 51–64.

Haagen, C. H. Social and psychological characteristics associated with the use of marijuana by college men. Middletown, Conn.: Wesleyan University, Jan. 1970.

Hager, D. L., Vener, A. M., & Stewart, C. S. Patterns of adolescent drug use in middle America. *Journal of Counseling Psychology,* 1971, 18(4), 292–297.

Hochman, J. L., & Brill, N. Q. Marijuana use and psychosocial adaption. Paper presented at American Psychiatric Association meeting, Washington, D.C., May 3, 1971.

Hoffer, E. *The true believer.* New York: Harper & Row, 1966.

Hofmann, A. The discovery of LSD and subsequent investigations on naturally occurring hallucinogens. In F. J. Ayd, Jr., & B. Blackwell (Eds.), *Discoveries in biological psychiatry.* Philadelphia: Lippincott, 1970.

Horowitz, M. J. Flashbacks: Recurrent intrusive images after the use of LSD. *American Journal of Psychiatry,* 1969, 126, 147–151.

Huxley, A. *The doors of perception.* New York: Harper & Row, 1954.

Josephson, E., Haberman, P., Zanes, A., & Elinson, J. Adolescent marijuana use: Report on a national survey. Paper presented at First International Conference on Student Drug Surveys, Newark, N.J., Sept. 14, 1971.

LaBarre, W. Primitive psychotherapy on native American cultures: Peyotism and confession. *Journal of Abnormal Social Psychology,* 1947, 24, 294-309.

Malleson, N. Acute adverse reactions to LSD in clinical and experimental use in the United Kingdom. *British Journal of Psychiatry,* 1971, 118, 229-230.

Marshman, J. A., & Gibbins, R. J. The credibility gap in the illicit drug market. *Addictions,* 1969, 16, 4.

McGlothlin, W. H. Marijuana: An analysis of use, distribution and control. *Contemporary Drug Problems. A Law Quarterly,* 1972, 1(3), 467-500.

McGlothlin, W. H. *Amphetamines, barbiturates and hallucinogens: An analysis of use, distribution and control.* SCID-TR-9. U.S. Bureau of Narcotics and Dangerous Drugs, 1973.

McGlothlin, W. H., & Arnold, D. O. LSD revisited: A ten-year follow-up of medical LSD use. *Archives of General Psychiatry,* 1971, 24, 35-49.

McGlothlin, W. H., Arnold, D. O., & Freedman, D. X. Organicity measures following repeated LSD ingestion. *Archives of General Psychiatry,* 1969, 21, 704-709.

McGlothlin, W. H., Cohen, S., & McGlothlin, M. S. Long lasting effects of LSD on normals. *Archives of General Psychiatry,* 1967, 17, 521-532.

McGlothlin, W. H., Jamison, K., & Rosenblatt, S. Marijuana and the use of other drugs. *Nature,* 1970, 228(5277), 1227-1228.

Mead, M. *The changing culture of an Indian tribe.* New York: Columbia University Press, 1932.

Mitchell, S. W. The effects of anahalonium lewinii (the mescal button). *British Medical Journal,* 1896, 2, 1625.

Mizner, C. L., Barter, J. T., & Werme, P. H. Patterns of drug use among college students: A preliminary report. *American Journal of Psychiatry,* 1970, 127(1), 55-64.

National Commission on Marihuana and Drug Abuse. *Marihuana: A signal of misunderstanding.* Appendix, Vol. II, Washington, D.C.: U.S. Government Printing Office, 1972.

Richards, R. N. MDA and its relationship to other psychedelics. *Addictions,* 1971, 18(3), 11-16.

Robbins, E., Frosch, W. A., & Stern, M. Further observations on untoward reactions to LSD. *American Journal of Psychiatry,* 1967, 124, 393-395.

Salzman, C., Lieff, J., Kochansky, G. E., & Schader, R. I. The psychology of hallucinogenic drug discontinuers. *American Journal of Psychiatry,* 1972, 129(6), 755-761.

Schultes, R. E. The aboriginal therapeutic uses of *lophophora williamsii. Cactus and Succulent Journal,* 1940, 12, 177-181.

Schultes, R. E. The appeal of peyote (*lophophoro williamsii*) as a medicine. *American Anthropologist,* 1938, 40, 698-715.

Sharpe, L. G., Otis, L. S., & Schusterman, R. J. Disruption of size discrimination in squirrel monkeys (*Saimiri sciureus*) by LSD-25. *Psychonomic Science,* 1967, 7, 103-104.

Sheppard, C. W., Gav, G. R., & Smith, D. E. The changing patterns of heroin addiction in the Haight-Ashbury subculture. *Journal of Psychedelic Drugs,* 1971, 3, 22-30.

Slotkin, J. S. *The peyote religion.* Glencoe, Ill.: The Free Press, 1956.

Smart, R. G., & Bateman, K. Unfavourable reactions to LSD: A review and analysis of the available case reports. *Canadian Medical Association Journal,* 1967, 97, 1214-1221.

Smith, M. G. Ethnology: A Negro peyote cult. *Journal of the Washington Academy of Science,* 1934, 24, 448-453.

Stanton, M. D., & Bardoni, A. Drug flashbacks: Reported frequency in a military population. *American Journal of Psychiatry*, 1972, **129**, 751–755.

Szara, S. The comparison of the psychotic effect of tryptamine derivatives with the effects of mescaline and LSD-25 in self experiments. In S. Garattini & V. Ghetti (Eds.), *Psychotropic drugs*. Amsterdam: Elsevier, 1957.

U.S. Bureau of Narcotics and Dangerous Drugs. *Microgram*, Nov. 1967, 1(1).

U.S. Bureau of Narcotics and Dangerous Drugs. *Microgram*, Jan. 1968, 1(3).

U.S. Bureau of Narcotics and Dangerous Drugs. *Microgram*, Feb. 1968, 1(5).

U.S. Bureau of Narcotics and Dangerous Drugs. BNDD Laboratory System's Workload, Fourth Quarter, FY, 1971. Unpublished manuscript, Nov. 24, 1971.

U.S. Congress, House of Representatives. *Crime in America—Illicit and Dangerous Drugs*. Hearings before the Select Committee on Crime, Oct. 23–27, 1969, San Francisco, 1970. Washington, D.C.: U.S. Government Printing Office,1970.

Walters, P. A., Jr., Goethals, G. W., & Pope, H. G., Jr. Drug use and life-style among 500 college undergraduates. *Archives of General Psychiatry*, 1972, **26**, 92–96.

White House Conference on Narcotic and Drug Abuse. Washington, D.C.: U.S. Government Printing Office, 1963.

Wolbach, A. B., Jr., Isbell, H., & Miner, E. I. Cross tolerance between mescaline and LSD-25 with and comparison of the mescaline and LSD reactions. *Psychopharmacologia*, 1962, **3**, 1–14.

Wright, M., & Hogan, T. P. Repeated LSD ingestion and performance on neuropsychological tests. *Journal of Nervous and Mental Disease*, 1972, **154**, 432–438.

14
THE EPIDEMIOLOGY OF STIMULANT ABUSE

Everett H. Ellinwood, Jr.
Behavioral Neuropharmacology Section
Duke University Medical Center

AMPHETAMINE ABUSE EPIDEMICS

As sudden as an explosion cocaine snuffing has spread as an epidemic of unsuspected danger; this is especially seen among the demimonde and artistic circles but also among university and college men. It is brought about usually by being led to it by others, more rarely by snuff powders for coryza which contain cocaine and can be obtained without a prescription [Bleuler, 1924].

It is said that we are doomed to repeat what we do not learn from history. Certainly this is true with drug abuse and is nowhere better illustrated than with sedative and stimulant abuse. With sedatives we went through wave after wave of "nonaddicting" new drugs; with amphetamine we have repeated the tragic experience of the 1890's with the stimulant cocaine. The safe, euphoriant, mental energizer that was a cure-all for depression, fatigue, phychasthenia, narcotic addiction, hangovers, and drunkenness has again proven to be a drug of marked abuse potential.

For 25 years, amphetamine abuse has had a curious tendency to appear suddenly in epidemic proportions in a given locale and to diminish just as rapidly to its original endemic level. Epidemics appeared in Japan in 1950-56, in Scandinavia (primarily Sweden) in 1964-68, and in the United States in 1965-69. According to Brill and Hirose (1969), factors involved in the Japanese epidemic included population migration, drug availability, and social upheaval. Recent experience in California has also demonstrated the importance of cultural disparity between generations and the popularization of the credo associated with the drug subcultures. Because California has often been the weathervane for nationwide changes in drug use, the rest of the United States may experience similar periodic outbreaks of stimulant abuse. Many knowledgeable students in the field are predicting a cocaine and amphetamine upsurge.

FACTORS IN ESTABLISHING AN EPIDEMIC

In summarizing the Japanese, Swedish, and American experience, several sequential factors seem to be involved in establishing a stimulant-abuse epidemic. These factors are as follows:

1. An initial oversupply of amphetamines that find their way into both the legal and illegal markets, often in injectable form.
2. The initiation or inoculation of large segments of the population to amphetamine effects from their use for medical purposes, for recreational purposes, or for their antifatigue properties.
3. Widespread dissemination of knowledge and at times proselytizing of the amphetamine experience.
4. The development of a core of chronic amphetamine abusers who establish a reliable illegal market for amphetamines.
5. Increasing use of the parenteral route for amphetamine administration.
6. The development of multiple "garage" laboratories manufacturing amphetamines to compensate for government curbs on the legal supply.

The environmental substrata on which this process takes place also have remarkable similarities in the three countries. All three countries have a cultural emphasis on personal productivity and aspirations. All have been involved in changing social values and patterns. Japan experienced a rather cataclysmic radical democratization of government; loosening of traditional authoritative family structure; and changes in economic, educational, and even moral aspects of the Japanese lifestyle (Brill & Hirose, 1969). In the United States and Japan there were population migrations into the areas where the epidemics hit the hardest; for example, young people flocked to Haight Ashbury in California, the state that was the major area of abuse in the United States.

Brill and Hirose (1969) described the Japanese experience as probably the most pure form of a drug epidemic that has ever been documented.

> The term epidemic is often applied to outbreaks of drug abuse, but it is not often that the interaction of the classic factors of host-agent and environment are as clearly marked as they were in the Japanese experience. In most outbreaks interpretations are difficult because the cases are relatively few, the spread insidious, unobserved, relatively slow. The situation is not totally new but rather an exacerbation of a long-standing series of drug problems—in the Japanese epidemic none of these issues pose serious difficulties of interpretation. Methamphetamine was new in the country and there had never been a problem with drug dependence of any kind in Japan and only towards the end of the epidemic did other drugs of dependence begin to play any significant role. The epidemic followed a clear course of spectacular increase with a sharp peak and rapid decrease after 1954–55 [pp. 179–180].

During World War II, after only 2-5 years of clinical experience with amphetamines, most combatants used amphetamines to counter fatigue. For example, over 72 million tablets were given to service personnel in Great Britain (Bett, Howells, & McDonald, 1955); Japan was no exception. At the end of hostilities, many Japanese drug houses had an oversupply of methamphetamine; the drug was released onto the market and apparently triggered the epidemic, which was later sustained by illegal manufacture of drugs. The drug-supply problem was compounded in 1949 when the Japanese government increased the ratio of intravenous (I.V.) ampules to oral medication, reasoning that I.V. use would occur only in hospitals. Instead, I.V. abuse of amphetamines increased. Amphetamine abuse in Japan was described by Brill and Hirose (1969) as primarily a disorder of young males between the ages of 12 and 25, usually with an onset between the ages of 16 and 20. As in the United States, there was a higher female/male ratio of drug offenders for amphetamines than for other types of drugs. Amphetamine abusers often had disturbed life patterns that could be traced back to the age of 10 years, and delinquent behavior often preceded drug use. The importance of the parenteral route of administration was documented by Tatetsu (1963), who was able to base a survey of prevalence in the slum area of Sanya on casual observations of the arms of persons coming to the public baths. In July 1954 the arms of 10.2% of the bathers bore injection marks, whereas in March 1955 only 1.1% showed such marks. (Using a similar method, examination of needle marks among arrestees, Bejerot (1970) was able to document the rise and fall of the Swedish amphetamine epidemic with a peak in 1968.)

Brill and Hirose (1969) described the cataclysmic social changes taking place in Japan at the time of the rise of the amphetamine epidemic. This was a nation in which the aftermath stresses of war were tremendous. Some of these stresses were due to the internal rearrangements of population: the major metropolitan areas lost as much as 60% of their population during the war, and a marked reversal of this trend followed the end of hostilities. Thus, by 1965, more than 50% of the population of Japan was living in urban centers. Brill and Hirose stated: "The epidemic also coincided with the time of the U.S. military occupation, complicated by major changes of ethnic, economic, social, educational and administrative and even moral aspects of Japanese life [pp. 186-187]." There was a marked decline in the traditional family control of the individual and a marked pressure on the Japanese populace to produce and to rebuild the war-torn country.

One question raised recently is whether the entertainment and news media contributed to the proselytizing of amphetamine abuse (as well as other drugs). Certainly the overdramatization and the undercurrents of excitement that the news media portrayed about drug use did contribute to its spread among naturally curious adolescents. The new experiences and levels of consciousness produced by drugs were alluded to in the news media as well as in music and other art forms. The cultural avant garde has usually tended to be the first users of various drugs; at times this group becomes the Pied Piper as well, as can be attested to by several songs that appeared during the height of drug popularity in the United States. Drug abuse, then, has a tendency to march down through middle-class strata to a final residence in those with more marginal social adaptions. This tendency was noted in Japan, where the first cases of amphetamine abuse were recognized among entertainers, artists, musicians, writers, and students. It soon spread to the entire population, but most heavily affected vagrants, the unemployed, and those who lived under marginal circumstances. For example, in Japan in 2 years prior to the general spread of amphetamine abuse, ASAI reported that among 88 motion-picture employees, he found 44 abusers of amphetamines and 11 addicts (Brill & Hirose, 1969). Tatetsu, Goto, and Fujiwara (1956), however, reported that those with disadvantageous social and economic conditions were most likely to abuse amphetamines. For example, the Korean minority, who comprised 0.6% of the population of Tokyo, accounted for 22% of the persons receiving social welfare, 67% of the illegal manufacturers of amphetamines, 58% of the sellers, and 30% of the offenders against possession-control laws (Tatetsu et al., 1956). Inghe (1969) reported that in Sweden during the mid-1940s, the first primary users of amphetamines were the Bohemian writers, actors, musicians, other artists, and their admirers. Much of the early use of amphetamines in the United States first appeared in entertainment and art enclaves in San Francisco, Los Angeles, and the Village in New York City. Many entertainers and actors use amphetamines prior to a performance and, when on a hectic schedule, in large doses. These same entertainers are often role models for whole segments of a generation of youth. Widespread knowledge of a charismatic hero's drug use by newspaper reports of arrest, undergound grapevines, and actual portrayal of use in various art forms certainly must have an impact on impressionable followers.

Superimposed on the subcultural use of amphetamines was the general widespread use among the major culture. In this country medically prescribed amphetamines, for a number of years, comprised 13%–15% of all psychoactive drugs sold by prescription—a percentage that is far out of proportion to needs, based on legitimate medical use of these drugs. Sadusk (1966) reported that there were enough amphetamines produced in the United States for each man, woman, and child to have 35 doses at 5 mg. each. As was mentioned earlier, at least part of this more widespread use of amphetamines is an expression of the general cultural emphasis of countries such as Japan, Sweden, and the United States on productivity and personal achievement. Indeed, amphetamines do increase productivity. Untold thousands of individuals in all these countries have used amphetamines primarily for this purpose, even though the rationale of weight reduction may have been used. Acceptance by the general culture is also noted in the widespread use by females. The female/male ratio of drug abusers is much higher with amphetamines than with other drugs including alcohol, perhaps because there are much greater numbers being inoculated through their use as diet pills. Recently the widespread acceptability of amphetamine use was demonstrated dramatically by reports of a physician prescribing injections for entertainment, literary, business, and political leaders, including possibly a U.S. president (Rensberger, 1972).

Several of these famous individuals described became dependent on the prescribed intravenous and intramuscular injections. Some became psychotic. The injections contained various vitamins as well as amphetamine. This physician (who purchased amphetamines at a rate of 80 g. per month) even appeared before a congressional committee where his biography included the following statement: "Dr. 'X'... has been particularly interested in using his methods to counteract the severe physical and emotional stress of those who live and work in environments of continual high pressure [quoted by Rensberger, 1972]." Another physician who treated several patients of "Dr. X" who became psychotic describes them: "They were people in high-powered industries who were constantly challenged to come up with greater and greater creative projects. They needed this kind of extra chemical push to meet the increasing demand."

These "super achievers" repeated the same pattern of abuse involvement that their famous creative counterparts (literary and scientific professional leaders) had undergone during the 1890s with the stimulant cocaine (Ellinwood, 1973). In both centuries the men involved represented the pinnacle or leading edge of the culture; they do not fit neatly into our usual stereotype of the drug abuser. Their case histories show how a culture based on achievement can actually foster certain types (e.g., simulant) of drug abuse. Even with "street" intravenous users, behavior is often a grandiose parody of super success. Smith (1969) described the frenetic, frequently fatal, attempts to achieve status, to become the biggest freak on the street (in the Haight Ashbury), to become the biggest hustler, to shoot the most methamphetamine, to get the biggest speed operation, or to dress in the most bizarre way. Fiddle (1968) also describes the overreaching speed freak. Thus responsibility for the endemic and epidemic abuse of amphetamines rests both in subcultural groups and the general culture, including its leaders.

The modern history of the use of stimulant drugs certainly demonstrates that they do indeed have multiple strong actions that are potentially useful. These actions include a depressant effect on appetite, an enhancing effect on vigilance and arousal level, an elevation of mood, a reactivation of the individual in the fatigue state, and an enhancement of athletic performance. As early as 1883, a German military surgeon, Aschenbrandt (1883) added cocaine to the drinking water of soldiers, unannounced to them during a military maneuver. Their performance was described as improved. Cocaine has long been used by the people of the Andes. Among the ancient Incas, long-distance messenger runners used cocaine to combat fatigue. And today cocaine is used by approximately 2 million people in the Andes for its antifatigue effect.

In general stimulants are used to accomplish the following:

1. Enhance motor performance, as in illegitimate use in athletic events.
2. Increase attention and vigilance especially when there are external or internal factors impinging on the normal state of arousal.
3. Depress appetite.
4. Enhance mood.
5. Produce euphoria (recreational use) or indeed, with I.V. use, produce an orgiastic-like state.

THE AMPHETAMINE ABUSER AND DISTINCT PATTERNS OF USE

There are at least two major routes of chronic amphetamine abuse: oral and intravenous. A person using the oral route of administration often takes the usually prescribed dose of the drug for several weeks before increasing the dose. He gradually increases his use of amphetamines over a period of weeks or months as tolerance develops. Increasingly he encounters insomnia and irritability at night and thus frequently uses sedatives or alcohol to sleep. Persons exhibiting this pattern can be described as follows:

1. Hundreds of housewives have succumbed to this pattern after initially being prescribed amphetamines for weight reduction.
2. Many businessmen and professionals use amphetamines for their anti-fatigue, activity-sustaining effect and for their weight-reduction effect.
3. Many students succumb to their abuse by initially using amphetamines to extend their study periods or to cram for exams. Often these are high-achieving students (partially because of previous accessability in medical clinics, medical and nursing students were quite vulnerable). Alternately, many students, through their initial student use and validation of the effects of amphetamines, set the stage for later abuse triggered by periods of stress.
4. Truckdrivers also have had a prevalent use of these drugs to sustain alertness over 24–48-hour periods in long-distance hauling.
5. There are considerable numbers of individuals who become attached to amphetamines through their initial use for kicks or a "high" in the oral form.

Amphetamines are used either alone or in combinations with other drugs including alcohol. (Amphetamine combinations with alcohol can maintain the person's arousal even though he consumes considerable quantities of alcohol.) There is a danger in this pattern in that these persons often become quite intoxicated but do not pass out and have gone on to indulge in criminal or violent activities that appear quite bizarre and may be associated with amnesia for the episode (Ellinwood, 1971).

Both oral and I.V. use of large doses of amphetamines produce a general sense of well being. Most amphetamine abusers initially note an increase in gregariousness and a sense of cleverness, "crystal-clear thinking," and invigo-rating aggressiveness, along with a feeling of ability and at times invulnera-bility. Any ambivalence, depression, psychasthenia, or fatigue is magically abolished. Because tolerance is quickly developed to these positive effects of the drug, one needs to increase the dosage to recreate the effects.

The other major pattern of use is one in which the individual injects I.V. doses of amphetamine (usually of methamphetamine in the United States) at short intervals and in immense quantities (up to 2,000 mg. per day) over a period of 4-6 days, during which times he does not sleep (Kramer, Fischman, & Littlefield, 1967). The extended sleepless periods cannot be explained simply as avoidance of the postamphetamine depression or as insomnia due to amphetamines. Many amphetamine users who do not become tremendously depressed still engage in extended periods of wakefulness. In addition, since most amphetamine users know the extent to which it produces insomnia, they are capable of handling this effect, either by stopping the dose at a point prior to sleep or by using sedatives. Many addicts, in explaining their prolonged periods of sleeplessness, state that the experience itself is an ineffable one in which there is a "need" to continue the experience. Quite often they are so totally engaged in the task at hand that they will continue to use amphetamines, thus prolonging their repetitious activities. Even when addicts have established a successful 24-hour cycle on oral amphetamines, they often go through periodic prolonged binges. These are at times remembered as intensely meaningful or significant experiences (and at times psychotic). The addict may spend the entire period engaged in repetitious tasks or series of activities or even a prolonged period of pursuing a central theme of thinking. He may go on an extended trip or even drive aimlessly for 2-3 days. In the social setting, the process may also take on an underserved intensity in which the persons "rap" on and on or pursue mutual activities for hours.

Gradually the user becomes more tense, tremorous, and irritable as the run progresses; at that point, he may stop using the drug, pass out from exhaustion, or take a sedative or narcotic. Then he usually sleeps for 24 to 48 hours, wakes up ravenously hungry, eats large quantities of food, and then starts the process all over again. Whereas the oral use of amphetamine produces a sustained sense of euphoria associated with an energizing effect, the I.V. use of amphetamine produces an immediate, ecstatic, exalting, orgiastic experience. This intensely euphoric feeling is described as an electrical shock running from the head to the abdomen to the groin; at other times, it is described as an expanding, flashing, buzzing, vibrating feeling. The effects are alluded to in the "street" names for amphetamine such as "splash," "spliven," "grease," and "rhythm." The I.V. use of cocaine produces a similar effect, but has a shorter duration.

Intravenous use of amphetamines in epidemic proportions had its first start in Japan following World War II. Although there was a moderate endemic use of I.V. amphetamine in this country, especially in New York City, San

Francisco, and Los Angeles, its use began to increase in the early 1960s, leading to establishment of cliques of amphetamine users in these cities.

Studies have characterized the I.V. amphetamine user differently, often dependent on sampling techniques, time period, and locale (Bejerot, 1970; Schick, Smith, & Myers, 1969). One important factor is the difference between samples taken during the endemic period versus those taken during peak epidemic years. During the peak Haight Ashbury experience, most I.V. users were 20–21-year-old middle-class persons with some college education; most had migrated to San Francisco, reflecting the flood of Flower Child initiates during those years. In contrast, Bejerot (1970) reported mean ages of 25–29 years in the peak years in Sweden. Studies from hospitals again reflect a different population of endemic users who have been selected for more borderline adaptations; this population often is older (Ellinwood, 1967). Other groups of I.V. users have (a) moved from I.V. use of other drugs, (b) are polydrug users, (c) have moved up from oral use of amphetamines, and (d) are part of the rapidly increasing number of cocaine users from what was only endemic use several years ago (this appears primarily related to the new supply routes from South America).

AMPHETAMINE INOCULATION OF A
LARGE POPULATION BASE

Both the amount of amphetamines production and the total number of prescriptions, including new prescriptions, give an indication of the overwhelming number of people who have been inoculated with amphetamines each year. ("Inoculation" means that the person has a chance to experience the euphoriant and energizing effects of amphetamine repeatedly over a period of time, usually 1–3 months.) From this inoculation period, a number of perhaps "addiction prone" persons will go on to abuse patterns. Dr. Mitchell Balter (unpublished report), in a series of studies of several years, has documented the extensive prescribing of amphetamines by American physicians. The majority (up to 80%) of these prescriptions are written for women between the ages of 20 and 49, primarily for controlling obesity. There has been a gradual decline for the past 10 years in the number of prescriptions written; and over the past year, there has been a dramatic drop based on physicians' alarm over the abuse potential. In 1967, at the height of the amphetamine-abuse epidemic, Balter reports that there were 31 million prescriptions for anorexic stimulant drugs. Of these, there were 14 million new prescriptions. Of this total for stimulant drugs, 23 million were prescribed for amphetamines and 10 million were new amphetamine prescriptions. At this rate 6%–8% of all adults over 18 years could have used amphetamines by prescription. Perhaps another 2% received them from informal but not necessarily illegal channels (for example, borrowing pills from a friend without a prescription). In 1970 the prescription rate for amphetamines dropped slightly to 28 million for amphetamines; 9.6 million were for new prescriptions. At this rate, considering new medical prescription alone, 5%-7% of the population might be inoculated each year. Over a number of years the cumulative effect would result in inoculating a large segment of the population. Chambers and Inciardi (1972), in a study based on a sample population of 7,500 (representing the 14 million people in New York State), confirmed that there are considerable proportions of the population that have used diet pills. They estimated the figure at 12%, and this did not include persons obtaining amphetamines from an illegal market.

OVERSUPPLY OF AMPHETAMINES

The actual amounts of amphetamine produced by legal pharmaceutical houses also document the oversupply of these drugs in the United States before 1972. (The Japanese wartime oversupply of methamphetamine has already been described as the trigger for their drug epidemic.) The supply of amphetamines recently has been curbed by the U.S. government to 20,700 lb. (Scoville, personal communication, 1972). This amount represents 18% of the 1971 supply of amphetamine, when the United States produced approximately 100,000 lb., enough to make 8 billion pills and capsules. The reduction in supply does not apply to other stimulant or anorexic drugs. Sources at the Food and Drug Administration (FDA) estimate that, originally, up to 90% of this supply went into the illegal market. If only 70% went into the illegal market from the estimated 9,356 kg. of amphetamine sulfate and 6,100 kg. of methamphetamine hydrochloride produced, this supply would be sufficient to sustain 150,000 amphetamine abusers at 200 mg. per day for a year. This dosage probably represents the average severe amphetamine habit. This level can produce the more severe difficulties discussed previously. Several variables must be considered in regard to the 200-mg/day dose for addicts. Addicts do not use drugs continuously throughout the year; at times, they rest for periods depending on the pattern of abuse. For example, the "run use" of amphetamines is often a cycle of 4 days of use and 2 days of rest without amphetamines. Thus a person might use 300–400 mg. per day but have rest periods in between. At any rate, a 200-mg/day dose provides 75 g. amphetamine per year. Of course, this amount will not sustain a high-dose I.V. user; but he primarily uses street drugs, anyway. The 150,000 addicts do not include the number supplied from illegal "garage" laboratories. Production of amphetamine is a relatively simple task and can be accomplished by any bathroom laboratory. Even if there were only 150,000 addicts, this number would represent approximately one-half to one-fourth the number of estimated heroin addicts in the United States; yet heroin addiction has received by far the most attention.

As legal supplies of amphetamines are curbed, garage laboratories undoubtedly will take over as a source for amphetamines. The reduction of legal supplies, however, likely will reduce both the number of "straight" middle-class users of amphetamines and the number of people being inoculated with the amphetamine experience. It might be predicted that amphetamine use will go farther underground and will tend to be more of a phenomenon of subcultural or criminal populations, as is the case with narcotic abuse. We can certainly expect that a change in the source of supplies of amphetamines, will change the nature of amphetamine-abuse patterns. In the future, history may record the experience with amphetamines in a very similar fashion to the changes that took place following the Harrison Act, which made general narcotic use illegal and placed tight controls on medical use. At that time most of the approximately 5% of the population using narcotic drugs stopped using them, and narcotic usage came to reside primarily in the subcultural and criminal populations.

ILLEGAL SUPPLY OF DRUGS
FROM LEGAL SOURCES

Fleming (1960) reported that there was an extensive bootlegging of legal amphetamines to truckdrivers in the United States. More than 200 operators at truckstops were selling tablets, and some operators had extensive supplies. The ease with which amphetamines as well as sedatives could be obtained legally in the United States was dramatized by a television producer (Walsh, 1964), who set up a fictitious company in Manhattan and was able to obtain from manufacturers the equivalent of more than 1 million standard tablets worth nearly $500,000 in the black market. Nine of the 10 companies from which the drugs were ordered delivered them without asking for validation of license or FDA registration. In addition to distribution through fictitious distribution companies similar to the one demonstrated, there was considerable diversion of legitimate amphetamines into the black market via looting of trucks carrying legitimate supplies. Obviously, the need for present controls on amphetamines has been repeatedly documented.

INCIDENCE OF AMPHETAMINE ABUSE

There are no adequate incident studies for either the epidemic or the endemic abuse of amphetamines. Most data have been gathered from biased samples or are based on estimates of information on legal supplies (as discussed previously). These studies, however, provide a glimpse of amphetamine abuse from several vantage points. In 1954, at the peak of the Japanese epidemic, it was estimated that 2 million persons were involved (550,000 were addicts) of a population of 88.5 million (Bejerot, 1970; Brill & Hirose, 1969). Approximately 55,000 of these individuals were arrested for violation of the amphetamine-control laws (Brill & Hirose, 1969). In 1954 it was estimated that 1% of the entire population of the city of Kurune and about 5% of the population between 16 and 25 years of age were actively addicted (Masaki, 1956). In certain slum areas of the major cities of Japan, 10%-35% of those coming to the public baths had needle marks on their arms from I.V. use of amphetamines (Brill & Hirose, 1969).

In western countries, there has been a major concern with amphetamine abuse: there has been a higher incidence of admission to psychiatric hospitals due to amphetamine-produced psychosis as well as other manifestations of abuse. The following studies demonstrated that amphetamines contribute significantly to psychiatric admissions. In Northern Ireland, McConnell (1963) found that 2% of those admitted to psychiatric wards had symptoms related to amphetamine abuse. Johnson and Milner (1966) found that 3.5% of psychiatric admissions in England had symptoms related to amphetamine abuse. During peak years of amphetamine use in Los Angeles, Rockwell and Ostwald (1968) found that 15% of those coming to a psyhciatric unit had amphetamine in their urine. Scott and Willcox (1965), even at this early date, found that 18% of young people coming to a juvenile detention home in London had amphetamine in their urine. Even though these samples do not provide one with a basis for generalization, they do demonstrate the periodic widespread use and complications of amphetamines.

PHYSICAL AND PSYCHOLOGICAL MORBIDITY OF AMPHETAMINE ABUSE: IMPACT ON THE INDIVIDUAL

Does Speed Kill?

An extensive discussion will not be attempted concerning the physical and psychological impact on the person during the ongoing process of amphetamine abuse (for a review, see Ellinwood, 1969, 1973; Kalant, 1966). This section examines the residual or chronic consequences to the individual. The phrase "speed kills," like many aspects of amphetamine use, has multi-determined meanings. "Street" amphetamine users interpret this slogan in three ways:

1. There is an increase in violence and homicide associated with use.
2. The user either dies from an overdose or has an accelerated mortality.
3. Amphetamine kills one's soul or psychological being.

Physical Effects on the User

Amphetamine addicts often announce dramatically that they do not expect to live more than 2 or 3 years. From their accounts, one gets the impression that the amphetamine addict burns himself out. This is incorporated into the credo of many speed users and the image they present to others. There is also a general uneasy consensus among those who work with high-I.V.-dose amphetamine addicts that life expectancy may be short. Fatalities due to acute overdose, however, are not reported frequently, and there are no adequate morbidity studies. Inghe (1969) reports an increased mortality rate among those who were given legal prescriptions for central stimulants in the 1965-67 Swedish series. The increase was a slight one, perhaps because it represents only the mortality rate for potential amphetamine abusers, not acutal abusers. Although there have been few reported cases of death directly attributable to acute and chronic amphetamine abuse, Clement, Solursh, and Van Arnst (1970) noted a number of fatal cases on the streets of Toronto, apparently related to amphetamine abuse but largely unprovable. In these cases, at autopsy pathological evidence of death directly due to amphetamines was usually rare. In fact, the more devastating physical effects of amphetamine abuse are in general rarely reported in the literature.

Subarachnoid hemorrhage from aneurysms, arterio-venous malformations and intercerebral hematoma formation (Weiss, Raskind, Morganstern, Pytlyk, & Baiz, 1970) have been reported as a complication of amphetamine abuse, probably secondary to hypertension (Goodman & Beker, 1970; Kane, Keeler, & Riefler, 1969; Rumbaugh, Bergeron, Fang, & McCormick, 1971). Cerebral vascular thrombosis with paralysis also has been reported in otherwise normal young persons (Kane et al., 1969). With cases of fatal amphetamine intoxication (without cerebral vascular accidents) usually associated with hyperpyrexia and cardiovascular collapse, the significant findings most often described are diffuse petechial hemorrhages, cerebral edema, acute internal hydrocephalus with dilated ventricles, pulmonary edema and renal tubular degeneration (Harvey, Todd, & Howard, 1949; Pretorius, 1953; Zalis & Parmley, 1963). The microhemorrhages at times extend to the viscera, pericardial sac, epicardium, and the gastric muscosa.

In addition to the specific drug effect of amphetamine, I.V. users are subject to all the general medical complications of nonsterile I.V. use of drugs of unknown quality, similar to those occurring with narcotic use. Some of these complications are overdose, multiple embolic thrombosis, hepatitis, pneumonia, embolic pneumonia, lung abscess, endocarditis, tetanus, syphilis, local sepsis at injection sites, and generalized septicemia.

The slow death of one's soul or "psychological being" is certainly controversial, but some clinical investigators report residual psychological effects following chronic amphetamine use. The residual effects of chronic amphetamine abuse could indeed be a true interplay of structural-physiological changes associated with concurrent psychological changes. Both effects possibly could be independent, but most often they are mutually interacting. Ellinwood and Escalante (1970), studying experimental animals given chronic doses of methamphetamine, found that the neuronal chromatolysis in central nervous system (CNS) areas (e.g., reticular-activating system) was related to alerting and emotional arousal. This finding may be similar to that of a longer term followup (Tatetsu et al., 1966; Utena, 1966) of subjects who reported the following symptoms as persisting for several months or years: loss of initiative, emotional flattening, and apathy. In addition, these effects might be due to chronic CNS insult. (Brain damage on the basis of cerebral vascular accidents as well as multiple petechial hemorrhages has been discussed previously. The adynamia described by the Japanese is similar to the frequent description of the apathetic "spaced out" postamphetamine users in the United States (Ellinwood, unpublished results, 1971). Postamphetamine addicts often describe a rather emotionally colorless life in which there is little or no desire. At times they lose their train of thought (the emotional themes upon which thought processes usually ride appear to be transient and weak). In some there is a deficit in emotional memory; i.e., events and interactions usually remembered because they are emotionally important are not retained by these persons. Documentary evidence for these clinical impressions is lacking (most IQ tests are in the normal range), but Rylander (1969) reported that 14 of 50 advanced addicts showed impaired immediate and long-term memory functions on testing.

Utena (1966) emphasized the increased potential for psychopathic or psychotic reactions similar to those induced by amphetamines to recur not only on reintroduction of amphetamine but also in abstinent persons under stress. Such a tendency to relapse under both physical and psychological stress was found in one-fourth of the residual cases who were admitted to the Matsuzawa Hospital. In this study, amphetamine psychosis showed a schizophrenic-like picture in the early stages of the illness, frequently left residual states, and had a peculiar tendency to relapse. In view of this pattern, Utena suggested strongly that chronic intoxication may play some causative role in producing the longer lasting postamphetamine schizophrenic-like picture that the Japanese have so frequently reported. In addition, many western observers think that a number of borderline or, indeed, simply vulnerable persons are pushed over, with amphetamine abuse, into chronic psychosis; without such abuse, these people probably would have made a marginally successful adjustment (Ellinwood, 1967, 1969, 1972b).

A similar picture appears to be emerging associated with chronic use of psychedelic drugs. Bowers (1972) states:

Hollisters' assertion that it is unlikely that one could produce a chronic psychosis by most known chemical agents seems untenable today. Experience with casualities from the psychedelic drug scene has established the fact that the illicit drugs of choice (LSD, mescaline, psilocybin) can by single or repeated administration lead to a syndrome which behaves much like nondrug-induced psychosis in the long run as well as the short run [p. 439].

An interesting question arises as to what becomes of the relatively fixed delusions of chronic amphetamine abusers who do not remain psychotic in other ways. The fixed delusions can be distinguished from the more gross, all-prevailing delusions that amphetamine psychotics demonstrate. Most hallucinations subside within 2-3 days after the last dose of amphetamine, and delusions typically resolve themselves within a week or two. There are groups of carefully studied individuals, however, who have residual delusions in what is otherwise a clear and rational consciousness; these delusions persist for periods of at least a year (Ellinwood, 1967, 1971, 1972b). Even when the delusions were discussed in terms of their occurence during the amphetamine intoxication period, these persons held to the reality of these experiences and beliefs. They understood fully the questionable validity of these delusions by others. Additional evidence of residual psychological effects were noted after examination with the Minnesota Multiphasic Personality Inventory (MMPI) in chronic amphetamine abusers. These effects were significantly different from those in other types of addicts, especially increases on the schizophrenic and psychasthenic scale. These scales indicate there is some degree of residual bizarre thinking associated with emotional apathy (Ellinwood, 1967).

Violence and Homicide
Associated with Use

Violence related to amphetamine abuse is widely held to occur, yet it is not a completely documented phenomena. To provide some balance of the effects of amphetamine on aggressive and violent behavior, effects of other drugs are briefly noted. The consensus among those who work closely with problems of drug abuse is that opiates do not induce unwarranted violence and, in fact, are likely to inhibit tendencies toward violence, even though addicts are frequently involved in potentially explosive criminal situations (Kolb, 1925). On the other hand, for years alcohol and sedatives have been associated with an increase in violence that is thought to be secondary to a lowering of impulse control (Guize, Taulson, & Catfield, 1962). Reports from law-enforcement personnel and psychiatrists, as well as from drug users themselves, have indicated that amphetamine may also be related to aggressive behavior, perhaps more specifically than is any other group of drugs. That is, amphetamine actually may induce aggression, rather than simply lower impulse control (Ellinwood, 1969, 1971; Kramer, 1969; Smith, 1972). Often the amphetamine-induced paranoid ideation or emotional lability leads to a violent act or even homicide (Ellinwood, 1971).

Not infrequently the amphetamine abuser committing homicide is attacking the imagined assaillant created in his paranoid, delusional thinking. The violent act may take place in a state of terror and panic, often secondary to misinterpretation of events or delusions. Perhaps equally important is the influence of amphetamines in creating (a) impulsive reactiveness and (b) a lability of mood, the user abruptly vacillating from a warm congeniality to fiercely hostile moods, for the most trivial of reasons (Ellinwood, 1971; Kramer, 1969). The drug subculture amphetamine abuser, of course, is involved frequently in criminal activity to support his drug use; he may suddenly panic and react violently while involved in an armed robbery. At times this reaction is touched off by bizarre feelings, such as his being furiously angry because the storekeeper "smiled at me." In one recent study of amphetamine abusers (Ellinwood, 1971), 12 of 13 persons committing homicide were carrying concealed weapons at the time. Many speed users carry weapons ostensively for a variety of reasons, such as the following: (a) for use in armed robbery; (b) because of the user's suspiciousness and fears—often the individual has heard someone breaking in at night, or he becomes increasingly fearful of his persecutors and begins carrying a gun; and (c) there is a certain amount of "cowboy and Indian" braggadocio involved in carrying guns by speed users. Anyone working with amphetamine addicts hears stories of persons sitting all night with a loaded gun waiting for fantasy intruders to enter. Under these conditions they have been known to shoot at imagined noises or images (Ellinwood, 1971).

Reports of violence associated with amphetamine abuse are not peculiar to the United States. From Sweden there were similar reports of aggression as well as of homicide (Rylander, 1969). Rylander reports that there were three murders, one manslaughter, and 21 assault-and-battery crimes by the 146 stimulant addicts admitted to his Swedish Forensic Psychiatric Clinic. There were 109 crimes against property, some of which included associated aggression. In addition, during the Japanese epidemic of amphetamine abuse, Noda (1950) reported that in a 2-month period 31 of 60 convicted murderers had some connection with the misuse of amphetamines. In his original monograph on amphetamine psychosis in England, Connell (1958) stated that hostile aggressive behavior was observed in 22% of subjects.

Nevertheless, the relationship of amphetamines to crimes of violence is not an overwhelming one, when surveyed from incidence studies. Blum (1967) concluded, "research done to date directly contradicts the claims linking amphetamine abuse either to crimes of violence, sexual crimes or to accidents [p. 30]." In reviewing the California Youth Authority data of Roberts, however, Blum (1969) found that there was a nonstatistically significant involvement of amphetamine users in assaults. A study of drug use in arrested individuals in six metropolitan areas (Eckerman, Bates, Rachel, & Poole, 1971) indicated amphetamines were the fifth most commonly used drug and were the most underreported by arrestees, in that only nine of 30 arrestees who had positive urine samples for amphetamines admitted to their use. This study indicated that arrests for criminal homicide, forceful rape, and assaults had a greater proportion of total arrests for current users of amphetamine (12.1%) than for the "current users" of heroin (8.5%), morphine (8.8%), cocaine (9.0%), and marijuana (11.6%), but were less than for barbiturates (17.2%). Arrests for Crimes Against the Person (homicide, rape, and assault) among "current amphetamine users" were less frequent than among a group of nondrug users. It must be kept in mind that this is an incidence study from arrestees, not from a general population. Eckerman et al. (1971) concluded from this study:

> Based on the results of this study there are only two drugs of the eleven drug substances included for which it is recommended that more intensive investigation

be undertaken. These are barbiturates and amphetamines. There simply is not sufficient data to say anything definitive, but there did appear to be an unusually high concentration of Index Crime arrest charges among "amphetamine users" when compared with those identified as "users" of other drugs.

EFFECTS ON SOCIETY

Traditionally the question of social impact of drug abuse raises several issues:

1. Threat of contagion or involvement of adolescents and young adults into the drug-abuse process.
2. Crime-inducing characteristics of drug abuse.
3. Its effect on violent behavior or aberrant sexual behavior.
4. Production of social and economic invalids.
5. Provision of a medical disease reservoir and source of contamination by contact through common needle use.

With amphetamine use there is the danger of a rapid epidemic-like process that can sweep thousands into its path. Crime-inducing aspects of amphetamine abuse have been recognized by the Japanese (Noda, 1950) and the Swedish. Inghe (1969) described an "aflameness" to criminal activity. Smith (1969, 1972) described the illegal marketplace for amphetamines in the United States and the capacity of this marketplace to rapidly criminalize great numbers of middle-class youngsters. Amphetamine abuse is known to induce violence, particularly among violence-prone cliques such as motorcycle gangs. "Hells Angels," for example are known for their speed use. The interaction of amphetamine in such groups who already have the potential for violence is alarming especially when amphetamine is combined with large quantities of alcohol. Swedish (Inghe, 1969) and Japanese (Tatetsu et al., 1956; Utena, 1966) investigators describe the production of social and psychiatric invalids as the main residual problems of amphetamine abuse. Relatively little study has been applied to this subject in the United States. In addition, the I.V.-using, speed subculture certainly is a potent reservoir for such diseases as hepatitis, syphilis, and a host of other less common communicable diseases.

The impact of amphetamine abuse on society cannot be measured solely in terms of statistics. Amphetamine abuse also affects the ideas and feelings that a culture has about itself. To be accurate, one should consider the interplay of drug subcultures against the major culture and especially the effect of this dissonance on the social value systems that hold a society together—the "cultural glue." In the past, when the heroin subculture welded together around the use of this drug, often a criminally oriented group developed. This process is perhaps the primary means of establishing an anticulture group. The new amphetamine subcultural groups, although not infrequently criminal, are different from the heroin subculture. Like the 18th century sadists and the 11th century witches, the amphetamine subculture has often turned to more bizarre forms of anticultural value systems (Ellinwood, 1972).

In previous, church-dominated eras, black mass performed by individuals professing the role of witches was one such protest that reversed the prevailing cultural images. Crosses were inverted, urine was substituted for wine, white was transformed to black, virgins were raped, and Lucifer was substituted for Christ. Particpants enhanced the experience with a hallucinogenic witches' brew containing, among other ingredients, belladonna. There is no doubt that the participants derived a great emotional charge from this violation of the Christian ceremony. At present, if a person is having difficulty identifying with the general culture, initiation into the speed clique or into Hell's Angels could provide a similar solid negative identity; most participants describe these experiences as meaningful or intense. The values most antithetical to our prevailing culture are not religious but are aimed at (a) the success orientation; (b) the sterile, clean, immaculate nature of our middle-class life; (c) the less than overwhelmingly humanistic orientation of our major social institutions; and (d) rationalism itself. Excessive drug use and loyal opposition to the established culture often appear to go hand in glove and, in fact, tend to potentiate each other.

Smith (1969) describes this bizarre behavior as status endowing in the speed scene; the names members give themselves reflect this orientation, such as "Mad Bruce," "Dr. Zoom," "Crazy Tom," "Mr. Clean," "Super Crank," and "Nickidrene." One such group wore quasi-military uniforms and labeled themselves the "Methedrine Marauders" or "Crank Commandos." (The recent movie *A Clockwork Orange* portrays an anticulture with an orientation not toward financially rewarding crime, but toward bizarre but success-oriented hectic activity and violence raised to an art form.) In contrast to a more primitive society, sophisticated societies tolerate considerable discordance of values from subcultural groups; however, there may be limits to which these dissonant strains can be withstood before societal organization begins to suffer.

AMPHETAMINE-INDUCED OVEREVALUATION OF PERCEPTS AND CONCEPTS: THE SUDDEN NEW VALUES AND THEIR CONTAGION

Even within the individual amphetamine addict one can trace the beginnings and spread of a common value-system change tightly held by a subcultural group which establishes an overwhelming feeling of camaraderie. One repeated observation that becomes more noticeable as the individual abuser becomes progressively psychotic is the increased intensity of feelings associated with perception and thinking. Even some nonpsychotic amphetamine abusers state that they have an intense sense of reality, portentiousness, and significance associated with common ordinary objects, the perception of an event, and, indeed, the importance of their own thinking.

This hypercathexis of objects and events is also associated with an intense curiosity. Events and casual objects not only represent themselves, but they are signs and clues for deeper significance. Thinking also may become overly involved—manifested primarily in usually unsophisticated philosophical concerns dealing with "beginnings, meanings, and essences." Revelation of "significant" illogical insights are frequently experienced (Ellinwood, 1967).

These often are pseudoprofound experiences that usher in prolonged periods of both real and psychotic or naïve thinking. The overevaluation of one's thoughts and environment has consequences other than more psychotic thinking. Amphetamine addicts overvalue their dirty unkempt surroundings; they tend to place great significance on their many meaningless stereotyped tasks. This overevaluation of the person's way of life and its crazes and fads often continues to have a pull on him even after he is abstinent from amphetamines. The subcultural group thinking, even though it may also be quite bizarre, can become laden with significance; and the person often feels quite strongly about what appears to be absurd values or philosophy. (Of course, history is filled with innumerable accounts of this happening without stimulant drugs, but with the drugs it is more blatant, spontaneous, and often leaderless.) Future research is certainly needed to analyze the characteristics of group processes and dynamics under the influence of drugs. Amphetamine users will prove to be an interesting group to study.

AMPHETAMINE SUBCULTURAL GROUPS: THEIR CRAZES

There have not been adequate field studies to demonstrate the contagiousness of amphetamine-induced ideas and behavior. Some reports, however, indicate that the spread of these behaviors can be quite rapid. Fiddle (1968) provided several excellent examples of subcultural organization of amphetamine users around bizarre goals and "holy grails." He described several bizarre fads or "crazes" through which the amphetamine abusers socialize. One such craze in Greenwich Village was organized around the collecting of stones, which started when one amphetamine addict suddenly overvalued stones—which he perceived as gems—and began searching for stones in parks and elsewhere. He was convinced that if he kept digging and dug deep enough he would find the "stone of stones." When he first began collecting, the members of his circle laughed at him; however, they finally became curious, joined in the hunt and then became dedicated collectors. This group activity lasted 3 years, during which time they continually engaged in a hyperactive quest for stones that they believed had magical or at least mysterious quality. This quest led to stealing and bartering for stones and the establishment of a flourishing economy. Persons involved in this craze were not teenagers, but men and women in their 20's, 30's, and 40's. The pace was often furious; at times, for several days and nights, they would partake in an endless round of activities that subsided only when they all became physically exhausted. Fiddle describes other groups of "intelligensia" (using amphetamines) in the

Village who would hunt for mystical meanings in objects such as Japanese musical instruments and Buddist tombs, search in Chinese texts for so-called meaning, and weave the whole into an elaborate time-stuffing mumbo-jumbo that kept everyone on the precipice of meaning. At times the group is held together almost with a religious awe, often with an intensity of feeling that something sacred was about to happen.

Thus, amphetamine may have a special place in a contemporary society that is imbued with the meaninglessness of existence. Amphetamine certainly cures this problem. The difficulty resides in the indiscriminate attachment of portentious meaning to both the bizarre and the real.

If individuals can develop delusions with amphetamine abuse, then can more "realistic" group beliefs be far behind? This may in fact be the real danger of amphetamine abuse, especially in group activities where belief systems are mutually reinforced by both the group and the intense feelings of reality induced by the drug itself. Thus, bizarre beliefs can become a "reality" under these conditions. The potential danger to society is in the process of seeding it with too many marginal and bizarre beliefs or value systems. On the other hand, such crisis cults tend to arise when the dominant culture is not serving the needs of specific groups (Labarre, 1970). Certainly, the existence of such cults seems to imply that the general culture needs to do some "soul searching."

THE AGENT'S ABUSE POTENTIAL

The literature available indicates that there is a marked abuse liability with amphetamines under certain circumstances. The abuse potential of amphetamines and other psychomotor stimulant drugs can be documented both from laboratory studies and from clinical case reports. First, laboratory evidence comes primarily from self-administration studies in which animals perform a lever-press response to obtain intravenous injections of drugs. Under these conditions, rats (Pickens, 1968) and monkeys (Balster & Schuster, 1973; Deneau, Yanagita, & Seevers, 1964) will initiate and maintain responding for amphetamine injections. The remarkably large amounts of amphetamine that monkeys will self-inject over short periods of time after only a brief experience with this drug demonstrates that this aspect of amphetamine-abuse potential compares with narcotics. The response patterns, pharmacological response, and toxicity are strikingly similar to those seen in humans who abuse amphetamines and are distinct from narcotics (Schuster, Woods, & Seevers, 1969). Many animals, when left in a free-choice situation, will continue to inject until they kill themselves. The second line of evidence comes from the numerous case reports, both published and unpublished, that attest to amphetamine-addiction liability. In many cases the latency from the first amphetamine experience to abuse cycle is a very short period, often within 2-6 months. A third indicator is the rapidity with which the Japanese experienced a national epidemic of amphetamine abuse; that this epidemic occurred in a country that has never had a significant alcohol or drug abuse problem in the past (Brill & Hirose, 1969) is an index of the abuse potential of amphetamines. Similar but less drastic epidemics were noted in the United States and Sweden.

Abuse potential for amphetamine, as for other drugs, can only be properly assessed when broken down according to its different routes of administration. Any amphetamine addict can tell you that the I.V. route is the most addicting in that it produces the intense orgiastic experience that neither oral administration nor "snorting" can produce. Case histories from persons who have initially experimented with the I.V. route of administration illustrate the very short latency periods, 1–2 months, necessary to establish an abuse cycle. With oral medication, one is, of course, concerned with whether the doses used were the usual therapeutic doses or much higher doses used at times for "recreational" purposes. Regular administration of therapeutic doses of amphetamine over a period of 6 weeks or less probably does not have an overwhelming abuse potential, but there are no quantitative data, other than case reports, to support this contention. (If one wanted to engage in mathematical juggling one could take the figure 150,000, mentioned earlier as a possible number of amphetamine abusers in this country, divide by the 9.6 million new prescriptions per year, and arrive with the rough figure of 1.5%. This figure may be grossly high; but if it is anywhere near correct, then the prescribing of amphetamine for obesity needs to be seriously reevaluated. This inaccurate figure is presented to demonstrate the need for accurate incidence studies.) Thus the abuse potential for amphetamine is dependent on several factors including (a) route of administration and dose level, indicating the intensity of the experience; (b) subcultural or group reinforcement of the drug use; (c) early establishment of a drug-induced exhaustion-depression cycle (this is dependent on both drug dosage and duration of drug-use cycle); (d) early age of initiation; (e) use by persons who have chronic fatigue. These people tend to establish an insidious cycle of need based more on depression and inability to cope.

Finally, to define more accurately the abuse characteristics of amphetamine, one needs to distinguish between abuse potential and what Ellinwood (1973) has described as abuse involvement and abuse persistence. Abuse potential is defined primarily as the tendency for a certain percentage of individuals taking amphetamines to fall into abuse patterns. Abuse involvement is used to describe the degree to which the person who has established an abuse pattern is overwhelmingly involved with the use of amphetamines in the face of known devastating and dangerous effects. A marked degree of abuse involvement implies that the person is unable voluntarily to pull himself out of this pattern of use. With amphetamine, one does note a marked abuse involvement. Often the person stops only after an abrupt altercation, incarceration, or psychotic experience. The overwhelming involvement is especially true of the high-dose amphetamine user, but also is noted with abusers using the oral route. Abuse persistence is the long-term tenacity that the pattern of abuse appears to have on the person. As with narcotic drugs, amphetamines demonstrate some capacity for a resolute grip on the person even after long periods of abstinence. This stubborn, enduring quality of the amphetamine habit is not as great as that with heroin, especially after 1 or 2 years. In fact, there is a tendency for the amphetamine addict to "burn out" within 2-3 years or, alternately, to experience a psychosis and stop the drug habit. In contrast, the heroin addict is usually thought of as taking 8-16 years to "burn out" or to run his course.

In summary, amphetamine has a moderate to severe addiction-abuse potential, depending on the route of administration. Amphetamine certainly is not overwhelmingly addicting if one considers the number of people who are inoculated with the experience each year (perhaps the same could have been said for narcotics prior to the Harrison Act). Abuse involvement appears to be remarkably high with amphetamines: once the person has developed an abuse pattern, he becomes severely dependent and entrenched. Abuse persistence is not as great with heroin, and there is a tendency for amphetamine addicts to burn out within 2-3 years.

CONCLUSIONS: THE NEED FOR MORE DEFINITIVE STUDIES

The literature on amphetamine abuse indicates that abuse of this drug tends to develop along the lines of an epidemic and that more incisive studies are needed to define the nature of these epidemics as well as the endemic condition. Compared with other epidemics, the analagous conditions underlying the spread of amphetamine abuse are as follows:

1. Temporal characteristics are consistent with those of many infectious epidemics.

2. The spread of amphetamine abuse is highly contagious at certain phases of the "epidemic."

3. The ample initial supply or oversupply of the drug "agent" often triggers the initial abuse phase.

4. The environmental-cultural setting often has common factors across amphetamine epidemics in different countries.

5. Initiation of the peak phase of the "epidemic" follows the establishment of an "agent reservoir" or adequate market of the drug from illegal laboratories. (See Figure 1.)

Further knowledge of and understanding of these aspects of the spread of amphetamine abuse will provide us with a base to develop early intervention techniques.

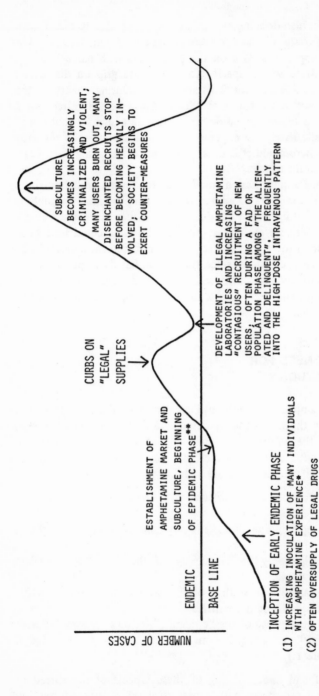

FIG. 1. Model amphetamine epidemic.

Two types of studies are lacking in our current state of the art: (*a*) good longitudinal studies that trace the beginnings of an amphetamine epidemic and then follow this process and (*b*) the development of means of accomplishing adequate incident studies from the general population. Perhaps another type of study is needed: a quantitative documentation of the means by which amphetamine abusers are inoculated; i.e., the number who are initiated to amphetamine use through prescription of amphetamines for obesity versus the use of these drugs for recreational purposes. There are many problems involved in accomplishing adequate studies. As with many epidemiological studies in psychiatry, the study of amphetamine abuse suffers from a lack of an adequate definition of the illness and the various types and stages. For example, we need to be able to adequately separate the types: e.g., high dose, I.V. abuse with its 4-day cycle; the lower dose oral abuse with a daily cycle; and various stages in between. We also need to determine whether the abuser is surreptitiously using the drug from legal sources or whether he belongs to a subcultural group obtaining his supply of drugs from an illegal market. In properly establishing the diagnosis, we may need to resort to a weighted decision process similar to that used in the diagnosis of rheumatic fever. Diagnosis is complicated because many amphetamine abusers do not admit to use and urine testing is not always the answer as it is with heroin, in that the person is often not using amphetamines continuously as he is with a dependence-producing drug like heroin. Thus, a test should be developed similar to those used to detect heroin abuse, syphilis, or tuberculosis. A physiological test such as the development of tolerance to blood-pressure effects of catecholamine-like drugs might be an answer (Balster, R., personal communication, 1973). Additional corroborating tests are needed such as a form of the Minnesota Multiphasic Personality Inventory, on which amphetamine abusers usually have quite distinctive scores (Ellinwood, 1967).

One of the major difficulties is that investigation of the early subcultural group is like studying a floating crap game. Although frequently quite a cohesive group, they are more often constantly on the move and are difficult to keep up with. Smith (1969, 1972), Carey and Mandel (1969), and Griffith (1966) have conducted studies that perhaps are appropriate. These investigators gathered information through the participant-observation method and provided an excellent phenomenological description of the developing amphetamine-abuse process. This type of study, however, does not provide a quantitative assessment with adequate sampling. Study of supply routes of amphetamine has become much more difficult now that amphetamines have gone underground. At one point it was relatively easy to trace out these supply routes when legal prosecution of the case was not so persistent.

An accurate assessment of the endemic use of amphetamines in the United States is needed; such use should be monitored carefully and over an extended period of time. Especially needed are more studies like that of Balter (personal communication, 1973) on the prescription habits of physicians. Assessment of endemic use may provide the clue to the initiation of new amphetamine-abuse epidemics in various regions of the United States. Using such methods in 1948–49 the Danish Board of Health controlled an incipient epidemic (Bejerot, 1970). After World War II Denmark experienced a remarkable increase in amphetamine addiction; however, extensive investigations of prescriptions were introduced. Bejerot states that in this way the Danes could diagnose a large number of amphetamine addicts and could discover a considerable number of physicians with less than responsible prescribing practices. Close surveillance and supervision was provided for addicts and physicians.

> Since no large addict market had time to be established on the basis of generous prescriptions and since many of those abusing amphetamines had not become chronically addicted, when the control system began to function in 1950, no prerequisites for an illegal drug market of any significance arose in Denmark [Bejerot, 1970, p. 71].

Such studies coupled with careful surveillance of manufactured stimulants, following them to their final destination in legitimate pharmacies, would provide an effective early intervention.

Finally, perhaps we should recognize that overuse of stimulants is a price we pay for living in a highly competitive, achievement-oriented industrial society. Think of the huge quantities of coffee, tea, and tobacco consumed by modern man to maintain his programed activity; we would certainly be in trouble if these drugs had a high abuse potential. In that it is unlikely that we will dramatically alter our cultural vector in the next few years, perhaps we need a better understanding of how the individual can best come to an equilibrium between his inherited system and modern society (Ellinwood, 1972a). We should keep in mind the more natural forms of behavioral scheduling found in nonindustrial societies; we might note that the more intense periods of activity are broken up by spiritual, somnulant as well as nutrient repast. Our biological nature is not one easily programed to sustain long periods of alert, confining activity. Long periods of arousal in nonmeaningful tasks is probably the most unnatural aspect of modern life, yet comprises an inordinately large part of our everyday experience, e.g., driving and assembly-line working. Russo (1968) expresses one aspect of this condition in his paraphrasing of Thomas de Quincey, author of *Confessions of an English Opium Eater:*

> As early as 1845 de Quincey . . . predicted the psychological effects of industrial urban society and related them to the use of drugs. In Suspira de Profundis he predicted the fierce condition of eternal hurry . . . [is] likely to defeat the grandeur which is latent in all men, and argued that without sufficient opportunity for solitude and reverie man loses his capacity to dream splendidly. Without it man lacks the means to invest his life with meaning and enhance his experiences by the creative forces of his imagination [p. 1].

REFERENCES

Aschenbrandt, T. Die physiologische Wirkung und die Bedeutung des Cocainmuriat auf dem menschlichen Organismus. *Deutsche Medizinische Wochenschrift*, 1883, 12, 730–732.

Balster, R. L., & Schuster, C. R. A comparison of d-amphetamine, l-amphetamine, and methamphetamine self-administration in Rhesus monkeys. *Pharmacology Biochemistry and Behavior*, 1973, 1, 67–71.

Bejerot, N. *Addiction and society*. Springfield, Ill.: Charles C Thomas, 1970.

Bett, W., Howells, L., & McDonald, A. Amphetamine in clinical medicine. A survey of the literature. *Postgraduate Medical Journal*, 1955, 2, 205–222.

Bleuler, E. *Textbook of psychiatry*. (Authorized English ed. by A. Brill) New York: MacMillan, 1924.

Blum, R. H. Mind-altering drugs and dangerous behavior: Dangerous drugs. In the President's Commission on Law Enforcement and Administration of Justice, Task Force Report: *Narcotics and drug abuse*. Washington, D.C.: U.S. Government Printing Office, 1967.

Blum, R. H. Drugs and violence. In *Crimes of violence*. A Staff Report to the National Commission on the Causes and Prevention of Violence, Vol. 13, p. 32. Washington, D.C., U.S. Government Printing Office, 1969.

Bowers, M. B., Jr. Acute psychosis induced by psychotomimetic drug abuse: I. Clinical findings. *Archives of General Psychiatry*, 1972, 27, 437–440.

Brill, H., & Hirose, T. The rise and fall of a methamphetamine epidemic: Japan, 1945-1955. *Seminars in Psychiatry*, 1969, 1, 179–194.

Carey, J. T., & Mandel, J. The bay area speed scene. *Journal of Health and Social Behavior*, 1969, 9, 164–174.

Chambers, C., & Inciardi, J. Epidemiology of polydrug use. Presentation to the District of Columbia Family Practice Association, Maryland, Virginia, 1972.

Clement, W., Solursh, L., & Van Arnst, W. Abuse of amphetamine and amphetamine-like drugs. *Mental Health Digest*, 1970, 2, 9.

Connell, P. H. Amphetamine psychosis. *Institute of Psychiatry, Maudsley Monographs*, No. 5. London: Oxford University Press., 1958.

Deneau, G. A., Yanagita, T., & Seevers, M. H. Psychogenic dependence to a variety of drugs in the monkey. *Pharmacologia*, 1964, 6, 183. (Abstract)

Eckerman, W. C., Bates, J. D., Rachel, J. V., & Poole, W. K. *Drug usage and arrest charges. A study of drug usage and arrest charges among arrestees in six metropolitan areas of the United States*. Bureau of Narcotics and Dangerous Drugs, U.S. Department of Justice. Washington, D.C.: U.S. Government Printing Office, 1971.

Ellinwood, E. H., Jr. Amphetamine psychosis – a description of the individuals and the process, *Journal of Nervous and Mental Disease*, 1967, 144, 273–283.

Ellinwood, E. H., Jr. Amphetamine psychosis: A multi-dimensional process. *Seminars in Psychiatry*, 1969, 1, 208–226.

Ellinwood, E. H., Jr. Assault and homicide associated with amphetamine abuse, *American Journal of Psychiatry*, 1971, 127(9), 1170–1175.

Ellinwood, E. H., Jr. Cultural disparity between generations and drug use. In L. Miller (Ed.), *Drug addiction; Clinical and sociolegal aspects*. New York: Futura Publishing Co., 1972.(a)

Ellinwood, E. H., Jr. Discussion. In E. H. Ellinwood & S. Cohen (Eds.), *Current concepts of amphetamine abuse*. National Institute of Mental Health, U.S. Department of Health, Education, and Welfare. Washington, D.C.: U.S. Government Printing Office, 1972.(b)

Ellinwood, E. H., Jr.: The amphetamines and related stimulants. National Commission on Marihuana and Drug Abuse Report, Section on stimulant drugs. Washington, D.C.: U.S. Government Printing Office, 1973.

Ellinwood, E. H., Jr., & Cohen, S. Meetings: Amphetamine abuse. *Science*, 1971, 171, 420–421.

Ellinwood, E. H., & Escalante, O. D. Central nervous system cytopathological changes in cats with chronic methedrine intoxication. *Brain Research*, 1970, 21, 555.

Fiddle, S. Circles beyond the circumference; Some hunches about amphetamine abuse. In J. Russo (Ed.), *Amphetamine abuse*. Springfield, Ill.: Charles C Thomas, 1968.

Fleming, A. S. Amphetamines drugs. *Public Health Reports,* 1960, 75, 49-50.

Goodman, S. J., & Beker, D. P. Intercranial hemorrhage associated with amphetamine abuse, *Journal of the American Medical Association,* 1970, 212, 428.

Griffith, J. A study of illicit amphetamine drug traffic in Oklahoma City. *American Journal of Psychiatry,* 1966, 123, 560.

Guize, S. E., Taulson, V., & Catfield, P. Psychiatric illness in crime with particular reference to alcohol. A study of 223 criminals. *Journal of Nervous and Mental Disease,* 1962, 134, 512-521.

Harvey, K. J., Todd, C. W., & Howard, J. W. Fatality associated with benzedrine ingestion. *Delaware Medical Journal,* 1949, 21, 111-115.

Inghe, G. The present state of abuse and addiction to stimulant drugs in Sweden. In F. Sjoquist & M. Tottie (Eds.), *Abuse of central stimulants.* New York: Raven Press, 1969.

Johnson, J., & Milner, G. Amphetamine intoxication and dependence in admission to a psychiatric unit. *British Journal of Psychiatry,* 1966, 112, 617-619.

Kalant, O. *The amphetamines.* Springfield, Ill.: Charles C Thomas, 1966.

Kane, E. F. J., Keeler, M. F., & Reifler, C. B. Neurological crises following methamphetamine. *Journal of the American Medical Association,* 1969, 210, 556-557.

Kolb, L. Drug addiction in relation to crime. *Mental Hygiene,* 1925, 9, 74-89.

Kramer, J. C. Introduction to amphetamine abuse. *Journal of Psychedelic Drugs,* 1969, 2, 1-16.

Kramer, J. C., Fischman, V. S., & Littlefield, D. C. Amphetamine abuse—pattern and effects of high doses taken intravenously. *Journal of the American Medical Association,* 1967, 201, 305-309.

LaBarre, W. *The ghost dance.* Garden City, N.Y.: Doubleday, 1970.

Masaki, T. Amphetamine problem in Japan, World Health Organization, Technical Report Service, 1956, 102, 14-21.

McConnell, W. B. Amphetamine substances in mental illness in Northern Ireland, *British Journal of Psychiatry,* 1963, 109, 218-224.

Noda, H. Concerning wake-amine intoxication. *Kurume Igakkai Zasshi,* 1950, 13, 294-298.

Pickens, R. Self-administration of stimulants by rats. *International Journal of the Addictions,* 1968, 3(1), 215-221.

Pretorius, H. P. J. Dexedrine intoxication in children: Two cases, one fatal. *South African Medical Journal,* 1953, 27, 945-948.

Rensberger, B. Amphetamines used by a physician to lift moods of famous patients. *New York Times,* Dec. 4. 1972.

Rockwell, D. A., & Ostwald, P. Amphetamine use and abuse in psychiatric patients. *Archives of General Psychiatry,* 1968, 18, 612-616.

Rumbaugh, C. L., Bergeron, R. T., Fang, F. C. H. F., & McCormick, R. Cerebral angiographic changes in the drug abuse patient. *Radiology,* 1971, 101, 335-344.

Russo, J. R. Cultural omen or contemporary problem. In J. Russo (Ed.), *Amphetamine abuse.* Springfield, Ill.: Charles C Thomas, 1968.

Rylander, G. Clinical and medical criminal aspects of addiction to central stimulating drugs. In F. Sjoqvist & M. Tottie (Eds.), *Abuse of central stimulants.* New York: Raven Press, 1969.

Sadusk, J. F. Non-narcotic addiction. Size and extent of problem. *Journal of the American Medical Association,* 1966, 196, 707-709.

Schuster, C. R., Woods, J. H., & Seevers, M. H. Self-administration of central stimulants by the monkey. In F. Sjoqvist and M. Tottie, (Eds.), *Abuse of central stimulants.* New York: Raven Press, 1969.

Scott, P. D., & Willcox, D. R. C. Delinquency and amphetamines. *British Journal of Psychiatry,* 1965, 111, 865-875.

Schick, J. F. E., Smith, D. E., & Myers, F. H. Use of amphetamines in the Haight Ashbury subculture, *Journal of Psychedelic Drugs,* 1969, **2**, 139-170.

Smith. R. Traffic in speed: Illegal manufacture and distribution. *Journal of Psychedelic Drugs.* 1969, **2**, 30-42.

Smith, R. Compulsive methamphetamine abuse and violence in the Haight Ashbury district. In E. H. Ellinwood & S. Cohen (Eds.), *Current concepts of amphetamine abuse.* National Institute of Mental Health, U.S. Department of Health, Education, and Welfare. Washington, D.C.: U.S. Government Printing Office, 1972.

Tatetsu, S. Methamphetamine psychosis. *Folia Psychiatrica et Neurologica Japonica* (Suppl.), 1963, **7**, 377-380.

Tatetsu, S., Goto, A., & Fujiwara, T. *The awakening drug intoxication,* Tokyo: Igakushoin, 1956.

Utena, H. Behavioral aberrations in methamphetamine intoxicated animals and chemical correlates in the brain. *Progress in Brain Research,* 1966, **21B**, 1902.

Walsh, J. Psychotoxic drugs; Dodd bill passes Senate and comes to rest in the House; Critics are sharpening their knives, *Science,* 1964, **145**, 14-18.

Weiss, S. R., Raskind, R., Morganstern, N. L., Pytlyk, P. J., & Baiz, T. C. Intracerebral subarachnoid hemmorrhage following use of methamphetamine. *International Surgery,* 1970, **53**, 123-127.

Zalis, E. G., & Parmley, L. F. Fatal amphetamine poisoning. *Archives of Internal Medicine,* 1963, **112**, 822-826.

PART V
PSYCHOTHERAPEUTIC DRUGS

15
AN OVERVIEW OF PSYCHOTHERAPEUTIC DRUG USE IN THE UNITED STATES

Glen D. Mellinger, Mitchell B. Balter,
Hugh J. Parry, Dean I. Manheimer,
and Ira H. Cisin[1]

INTRODUCTION

This report shifts attention from the illicit use of mood-changing drugs, with which most of the other studies in the present volume are concerned, to the legal use of mood-changing drugs for medical or quasi-medical reasons. To emphasize this distinction, this report uses the term "psychotherapeutic" to refer to those mood-changing drugs that (*a*) are used as medicines to alleviate psychic distress, or as adjunctive treatment of various physical disorders; and (*b*) are typically acquired through a doctor's prescription or over the counter at a drugstore.

Although this discussion concerns behavior of patients and physicians that is perfectly legal, the use of psychotherapeutic drugs in medical practice has become almost as controversial as the use of illicit drugs.

At one level, there is an explicit and thoroughly legitimate concern about the medical consequences of using psychotherapeutic drugs—especially the fear that prolonged use of these drugs may have adverse physical or psychological consequences that may outweigh their benefits (Lennard, Epstein, Berstein, & Ranson, 1971; Rogers, 1971). This issue confronts the physician in his daily practice as he makes a complex set of judgments about the character of the patient, the severity of his distress, and the availability of acceptable

[1] Glen D. Mellinger and Dean I. Manheimer are at the Institute for Research in Social Behavior, Berkeley, California; Mitchell B. Balter is at the Psychopharmacology Research Branch, National Institute of Mental Health, Washington, D. C.; and Hugh J. Parry and Ira H. Cisin are at the Social Research Group, The George Washington University, Washington, D.C.

alternatives in dealing with that distress. He is also faced with the further possibility that *not* using psychotherapeutic drugs may have worse consequences (e.g., inability to function tolerably at work or home, alcoholism, or suicide) than even heavy and prolonged use of these drugs would have.

Quite apart from questions of medical practice and medical philosophy, there are other even deeper issues in the debate that often remain hidden. These issues have to do with fundamental societal values usually associated with the Puritan Ethic—for example, the fear that widespread use of psychotherapeutic (not to mention illicit) drugs both foretells and contributes to a major breakdown in American moral character. This fear is expressed in the beliefs, held by many, that use of psychotherapeutic drugs reflects personal weakness and undermines values traditionally placed on self-reliance, self-control, and will power to cope with one's problems. Klerman (1971, 1972) has applied the term "pharmacological Calvinism" to this cluster of values.

Corollary to these beliefs are two often-stated assertions: (*a*) that psychotherapeutic drugs are widely prescribed for conditions that do not merit treatment; and (*b*) that use of medications to provide symptomatic relief invariably reduces the motivation or ability to deal with the problem giving rise to the symptom. The first is a statement of opinion that clearly reflects a traditional stoical value orientation regarding the legitimacy of emotional distress as a medical problem, and the moral propriety of relieving (rather than enduring) distress that results from everyday problems of living (Lennard et al., 1971; Rogers, 1971). As such, it is not subject to empirical verification. The second assertion is an hypothesis that is subject to verification and should indeed be tested in the near future.

To date most of the discussion of these issues has occurred largely in the absence of adequate and pertinent data. There have been many claims about the potential dangers inherent in current prescribing practices and frequent assertions that we are becoming an "over-medicated society" (Berg, 1971; Lennard et al., 1971; Rogers, 1971). Until very recently, however, there has been little solid evidence regarding questions such as: How many people are using medically prescribed mood-changing drugs? How often and over what periods of time are these drugs being used? How prevalent are the emotional and somatic disorders for which use is indicated? How severely distressed are those who obtain drug treatment? What are the attitudes and beliefs of the American people regarding use of psychotherapeutic drugs, and how are these beliefs related both to drug use and to more general social values? The objective of this report is to review the evidence now available regarding these issues.

CLASSIFICATION OF PSYCHOTHERAPEUTIC DRUGS

Because of the great variety of mood-changing drugs available through medical and other channels, it is imperative to identify as precisely as possible the type, class, and source of drugs with which a study is concerned.

Operationally, this study defines psychotherapeutic drugs as (a) all prescription (Rx) drugs that could be assigned to any one of the six major therapeutic classes shown in Table 1 and (b) drugs that can be legally purchased directly over the counter (OTC) without a prescription and are advertised and marketed as stimulants, tranquilizers, or sleeping pills. This report was concerned primarily with psychotherapeutic drugs that were

TABLE 1

Classification of Psychotherapeutic Drugs

Prescription (Rx) drugs	Examples: Generic names	Examples: Trade names
Major tranquilizers		
Phenothiazine derivatives	Chlorpromazine, thioridazine	Thorazine, Mellaril
Butyrophenones	Haloperidol	Haldol
Thioxanthenes	Thiothixene, chlorprothixene	Navane, Taractan
Minor tranquilizers		
Substituted diols	Meprobamate, tybamate	Equanil, Miltown, Tybatran
Benzodiazepines	Chlordiazepoxide, diazepam, oxazepam	Librium, Valium, Serax
Miscellaneous	Hydroxyzine, buclizine	Atarax, Softran
Antidepressants		
Tricyclics	Impramine, amitriptyline	Tofranil, Elavil
Monoamine oxidase (MAO) inhibitors	Isocarboxazid, phenelzine	Marplan, Nardil
Others	Methylphenidate, combination of amitriptyline and per-phenazine	Ritalin, Triavil, Etrafon
Stimulants		
Amphetamines	Dextroamphetamine (and combinations), methamphetamine	Dexedrine, Dexamyl, Desoxyn
Others	Deanol, pentylenetetrazol (and combinations)	Deaner, Metrazol
Sedatives		
Barbiturates (long-acting and intermediate-acting)	Phenobarbital, butabarbital	Eskabarb, Buticaps
Others	Bromisovalum	Bromural
Hypnotics		
Barbiturates (short-acting)	Secobarbital, pentobarbital	Seconal, Nembutal
Others	Glutethimide, ethchlorvynol	Doriden, Placidyl
Over-the-counter (OTC) drugs		
Stimulants	Caffeine	No-doz, Vivarin, No-nod
Tranquilizers	Scopolamine and/or metha-pyrilene	Cope, Nervine, Compoz
Sleeping pills	Scopolamine and/or metha-pyrilene	Sleep-Eze, Mr. Sleep, Sominex, Nytol

prescribed or administered by a physician in outpatient (i.e., nonhospital) practice. Parry, Balter, Mellinger, Cisin, and Manheimer (1973) presented more detailed data on use of OTC drugs elsewhere.

The classification of prescription drugs is based primarily on *desired clinical action* (i.e., the main purposes for which the drugs are actually prescribed) and secondarily on chemical structure and pharmacological effects. Thus, the classification of "stimulants" includes both amphetamines and nonamphetamines, but hypnotic sedatives are distinguished from those used mainly for daytime sedation. Other classifications (e.g., Chambers, 1971) emphasize chemical structure and distinguish for example, between barbiturates and other sedatives, regardless of their use to produce daytime or nighttime sedation. Each method of classification has advantages and limitations. Drug function is emphasized here because it is probably more highly related to user characteristics (such as age, sex, and socioeconomic status) than is the chemical structure of the drug.

Any classification, of course, must be somewhat arbitrary. Two examples illustrate the point: antispasmodics (GI) and stimulants. Antispasmodics pose a definitional problem for two reasons: first, they are indicated primarily for treatment of gastrointestinal symptoms that may have psychic origins; and, second, they are sometimes produced in combination with low dosages of sedatives or tranquilizers. The classification excludes these combination drugs because their intended action is directed mainly at the somatic disorder and their effect on mood is minimal. Stimulants also pose a definitional problem because, like GI disorders, obesity may have a psychic component. In this case, however, this drug class is included because stimulants have a pronounced effect on the central nervous system and are often *used* specifically to affect mood even though they are usually *prescribed* to help control obesity.

In trying to answer the question, "How many people are using psychotherapeutic drugs?," four other definitional issues have to be carefully distinguished:

1. Drug *type* (i.e., prescription vs. OTC).
2. Drug *source* (i.e., from a physician, drugstore or other source).
3. *Time period* for which prevalence estimates are obtained (e.g., 1 week, 1 year, ever).
4. *Levels of use* (e.g., "once or twice," "intermittently," "regularly over some period of time," and so on).

Failure to distinguish these issues can produce bizarre conclusions. Some time ago, Parry (1971) delivered a paper in which he reported that about one-half of American adults had, at one time or another, used a psychotherapeutic drug. A few months later, an article (Berg, 1971) appeared in a popular women's magazine interpreting this finding to the effect that "45 million American women have been swallowing tranquilizers on their doctors' orders."

This conclusion conveniently overlooked several facts about the data on which it was based: (a) it included *all* classes of drugs shown in Chart I, not just tranquilizers; (b) it included drugs that were acquired OTC and illicitly, as well as those prescribed by a physician; (c) it included drugs that had been used only once or twice; and (d) it included drugs that had been last used years ago. By overlooking these "details" the article produced an estimate about five times greater than the facts would warrant. This experience illustrates the current tendency to sensationalize the issue of psychotherapeutic drug use.

BACKGROUND DATA FROM DRUGSTORE AND PHYSICIANS' RECORDS

As Balter and Levine (1973) noted, it is difficult, "to arrive at a comprehensive quantitative description of psychotherapeutic drug usage in the United States . . . because there is no central source of information or unitary data collection system that encompasses the physician, the drug store, and the consumer, i.e., the patient and others in the general population who use drugs." The difficulty is compounded by the fact that the patient who receives a prescription has options regarding whether to fill the prescription, whether to use all of the medication provided, and whether to obtain all the refills permitted.

Given this situation, the kind of quantitative descriptions Balter and Levine discussed require data from two types of sources: medical and prescription records and sample surveys of persons (including both patients and non-patients) in the general population. Regarding the first source, medical and prescription records, the most useful for the present study were data from the following:

1. The National Prescription Audit (NPA) of Gosselin and Company[2]—a biweekly audit of prescriptions filled in a sample ($N = 800$) of U.S. drugstores.

2. Audatrex of Gosselin and Company—a continuous audit of prescriptions issued by a panel of 500 physicians in 27 key cities in the United States.

3. The National Disease and Therapeutic Index (NDTI) of Lea and Associates[3]—a reporting service that monitors the medical behavior of a national sample of physicians in private practice.

Trends in Retail Sales of Prescription Psychotherapeutic Drugs

On the basis of projections from the NPA data, Balter and Levine (1973) estimated that 214 million prescriptions (both new and refill) for

[2] Gosselin and Company, Dedham, Mass.
[3] Lea and Associates, Ambler, Pa.

psychotherapeutic drugs were filled in U.S. drugstores during 1970 at a retail cost of $972 million. These 214 million prescriptions accounted for approximately 17% of the total of 1.3 billion prescriptions for all drugs and a slightly higher proportion of the $5.6 billion spent. Thirty-eight percent of prescriptions for psychotherapeutic drugs were new prescriptions; 62% were refills.

Antianxiety agents alone accounted for almost 39% of all prescriptions for psychotherapeutic agents, more than twice the total of 18% accounted for by the next highest class, hypnotics. Stimulants constituted 13% of the total. Antidepressants, the least widely used class of drugs, accounted for approximately 9% of prescriptions for psychotherapeutic agents, while the figures for antipsychotics (10%) and sedatives (11%), mainly phenobarbital, were only slightly higher. Three drugs—Librium, Valium, and meprobamate—accounted for 89% of all prescriptions for antianxiety agents filled in U.S. drugstores and a similar percentage of the consumer spending.

Between 1964 and 1970 the number of prescriptions for all psychotherapeutic drugs filled in U.S. drugstores rose from 149 million to 214 million, an overall increase of 44%. During that same period prescriptions for nonpsychotropic drugs increased at a higher rate, 48%.

This average yearly increase of slightly over 7% in the combined total for all psychotherapeutic drugs, however, is not typical of the growth rate for any of the individual drug classes. In the 6-year period 1964–70, the number of prescriptions filled in drugstores for antidepressants increased by 108%. In that same period, prescription totals for the antianxiety agents increased by 84%, and those for antipsychotics grew by 53%. The growth of the antidepressants can be traced to a rapid increase in the popularity of the perphenazine-amitryptyline combinations that were first marketed in 1964.

There was also a 28% increase in the prescriptions for hypnotics, but mainly in the nonbarbiturate subclass.

The 1970 total of 28.2 million prescriptions for stimulants, primarily amphetamines, was a mere 6% greater than the 1964 figure. The total for sedatives, primarily phenobarbital, actually declined slightly from 24.1 million in 1964 to 23.8 million in 1970.

With the current concern about the overprescribing of barbiturates and amphetamines, it should be pointed out that in the United States prescriptions filled for these two groups of drugs have been relatively constant over the past 8–10 years. Given an annual increase in population, the annual figures for the barbiturates and amphetamines are indicative of a steady decline in their use that probably antedates current concerns about the use of psychotherapeutic drugs.

Contribution of Various Physician
Specialties to Volume of Prescribing

Since the process of drug acquisition and use begins with the physician, it is important to know the extent to which the various physician specialties contribute to the prescribing of psychotherapeutic drugs for outpatients.

First, general practitioners accounted for a large share of the prescribing of psychotherapeutic drugs. Data from the NDTI on new therapy with out-patients showed that general practitioners accounted for 50% of the new therapy involving psychotherapeutic drugs. Although this physician group represents only 31% of all physicians, it accounts for 38% of all patient visits.

Second, psychiatrists and neurologists accounted for only 5% of the total for new therapy with these drugs, a figure that was about equal to their representation in the physician population and was clearly small in terms of the total utilization of these agents among outpatients. When all therapy (new and continuing) was considered, the figure rose to 17%, thus reflecting the chronicity of conditions treated by psychiatrists and neurologists. Nonetheless, it is quite apparent that in the U.S. the bulk of the prescribing of psychotherapeutic drugs is in the hands of nonpsychiatrists.

How Psychotherapeutic Drugs Are Prescribed

A detailed analysis of Audatrex data indicated that patterns of prescribing by physicians in private practice were generally quite conservative. Regarding prescriptions for short-acting barbiturate hypnotics, in 71% of prescriptions no refills were permitted; for amphetamines, the corresponding figure was 76%; for antianxiety agents, 60%.

When refills were permitted, both the number of refills and quantity of drug per prescription tended to be small. The median number of days of therapy permitted on the original prescription plus refills was far from excessive, and extremes were rare. In the case of antianxiety agents, 60% of the prescriptions allowed 1 month or less of daily therapy, and 89% allowed 2 months or less. Similar figures for the amphetamines were as follows: 64%, 1 month or less; 80%, 2 months or less. Less than half the patients received a psychotherapeutic drug on the first visit for a new diagnosis; and most of the patients being placed on drugs were previously known or seen by the doctor. Patients were seldom given options to raise or lower dosages.

Although certainly there are transgressions in prescribing, these data do not argue that physicians in private practice are generally uninformed or unsophisticated about the dangers of drug dependence or cavalier in their prescribing habits. From observations of these and other data, private medical practitioners in many respects might be better characterized as cautious and orthodox to the point of inflexibility. This conservative picture, of course, does not rule out the possibility that a deviant physician or group of physicians could do a great deal of harm in a particular locale. The private practitioner in the United States, however, does not seem to be either a major or a significant contributor to the core problems of drug dependence.

Purposes for Which Drugs Are Prescribed

In the popular view, the use of psychotherapeutic drugs is almost exclusively associated with the treatment of mental disorders. The fact is, however, that in the United States the most widely used psychotherapeutic drugs are frequently prescribed in cases where the physician has diagnosed and is treating some physical condition, though it may originate in emotional distress or be further aggravated by or result in emotional distress. Illustrations come easily to mind: cardiovascular disorders, ulcers, painful arthritic conditions, acute dermatitis, and a host of other physical ailments.

In the case of the antianxiety agents (minor tranquilizers), the class of psychotherapeutic drug most commonly prescribed, data on outpatients from the NDTI show that in only a little more than one-third of the instances of new therapy was treatment directed to persons with a specific diagnosis of mental disorder. Even when "senility" was included in the mental-disorder category, it was found that the proportion of all new therapy with antianxiety agents associated with the treatment of mental disorders was just over 50%. Thus, new therapy with antianxiety agents is about as likely to be directed to patients with a primary diagnosis of physical disorder as it is to patients with a primary diagnosis of mental disorder.

Additional data from the same source, however, show that in most instances when a physician prescribed psychotherapeutic drugs (other than amphetamines) his *specific therapeutic intent,* as distinct from his *primary diagnosis,* was to alleviate or prevent *symptoms* of psychic or emotional distress.

The great diversity in the diagnoses and conditions being treated with psychotherapeutic drugs must be kept in mind when interpreting prevalence rates and usage patterns.

METHODOLOGY OF THE NATIONAL SURVEY

The chief limitation of medical and prescription audits is that they describe what happens only up to the point that the prescription is written or filled. They tell us little or nothing about the persons for whom prescriptions are written, whether they use these and other drugs, and how they use drugs. To obtain this kind of information, it becomes necessary to use household sample surveys.

As a source of data on psychotherapeutic drug use, the household sample survey offers the only feasible way at present to determine prevalence of use in the general population. A further advantage of this kind of survey is that one can compare the characteristics of users and non-users and thereby learn a great deal about the motivations, situations, and, ultimately, consequences associated with drug use.

The national survey discussed here was the most recent in a series of studies beginning in 1966. The studies were planned and carried out jointly by two research teams: The Social Research Group of The George Washington University (Washington, D.C.) and the Institute for Research in Social

Behavior (Berkeley, Calif.), with the support and close collaboration of the Psychopharmacology Research Branch, National Institute of Mental Health.[4] This series of studies was conducted in sequence so that each would benefit from the experience of the other. The Institute for Research in Social Behavior conducted two community surveys in the San Francisco Bay area (Cisin & Manheimer, 1971; Manheimer, Mellinger, & Balter, 1969; Mellinger, 1971; Mellinger, Balter, & Manheimer, 1971) and has been instrumental in developing the basic instruments and procedures for collecting data about psychotherapeutic drug use. The Social Research Group conducted a full-scale, rigorous study to measure the level of validity of sample survey techniques for obtaining data on drug use (Parry, Balter, & Cisin, 1970-71). Data for the nationwide study were collected under the direction of the Social Research Group; analysis of these data was carried out jointly by the two research teams.

Data were obtained in personal interviews with 2,552 persons aged 18-74 years living in the contiguous United States. Respondents were selected by rigorous probability sampling methods to form a cross-section of American adults living in households. Completed interviews slightly surpassed 85% of the originally designated sample.

Interviews lasted between 60 and 90 minutes, depending on the psycho-therapeutic drug history of the respondents. The range of questions covered the use of prescription and nonprescription drugs, sources of the drugs, ailments for which they were prescribed, and the duration and frequency of use of each drug. Data also were acquired concerning the personal and social characteristics of respondents, and respondents' current state of health, their attitudes toward psychotherapeutic drugs, their general values, their recent exposure to stressful experiences, and the various psychic and somatic symptoms to which they are subject.

As in any empirical research, it is essential to understand the methods used so that one can assess the validity of the results and properly interpret their meaning and implications. In household sample surveys the major issues to be considered are (a) *sampling*—i.e., how respondents were selected for inclusion in the study and (b) *data collection*—i.e., what questions were asked and how interviewers were selected, trained, and so on.

Sampling

The national study was based on strict probability sampling in which each person in the study population (in this case, all American adults living in

[4] These studies were conducted under grants MH-12591 and MH-12590. The former was awarded originally to the Family Research Center, Langley Porter Neuropsychiatric Institute, California Department of Mental Hygiene. The grant was subsequently transferred to the Institute for Research in Social Behavior, an independent, nonprofit organization, which is the successor to the Family Research Center. The latter grant was awarded to the Social Research Group of The George Washington University.

households at the time of the survey) has a determinable probability of being included in the sample. Since there is no "list" of persons in the population from which samples can be selected, surveys such as this use a technique known as area sampling. The process involves a series of sampling stages. In the first stage, all areas in the country with known population size [e.g., standard metropolitan statistical areas (SMSA's) and counties] are listed, and a sample of such areas is selected by a random procedure. In successive stages, census tracts, blocks (or equivalent smaller areas), and then households are selected randomly. Only one person is selected in each household. Thus, in households with more than one eligible person (any adult resident in the age range 18–74), one respondent is selected, again at random. In tabulating the results, each respondent is weighted inversely to his probability of being selected.

Once the person is selected, no one else can be substituted for the designated respondent, and every effort is made to locate and interview that person, even if many call-backs are required. The logic of survey sampling also requires that interviews be completed with the highest possible percentage of designated respondents. These requirements of probability sampling are exceedingly important because they avoid biasing the sample in favor of people who are more cooperative, more often at home, or who may differ in other important respects from the rest of the population. These requirements also explain why probability methods are considerably more expensive than other, short-cut methods of selecting respondents.

The use of volunteers as respondents, for example, is clearly unacceptable because of the biases usually associated with self-selection. Various forms of "quota" and "modified probability" sampling (in which the interviewer selects respondents so as to match the population with respect to certain prespecified characteristics such as age and sex) are often used to avoid expensive call-backs. But such samples are no more acceptable than the use of volunteers: the quota method merely substitutes the unknown bias of the interviewer in selecting respondents for the unknown self-selection bias of the volunteer respondent. Manheimer and Hyman (1949) demonstrated how sampling bias can result from the reluctance of interviewers to interview certain kinds of respondents.

In short, this study used probability sampling because it is the only method that satisfies the statistical requirements for unbiased estimates (as well as for significance testing) and thereby permits probability statements about the accuracy of survey results. For example, 22% of the persons interviewed in this study reported using at least one medically prescribed psychotherapeutic drug during the year prior to interview. Given the size of the sample (2,552 persons), the probability is .95 that one would have obtained a figure between 20% and 24% (22% ± 2%) if all persons in the study population had been interviewed.

One other point should be mentioned. The study population, as defined, excluded persons who were institutionalized at the time of the survey. Results of this study therefore underestimate somewhat the number of persons using certain types of psychotherapeutic drugs, especially the more potent major tranquilizers and antidepressants that are commonly used in treating hospitalized mental patients.

Data Collection

Another set of methodological issues involves the procedures used to collect data, i.e., the strategy of interviewing and the design of the interview schedule or other instrument. A related matter concerns the selection, training, and supervision of interviewers whose performance in the interviewing situation is all important in determining the quality of the data obtained (Kahn & Cannell, 1962). Supervision procedures for this study, for example, included regular briefings in which each interviewer's work was carefully edited and reviewed with him, periodic quizzes dealing with problem areas, postcard or telephone follow-up with respondents to verify work completed, and so on (Manheimer, Mellinger, Somers, & Kleman, 1972).

The issue of interview strategy and questionnaire design is especially pertinent to two problems that characterize psychotherapeutic drug use: (a) the difficulty respondents may have in recalling and identifying drugs they have used and (b) the reluctance they may have in admitting behavior that many people regard as at least somewhat reprehensible.

In asking respondents to recall and identify psychotherapeutic drugs they have used in the past, the usual problems of forgetfulness are magnified by the diversity of products available, the esoteric names assigned to them, and the fact that physicians often choose to withhold from patients the name and desired action of drugs they prescribe. Even when respondents are knowledgeable about psychotherapeutic drugs and have used these drugs themselves, there is good reason to believe that there is some stigma attached to using drugs, including those medically prescribed. The prevalence of negative attitudes regarding drug use makes it likely that some, perhaps many, drug users feel guilty about using drugs and therefore are reluctant to admit having done so.

These problems of recalling, identifying and admitting drug use were encountered in the extensive pretesting for two community surveys that preceded the national study. As a result, nearly a year was spent in developing and testing the data collection procedure finally used. The procedures involved the following strategy.

1. To minimize any reluctance respondents might have to *admit* using drugs, an interviewing procedure was specifically designed to establish and maintain good rapport. The study was introduced as "a survey on health problems and how people cope with them," rather than as a drug survey. Questions about drug use were preceded by a series of "warm-up" questions about the respondent's health, medical care behavior, and symptoms of psychic and somatic distress.

2. The procedure and the questions concerning use of psychotherapeutic drugs were also essential in helping respondents to *recall and identify* drugs they had used. The questioning was designed to identify, *by name,* each psychotherapeutic drug a respondent had used, and involved three aids to recall: (*a*) a description of the function that each class of psychotherapeutic drug is intended to serve, (*b*) the name of the drug class, and (*c*) a "drug recognition chart" that depicted, life-sized and in color, more than 120 different psychotherapeutic drugs in their various forms and strengths. The drug chart provided still another aid to recall by listing the *name* of each drug pictured.[5,6]

The questioning procedure may be illustrated for the tranquilizer/sedative class. While showing a respondent the chart for drugs in this class, the interviewer said: "Now I'm going to ask you about the kinds of pills or medicines that many people take to calm down, to relax, or to reduce nervous tension. These are often called tranquilizers or sedatives. Have you ever taken any of these—or any pills *or medicines* like them—for any reason?"

About 5% of the respondents who had used drugs were not able to identify the name of one or more drugs they had used. Less difficulty was experienced in identifying drugs used recently, of course, than in identifying those used in the distant past.

Having devoted a great deal of time and effort to developing these methods of collecting data on psychotherapeutic drug use, the next step was to conduct a large-scale and systematic validation study during the winter-spring of 1968-69 to test the effectiveness of these methods. The methods of the validation study have been described in detail by Parry et al. (1970-71). Briefly, the study design involved interviewing six different groups of persons (three experimental and three control groups) known to have obtained at least one drug prescription prior to the interview. The six groups, ranging in size from 121 to 199 cases, differed with respect to (*a*) type of drug prescribed, (*b*) length of time since the prescription was filled, and (*c*) method of interviewing. Interviewers were unaware of the purpose of the study and did not know that all respondents had actively filled prescriptions. The major findings of the validation study were as follows:

1. There was indeed some underreporting of psychotherapeutic drug use, but the level of underreporting was not high enough to alter any conclusions based on the results reported here.

[5]Obtaining, insofar as possible, the specific name of each drug used was important for the following reason. Although the main concern originally was to reduce the amount of *underreporting* by respondents, pretesting experience demonstrated that *overreporting* was also a problem. Thus some respondents answered the question about tranquilizers with "aspirin" or even "dexedrine." Only by asking the specific identification question could these responses be assigned to the correct drug class.

[6]Grateful acknowledgment is given the technical assistance of Smith, Klien & French, Inc., in designing and producing the drug recognition chart used in the national survey.

2. The percentage of accurate responses was higher for some classes of drugs than for others.

3. Interviewing methods used in the national study produced a significantly higher level of validity than did simpler and more direct methods commonly used in surveys.

With respect to the first two points, Parry et al. (1970–71) found that the percentages of completely valid responses were 67 for stimulants, 72 for sedatives, and 83 for minor tranquilizers. These findings indicate that the number of persons using any given class of psychotherapeutic drug is actually somewhat higher than the figure given in the following section. For example, the prevalence figure of 15% for minor tranquilizers should probably be something more like 18%, and the figure of 5% for stimulants should be more like 7% or 8%.

For the three drug classes combined, the validity study found that 74% of the psychotherapeutic drug users gave completely valid responses regarding the class they had used. Another 8% reported using a psychotherapeutic drug, although they identified the class incorrectly. Thus one can assume a validity level of approximately 82% for the estimate that 22% of American adults used some type of medically prescribed psychotherapeutic drug during the past year (i.e., the year prior to interview). The actual percentage is therefore probably closer to 27, or about one-fourth of the adult population.

SURVEY DATA: PREVALENCE OF USE

This section summarizes and discusses some of the major findings from the national survey regarding the prevalence of psychotherapeutic drug use. The findings were reported in greater detail by Parry et al. (1973).

Medically Prescribed and Over-The-Counter Drugs

Table 2, based on the national household sample survey, shows that 31% of American adults reported using one or more psychotherapeutic drugs during the "past year," i.e., the year prior to the interview. Twenty-two percent used a medically prescribed drug; 12% used an OTC surrogate. These last two figures include 3% who used both a prescribed drug and an OTC drug.

The percentage of women using a prescribed drug is much greater than the percentage for men: 29% to 13%. But the percentages using OTC drugs are identical (12%) for men and women.[7]

In addition to this sharp sex difference in use of prescribed as compared with OTC drugs, there are equally sharp differences with respect to age. Thus the use of medically prescribed psychotherapeutic drugs is more prevalent

[7] Although women are *more* likely than men to use medically prescribed drugs, and *equally* like to use OTC drugs, Cahalan and Cisin (1968) report that women are *less* likely than men to use alcohol. The implications of these differential patterns in use of various types of drugs by men and women are discussed later.

TABLE 2

Use of Medically Prescribed (Rx) and Over-the-Counter (OTC)
Psychotherapeutic Drugs During the Past Year, by Age and Sex

Sex of user and type of drug use[a]	Percent using past year, by age group (in years)				
	18–29	30–44	45–59	60–74	All persons
All persons					
Rx only	12	20	22	24	19
Rx and OTC	3	4	2	3	3
OTC only	20	6	4	5	9
Total, either Rx or OTC	35	30	28	32	31
Total who used none	65	70	72	68	69
Total	100	100	100	100	100
(No. of persons)	(581)	(693)	(728)	(550)	(2,552)
Men					
Rx only	3	11	13	19	11
Rx and OTC	3	1	1	2	2
OTC only	23	6	3	7	10
Total, either Rx or OTC	29	18	18	28	22
Total who used none	71	82	82	72	78
Total	100	100	100	100	100
(No. of persons)	(241)	(282)	(308)	(218)	(1,049)
Women					
Rx only	19	26	29	28	25
Rx and OTC	4	6	2	3	4
OTC only	17	7	5	4	8
Total, either Rx or OTC	40	38	36	35	38
Total who used none	60	62	64	65	62
Total	100	100	100	100	100
(No. of persons)	(340)	(411)	(420)	(332)	(1,503)

Source: National Survey, 1970–71.

[a]Figures in this table for Rx drugs refer to the use of drugs obtained through conventional medical channels, excluding hospital use.

among older than among younger people; but the reverse is true for OTC drugs, which are most likely to be used by persons aged 18-29. In fact, among 18-29-year-old men there are many more using OTC drugs (26%) than there are using prescribed drugs (6%). Moreover, in this age group, the percentage of men using OTC drugs is somewhat higher than the percentage of women: 26% to 21%.

Therapeutic Classes of Medically Prescribed Drugs

Table 3, based on data from the national survey, shows the percentage of American adults using medically prescribed drugs in the various classes of psychotherapeutic drugs. Two drug classes, minor tranquilizers and daytime sedatives, were combined. First, daytime sedatives (mostly phenobarbital) are often used for the same purpose as minor tranquilizers, i.e., to calm and relax. Second, a few respondents were unable to identify or name the drug they had used and could only report, for example, that they had used a drug "to calm my nerves." About 80% of this combined class, however, is made up of minor tranquilizers.

The major findings in Table 3 are as follows. Fifteen percent of American adults (ages 18-74) reported using a minor tranquilizer or daytime sedative

TABLE 3

Use of Prescription Psychotherapeutic Drugs During
Past Year, by Drug Class and Sex

Drug class[a]	Percent of users, by sex		
	Men	Women	All persons
Minor tranquilizer/sedative	8	20	15
Stimulant	2	8	5
Hypnotic	3	4	3
Antidepressant	2	2	2
Major tranquilizer	1	2	1
Total who used any[b]	13	29	22
Total who used none	87	71	78
Total	100	100	100
(No. of persons)	(1,049)	(1,503)	(2,552)

Source: National Survey, 1970-71.

[a]Figures in this table refer to the use of Rx drugs obtained through conventional medical channels, excluding hospital use.

[b]Percentages for separate classes add to more than the percentage of persons using "any" because some persons used drugs of more than 1 class. These amounted to 3% of the men and 4% of the women.

during the past year, and 5% reported using stimulants, the next most widely used class. For both classes use is much more common among women than it is among men. In fact, use of minor tranquilizers, daytime sedatives, and stimulants accounts for viturally all the male-female difference in use of psychotherapeutic drugs reported in Table 2. Use of hypnotics and anti-depressants is about equally widespread among men and women.

Table 4 shows prevalence data for the various drug classes according to sex and age. Use of medically prescribed psychotherapeutic drugs is more prevalent among older than among younger persons. Of the men aged 60-74, 21% used some medically prescribed drug during the past year, as compared with only 6% of those in the 18-29-year group. There is a similar but less sharp difference among women, except that prevalence levels are constant across the three older age groups. Thus, the difference in rates between men and women are greatest (about 4:1 in favor of women) in the 18-29 age group and decline to 3:2 by ages 60-74.

The increasing prevalence of use with age is due almost entirely to antianxiety drugs and hypnotics. Among women, use of stimulants shows the reverse pattern; i.e., use is more prevalent among younger women (ages 18-44) than among those who are older. Although use of medically prescribed stimulants is uncommon among men, prevalence is, if anything, highest during middle age (30-59 years). These findings support the impression that women are mainly concerned with weight, for cosmetic reasons, when they are young, whereas men become weight conscious, for health reasons, when they are somewhat older.

Levels of Use of Medically Prescribed Drugs

The data so far considered only the number of persons using drugs, regardless of the frequency, regularity, or duration of use. A small percentage of persons could account for a large percentage of the total volume of use. Conversely, a large number of persons who use drugs infrequently cannot be considered a "heavy" drug using population. For these reasons, it is important to consider how often people use psychotherapeutic drugs and over what periods of time.

Deciding how to measure levels of use was one of the most difficult problems faced in the survey because of the tremendous variety of patterns of use found in the data. After trying several possible methods of classification, the investigators devised a "duration-frequency" index that is relatively simple, yet does reasonable justice to the complexity of the data. For each class of drug, the classification procedure identifies the maximum level of use attained by each individual in terms of the longest duration of daily use or the greatest frequency of intermittent use.

All persons who had used one or more drugs in a particular class, e.g., hypnotics, in the past year were identified and scored for the highest level of use *ever* attained on drugs in that class. (There was one exception to this rule:

TABLE 4

Use of Prescription Psychotherapeutic Drugs During Past Year,
by Drug Class, Sex, and Age

Sex of user and drug class[a]	Percent using past year, by age group (in years)				
	18-29	30-44	45-59	60-74	All persons
Men					
Minor tranquilizer/sedative	5	7	9	11	8
Stimulant	1	2	2	1	2
Hypnotic	1	1	2	7	3
Antidepressant	–	2	1	4	2
Major tranquilizer	(b)	1	1	(b)	1
Total who used any[c]	6	12	14	21	13
Total who used none	94	88	86	79	87
Total	100	100	100	100	100
(No. of persons)	(241)	(282)	(308)	(218)	(1,049)
Women					
Minor tranquilizer/sedative	12	21	22	25	20
Stimulant	10	11	6	3	8
Hypnotic	3	3	4	8	4
Antidepressant	2	2	2	2	2
Major tranquilizer	1	2	2	2	2
Total who used any[c]	23	32	31	32	29
Total who used none	77	68	69	68	71
Total	100	100	100	100	100
(No. of persons)	(340)	(411)	(420)	(332)	(1,503)

Source: National Survey, 1970–71.

[a]Figures in this table refer to the use of Rx drugs obtained through conventional medical channels, excluding hospital use.

[b]Less than 0.5%.

[c]Percentages for separate classes add to more than the percent of persons using "any" because some persons used drugs in more than one class.

in assigning a "level of use" score to each person for each drug class, it was decided to exclude other drugs in that class last used more than 2 years prior to the survey.) For past-year drug users, this measure thus emphasizes their *history* of experience with drugs last used in the recent past. It should be noted that a person's *past-year* level of use may in fact be lower than the maximum level on which his classification is based.

Persons who had used drugs during the past year were thus assigned to one of the following groups:

- *High*—those whose maximum pattern involved regular daily use for at least 2 months.
- *Medium*—those whose maximum pattern involved regular daily use for a period of at least 1 week but less than 2 months and those whose maximum pattern involved intermittent use on at least 31 occasions.
- *Low*—those whose maximum pattern involved regular daily use for less than 1 week and those whose maximum pattern involved intermittent use on fewer than 31 occasions.

Table 5, based on the national study, shows the highest level of use ever attained by persons who used psychotherapeutic drugs during the past year.

Using this classification procedure, the left-hand columns in Table 5 show that 8% of the adult population were classified as high-level users; i.e., they used medically prescribed mood-changing drugs during the past year *and*, at some time, used such drugs regularly (daily or almost daily) for a period of at least 2 months. (Most of these persons, in fact, used a drug in this fashion for 6 months or longer.) About equal percentages of persons were classified as medium- or low-level users.

Women were much more likely than men to be classified as high-level users. Apparently, this simply reflects the fact that, in general, women are more

TABLE 5

Highest Level of Use Ever Attained by Persons Who Used Prescription Drugs During Past Year, by Sex

Level of use[a]	Total sample			Users only		
	Men	Women	All persons	Men	Women	All users
High	5	10	8	41	36	37
Medium	4	10	7	30	34	33
Low	4	8	6	27	28	27
Missing information	([b])	1	([b])	1	2	2
Total who used any	13	29	22	100	100	100
Total who used none	87	71	78	–	–	–
Total	100	100	100	100	100	100
(No. of persons)	(1,049)	(1,503)	(2,552)	(135)	(456)	(591)

Source: National Survey, 1970–71.

[a]Figures in this table refer to the use of Rx drugs obtained through conventional medical channels, excluding hospital use.

[b]Less than 0.5%.

likely to use psychotherapeutic drugs. In fact, when we look at the distribution of use among the users only (right hand columns), men are slightly more likely to be high-level users than are women. And, for the majority (60%) of psychotherapeutic drug users, the highest level of use attained involved either intermittent use or regular use for periods of less than 2 months.

Table 6 summarizes, by selected demographic subgroups (a) the prevalence of use of medically prescribed psychotherapeutic drugs and (b) the prevalence of high-level use. Findings are as follows:

1. Prevalence of high levels of use is significantly higher among people living in the West than among people living in the rest of the country. This difference is about what one would expect given the total number of people using medically prescribed psychotherapeutic drugs in the four regional groups.

2. Prevalence of high levels of use is higher in the three older age groups (30–74 years)—about 1 in 10—than in the youngest (18–29 years) age group where it is only 1 in 20. Given the number of persons using psychotherapeutic drugs, however, these rates of high–level use are somewhat higher than one would expect in the two middle-aged groups (30–59 years) and somewhat lower in the oldest and youngest groups.

3. Contrary to expectations, there are only small differences in prevalence among the various socioeconomic status (SES) groups. Closer examination of the table reveals, however, that almost one-half of the users in the lowest SES stratum are classified as high-level users, whereas less than one-third of the users in the highest stratum are so classified. In other words, rate of use is about equal across the various SES strata; but if a person is a user, then the probability that he will be a high-level user is greater in the lower SES group.

This last finding suggests that, among the lowest SES levels, the use of psychotherapeutic drugs does not begin until symptoms are more serious and that, consequently, the drugs must be taken over longer periods of time. This pattern of delayed medical treatment would in turn be associated with less economic access to medical facilities, less information about facilities, and perhaps a lifestyle in which seeking a physician is reserved for relatively serious symptoms. One might also speculate that among these poorer respondents, the life stresses associated with psychic symptoms are more likely to be situational and continuous, e.g., poverty, debt, and unemployment.

Use of Alcohol and Use of Medically Prescribed Drugs

In public discussions of drug use and drug abuse, it is often overlooked that alcohol continues to be the most widely used (and abused) psychotropic drug in American society. Inasmuch as alcohol has pharmacological effects similar to those of sedatives, hypnotics, and minor tranquilizers, it is

TABLE 6

Prevalence of Past Year Use and High-Level Use of Medically
Prescribed Psychotherapeutic Drugs Among Subgroups
in the Population

Population subgroup[a]	Percent using drugs among all persons in each subgroup		Number in subgroup
	Using at high level	Using	
All persons	8	22	2,552
Region:			
Northeast	7	18	623
North Central	7	22	798
South	8	22	779
West	12	30	352
Age, in years:			
18–29	5	15	581
30–44	10	24	693
45–59	10	23	728
60–74	9	27	550
Index of Social Position (ISP)[b]:			
Highest	7	23	634
Second quartile	8	24	675
Third quartile	8	21	673
Lowest	10	21	545

Source: National Survey, 1970–71.

[a]Figures in this table refer to the use of Rx drugs obtained through conventional medical channels, excluding hospital use.

[b]Index of Social Position, combining education and occupation, is based on the standard Hollingshead scoring. His groups were combined into rough quartiles for the purpose of analysis.

reasonable to suppose that alcohol and these particular psychotherapeutic drugs sometimes provide *alternative* ways of coping with emotional distress. Of course, alcohol often serves functions other than, or in addition to, coping with distress. In particular, it is often used as a social-recreational drug in much the same way that marijuana has come to be used by many young people.

Nevertheless, the pharmacological similarities between alcohol and psycho-therapeutic drugs suggest that persons seeking to alleviate emotional distress could make a choice between the two types of drugs. The choice is probably contingent on several factors, including (*a*) acceptance of and access to the medical system as an appropriate source of help in dealing with emotional distress and (b) relevant norms of one's age-sex reference groups regarding the propriety of using alcohol versus medically prescribed drugs.

In general, use of alcohol is most prevalent among groups of people who are least likely to use medically prescribed mood-changing drugs, and vice versa (Table 7). As shown in Table 2, use of prescribed drugs (a) is much more prevalent among women than it is among men and (b) increases sharply with age. Table 7 shows that, for alcohol, the direction of these relations to sex and age are reversed: men are more likely than women to use alcohol (77% to 63%), and prevalence of alcohol use declines with age.

In addition, use of alcohol is much more widespread than use of prescribed psychotherapeutic drugs: 69% of American adults used alcohol during the past year as compared with 22% who used prescribed psychotherapeutic drugs. There is some overlap in the use of these drugs and the use of alcohol: 15% reported using both types of drugs during the past year, although the use did not necessarily occur simultaneously. Only 7% used prescribed psychotherapeutic drugs and not alcohol.

Discussion

Sharp differences are found in prevalence of use of the various types of drugs (including alcohol) among the various age-sex groups in the population.

Women, for example, are much more likely than men to use medically prescribed psychotherapeutic drugs. This difference is undoubtedly due to three factors:

1. As discussed in a later section, women are more likely than men to report the kinds of emotional distress for which the common psychotherapeutic drugs are indicated.

2. Women are also more likely than men to seek medical care and thus to gain access to the prescribing system.

3. American society is generally less tolerant regarding the use of alcohol by women than by men, and women are therefore less likely to drink than men are.

The reverse side of the coin may be that doctor-going implies an admission of weakness which, in our culture, is generally less acceptable for men than it is for women. Thus for men, alcohol to some extent seems to serve as a readily available and less ego-threatening alternative to the psychotherapeutic drugs.

The relation of age to drug use presents a somewhat different situation. Use of medically prescribed psychotherapeutic drugs becomes more prevalent with increasing age, whereas use of alcohol and use of OTC drugs declines with age. It should be noted that the more widespread use of the prescribed drugs among older people cannot be explained in terms of the prevalence of emotional distress. In fact, high levels of psychic distress tend to be reported more often by younger than by older people. Older people, however, are more

TABLE 7

Use of Any Medically Prescribed Psychotherapeutic Drug and/or
Alcohol During Past Year, by Age and Sex

Sex of user and drug used[a]	Percent using past year, by age group (in years)				
	18–29	30–44	45–59	60–74	All persons
Men					
Rx only	([b])	1	4	7	3
Rx and alcohol	5	11	11	14	10
Alcohol only	82	69	63	50	67
Total who used either	88	82	78	71	80
Total who used none	12	18	22	29	20
Total	100	100	100	100	100
(No. of persons)	(241)	(282)	(308)	(218)	(1,049)
Women					
Rx	6	9	13	15	10
Rx and alcohol	17	23	18	16	19
Alcohol only	56	48	40	27	44
Total who used either	78	80	71	58	73
Total who used none	22	20	29	42	27
Total	100	100	100	100	100
(No. of persons)	(340)	(411)	(420)	(332)	(1,503)
All persons					
Rx	3	6	9	11	7
Rx and alcohol	12	18	15	15	15
Alcohol only	67	57	51	38	54
Total who used either	83	80	74	64	76
Total who used none	17	20	26	36	24
Total	100	100	100	100	100
(No. of persons)	(581)	(693)	(728)	(550)	(2,552)

Source: National Survey, 1970–71.

[a]Figures in this table refer to the use of Rx drugs obtained through conventional medical channels, excluding hospital use.

[b]Less than 0.5%.

likely than others to seek medical care and, in particular, to make repeated visits to the doctor (National Center for Health Statistics, U.S. Department of Health, Education, and Welfare. Unpublished data from National Health Survey, 1972). Their greater access to psychotherapeutic drugs through the medical system thus provides a conventional (and thus acceptable) means of coping with emotional distress, especially when it occurs concomitantly with physical ailments. To some extent, though only partially, the more widespread use of prescribed psychotherapeutic drugs among older people thus offsets the relatively low prevalence of alcohol use in this group.

At the other end of the age continuum, 18–29 years, there is a striking preference in favor of nonmedical sources for obtaining drugs. This preference, especially among men, extends to alcohol, OTC drugs, and, as shown elsewhere (Mellinger, 1971; Mellinger et al., 1971), to prescription drugs obtained outside the medical system. It also extends, of course, to illicit drugs. Unfortunately, data are unavailable with which to explore this nonmedical preference among young people; it remains to be seen to what extent it reflects a rejection of the medical system as an appropriate place to seek help for one's emotional problems.

SURVEY DATA: EMOTIONAL DISTRESS AND LIFE CRISIS

Given that 22% of the adult population of the United States used medically prescribed mood-changing drugs at some time during a 1-year period, it is important to ask how widespread the "disorder" is for which these drugs are primarily indicated?

The disorder in this case is emotional distress, primarily anxiety and depression because most of the persons who use psychotherapeutic drugs are using minor tranquilizers, daytime sedatives, hypnotics and antidepressants. To further understand emotional distress, and the use of drugs to cope with it, it is also important to know something about the stressful situations that may give rise to anxiety and depression. For these reasons, the national survey included data on the most common symptoms of emotional distress and also on crisis situations that may have occurred in the lives of respondents.

Methods

Data on emotional distress were obtained by means of a shortened version of a well-developed symptom checklist that was used in a series of drug-evaluation studies with psychiatric clinic outpatients (Lipman, Covi, Rickels, Uhlenhuth, & Lazar, 1968). Items in the list focused on symptoms of neurosis (e.g., feeling depressed, anxious, etc.) rather than symptoms typical of more serious but less common psychiatric disorders. For each symptom all respondents were asked whether they had been bothered by the feeling during the past year and, if so, how much it had bothered them. Only 11% of the sample said they had experienced no distress at all on any of the 19 items that went into the measure of psychic distress.

The use of symptom checklists in cross-section surveys presents certain problems of interpretation that are much less likely to occur when the same kinds of self-report questions are used with clinic patients. In particular, a survey respondent may report being troubled by a "symptom" that has nothing to do with any underlying psychic disorder. (He may have trouble sleeping, for example, because he has noisy neighbors.) Therefore, an indexing procedure was devised to minimize the possible effects of such artifactual influences.

The essence of the procedure was that the investigators looked for *combinations* of symptoms that have clinical significance. First, each respondent was scored on each of four indexes: mood anxiety, mood depression, anergia, and impaired cognitive functioning. Second, for each index a minimum threshold of "high distress" was established that took account of both number and severity of symptoms. (On the four-item depression index, for example, a respondent achieved the minimum criterion for high distress if he reported either a great deal of distress on one item and some distress on another, or if he reported some distress on three items.) Third, a respondent was classified as "high distress" if he met the minimum threshold on at least two of the four indexes; one of the four had to be mood anxiety or mood depression.

Fortunately, the validity of these procedures could be evaluated because the questions on the symptom checklist had also been asked of the large sample of outpatients who were accepted, after psychiatric screening, in the multiclinic studies (Lipman et al., 1968). Therefore, the same indexing procedures used in the national study could be applied to the clinic outpatient data; and, thereby, the high distress group could be compared with 1,077 anxious-neurotic outpatients.

Persons classified as high on psychic distress fell well within the range of scores for the clinic samples, although—not surprisingly—the outpatients included a higher percentage of persons with exceedingly high scores than did the high-distress survey respondents. These results demonstrate that the criteria of high distress were sufficiently stringent to achieve the objective, i.e., to identify a group of persons who appear, by actual clinical standards, to be truly distressed.

In addition to data on emotional distress, the study also obtained data on the number and severity of life crises a person had experienced in the year or so prior to interview. For this purpose, an instrument developed by Holmes and Rahe (1967), known as the Social Readjustment Rating Scale, was adapted. This instrument lists 43 events ranging in severity from death of a spouse to minor violations of the law. In developing the scale, Holmes and Rahe asked a panel of judges to rate the severity of each event (in terms of the amount of personal and social readjustment it would require) on a scale of

1-100, using marriage, with a life crisis score of 50, as an anchoring point. Each item was assigned a life crisis score based on the panel's ratings.

In adapting the instrument to the present study, the number of items was reduced from 43 to 32, eliminating some of the least severe items. As with the symptom checklist, each respondent was asked to respond to each item and to indicate whether the event had occurred during the past year or so. Each respondent's total score is the sum of the life crisis units assigned to the events he had experienced.

Again, rigorous criteria were applied in classifying people as high on the index of life crisis. To be classified as high, a person had to report a total of 150 life crisis units. Thus death of a spouse, the most highly weighted item with 100 units, would not suffice by itself to justify a high rating.

Findings

Table 8 shows that 27% of American adults are classed as high on the index of psychic distress and 33% are classed as high on the life crisis scale. If anything, these figures underestimate the extent to which people experience emotional distress or life crises during the course of a year. Many more had experienced moderate to severe psychic distress on one or several items, for example, but were not classified as high on the index because their responses did not meet the pattern criteria.

TABLE 8

Percentage of Persons Classified as High on Index of Psychic
Distress and Index of Life Crisis, by Age and Sex

Sex of user and index	Age group (in years)				
	18-29	30-44	45-59	60-74	All persons
All persons:					
Psychic distress	31	29	26	22	27
Life crisis	51	33	26	15	33
(No. in group)	(581)	(693)	(728)	(550)	(2,552)
Men:					
Psychic distress	24	21	15	18	19
Life crisis	51	31	19	13	29
(No. in group)	(241)	(282)	(308)	(218)	(1,049)
Women:					
Psychic distress	36	35	35	25	34
Life crisis	52	34	32	17	35
(No. in group)	(340)	(411)	(420)	(332)	(1,503)

Source: National Survey, 1970-71.

Women are more likely than men to be classified as high on psychic distress (34% to 19%), but only somewhat more likely to be high on life crisis (35% to 29%).

Life crisis is strongly and negatively related to age, among both men and women. Fifty-one percent of 18–29-year-old respondents reported a high level of life crisis, as compared with only 15% of those aged 60–74. This relation undoubtedly reflects the fact that the list of life crises taken from Holmes and Rahe includes many *transition* situations (marriage, change of residence, change of job, and so on) that are encountered more frequently by young people. The list does not include some of the continuing or chronic conditions and situations that are more common among older people (declining vigor and competence, loneliness, and the like) and that may be equally stressful.

Psychic distress is also negatively related to age—young people were more likely to report a high level of distress than older people were—but the relation is not as strong as it is for life crisis.

Table 9 shows that both psychic distress and life crisis are positively related to psychotherapeutic drug use. For example, among the 211 men classified as high on the psychic distress index, 25% had used medically prescribed psychotherapeutic drugs during the past year—as compared with only 7% among those classified as low on the index. Unfortunately, the data do not indicate whether these low distress persons were using the drug as adjunctive treatment for some physical ailment.

Psychic distress appears to be more strongly related to psychotherapeutic drug use than is life crisis. And a separate analysis, not shown here, indicates that life crisis is related to drug use among people whose level of psychic distress is high, but not among those who report a low level of distress.

In view of frequent claims that Americans are overly prone to resort to psychotherapeutic drugs, it is of interest that even among persons reporting a high level of psychic distress, a substantial majority did not use such drugs during the past year (Table 9). Thus 75% of the high-distress men and 65% of the high-distress women did not use medically prescribed psychotherapeutic drugs during the year prior to interview.

There is one other important finding, which is based on the data in Table 9 but which is not directly apparent in the table: Of the persons who used prescribed psychotherapeutic drugs in the past year, the majority (65%) were classified as high on the index of psychic distress or on the index of life crisis or on both. The figure is even higher (almost 8 out of 10) in the relatively small group of persons who used psychotherapeutic drugs regularly for 2 *months* or longer.

In short, while the majority of persons who used psychotherapeutic drugs reported a high level of distress, the majority of highly distressed persons did *not* use such drugs.

TABLE 9

Use of Medically Prescribed Psychotherapeutic Drugs During the
Past Year, by Level of Psychic Distress, Level of Life
Crisis, and Sex

Level	Men		Women	
	Percent using[a]	No. in group	Percent using[a]	No. in group
Psychic distress:				
High	25	211	35	506
Medium	12	266	22	430
Low	7	572	14	567
Life crisis:				
High	14	310	27	510
Medium	13	434	24	627
Low	7	295	16	352

Source: National Survey, 1970-71.

[a]Stimulants have been excluded from the figures for Rx drug use because this class of
drugs is generally not used to cope with psychic distress as it is defined here.

SURVEY DATA: ATTITUDES REGARDING USE
OF PSYCHOTHERAPEUTIC DRUGS

Previous sections showed that (a) the majority of persons who reported a
high level of psychic distress or life crisis did not use medically prescribed
psychotherapeutic drugs during the past year and (b) people who did use such
drugs typically used them intermittently or for relatively short periods of
time. These findings suggest that many people have fairly strong reservations
about using psychotherapeutic drugs. This expectation is definitely borne out
by data from the national survey. These findings are in sharp contrast with
the currently widespread impression that vast numbers of Americans are
eagerly resorting to medically prescribed mood-changing drugs (especially
tranquilizers) as an instant solution to all of life's problems.

In the national survey, respondents were asked a detailed set of questions
pertaining to attitudes about use of psychotherapeutic drugs. The investigators
chose to ask about tranquilizers because they are the most frequently used
and most highly publicized of the prescription psychotherapeutic drugs. The
first question asked was, "What does the term 'tranquilizer' mean to you—that
is, just what would you say a tranquilizer drug or pill is?" Later in the
interview, after the series of questions about use of psychotherapeutic drugs,
respondents were asked questions designed to assess attitudes and beliefs
about use. This section presents a summary of results reported in more detail
by Manheimer, Davidson, Balter, Mellinger, Cisin, and Parry (1973).

Knowledge About Tranquilizers

Most people did know what effect a tranquilizer has. When asked to describe what the word "tranquilizer" meant, almost 70% gave definitions that explicitly mentioned a tranquilizer's desired action—to calm, to relax, or to relieve tension or anxiety. Only 11% said they did not know what a tranquilizer was; an additional 3% gave definitions that were clearly incorrect. The remainder responded either in terms of value judgements or in vague terms that applied as well to other drugs as to tranquilizers.

Not surprisingly, knowledge about tranquilizers is partly a function of age and education. For example, 23% of those aged 60–74 said they did not know what a tranquilizer was, in contrast to 4% of the 18–29-year-olds. And while 22% of those with less than a high school education said they were unable to define a tranquilizer, the corresponding number among college-educated persons was only 3%.

All attitude data reported here exclude respondents who said they did not know what a tranquilizer was.

Attitudes and Beliefs About Tranquilizers

Respondents were asked whether they agreed or disagreed with a wide range of statements about minor tranquilizers. These statements were presented in self-administered form and were preceded by the following instructions:

> Now I'm going to give you a list of statements people have made about tranquilizers—that is, pills such as Miltown, Equanil, and Librium that can be used to calm you down, or keep you from getting nervous or upset. As you read each statement, please circle the number of one of the items underneath it to tell whether you agree strongly, agree, disagree, or disagree strongly.

The statements were constructed to bear directly on a number of issues regarding use of psychotherapeutic drugs. With respect to *efficacy,* most respondents (74%) agreed with the statement that "tranquilizers work very well to make a person more calm and relaxed."

On two other issues, however, there is evidence of considerable conservatism in views about the morality of using psychotherapeutic drugs. For example, substantial majorities have doubts about the effects of tranquilizers on *a person's self-awareness and ability to solve his own problems:* 69% agreed that "tranquilizers don't really cure anything, they just cover up the real trouble"; and 57% agreed that "using tranquilizers just prevents people from working out their problems for themselves." On the other issue, *self-reliance and strength of character,* almost 90% agreed that "it is better to use will power to solve problems than it is to use tranquilizers"; and a sizeable number (40%) agreed that "taking tranquilizers is a sign of weakness." Together, these beliefs lend strong support to Klerman's (1971, 1972) observations about "pharmacological Calvinism."

Two items dealt with the related issue of *control over behavior and mood*. The items are: "Tranquilizers cause people to lose some control over what they do" (61% agreed) and "Tranquilizers can change your mood so that you just don't care about anything" (66% agreed). The first of these statements partly expresses the belief that tranquilizers can affect mental alertness and physical performance by virtue of their side effects. However, both statements seem to reflect the belief that tranquilizers diminish one's drive, effectiveness, and sense of responsibility. Support for this latter interpretation can be found in the correlations of these items with the more obviously moralistic ones, e.g., "taking tranquilizers is a sign of weakness." One respondent's remark typifies this viewpoint. "I want to be in full control of myself right or wrong so I don't want some chemical to do something to my system over which I don't have control."

Other issues on which many Americans have doubts about using tranquilizers involve *short-term side effects* (e.g., 73% agreed with the statement that "tranquilizers often have bad side effects—such as making a person very sleepy or sick to the stomach"), *long-term adverse effects* (e.g., 80% agreed that "long-term use of tranquilizers may cause real physical harm to your body"), and various *consumer concerns*. To illustrate the latter, 57% agreed that "tranquilizers often get on the market before they are thoroughly tested to be sure they are safe," and 59% agreed that "many doctors prescribe tranquilizers more than they should."

On the whole, then, Americans generally believe that tranquilizers are effective; but they have serious questions about the morality of using tranquilizers and doubts about their physical safety. Although these beliefs are by no means unanimous, the degree to which they are held is remarkably similar across subgroups of the population defined by characteristics such as sex, age, education, income, and region of the country.

The few clear-cut differences found among demographic groups pertained to moral issues associated with tranquilizer use. Those with the least education were the most likely to agree that using tranquilizers indicates weakness of character and that their use prevents a person from solving his problems himself.

Attitudes Toward Tranquilizers in Relation to Values

The investigators also were interested in the extent to which the various specific attitudes toward tranquilizers are related to more general value orientations or a broader social ethic—in particular, values reflecting the work-achievement-success and do-not-complain orientation commonly associated with the Protestant Ethic.

As expected, it was found that a stoicism-traditionalism index[8] reflecting these values was strongly and positively related to the attitude items

---

[8] The stoicism-traditionalism index is described by Manheimer, Davidson, Balter, Mellinger, Cisin, and Parry (1973).

embodying the essence of "pharmacological Calvinism"—e.g., tranquilizer use is a sign of weakness. It is interesting, however, that the stoicism-traditionalism index is virtually unrelated to the attitude items pertaining to the physical dangers in using tranquilizers.

Attitudes Toward Tranquilizers Among Users

Having found that the majority of American adults express attitudes regarding tranquilizers that are essentially conservative, the investigators were then interested in the extent to which persons who have used medically prescribed tranquilizers share these same attitudes.

Even though differences in attitudes between users and non-users are pronounced, large proportions of the persons who use medically prescribed tranquilizers hold unfavorable attitudes about using these drugs. Forty-two percent of the users agreed that "using tranquilizers just prevents people from working out their problems for themselves"; and slightly more than 60% agreed that "tranquilizers don't really cure anything, they just cover up the real trouble." In addition, almost 50% of the users agreed that "tranquilizers cause people to lose some control over what they do." An even higher proportion (74%) felt that long-term use of tranquilizers could be physically harmful.

These findings argue strongly that people are not being misled into believing that tranquilizers are a panacea. Even among users, large numbers have doubts about the safety and morality of use, a finding that undoubtedly helps to explain the generally conservative patterns of use found among users of medically prescribed psychotherapeutic drugs.

CONCLUSIONS

A great deal of data has been presented regarding the use of psychotherapeutic drugs. Nevertheless, the first conclusion must be that there is still much to be learned, especially about the short and long-term consequences of using these drugs. What happens to people who use medically prescribed mood-changing drugs over substantial periods of time? While using drugs, does their ability to function in the family or work situation improve or deteriorate, as compared with their ability to function *before* using drugs? How is personal growth and development affected by use of psychotherapeutic drugs, as compared with non-use under conditions of moderate or severe emotional distress?

Answers are also needed to the question: What viable alternatives are there to psychotherapeutic drug use? If such alternatives really exist, are they demonstrably more effective than psychotherapeutic medication? Are they reasonably accessible and economically feasible?

In short, more data are needed on the relative human costs and benefits of using psychotherapeutic drugs, using other alternatives (possibly in combination with drugs), or doing nothing.

A previous section discussed the widespread belief that use of medications to relieve symptoms automatically reduces the motivation or ability to deal with the underlying problem. This is a reasonable hypothesis, but it has never been adequately tested. Furthermore, it overlooks an equally reasonable hypothesis: the symptom itself may impair an individual's ability to deal constructively with his underlying problems. Unfettered anxiety is surely *not* conducive to coping realistically with life's problems. Because these hypotheses are central to the currently popular arguments against use of psychotherapeutic drugs, studies in this area are urgently needed.

Clearly, prospective studies would be required. Klerman (1971) suggested two possibilities involving use of drugs for women in labor and for people who have experienced grief. In terms of subsequent relationships with her infant, for example, is it better for the mother to have to work through all of the anxieties of childbirth, or to moderate these anxieties with medication? It would be relatively simple, Klerman proposes, to design controlled studies to determine the consequences of using drugs in these kinds of situations.

It also would be useful to extend this concept to include longitudinal studies that would begin by identifying people in the general population who report a high degree of distress but who do not, at the time of a first interview, use drugs. The initial interview would also determine their level of functioning in the family, on the job, in other areas of health, etc. Since some portion of these high-distress persons would be expected to begin using drugs at a later date, follow-up interviews could provide data on changing levels of functioning associated with use of drugs under varying conditions of use and administration.

Meanwhile, the studies reported here have added a great deal to knowledge about the extent and nature of psychotherapeutic drug use in the United States. The data presented here are much more suggestive of a medical or illness model of behavior than they are of a deviance model or even a "self-indulgent consumer" model.

It was shown, for example, that emotional distress and the occurrence of life crises are strongly related to the use of medically prescribed psychotherapeutic drugs, and that the majority of persons using these drugs are highly distressed. Data from prescription records also show that psychotherapeutic drugs are often prescribed as adjunctive treatment for a great variety of physical ailments.

Granted, there are some who would not regard emotional distress as necessarily an "illness," in the traditional sense (especially if it stems from the everyday trials and tribulations of living), and who would therefore argue that it is inappropriate to use medications for treating it (e.g., Lennard et al., 1971). In this respect, the controversy over the use of mood-changing drugs in medicine amounts to differing social and personal values regarding (*a*) the legitimacy of psychic "disease," (*b*) personal criteria of illness, and (*c*) philosophy of medical practice. Empirical data cannot *resolve* a controversy over values, but can help by demonstrating the consequences of adopting one position rather than others.

There are other ways in which the data in the present report suggest a medical rather than a deviance model. Persons who use medically prescribed psychotherapeutic drugs (a) tend to be middle-aged and older, rather than young, (b) generally hold conservative attitudes regarding use of drugs, and (c) typically use drugs intermittently or for relatively short periods of time. These patterns of use, in particular, are consistent with a medical model in which treatment is associated with brief or intermittent episodes of distress and is discontinued when the treatment produces its desired effect or the conditions producing the symptoms subside.[9]

The medical model suggested by the data is also one in which behavior is, for the most part, *elective*. Although the emotional conditions associated with use of psychotherapeutic drugs may become disabling, they are seldom fatal. Up to a certain level of distress, therefore, the afflicted person can make choices about whether to use psychotherapeutic drugs and how to use them. Thus, insofar as his behavior is elective, it is also *selective*. The selectivity of drug-using behavior is evident in the finding that the *treated* prevalence of emotional distress in the population does not always correspond with the distribution of the disorder itself. For example, the prevalence of emotional distress is quite high among young men, but the prevalence of prescribed drug use is very low. It is this selective factor in drug-using behavior that focuses our attention on the cultural values that determine which persons seek help in the medical system, which ones acquire drugs, and which ones use drugs in various ways.

Finally, the present report showed that about one-fourth of the adult population of the United States used medically prescribed psychotherapeutic drugs during the year prior to study. In addition, although it has been widely publicized that recent years have seen an increase in the volume of prescribing of psychotherapeutic drugs, it was shown here that, since 1964, the rate of increase has been lower than that for prescription drugs in general.

In short, data reported here present less cause for alarm than some critics would have one believe. Generally speaking, usage patterns appear to be cautious and appropriate to level of distress or life crisis, and prevailing attitudes toward the use of drugs are predominantly conservative. This is not to say that there are no problems with the overuse or misuse of psychotherapeutic drugs. There may well be persons who use psychothera-peutic drugs when they might be coping with their problems more effectively in other ways. There is little question that physicians should be more

---

[9] It must be remembered, of course, that most drug data shown here reflect the preponderance of minor tranquilizer and sedative use. Other data (Parry et al., 1973) indicate that the more potent drugs (major tranquilizers and antidepressants), which are indicated for conditions that tend to be chronic, are used more regularly over longer periods of time. These drugs, however, are used by many fewer people.

knowledgeable than they are about diagnosing emotional disorders and prescribing psychotherapeutic drugs and that pharmaceutical houses could be doing a better job of educating physicians than they have done in the past.

Nevertheless, the investigators are greatly concerned about the prevailing tendency to sensationalize and polarize the issues surrounding psychotherapeutic drug use. An unfortunate result of this tendency may be to thoughtlessly and arbitrarily curtail the judicious medical use of psychotherapeutic drugs to relieve human suffering.[10]

REFERENCES

Balter, M. B., & Levine, J. Character and extent of psychotherapeutic drug usage in the United States. *Proceedings of the 5th World Congress of Psychiatry*, Mexico, 1971. Excerpta Medica; Amsterdam, Sept. 1973.

Berg, R. H. The over-medicated woman. *McCall's*, Sept. 1971, 67, 109–111.

Cahalan, D., & Cisin, I. H. American drinking practices: Summary of findings from a national probability sample: I. Extent of drinking by population subgroups. *Quarterly Journal of the Study of Alcohol*, 1968, 29, 130–151.

Chambers, C. D. An assessment of drug use in the general population, Special Report No. 1. Drug use in New York State. New York State Narcotic Addiction Control Commission, 1971.

Cisin, I. H., & Manheimer, D. I. Marijuana use among adults in a large city and suburb. *Annals of the New York Academy of Sciences*, 1971, 191, 222–234.

Holmes, T. H., & Rahe, R. H. The social readjustment rating scale. *Journal of Psychosomatic Research*, 1967, 11, 213–218.

Kahn, R. L., & Cannell, C. F. *The dynamics of interviewing*. New York: Wiley, 1962.

Klerman, G. L. A reaffirmation of the efficacy of psychoactive drugs. *Journal of Drug Issues*, 1971, 1, 312–319.

Klerman, G. L. Psychotropic hedonism vs. pharmacological Calvinism. *Hastings Center Report*, 1972, 2(4), 1–3.

Lennard, H. L., Epstein, L. J., Bernstein, A., & Ranson, D. E. *Mystification and drug misuse*. San Francisco: Jossey-Bass, 1971.

Lipman, R. S., Covi, L., Rickels, K., Uhlenhuth, E. H., & Lazar, R. Selected measures of change in outpatient drug evaluation. *Psychopharmacology: A Review of Progress, 1957–1967*. (PHS Pub. No. 1836, 249–254) Washington, D.C.: U.S. Government Printing Office, 1968.

Manheimer, D. I., Davidson, S. T., Balter, M. B., Mellinger, G. D. Cisin, I. H., & Parry, H. J. Popular beliefs and attitudes about tranquilizers. *American Journal of Psychiatry*, 1973, 130(11), 1246–1253.

Manheimer, D. I., & Hyman, H. Interviewer performance in area sampling. *Public Opinion Quarterly*, 1949, 13, 83–92.

Manheimer, D. I., Mellinger, G. D., & Balter, M. B. Marijuana use among urban adults. *Science*, 1969, 166(3912), 1544–1545.

[10] Portions of the material in this chapter have appeared in the *Proceedings of the 5th World Congress of Psychiatry*, Mexico, 1971, Excerpta Medica, Amsterdam, Sept. 1973; *American Journal of Psychiatry*, 1973, 130 (11), 1246–1253 (copyright 1973 by the American Psychiatric Association); and *Archives of General Psychiatry*, 1973, 28, 769–784 (copyright 1973 by the American Medical Association) and are used with the permission of the publishers.

Manheimer, D. I., Mellinger, G. D., Somers, R. H., & Kleman, M. T. Technical and ethical considerations in data collection. *Drug Forum: The Journal of Human Issues,* 1972, 1(4), 323-333.

Mellinger, G. D. "Psychotherapeutic drug use among adults: A model for young drug users? *Journal of Drug Issues,* 1971, 1, 274-286.

Mellinger, G. D., Balter, M. B., & Manheimer, D. I. Patterns of psychotherapeutic drug use among adults in San Francisco. *Archives of General Psychiatry,* 1971, 25, 385-394.

Parry, H. J. Patterns of psychotropic drug use among American adults. *Journal of Drug Issues,* 1971, 1, 269-273.

Parry, H. J., Balter, M. B., & Cisin, I. H. Primary levels of underreporting psychotropic drug use. *Public Opinion Quarterly,* 1970-71, 34, 582-592.

Parry, H. J., Balter, M. B., Mellinger, G. D., Cisin, I. H., & Manheimer, D. I. National patterns of psychotherapeutic drug use. *Archives of General Psychiatry,* 1973, 28, 769-784.

Rogers, J. M. Stimulus/response: Drug abuse by prescription. *Psychology Today,* 1971, 5(4), 16-24.

AUTHOR INDEX

Numbers in italics refer to the pages on which the complete references are cited.

SUBJECT INDEX